LEVELS OF THE HEART
LATAIF AL QALB

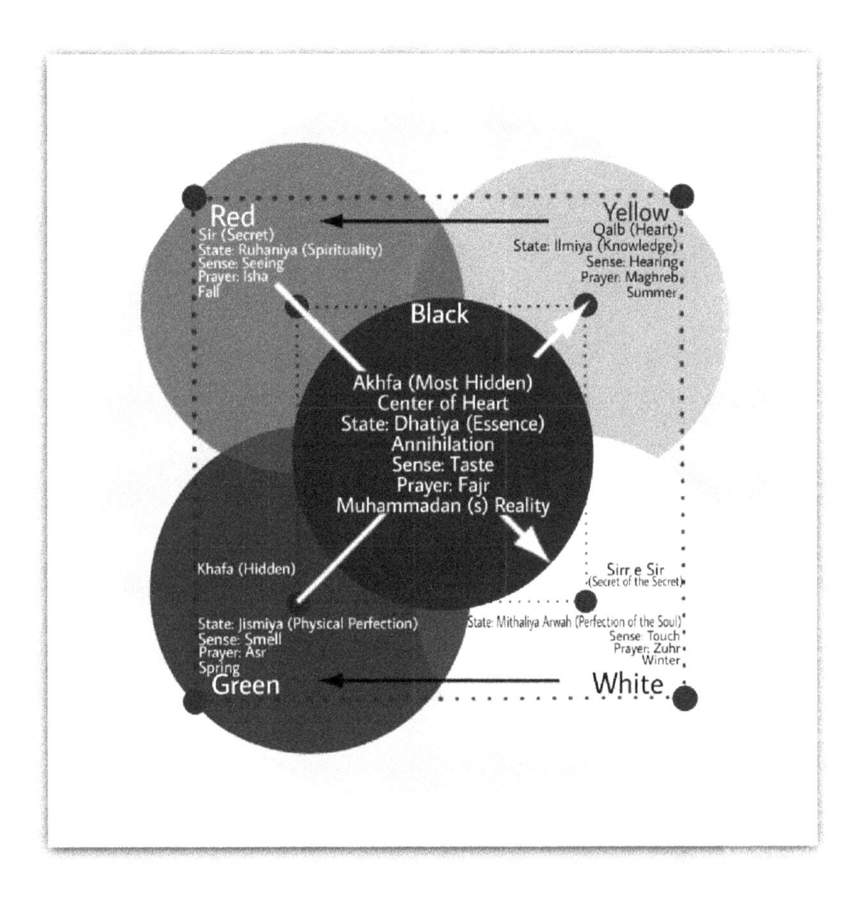

LEVELS OF THE HEART
LATAIF AL QALB لطائف القلب

BY
SHAYKH NURJAN MIRAHMADI

PUBLISHED BY THE
NAQSHBANDI CENTER OF VANCOUVER

ISBN: 978-0-9958709-2-5

Published and Distributed by:

Naqshbandi Center of Vancouver

3660 East Hastings

Vancouver, BC V5K 4Z7 Canada

Tel: (604) 558-4455

Web: nurmuhammad.com

First Edition: June 2017

TABLE OF CONTENTS

ABOUT THE AUTHOR

PROFILE

For the past two decades, Shaykh Nurjan Mirahmadi has worked hard to spread the true Islamic teachings of love, acceptance, respect and peace throughout the world and opposes extremism in all its forms. An expert on Islamic spirituality, he has studied with some of the world's leading Islamic scholars of our time.

Shaykh Mirahmadi has also founded numerous educational and charitable organizations. He has travelled extensively throughout the world learning and teaching Islamic meditation and healing, understanding the channeling of Divine energy, discipline of the self, and the process of self-realization. He teaches these spiritual arts to groups around the world, regardless of religious denomination.

BACKGROUND

Shaykh Nurjan Mirahmadi studied Business Management at the University of Southern California. He then established and managed a successful healthcare company and imaging centers throughout Southern California. Having achieved business success at a remarkably young age, Shaykh Nurjan Mirahmadi shifted his focus from the private sector to the world of spirituality. In 1994 he pursued his religious studies and devoted himself to be of service to those in need. He combined his personal drive and financial talents to work for the less fortunate and founded an international relief organization, a spiritual healing center, and a religious social group for at risk youth.

In 1995, he became a protégé of Mawlana Shaykh Hisham Kabbani for in-depth studies in Islamic spirituality known as Sufism. He studied and accompanied Shaykh Kabbani on many tours and learned about Sufi practices around the world. Together with Shaykh Kabbani, he has established a number of other Islamic educational organizations and relief programs throughout the world.

Shaykh Nurjan Mirahmadi has received written *ijazas* (authorization) to be a Spiritual guide, from two of the World Leaders of the Naqshbandi Nazimiya Sufi Order; Sultan al-Awliya Shaykh Muhammad Nazim al-Haqqani ق and Mawlana Shaykh Muhammad Hisham Kabbani. He is authorized to teach, guide, and counsel religious students around the world to Islamic Spirituality.

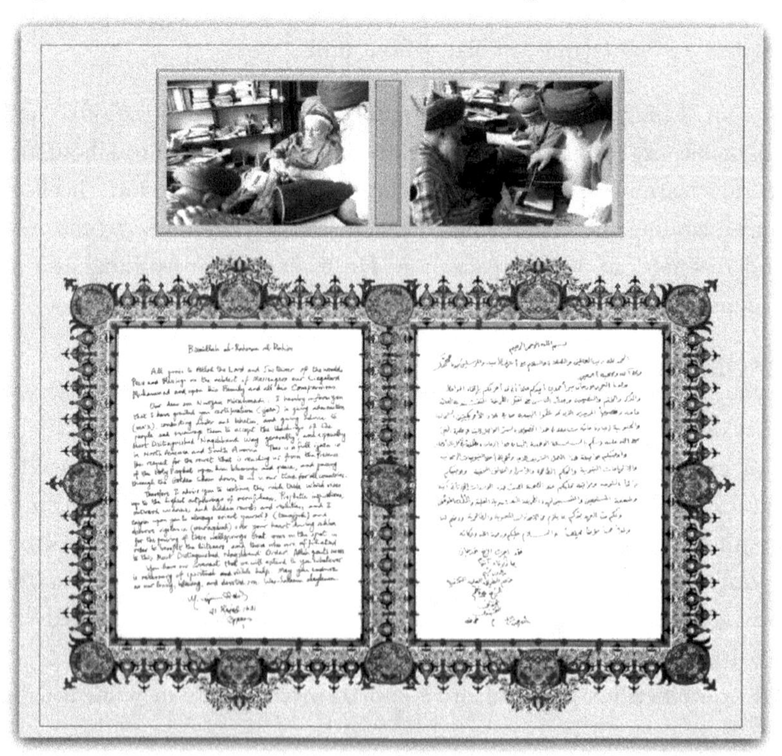

Shaykh Nurjan Mirahmadi has taught and travelled extensively throughout the world from Uzbekistan to Singapore, Thailand, Indonesia, Cyprus, Argentina, Peru, and North America. He teaches the spiritual sciences of Classical Islam, including meditation (*tafakkur*), subtle energy points (*lataif*), Islamic healing, the secrets of letters and numbers (*ilm huroof*), disciplining the self (*tarbiyya*), and the process of self-realization (*marif'ah*). He teaches the Muslim communities the prophetic ways of being kind, respectful and live in harmony with people. He emphasizes on good manners and respect, and often reminds his students that the spiritual journey begins from within and "You can't give what you don't have."

ACCOMPLISHMENTS

One of Shaykh Nurjan's greatest accomplishments has been the worldwide dissemination of the spiritual teachings of Classical Islam through his books and online presence. The Prophet Muhammad صلى الله عليه وسلم has told us, "Speak to people according to their levels." In an era of social media, Shaykh Nurjan's ability to reach a new generation of spiritual seekers through the Internet has been remarkable. His *NurMuhammad.com* website alone has over 1,500 unique visitors each day, and since its inception has seen more than 200,000 downloads of the book *"Dailal Khairat"*, 1.5 Million free downloads of *Naqshbandi Muraqabah*, and another 700,000 downloads of the *Naqshbandi Book of Devotions (Awrad)*, as well as many more articles. As of June 2017, his Facebook pages "Shaykh Nurjan Mirahmadi" and "Nur Muhammad" combined have over 850,000 likes and followers. Furthermore, his YouTube Channel "The Muhammadan Way" has over 2 million views, and his Google page, "Shaykh Sayed Nurjan Mirahmadi" has over 2.7 million views.

Shaykh Nurjan Mirahmadi focuses on the worldwide social media presence working on ways to bring knowledge to all seekers around the world. In 2015 he launched an Online University, called "SimplyIman.org", to spread these traditional Spiritual Islamic teachings even further and make it accessible to all seekers around the world.

For over 20 years Shaykh Nurjan has dedicated his life to spreading the true Islamic teachings of love, acceptance, respect and peace. He has established several non-profit organizations since the early 1990s and, over the past ten years, he has founded numerous educational and charitable organizations. In the Greater Vancouver region alone, he has established the following:

Divine Love: Hub-E-Rasul TV Series – launched in May 2017, this weekly half-hour Islamic television show covers a wide range of topics, focusing on spreading Prophet Muhammad's ﷺ message that Islam is a religion based on peace, love, tolerance and acceptance.

The show airs every Saturday at 1:30 pm (PST) on Joytv, reaching 7 million viewers Canada-wide. It reaches the online community through social media and through its website **huberasul.net.** For a full channel listing please visit **www.huberasul.net/schedule.**

Muhummadan Way App – a comprehensive resource of Islamic information for all mobile devices. Created for both Muslims and non-Muslims, it provides users with a wealth of knowledge including access to books, supplications, prayer times, month-specific practices, a media library of audio and video files, an events calendar, and much more.

Ahle Sunnah wal Jama of BC – this organization is a resource for authentic content, books, and articles from the Qur'an & Sunnah from around the world. It works in collaboration with the well-known international organizations, Al Azhar University of Cairo, Dar al Ifta of Egypt and Islamic Supreme Council of North America.

Hub-E-Rasul ﷺ Conference – monthly Milad & Mehfil-e-Dhikr events are organized and held throughout the Lower Mainland. The aim is to revive the teachings of the Qur'an and Sunnah by celebrating holy events in true Islamic spirit (*Isra wal Mi'raj, Laylatul Bara'h, Laylatul Qadr, Milad un-Nabi* etc.)

Naqshbandi Nazimiya Islamic Centre of Vancouver – this Centre is a place for people of all faiths and beliefs to attend weekly *dhikr* programs (circles of remembrance) three times a week (Thursdays, Fridays, and Saturdays). Shaykh Nurjan teaches above and beyond the principles of Islam including the deep realities of *maqam al-iman* (belief) and *maqam al-ihsan* (excellence of character).

SMC – an outreach organization that spreads teachings to the Western audience including concepts such as meditation and charity. It reaches out to other faiths to increase peace, love, and acceptance in the interfaith environment.

Simply Iman Cloud University – an international online platform allowing people from around the world to pursue studies in various aspects of faith and spirituality from a classical Islamic perspective. Students have the opportunity to learn at their own pace and engage in an open dialogue with a teacher in real-time.

Fatima Zahra Helping Hand – this charity organization runs a food program every two weeks which feeds more than 500 less fortunate people in the downtown eastside of Vancouver. It also collects clothing and non-perishable food items for the BC Muslim Food Bank and the Burnaby Homeless Shelter.

Shaykh Nurjan's Published Books – these titles are available at all major retailers and online.

- **Secret Realities of Hajj**
- **The Healing Power of Sufi Meditation**

Shaykh Nurjan has also established an international presence through many social media outlets including:

- **FaceBook (Shaykh Nurjan Mirahmadi)** with over 850,000 likes
- **YouTube Channel (NurMir)** with over 600 videos
- **NurMuhammad.com,** a comprehensive website containing many resources covering the deep realities of classical Islam.

Shaykh Nurjan's sincere mission is to spread the love of Sayyidina Muhammad ﷺ throughout the city for our families and children. If you would like to be a shareholder in all these blessings we invite you to support our Center by any means possible. We hope to strengthen our efforts by joining our hands in raising the Honourable Flag of Sayyidina Muhammad ﷺ.

UNIVERSALLY RECOGNIZED SYMBOLS

The following Arabic and English symbols connote sacredness and are universally recognized by Muslims:

The symbol عزّ وجلّ represents *Azza wa Jal*, a high form of praise reserved for God alone, which is customarily recited after reading or pronouncing the common name Allah, and any of the ninety-nine Islamic Holy Names of God.

The symbol صلى الله عليه وسلم represents *sall Allahu 'alayhi wa salaam* (God's blessings and greetings of peace be upon the Prophet), which is customarily recited after reading or pronouncing the holy name of the Prophet Muhammad صلى الله عليه وسلم.

The symbol عليه السلام represents *'alayhi 's-salam* (peace be upon him/her), which is customarily recited after reading or pronouncing the sanctified names of prophets, Prophet Muhammad's صلى الله عليه وسلم family members, and the angels.

The symbol رضي الله عنه represents *radi-allahu 'anh/'anha* (may God be pleased with him/her), which is customarily recited after reading or pronouncing the holy names of Prophet Muhammad's صلى الله عليه وسلم Companions.

The symbol ق represents *qaddas-allahu sirrah* (may God sanctify his or her secret), which is customarily recited after reading or pronouncing the name of a saint.

INTRODUCTION TO THE LEVELS OF THE HEART *LATAIF AL QALB* لطائف القلب

ACCORDING TO THE CLASSICAL ISLAMIC TEACHINGS

اَعُوْذُ بِاللهِ مِنَ الشَّيْطَانِ الرَّجِيْمِ
بِسْمِ اللهِ الرَّحْمَنِ الرَّحِيْم

A'udhu Billahi Minash Shaytanir Rajeem
Bismillahir Rahmanir Raheem

I seek refuge in Allah from Satan, the rejected one
In the Name of Allah, the Most Beneficent, the Most Merciful

Alhamdulillah (Praise be to Allah), that Allah عزّ وجلّ guided us to the love of Sayyidina Muhammad صلى الله عليه وسلم and into the hands of *awliyaullah* (saints), and their *uloom* and knowledges to take us towards the *marif'ah* (Gnosticism) and heavenly realities.

From the teachings of the Heart *(Lataif al Qalb)*, and these are subtle energy points upon the chest, upon the heart, that open the heart into the Divinely Presence. The Levels of the Heart, the subtle energies, and the reality of the heart, is the way and the door to the Divinely Presence. It is a timeless reality.

"These five stations of the heart are the center of the nine points, which represent the locus of revelation and inspiration of the Divine Presence in the heart of the human being. These nine points are located on the chest of each person and they represent nine different hidden states in every human being. Every state is connected to a saint, who has the authority to control that point. If the seeker in the Naqshbandi Way is able to unveil and to make spiritual contact with the authorized master controlling these points, he may be given knowledge of and power to use these nine points, *Latifah*/Chakra." (*From The Naqshbandi Sufi Way Book By Mawlana Shaykh Hisham Kabbani).*

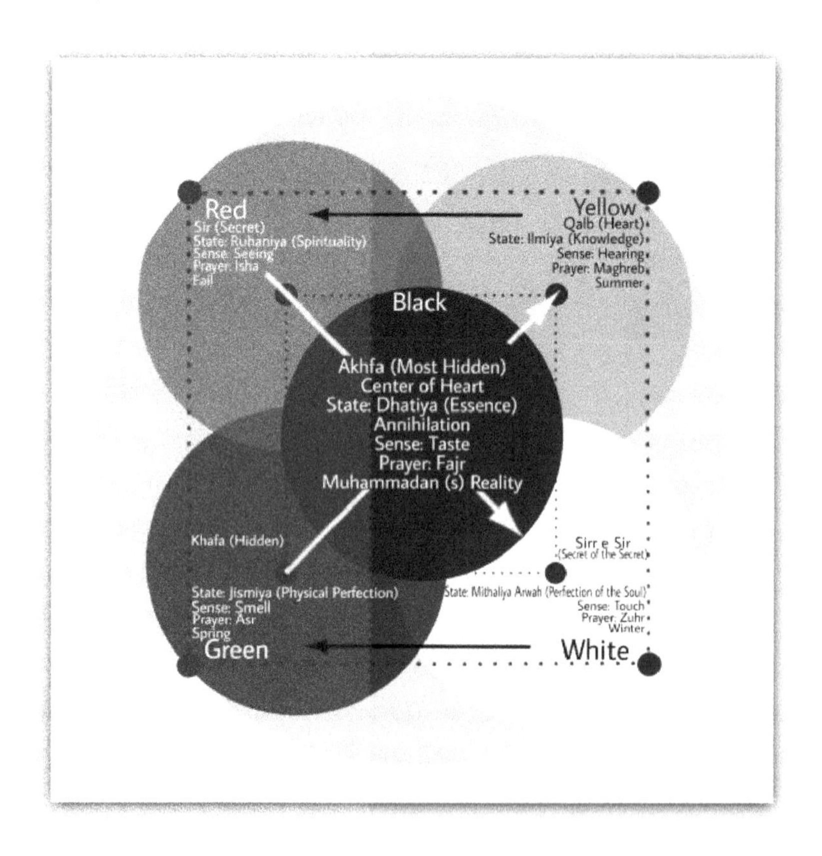

The guides begin to teach us how to enter into the heart and to the realities, the timeless realities of Allah's عزَّ وجلَّ Divinely Lights. That this goes from left to right. It starts from my heart, the first station of the Heart *(Qalb),* [on left side of chest] and it goes to the right side, the second station, the Secret *(Sir).*

It is an eternal hourglass like an eternity. It goes from the First Station of the Heart *(Qalb)*, to the Secret *(Sir),* the Second Station. The Secret *(Sir)* has to pass through the center, the Most Hidden (*Akhfa*) to get to the Third Station of the Secret of the Secret *(Sirr e Sir)*, then to the Fourth Station, the Hidden *(Khafa).* The Hidden *(Khafa)* passes again through the Fifth Station, the Most Hidden (*Akhfa*), back to the Heart (Q*alb),* the First Station. It is like an hourglass that it goes left, right, cut down, again to the right and back up. So it's like a figure 8 across the chest or across the heart but has a deep reality and everything that we are moving towards in the oceans of reality.

1. First Level: Station of the Heart, *Qalb* قلب

The first station of the heart is called the Heart (*Qalb* **قلب**) and it represents knowledge. Prophet Adam عليه السلام is responsible for this station as he was taught all the names and realities *(Qur'an, 2:31).* Allah عزَّ وجلَّ has honoured human beings due to that divinely knowledge.

Stage of Star Formation: **The Sun.** The Sun is the gravitational center of the solar system. Its gravitational pull is what keeps the planets in place in their orbits. It pours life-giving light, heat, and energy on Earth.

2. Second Level: Station of the Secret, *Sir* سر

The Secret (*Sir* سر) is the second station of the heart. It represents the spiritual vision. Prophet Nuh (Noah) عليه السلام is responsible for this station of teaching which includes building faith, and safety from ignorance.

Stage of Star Formation: **Red Giant.** The sun will expand to about a 100 – 1000 times its current size and it will become a Red Giant Star that will be 2,000 – 1 Million times more luminous than our Sun.

3. Third Level: Station of the Secret of the Secret, *Sirr e Sir* سر السر

The Secret of the Secret *(Sirr e Sir* سر السر) is the third station of the heart. It represents the spiritual perfection and certainty (*Ya'qeen*). Prophet Abraham عليه السلام and Prophet Moses عليه السلام are responsible for this Station. They are teaching about the secret of the Divine Fire and how to turn the fire of anger into the fire of the Divine Love.

Stage of Star Formation: **White Dwarf.** When the Red Giant passes the Planetary Nebula (*Nabiullah* (Prophet of Allah), the Most Hidden), what remains of it is a White Dwarf. This is a very small, hot star. White dwarfs have a mass of the Sun, but only 1% of the Sun's luminosity and diameter, approximately the diameter of the Earth. They have a very high density due to gravitational effects, i.e. one spoonful has a mass of several tonnes.

4. Fourth Level: Station of the Hidden, *Khafa* خفا /خفي

The Hidden *(Khafa* خفا) is the fourth station of the heart. It represents physical perfection and the reality of *Insan Kamil* (Perfected Being). It is under the authority of Sayyidina Isa (Jesus) عليه السلام. He represents the spiritual understanding, reviving the dead, resurrection, and *Qiyamah* (The Day of Resurrection).

Stage of Star Formation: **Neutron Star - Green Pulsar.** These stars are produced when a supernova explodes, forcing the protons and electrons to combine to produce a neutron star. Neutron stars are very dense with a mass of three times the Sun but a diameter of only 20 km. Pulsars are believed to be neutron stars that are spinning very rapidly.

5. Fifth Level: Station of the Most Hidden, *Akhfa* أخفاء

The Most Hidden *(Akhfa* أخفاء) is the fifth station of the heart and it is black because it represents *fana* (annihilation). It is under the authority of Sayyidina Muhammad ﷺ as he was the one who was raised up to the Divine Presence, in the Night of Ascension *(Isra wal Mi'raj)*. The Arabic letter of Alif ا in *Akhfa* أخفا denotes *'Izzat Allah* (Allah's Honor) as it does in the words of *Islam* اسلام, *Iman* ايمان, and *Ihsan* احسان.

<u>Stage of Star Formation:</u> **<u>Black Hole.</u>** Black holes are believed to form from massive stars at the end of their lifetimes. The gravitational pull in a black hole is so great that nothing can escape from it, not even light. Since no light can get out, people can't see black holes. Black holes can often suck neighbouring matter into them including stars.

Star Formation information from:

The Open University. (2016) *The Life Cycle of a Star.* Retrieved from http://www.telescope.org/pparc/res8.html

Subhana rabbika rabil 'izzati 'ama yasifoon, Wa salamun 'alal mursaleen wal hamdulillahi rabbil 'alameen. Bi hurmati Muhammadil Mustafa wa bi siratil Suratil Fatiha.

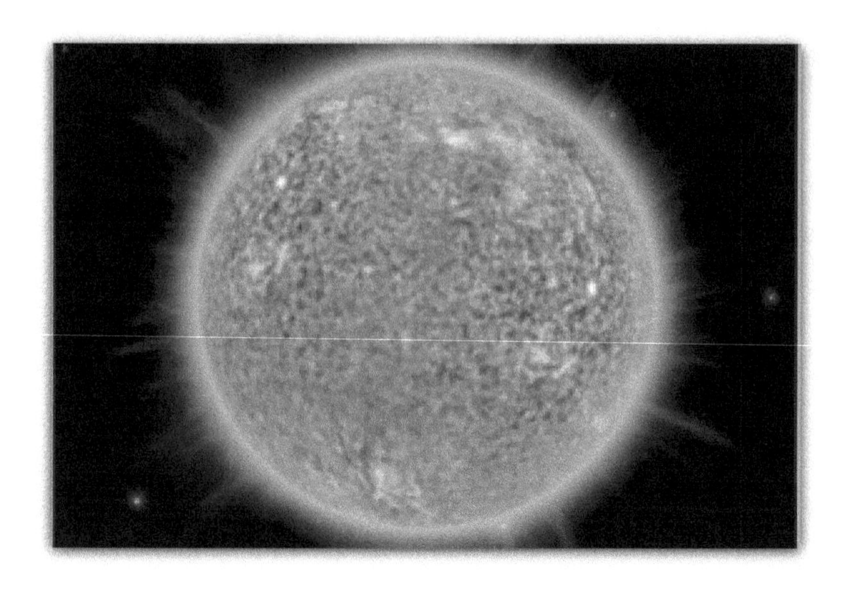

THE HEART

SUN – THE CENTER OF THE UNIVERSE

قَلْبَ الْمُؤْمِنْ بَيْتُ الرَّبْ

"Qalb al mu'min baytur rabb."

"The heart of the believer is the House of the Lord."

(Hadith Qudsi, Prophet Muhammad ﷺ)

...أَن طَهِّرَا بَيْتِيَ لِلطَّائِفِينَ وَالْعَاكِفِينَ وَالرُّكَّعِ السُّجُودِ ١٢٥

2:125 – "...An Tahhir baytee liTayifeena, wal 'Aakifeena, wa ruka'is sujood." (Surah Al-Baqarah)

"...Purify/Sanctify My House for those who perform Tawaf (circumambulation) and those who seclude themselves for devotion, and bow and prostrate [in prayer]." (The Cow, 2:125)

FIRST LEVEL THE HEART

STATION OF *QALB* قلب

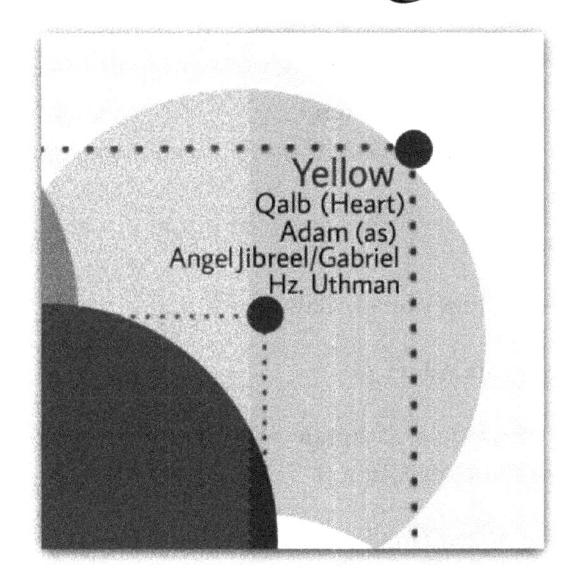

DIVINELY KNOWLEDGE

The Station of the *Qalb* (Heart) is symbolized by the Sun. The Sun is the center of the Universe and it holds the Solar System together with its gravitational pull. It pours life-giving light, heat, and energy on Earth. The Heart is the center of our inner universe. The first sense to open in the levels of the heart is the Hearing. The door to the soul is hearing. The *Qalb* is the state of *Ilmiya* (knowledge), and this is where all the divinely knowledge comes first.

Realities of the First Level of the Heart *Qalb* (Heart)

State: ***Ilmiya* (Knowledge)**

Sense: **Hearing**

Stage of Star Formation: **the Sun**

Colour: **Yellow**

Season: **Summer**

Archangel: **Sayyidina Jibreel/Gabriel** عليه السلام

Prophet: **Sayyidina Adam** عليه السلام

Companion: **Sayyidina Uthman al Ghani** عليه السلام – ***Jami'ul Qur'an* (Compiler of the Holy Qur'an)**

Pillar of Islam: ***Shahadah* (Testimony of Faith)**

Salat (Prayer time): ***Maghrib* (Evening) – After sunset**

Dhikr: ***SubhanAllah* (Glory be to Allah)**

Seek Support: ***Ya Sayyid* (O Master) – *Saliheen* (Righteous)**

6th Sense: **Spiritual Hearing**

HIGHLIGHTS OF THE STATION OF *QALB* (HEART)

- Station of *Qalb* (Heart) is the entry point to the reality
- Hearing is the door to the soul
- Sun is the source of Light and Power
- Sun is the Center of the Universe
- Heart is the Center of our Inner Universe
- Heart of the Believer is the House of God
- Vigilance of the Heart - Guard Your Heart
- Significance of the Heart in the Body
- Everything is Created from *NurMuhammad* صلى الله عليه وسلم
- Heart of Sayyidina Muhammad صلى الله عليه وسلم is the Ark of the Covenant
- Qur'an is emanating from the heart of Sayyidina Muhammad صلى الله عليه وسلم
- Sayyidina Jibreel (Gabriel) عليه السلام brings the Divinely Knowledge
- Adamic reality - He was taught all the Names
- Children of Adam are the Honoured Creation
- Angels bowed down to the Light and Knowledge that Sayyidina Adam عليه السلام carried
- Sayyidina Uthman عليه السلام was given the secret knowledge of Holy Qur'an
- *Shahada*– Testifying to the oneness of the Lord and accepting His Messenger, Sayyidina Muhammad صلى الله عليه وسلم
- Seek the righteous one for guidance

HEART – THE SUN OF THE BODY, THE HOUSE OF GOD

STATION OF THE *QALB* (HEART) IS THE ENTRY POINT

We move from the first station of *Qalb* (Heart), to the *Sir* (Secret) the second station, to the *Sirr e Sir* (Secret of the Secret), to *Khafa* (Hidden) and *Akhfa* (Most Hidden), which is black, and then annihilating and entering into the Divinely Presence. For now we focus just on the Heart; that the entry point for that understanding is the *Qalb* (Heart) and the secret of that color is yellow. Heart is the Sun of the universe within.

MAKE THE HEART THE HOUSE OF ALLAH عزَّ وجلَّ

When Allah عزَّ وجلَّ describes begin to purify My House, the *masjid* of Allah عزَّ وجلَّ.

أَن طَهِّرَا بَيْتِيَ لِلطَّائِفِينَ وَالْعَاكِفِينَ وَالرُّكَّعِ السُّجُودِ ١٢٥

2:125 – "…An Tahhir baytee liTayifeena, wal 'Aakifeena, wa ruka'is sujood." (Surah Al-Baqarah)

"...Purify/ Sanctify My House for those who perform Tawaf (circumambulation) and those who seclude themselves for devotion, and bow and prostrate [in prayer]." (The Cow, 2:125)

One is the exterior *masjid* (mosque) we build for Allah عزَّ وَجَلَّ, that we all want for our communities, but more important is that all the people who are involved in the *masjid* to also be building the *masjid* that He gave us within ourselves. It means that to make the heart of the believer the House of Allah عزَّ وَجَلَّ.

قَلْبَ الْمُؤْمِنْ بَيْتُ الرَّبْ

"Qalb al mu'min baytur rabb."

"The heart of the believer is the House of the Lord." (Hadith Qudsi)

Purify that house, sanctify that house, make *tawaf* around that house; this is the heart of the believer.

THERE WERE 360 IDOLS (FALSE GODS) IN *MAKKAH*

From *Awliya's* understanding and what Prophet صلى الله عليه وسلم gave from *Bismillahir Rahmanir Raheem, ati ullah atiur Rasula wa ulul amri minkum.*

يَاأَيُّهَا الَّذِينَ آمَنُوا أَطِيعُوااللَّه وَأَطِيعُوٱلرَّسُولَ وَأُوْلِي الأَمْرِ مِنْكُمْ...

4:59 – "Ya ayyu hal ladheena amanooAtiullaha, wa atiur Rasola, wa Ulil amre minkum..." (Surah An-Nisa)

"O You who have believed, Obey Allah, Obey the Messenger, and those in authority among you..." (The Women, 4:59)

In the understanding of the subtle energy points of the *lataif*, that we have 360 *lataifs* on the body. Also there were 360 idols in *Makkah*, which is not a random number. Everything Allah عزَّ وَجَلَّ describes is perfectly numbered.

لِّيَعْلَمَ أَن قَدْ أَبْلَغُوا رِسَالَاتِ رَبِّهِمْ وَأَحَاطَ بِمَا لَدَيْهِمْ وَأَحْصَىٰ كُلَّ شَيْءٍ عَدَدًا ٢٨

72:28 – "Liya'lama an qad ablaghoo risalati rabbihim wa ahata bima ladayhim wa ahsa kulla shay in 'adada." (Surah Al-Jinn)

"That He may know that they have conveyed the messages of their Lord; and He has encompassed whatever is with them and has enumerated all things in number." (The Jinn, 72:28)

It means the concept of the idol is the false god, that which you worship other than Allah عزّ وجلّ. It could be a desire, could be a deceit, could be a person, it could be anything that takes us away from the reality of worshipping Allah عزّ وجلّ.

KNOW THE *ARBAB* (LORDS) THAT GOVERN YOU

For *Ahlul Tazkiya,* the people who are trying to clean themselves, from holy *Hadith* of Prophet ﷺ, "Who knows himself will know His Lord."

مَنْ عَرَفَ نَفْسَهُ فَقَدْ عَرَفَ رَبَّهُ

"Man 'arafa nafsa hu faqad 'arafa Rabba hu."

"Who knows himself, knows his Lord." Prophet Muhammad ﷺ

Who does not know himself will not know his Lord. So we took a path in which we are trying to know ourselves. That way of knowing the self means you are going to find all the *rabs* (lords) and all the *arbab* (lords) that are governing *insaan* (human being). So there is not only one *rabbi al a'la* (The Lord Almighty). Allah عزّ وجلّ is the Creator! But there are many lords upon this heart, that are governing this body not to submit, not to pray, not to fast, and not to give in charity. Had we conquered these *rabs* and destroyed the false lords that govern this body, we could be walking on water. We should be seeing the Seven Heavens and hearing the *dhikr* of *Malaika*, angels.

It means if we didn't achieve that, then they are reminding us that there are many lords upon your heart. These were the idols that Prophet ﷺ was fighting. There were 360 idols in *Makkah. Makkah* is the state of the heart. 360 idols were blocking and encompassing *Makkah* because it is significant for the heart.

THE 360 ENERGY POINTS *(LATAIF)* IN THE BODY

This means that we have 360 *lataif* and energy points on the body, like satellite dishes of the body. Each one of them has an idol on its place that is trying to block us from submission to Allah عزّ وجلّ.

Our life is to destroy those idols, destroy those desires, destroy all those bad characteristics and perfect the whole 360 degrees that makes the circle. The circle, like the hand, that you want it to be *kamil*, perfected, and to understand the way of perfection.

So many people focus on teachings of the body and the form. They come and the guides begin to teach us that discipline the form with Islam, which means submission. It means use your practices to discipline the form and to bring the bad characteristics of the form down, and to begin to move into the oceans of realities and the oceans of light.

From the teachings of the *lataif* (Levels of the Heart), that they are subtle energy points upon the heart, that open the heart into the Divinely Presence. We must understand that our whole body is like satellite dishes, 360 different subtle energy points of the body that pick up these energies and they support us. It means that we are an energy being. The food that we eat is for the physicality but the spirituality and the energy and power that Allah عزّ وجلّ is sending is to the soul.

Everything is Based on the Levels of the Heart

For *Awliyaullah* (Saints), their focus is on the points within the chest, and the *Qalb* (heart). From the understanding of the *lataif*, and trying to focus on the *lataif*, knowledge of the *lataif*, and how important they are.

We have discussed in many other teachings that it has enormous layers of reality. Once you begin to study this concept of the *lataif* (Levels of the Heart), you see that many of the *dhikrs* are in this understanding. Our *salah* (daily prayer) is in this understanding; it means it holds the basis of moving into the Divinely Presence.

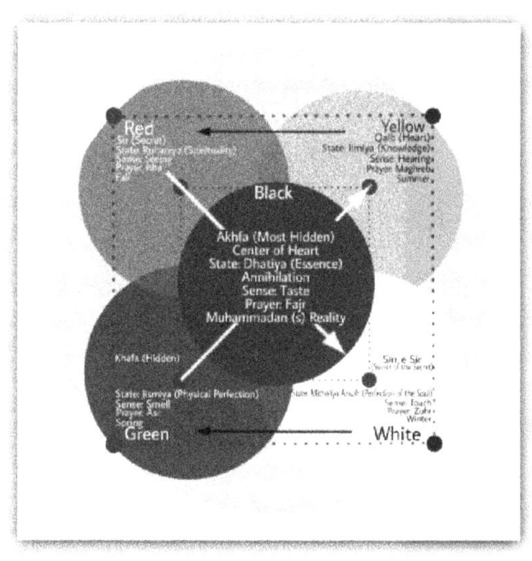

According to the Sufi tradition, everything in our lives is based on these *Lataif al Qalb*, (Levels of the Heart). You will go from yellow (the Heart) to red (the Secret); you pass the black (the Most Hidden), you go down to the white (the Secret of the Secret), then to the green (the Hidden), then to black (the Most Hidden), and then the whole ocean of blue that's all encompassing.

It means that everything in our life is going to be based on the understanding of these *lataifs* (Levels of the Heart); from the seasons to the timing of the day, to the reality of each of the prophets, to every colour and its significance. This means that many, many oceans of reality begin to open from that understanding, but again backed with all the chanting and practices.

There are ***Ashab Nabi*** **(Companions of Prophet Muhammad ﷺ):**

1. **Sayyidina Uthman** عليه السلام – Station of *Qalb* (Heart)

2. **Sayyidina Umar** عليه السلام – Station of *Sir* (Secret)

3. **Sayyidina Abu Bakr as-Siddiq** عليه السلام – Station of *Sirr e Sir* (Secret of the Secret)

4. **Sayyidina Ali** عليه السلام – Station of *Khafa* (Hidden)

5. **Sayyidina Muhammad** ﷺ – Station of *Akhfa* (Most Hidden)

There are ***Ahlul Bayt*** **(Family of Prophet Muhammad ﷺ):**

1. **Imam Hassan** عليه السلام – Station of *Qalb* (Heart)

2. **Imam Hussain** عليه السلام – Station of *Sir* (Secret)

3. **Sayyidatina Fatima** عليه السلام – Station of *Sirr e Sir* (Secret of the Secret)

4. **Sayyidina Ali** عليه السلام – Station of *Khafa* (Hidden)

5. **Sayyidina Muhammad** ﷺ – Station of *Akhfa* (Most Hidden)

Significance of the Heart Chakra

The Heart Purifies the Blood

We pray that the bad character goes and the Divine to be happy. If the Divine is happy, that heart chakra begins to open. If the heart chakra opens from the Divinely order, it will fix all the chakras, because it's the seed of energy.

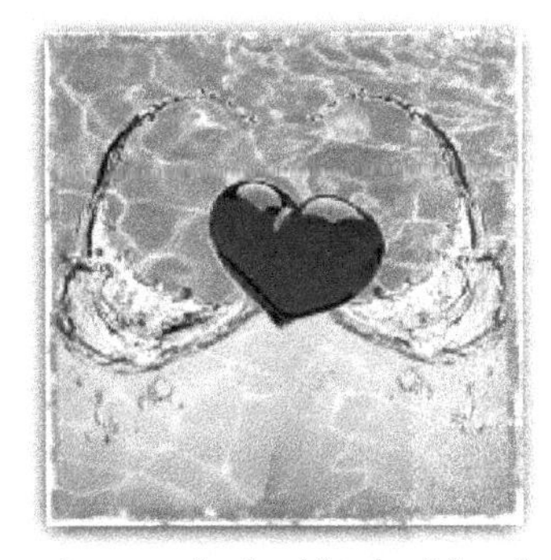

We said before when you breathe, your life is based on breath. All masters came and taught that our way is based on the breath. If you watch the physiology of the body, that when you breathe, that breath comes in and the lungs take the breath then they take the energy, the nourishment of that breath, and they send the blood directly into the heart. Then the heart now has to deal with the blood; the heart now has to process that breath. The heart has to then stamp that blood and send it to all the organs of the body.

Dirty Heart Contaminates the Whole Body

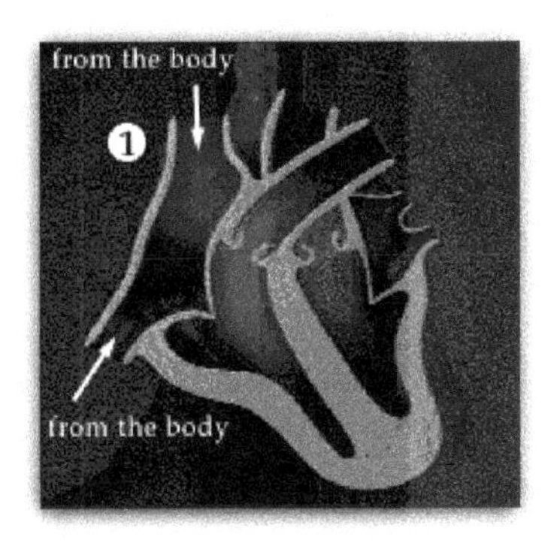

If contaminants are in the heart, it doesn't matter how well we breathe, how well we open up other chakras; it is still being stamped by what's within the heart. The seed of this power; if it's contaminated, dirtied or corrupted; it will corrupt the entire body, and darken the whole body.

أَلا وَإِنَّ فِى الْجَسَدِ مُضْغَةً إِذَا صَلَحَتْ صَلَحَ الْجَسَدُ كُلُّهُ، وَإِذَا فَسَدَتْ فَسَدَ الْجَسَدُ كُلُّهُ، أَلا وَهِى الْقَلْبُ

Qala Rasulullah ﷺ *– "Ala wa inna fil Jasadi mudghatan idha salahat salahal jasadu kulluho, wa idha fasadat fasadal jasadu kulluho, ala wa heyal Qalb."*

"There is a piece of flesh in the body, if it becomes good (reformed) the whole body becomes good but if it gets spoiled the whole body gets spoiled and that is the heart." Prophet Muhammad ﷺ.

The Sufis then focus on the heart and that is the most difficult *lataif* (chakra) to focus on because it requires passing security tests. The Divine tests before that light and these realities open. There are so many stages of testing because what God gives, He doesn't take away. Every stage of what He is going to give is going to be based on the perfection of character. Again, if that opens and begins to open, then begins the blossoming and the nourishing of the entire body; the entire body will benefit from all of those realities. Every *lataif*, every chakra, in the body will benefit from that reality.

Reality of Mirroring and Accompanying the Perfected Guides

In the old days, the teachers would give students mantras and different things to recite and they would go and work on themselves. That time doesn't exist anymore. People are too busy, too much in worldly affairs and worldly distractions. What's important now is the reality of mirrors and mirroring.

It means by keeping the company of the Shaykhs and the Shaykhs that kept the company of their Shaykhs, they are opening a reality of mirrors.

المؤمن مرآة المؤمن

"Al mu'min miratal mu'min."

"The believer is the mirror of the believer." Prophet Muhammad ﷺ
(Narrated by Abu Hurairah)

It means if you sit in the presence of a mirror long enough, it's going to reflect its reality upon you. All they ask from us is then that you do these chantings; you do these mantras to polish your mirror. As much as you are reciting, as much as you are reciting, then you are polishing, polishing, and polishing.

As we begin to polish and polish and polish, what happens is you will begin to take on the reflection of the master, the teachers. By keeping their company, by keeping our practices, by keeping our chanting, and by keeping our way is polishing, polishing, polishing, so that they can begin to reflect that perfection onto us.

The Spiritual Guides Dress Us From Their Knowledge

The knowledge of these different *lataifs* (chakras) is that when we polish and polish and polish and then seek out their knowledges, they begin to dress us from that reality. By studying one of their subjects or going into that understanding, you begin to open the soul to ask the Divine that, 'I heard about the *lataifs* of the heart, I heard about the chakras of the heart and I have from these Divinely knowledges.' The soul begins to ask the Divine Presence from those realities, 'Dress me from those realities'.

Subhana rabbika rabil 'izzati 'ama yasifoon, Wa salamun 'alal mursaleen wal hamdulillahi rabbil 'alameen. Bi hurmati Muhammadil Mustafa wa bi siratil Suratil Fatiha.

THE HEART OF SAYYIDINA MUHAMMAD ﷺ IS THE ARK OF THE COVENANT OF ALLAH عز وجل

إِنَّ اللَّهَ اشْتَرَىٰ مِنَ الْمُؤْمِنِينَ أَنفُسَهُمْ وَأَمْوَالَهُم بِأَنَّ لَهُمُ الْجَنَّةَ ... وَعْدًا عَلَيْهِ حَقًّا فِي التَّوْرَاةِ وَالْإِنجِيلِ وَالْقُرْآنِ وَمَنْ أَوْفَىٰ بِعَهْدِهِ مِنَ اللَّهِ فَاسْتَبْشِرُوا بِبَيْعِكُمُ الَّذِي بَايَعْتُم بِهِ وَذَٰلِكَ هُوَ الْفَوْزُ الْعَظِيمُ

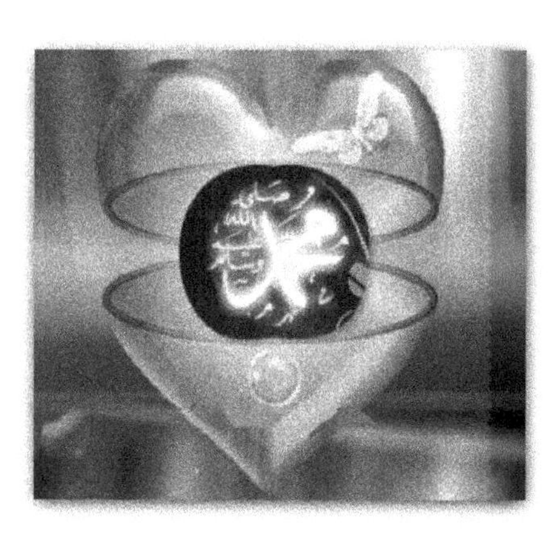

9:111 – "Inna Allaha Ashtara Minal Mu'umineena 'Anfusahum Wa 'Amwalahum Bi anna Lahumul Jannata, …Wa'dan 'Alayhi Haqqan fit Tawrati wal Injeeli wal Qur'ani, Wa Man Awfa Bi 'Ahdihi Mina Allahi, Fastabshiro Bi bay'ikum Al Ladhi Baaya'tum Bihi, Wa Dhalika Huwal Fawzul 'azeem." (Surah At-Tawbah)

"Indeed, Allah has purchased from the believers their lives and their properties [in exchange] for that they will have the Paradise…, a promise binding on Him in truth, in the Torah and the Gospel and the Qur'an. And who is more faithful to his Ahd (Covenant) than Allah? Then rejoice in your Bayat/Allegiance which you have fulfilled. And that is the great achievement." (The Repentance, 9:111)

NABI MUSA'S عليه السلام ARK OF THE COVENANT WAS SYMBOLIC

In the time of Nabi Musa عليه السلام, the *Ahd* (Covenant), was the Ark of the Covenant, because everything was an imitation for the arrival of Sayyidina Muhammad ﷺ. So they had the Tablets and they put it in a Box and the four angels held the Box and everywhere they moved they were victorious. That was symbolic of the Divine Presence at the *maqaam* (station) of Sayyidina Musa عليه السلام.

PROPHET MUHAMMAD'S ﷺ HEART IS THE ARK OF COVENANT

The greatness of Sayyidina Muhammad ﷺ is that he is the custodian of all realities. It means when he ﷺ arrived upon Earth, the real Covenant, the real *Ahad* of Allah عز وجل, opened upon Earth. That is the heart of the believer. This is the Covenant that Prophet ﷺ brought. Allah عز وجل says, "I am not in Heaven, I am not on Earth, I am not in that Box, I am not anywhere but I am in the heart of My Believer."

مَا وَسِعَنِيْ سَمَائِيْ ولا اَرْضِيْ وَلَكِنْ وَسِعَنِيْ قَلْبِ عَبْدِيْ اَلْمُؤْمِنْ

"Maa wasi`anee Samayee, wa la ardee, laakin wasi'anee qalbi 'Abdee al Mu'min."

"Neither My Heavens nor My Earth can contain Me, but the heart of my Believing Servant." (Hadith Qudsi conveyed by Prophet Muhammad ﷺ)

Allah's عز وجل only believer who arrived upon Earth is Sayyidina Muhammad ﷺ. The only believer which Allah عز وجل looks to is

Sayyidina Muhammad ﷺ. Sayyidina Muhammad ﷺ looks to all Creation. Allah's عز و جل *nazar* (gaze) is only upon Sayyidina Muhammad ﷺ.

It means then this heart and its *lataif* (energy points) is the Covenant of Allah عز و جل for *Ummati Muhammad* ﷺ. They don't have to look for a Box; they don't need angels to carry a Box for them to be victorious in battle. Where now that is what they are looking for; they are going to try to tear apart *Masjid al-Aqsa* to get to the Covenant, to get to their Box. They believe with that Box they should be victorious. But with the arrival of Sayyidina Muhammad ﷺ that Box was negated. What is victorious is the heart of the believer!

THE ANGELS GUARD THE HEART AND LEVELS OF THE HEART

That is why we study the Levels of the Heart and go into its teachings. These are the angels that are guarding; Sayyidina Jibreel عليه السلام at the First Station – the Heart (*Qalb*), Sayyidina Mikhail عليه السلام at the Second Station – the Secret (*Sir*), Sayyidina Izrail عليه السلام at the Third Station – the Secret of the Secret (*Sirr e Sir*), Sayyidina Israfil عليه السلام at the Fourth Station – the Hidden (*Khafa*). Then Sayyidina Malik عليه السلام is at the Fifth Station – the Most Hidden (*Akhfa*). He is at the center and the guardian, the enforcer for

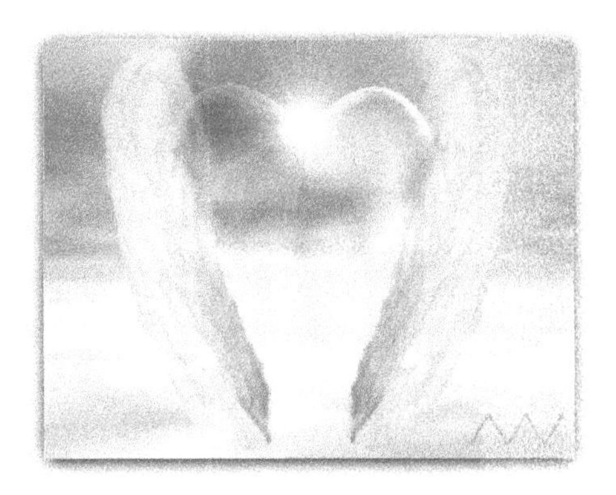

all of the *lataif* and Levels of the Heart. For, if anything should open of this heart, the guardians of Hell, Sayyidina Malik عليه السلام should be guarding that servant. It means they use Sayyidina Malik عليه السلام as a dragon that is upon them, a guardian for their presence on Earth. Otherwise these realities that open upon Earth, the *shayateen* (devils) would have destroyed them.

THE HEART CAN ONLY BE OPENED BY *IBADUR RAHMAN* (SERVANTS OF ALLAH, THE MOST COMPASSIONATE)

It means the Covenant, the *Ahd*, that they want for us to open is the reality of the heart; and how to focus upon the heart and how to open its realities.

إِنَّ الَّذِينَ يُبَايِعُونَكَ إِنَّمَا يُبَايِعُونَ اللَّـهَ يَدُ اللَّـهِ فَوْقَ أَيْدِيهِمْ ۚ فَمَن نَّكَثَ فَإِنَّمَا يَنكُثُ عَلَىٰ نَفْسِهِ ۖ وَمَنْ أَوْفَىٰ بِمَا عَاهَدَ عَلَيْهُ اللَّـهَ فَسَيُؤْتِيهِ أَجْرًا عَظِيمًا (١٠)

48:10 – "Innal ladheena yubayi'oonaka innama yubayi'on Allaha yadullahi fawqa aydeehim, faman nakatha fa innama yankuthu 'ala nafsihi, wa man awfa bima 'ahada 'alayhu Allaha fasayu teehi ajran 'azheema." (Surah Al-Fath)

"Indeed, those who give Bayat (pledge allegiance) to you, [O Muhammad] – they are actually giving Bayat (pledge allegiance) to Allah. The hand of Allah is over their hands. So he whoever breaks his pledge/oath, only breaks it to the detriment/Harm/loss of himself. And whoever fulfills their Covenant (Bayat) that which he has promised Allah – He will grant him a great reward."
(The Victory, 48:10)

The realities of the heart can only be opened by those who are *Ahlul Basirah* (Pious People with Spiritual Vision). From among a select group of *Ahlul Basirah*, there are some from *Ibadur Rahman* (Servants of the Most Compassionate). Allah عز وجل mentions, *"Allamal Qur'an. Khalaqal insan."*

الرَّحْمَـٰنُ (١) عَلَّمَ الْقُرْآنَ (٢) خَلَقَ الْإِنسَانَ (٣)

55:1-3 – "Ar Rahmaan. 'Allamal Qur'an. Khalaqal Insaan."
(Surah Ar-Rahman)

"The Most Merciful. (1) It is He Who has taught the Qur'an. (2) He has created Man. (3)" (The Beneficent, 55:1-3)

It is a description for a reality that Allah عزّ وجلّ has been given to them, that they are the custodians of the reality of the Holy Qur'an within their heart. We pray that Allah عزّ وجلّ keeps them amongst us. *Alhamdulillah* from *Ibadur Rahman* are Sultan al-Awliya Mawlana Shaykh AbdAllah Fa'iz ad-Daghestani ق, Sultan al-Awliya Mawlana Shaykh Muhammad Nazim Adil al-Haqqani ق and Sultan al-Awliya Mawlana Shaykh Hisham Kabbani. They are the custodians of that reality upon the Earth, which is far greater than any *tariqa* (spiritual path), and the names of *tariqas*, which mean nothing anymore.

Be "Muhammadiyoon"
Sayyidina Mahdi عليه السلام is Coming as Muhammadan Representative

The names of all *tariqas* are going to vanish. All that matters is to be *"Muhammadiyoon"*. Sayyidina Mahdi's عليه السلام arrival upon Earth is very close, very, very close. Many, many signs are moving very quickly upon Earth. Sayyidina Mahdi عليه السلام does not follow

any one's name and all names must follow Sayyidina Mahdi عليه السلام. He is the Muhammadan representative and the Muhammadan Way.

We pray that Allah عز و جل gives us life to see those days and prepares our hearts for the arrival of Sayyidina Mahdi عليه السلام. We pray that Allah عز و جل keeps us under the flag of Sayyidina Mahdi عليه السلام, the seven *Wazirs* (Ministers) of Sayyidina Mahdi عليه السلام, the *Khulafa* (Viceroy) of Sayyidina Mahdi عليه السلام and the *Nawab* of Sayyidina Mahdi عليه السلام.

The Moon Focuses Only on the Sun

For our focus is to be on what is real, and keep the company of those who are real. They *(Awliyaullah)* are fragranced from the presence of Sayyidina Muhammad ﷺ. They are fragranced from the lights of Sayyidina Muhammad ﷺ and their entire *nazar* (gaze) is upon Sayyidina Muhammad ﷺ.

Awliyaullah's (saints) whole *tafakkur*, contemplation, is to always be present in the presence of Sayyidina Muhammad ﷺ! If for a moment Prophet ﷺ should turn away from them, it would be better to be dead, that something must be wrong, and Prophet ﷺ must be upset.

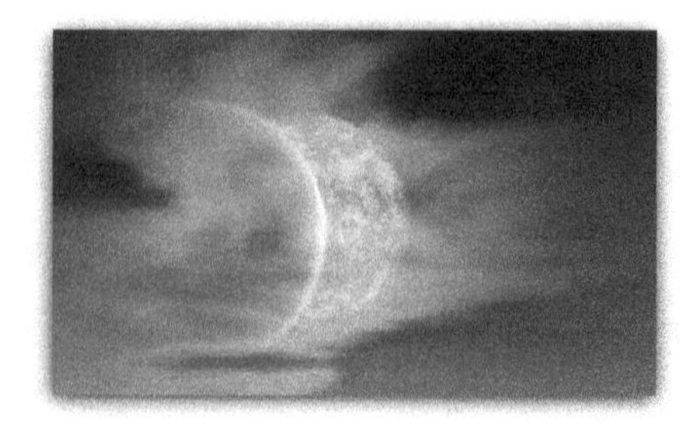

It means then, it gives us an understanding that those types of souls only focus on the 'Sun'. If you were to talk to the Moon, the Moon doesn't talk about Saturn, and Jupiter; it only knows what Allah عز و جل

wants it to know. It means it focuses on the Sun; it focuses on the Muhammadan Reality. It focuses on the love of Sayyidina Muhammad ﷺ, on how to achieve the love of Sayyidina Muhammad ﷺ so that we can achieve Allah's عَزَّ وَجَلَّ satisfaction. So to be dressed by that light, be blessed by that light and as a result of that light and blessings then you should be a reflection of that light because anything you focus on should be focusing on you.

It means if the focus is sincere, and the focus is towards Sayyidina Muhammad ﷺ then those beatific lights begin to dress the believer; the *Sunnah* of Prophet ﷺ begins to dress the believer and the eloquence of speech and softness of character begins to dress the believer.

ONLY *TAFAKKUR* (CONTEMPLATION) OPENS THE HEART

We pray that Allah عَزَّ وَجَلَّ dresses us and blesses us from these holy lights and allows us to reach that Covenant. And to take the steps necessary in which to open the heart and that is only through *tafakkur*, contemplation. Nothing in *had ad-dunya* (limit of the material world) is going to open those realities. This (opening) is from the *malakut* (heavens).

In days of difficulty the believers will go underground. The underground which is the reality of the Cave, is that they find no safety above on the surface of the world. The only safety they have is through their *tafakkur* (contemplation/meditation). By training on your *tafakkur*, contemplation, it becomes your life line. When you understand your life line and who is sending you support, you don't look left or right. Everything else is a distraction and many things can come into our life that will cut that life line.

It means by being from *Ahl at-Tafakkur* (People of Contemplation), they are guarding that life line with all their being. It means they sit and contemplate, train on how to negate themselves, and by negating themselves they are asking for the *madad* (support). They are asking for the support of Mawlana Shaykh Hisham Kabbani, the most powerful *Awliyaullah* (saint) on this Earth right now, where he carries the entire Earth beyond what we can imagine with our imagination.

When we call them *'Awliyaullah'* (saints) and we call them a *'Qutb'* and we call them *'al-Mutassarif'*, it means they inherit because Prophet ﷺ describes that, "My *Ulama* are inheritors of the prophets of *Bani Israel*."

عُلَمَاءِ وَرِثَةُ الأَنْبِيَاء

"Ulama e warithatul anbiya."

"The scholars are the inheritors of the prophets."

IBADUR RAHMAN ARE CUSTODIANS OF A VERY SPECIFIC LIGHT

The heart doesn't light by the brain; the heart can only light from *Ibad ar-Rahman* where Allah عزّ وجلّ says, "Whom We granted a light, We granted a light, whom We didn't give light, they have no light."

مَن يَهْدِ اللَّـهُ فَهُوَ الْمُهْتَدِ ۖ وَمَن يُضْلِلْ فَلَن تَجِدَ لَهُ وَلِيًّا مُّرْشِدًا ١٧

18:17 – "… man yahdillahu fahuwal Muhtadi, wa man yudlil falan tajida lahu waliyyan murshida." (Surah Al-Kahf)

"…He whom Allah, guides is rightly guided; but he whom Allah leaves to stray,- for him you will never find Saintly Guide to the Right Way." (The Cave, 18:17)

What He is talking from is the *Ibad ar-Rahman* (Servants of the Most Compassionate), that they are custodians of a very specific light. By keeping their company, and by keeping their practices, they are able to light the student through their *tafakkur*, and contemplation. They will be trained to carry the light, carry the light. If they (students) are able to keep themselves clean in that process then the permission comes from Prophet ﷺ and the heart will be lit. It means it will become the initial stage of a sun.

Subhana rabbika rabil 'izzati 'ama yasifoon, Wa salamun 'alal mursaleen wal hamdulillahi rabbil 'alameen. Bi hurmati Muhammadil Mustafa wa bi siratil Suratil Fatiha.

WUQUF AL QALB – VIGILANCE OF THE HEART

HEART IS THE SUN OF THE UNIVERSE

THE SUN, THE MOON, AND 11 STARS BOWING TO *AWLIYAULLAH* (SAINTS)

Prophet Yusuf (Joseph) عليه السلام comes into our life and teaches, that he said to his father, "*Yaa Baba,* I am having a dream that the 11 planets are bowing to me and the Sun and the Moon are bowing to me."

إِذْ قَالَ يُوسُفُ لِأَبِيهِ يَا أَبَتِ إِنِّي رَأَيْتُ أَحَدَ عَشَرَ كَوْكَبًا وَالشَّمْسَ وَالْقَمَرَ رَأَيْتُهُمْ لِي سَاجِدِينَ

12:4 – "Idh qala Yosufu li abeehi ya abati innee raaytu ahada Ashara kawkaban wash Shamsa wal Qamara raaytuhum le sajideen." (Surah Yusuf)

"[Of these stories mention] when Joseph said to his father, "O my father, indeed I have seen [in a dream] eleven stars and the sun and the moon; I saw them prostrating to me." (Joseph, 12:4)

Awliyaullah (saints) come into our life and teach, "That that is the reality of *Awliyaullah* (saints)." What did Prophet ﷺ describe from the prophets of *Bani Israel*? My *ulama* (scholars) inherit the realities and the stations of *Bani Israel* and the prophets of *Bani Israel*.

عُلَمَاءِ وَرِثَةُ الْأَنْبِيَاء

"Ulama e warithatul anbiya."

"The scholars are the inheritors of the prophets."

Allah ﷻ doesn't care for *dunya* (material world), He cares for the *malakut* (heavens) and the World of Light. When Allah ﷻ gives *Awliyaullah*, gives pious people, He doesn't give them cash; He doesn't give them an accounting license, He gives from His Heavens. He ﷻ says, this Heaven is under your control, these stars are under your control, this Moon is under your control, and this Sun is under your control.

وَسَخَّرَ لَكُم مَّا فِي السَّمَاوَاتِ وَمَا فِي الْأَرْضِ جَمِيعاً مِّنْهُ إِنَّ فِي ذَلِكَ لَآيَاتٍ لِّقَوْمٍ يَتَفَكَّرُونَ

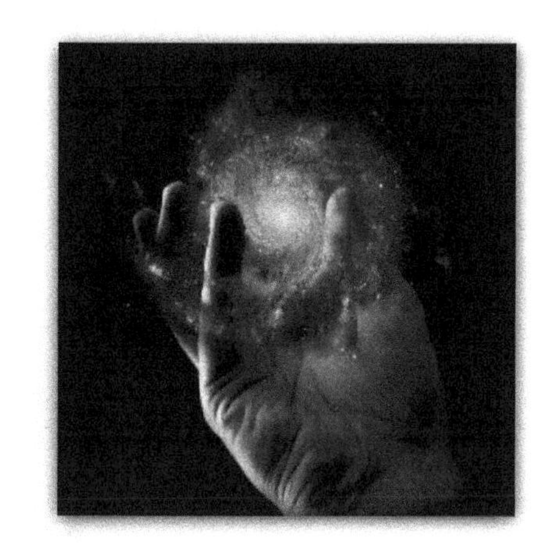

45:13 – "Wa sakhkhara lakum ma fis Samawati wa ma fil Ardi jamee'an minhu, inna fee dhalika la ayatin liqawmin yatafakkaron." (Surah Al-Jathiya)

"And He has subjected/gave the authority to you, as from Him, all that is in the heavens and on earth: Behold, in that are Signs indeed for those who do Tafakkur, reflect/Contemplate [Meditate]." (The Crouching, 45:13)

How many galaxies do we have within this universe? Billions! So Allah ﷻ is not running out. He says, I can bring a galaxy in an instant and you will be placed under control of it. That is what I want to give to you from the *mulk* of the Heavens, the *mulk* of *dunya* and then from the *malakut*, Heavens, which is *kulli shay* (all encompassing). Glory be to the hand that encompasses the *malakut* (heavens). That one holds everything.

فَسُبْحَانَ الَّذِي بِيَدِهِ مَلَكُوتُ كُلِّ شَيْءٍ وَإِلَيْهِ تُرْجَعُونَ (٨٣)

36:83 – "Fasubhanal ladhee biyadihi Malakutu kulli shay in wa ilayhi turja'oon." (Surah Yaseen)

"Therefore Glory be to Him in Whose hand is the [heavenly] dominion/ kingdom of all things, and to Him you will be returned." (Yaseen, 36:83)

Don't think that it is something small, that Allah ﷻ, *wa laqad karamna bani adam. (Holy Qur'an, 17:70)* He says, I want to give you what you can't imagine. What *Awliyaullah* are in charge of, I want to give that to you. I want these 11 planets and the Sun and the Moon to be at your feet, under your command but you must govern yourself accordingly.

The Universe Within

Sun (Heart), Moon (Face), and 11 Stars (Essential Organs)

What they begin to inspire, when you look within yourself and contemplate and meditate within yourself, that you have eleven essential organs. You have a heart which is your *shams* (sun), and you have a head, your brain, your face, which is your *qamar* (moon). So Allah ﷻ, just as every father says, if you can manage the small I will give you the big one to manage. But if you can't manage yourself, how am I going to give you the Heavens to be under your control?

Then our whole *tazkiya* (purification) is about understanding myself. What is the reality of my organs, what is the reality of my sun, and my heart? What is the reality of the moon that is my face?

The Condition of the Heart Affects the Whole Body

So then other people and other religions busy themselves in trying to open their energy and play with other planets because they work on a different system. *Awliyaullah* (saints) from Prophet ﷺ say, there is one focus for you, it is the heart. There is one piece of the flesh that if it is good, all of you is good; if it is bad, all of you is bad.

أَلا وَإِنَّ فِى الْجَسَدِ مُضْغَةً إِذَا صَلَحَتْ صَلَحَ الْجَسَدُ كُلُّهُ، وَإِذَا فَسَدَتْ فَسَدَ الْجَسَدُ كُلُّهُ، أَلا وَهِى الْقَلْبُ

"Ala wa inna fil Jasadi mudghatan idha salahat salahal jasadu kulluho, wa idha fasadat fasadal jasadu kulluho, ala wa heyal Qalb."

"There is a piece of flesh in the body, if it becomes good (reformed) the whole body becomes good but if it gets spoiled the whole body gets spoiled and that is the heart." (Prophet Muhammad ﷺ)

So he ﷺ taught them, taught the Companions, taught the *Ahl al-Bayt*, (his Family) and taught *Awliyaullah* (saints). You want to inherit from the Heavens? You want to inherit from the Heavens go into the heart; don't waste your time on anything else. This is not about the brain, this is not about the endocrine system, this is not about the liver; this is only about the heart. Conquer the heart, who governs the heart governs the entire body!

Our Way is *Waquf al Qalb* – Vigilance of the Heart

Then the way of *marif'ah* they begin to contemplate and look into the heart and they begin to observe all the desires of the heart. Be vigilant upon the heart that every word the *ulul amr* speak and teach, how is it affecting my heart? If my heart is palpitating and becoming nervous, something is wrong. It means *waquf*, vigilance of the heart; your whole life is about being vigilant with your heart. Every reality they are teaching, is it causing distress in the heart and why? Then there is something there, there is an issue. Is there a desire that governs the heart that is in conflict with what they are teaching of these realities?

It means our way is based then on complete vigilance over the heart. We are observing the heart and the desires and wants that are coming into the heart. It means how then to protect the heart and how then to bless and clean the heart? Where Allah عزَّ وجلَّ describes, this is My house. Clean it, wash it, bless it and circumambulate around it.

BE CAUTIOUS WHEN YOU DON'T WANT *DHIKRULLAH* (REMEMBRANCE OF ALLAH)

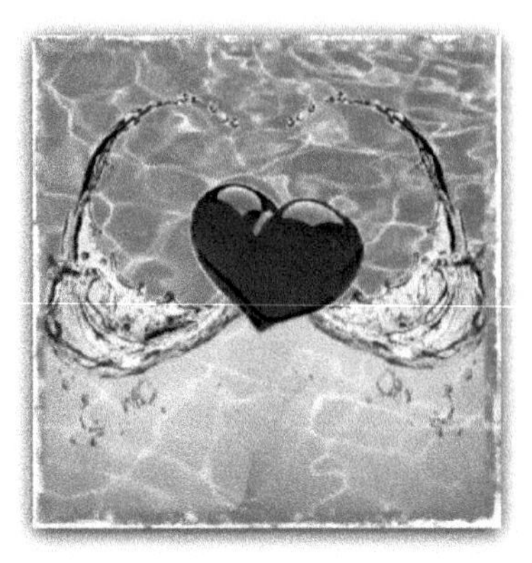

This is the heart. I wash my heart *bi dhikrullah*, I am going to wash my heart with praising upon Prophet ﷺ, with *majlis* of *dhikr* (remembrance). Only the *dhikr* and *awrad* has an energy that begins to purify the heart. It is not something easy. And if you are not capable of doing the *dhikr* and making the *salawat* (praisings on Prophet ﷺ), don't attribute it to yourself and say, "Yeah, you know, I couldn't do it." No, there is an even scarier thought that Allah ﷻ is not permitting you to mention His Name on your tongue or on your heart! That, you should be very scared of.

ALLAH ﷻ GIVES PERMISSION FOR HIS HOLY NAME TO BE MENTIONED

Allah ﷻ describes in *Surah An-Nur*: We allow Our Name to be mentioned in their homes.

فِي بُيُوتٍ أَذِنَ اللَّـهُ أَن تُرْفَعَ وَيُذْكَرَ فِيهَا اسْمُهُ يُسَبِّحُ لَهُ فِيهَا بِالْغُدُوِّ وَالْآصَالِ

24:36 – "Fee buyotin adhina Allahu an turfa'a wa yudhkara feeha ismuhu yusabbihu lahu feeha bilghuduwwi wal asal." (Surah An-Nur)

"(Lit is such a Light) in houses, which Allah has permitted to be raised to honour; and that His name be mentioned therein: In them He is glorified in the mornings and in the evenings, (again and again)." (The Light, 24:36)

Allah ﷻ says, We allow Our Name to be mentioned within their homes. Your home is your heart. If Allah ﷻ does not give permission there is no way you will mention His Name upon your tongue or your heart. That is scary.

That is when you begin to cry, "*Yaa Rabbi,* please inspire me to do my *awrad*, please inspire me to constantly make *darood shareef* and praise upon Sayyidina Muhammad ﷺ." My house is my heart; it's the only house that matters. Every other house may go in a tidal wave, may go in a *tufan,* or tornado, but what I am taking into this grave is this house. And Allah ﷻ says, then We have to allow Our Name to be mentioned within your heart. It means then my whole vigilance is, "*Yaa Rabbi,* please make me to have firmness in my *dhikr*. Make me to have firmness in the *salawat* upon Prophet ﷺ.

PROTECT YOUR HEART MORE THAN YOUR WEALTH

Ya Rabbi, let me be vigilant upon my heart and what is trying to come to my heart and what is trying to attack my heart. Your heart becomes more precious than your home.

You can see people and what they prioritize in life. If your home has twenty carats of diamonds and I drove by your house, I bet everything will have solid metal and be locked. All night long you will be thinking, "Someone is going to come and break through the window and steal everything. Where am I going to hide it (diamonds)? I will dig it in the ground." Dig, dig, dig, and then I will also make all the doors and windows with steel.

Allah ﷻ says, this is for *dunya* (material world); imagine what I am putting and bestowing of reality into your heart. Why are you so quick to put it everywhere so that it can be stolen? It means then pious people are vigilant of their heart. They don't go anywhere where it is not necessary to go. They don't open their heart where it is not necessary to open because they know that Allah ﷻ is depositing a treasure within the heart, and *Shaytan* (Satan) knows it and wants to just pick at it, and pick at it until you have *shak*, doubt in your belief. If doubt begins to enter into the belief, know that *Shaytan* is mining your heart. He is pulling it out, he has got all the treasures and it is a full on raid on your heart.

Be Careful Where You Go – Do They Take Your Light Or Give You Light

So they teach us, "Be vigilant of the heart. If you want these treasures to be placed upon the heart you have to have *istiqaamah* and have firmness in your belief, firmness in the practices, firmness in the *dhikr*, and firmness in the love of Prophet ﷺ." *Yaa Rabbi,* my path is to love Sayyidina Muhammad ﷺ more than I love myself.

All I want are the shining suns that represent the love of Sayyidina Muhammad ﷺ. I am not interested in sitting with anyone else because anyone else will take the jewels from my heart.

Some people go everywhere like it is a free *bazaar*. And you don't know who is putting jewels into your heart or who is taking the jewels from your heart because within two or three words of what they say you find yourself having doubt and darkness comes. So you don't just go anywhere, you don't just pray anywhere.

You want to make sure that is a shining sun and those are the lovers of Sayyidina Muhammad ﷺ. They are going to deposit the love of Sayyidina Muhammad ﷺ into my heart. If it is not, and they are not shining that light, they are going to send darkness into my heart. They are going to come against the *Sunnah*, they are going to come against the *Hadith*.

We said before, in your heart and in your mind don't ever say, "This is a weak *Hadith*." There is only a weak believer who is filled with *shak* and doubt. All they want now is to attack the *Sunnah* of Prophet ﷺ, attack the greatness of Sayyidina Muhammad ﷺ by constantly putting doubt, constantly putting doubt and they say, they are only *Ahl al-Qur'an*. This is *hizbush Shaytan* (party of Satan).

Qur'an does not open without the love of Sayyidina Muhammad ﷺ. We are not the people who have any doubt. If you don't understand that it came from Prophet ﷺ then you should be making *tafakkur*, contemplation, and connecting your heart with the heart of Sayyidina Muhammad ﷺ. He ﷺ will confirm within your heart exactly what it is and its reality!

Heart is the Real Sun

We took a path of how to open the heart and as soon as we open the heart, we realize the organs and their importance. Allah عزوجل is saying, if you don't have a Sun your galaxy is already dead; how are you going to manage My galaxy? So we go and say to the *shaykh*, "I wonder if this person was enlightened? He is watching TV and levitating off the ground, is he enlightened? Does he have spiritual power?" That is very easy for us if the person's heart is lit, and lit with faith that will dress all the organs. From the *Hadith* of Prophet ﷺ, if one piece (of the heart) is good, all of that person is good; if the heart is bad, all of it is bad.

أَلا وَإِنَّ فِى الْجَسَدِ مُضْغَةً إِذَا صَلَحَتْ صَلَحَ الْجَسَدُ كُلُّهُ، وَإِذَا فَسَدَتْ فَسَدَ الْجَسَدُ كُلُّهُ، أَلا وَهِى الْقَلْب

"Ala wa inna fil Jasadi mudghatan idha salahat salahal jasadu kulluho, wa idha fasadat fasadal jasadu kulluho, ala wa heyal Qalb."

"There is a piece of flesh in the body, if it becomes good (reformed) the whole body becomes good but if it gets spoiled the whole body gets spoiled Heart emanating light and that is the heart." (Prophet Muhammad ﷺ)

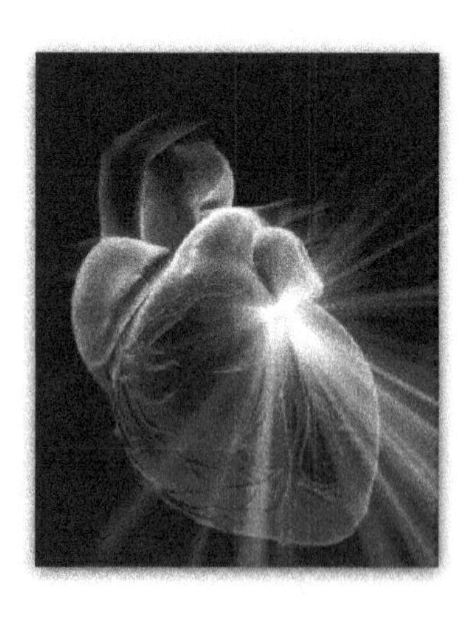

This means if the heart is lit, their galaxy has a Sun. Whatever practices they are doing, their heart is becoming stronger and stronger and stronger and what is the most favoured time for *Islam*? It's the full moon, the time of perfection, because the Moon is capturing all the light of the Sun.

So then they begin to teach, "If your heart is lit, and you lit the heart with *Awliyaullah*, lit it with *dhikr* (remembrance), lit it with the *salawat* (praising) for Prophet ﷺ, and lit it with *Islam*, and you are now entering the realities with *Iman* (faith), that heart is burning like a sun and your face is like a moon."

LIFE DEPENDS ON THE IMITATED SUN, IMAGINE THE POWER ALLAH ﷻ GAVE TO *AWLIYA*?

People of *tafakkur* (contemplation) stop there and make *tafakkur*. What power does the Sun have on Creation? If that is an imitated Sun and *Awliyaullah*, and pious people, if their hearts become a real Sun, that Allah ﷻ gives them *Nurul anwaar wa siratul asraar* (The light of the lights, the Secret of the Secrets). If that *nur* really opens within their heart what type of power does that light have? Don't you take your vision from the Sun? Don't you take your breath from the Sun? Isn't all the vegetation you are eating from the *shams* (sun)?

What then are you getting from the *Awliya* if their souls are more powerful than the Sun? Sayyidina Yusuf عليه السلام said, "They are all bowing down to me," which means 'my station is above their station'. What are you then taking from their souls, if their heart is emanating and dressing?

What do you take from the Moon? How it raises vegetation, how it brings the tides up and down; it means everything on this *dunya* is affected by that Moon. So it is not something small. It is so huge that *Shaytan's* only interest is to make sure nobody reaches that reality. If you should reach that reality you are more powerful than a thousand men on this *dunya*.

If your heart becomes a sun, it is a sun in which eyes can see. We talked about the Sun in the Heavens. How is it shining (continuously), then it has *layl* (night), then when it enters the Earth it is *nahar* (sunshine). The Sun is always shining but we don't have the eyes to see its light. Only when it enters *dunya* we can only see that line of it, that electromagnetic pulser. What it enters into *dunya* Allah ﷻ gave us the ability to see. So what light is Allah ﷻ sending upon the souls of *Awliya* (saints) and the realities of these souls? They open their heart and their heads become like a full Moon and every organ of their body is governed in its reality.

Your Breath is the Power of Your Heart, Your Sun

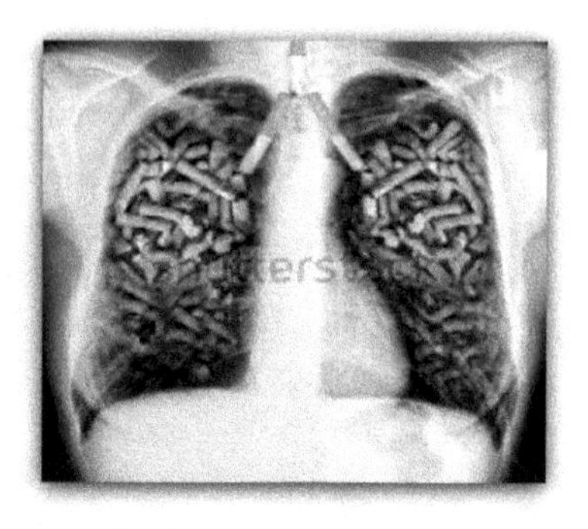

Then they come into your life (and teach) that within yourself is the Tree of Life, which are your lungs. And *nafas ar-Rahmah* (Breath of Mercy) is going to be the power and *Qudrah* for your entire galaxy because you want to inherit. "*Yaa Rabbi,* I want to inherit Your Heavens, I want to inherit Your Heavens." So then what are you doing smoking? You see some people saying, "Oh this is a big *shaykh* and he is (puffing) on a cigarette." His *sidratul muntaha* is on fire. What are you talking about? How is he a big *shaykh*? You think he is from *Awliyaullah*, that Allah ﷻ gave him to inherit from the Heavens, yet his Tree of Life is on fire? It's impossible.

Everything within our body is of importance. You are breathing in (for) this galaxy that Allah ﷻ gave to you, every breath of *nafas ar-Rahmah* that comes in. Our way is based on the power of that breath. That *nafas* is the power of your sun. It comes into the lungs and dresses from Allah's ﷻ *dhikr* and lights and *rahmah* (mercy). From that the blood takes it and goes into the heart.

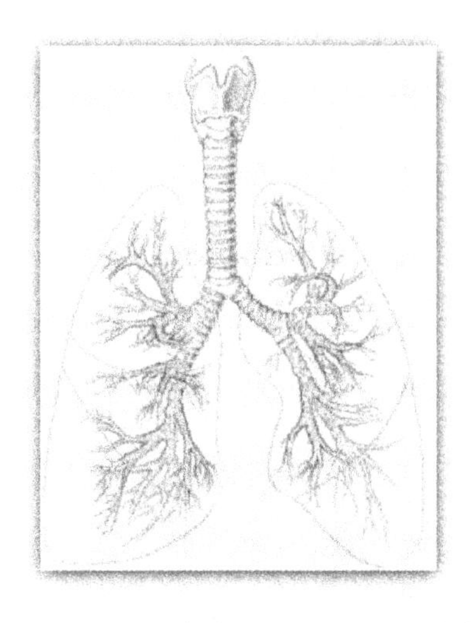

If your breath is bad your heart is destroyed, not the fragrance, but the quality of the breath. It means if the breath is not coming in pure and clean, the heart is destroyed. That pure and clean breath is what gives energy to the heart, gives the power to the heart. Then the lungs you see them as an upside down tree, why? Because this is the Tree of Life. Every life, every reality of yours, is coming through that breath. If you don't govern the breath and understand that breath, that it is a treasure from Allah ﷻ. *Awliyaullah* tell us there are 24,000 treasures in one day, 24,000 realities in one day. Every breath is with a *shukr* and thankfulness to Allah ﷻ.

Shaytan Wants to Destroy the Defense of Your Galaxy

It means then also guard your liver and kidneys. You understand that you have to govern your breath and no doubt *Shaytan* wants to come into my being, and how is he going to come into people's livers? By inspiring them to drink that which is not *halal* (permissible). When they drink something questionable or outright forbidden it is entering into the blood system, it is like *shayateen* (devils) that are attacking the body.

Shayateen want to destroy the defense of that galaxy. They know that if you become a powerful galaxy you are going to wreak havoc on the *shayateen* and their plans for *dunya*, but if you empower yourself it is a difficulty (for them). So they know that to destroy the liver, inspire him to drink that which is not acceptable allowing the *shayateen* inside the body and into the liver. The *shayateen* are coming within the blood and attacking the heart.

It means in every movement they are attacking the body, and they (*awliya*) begin to inspire and teach us, "Be careful of your breath, govern your breath that with the *Qudrah* of Allah ﷻ dressing you, you don't want anything forbidden within it."

SHAYTAN BROUGHT E-CIGARETTE AND *SHEESHA* TO KILL YOU FASTER

Shaytan is so obsessed with destroying *insaan* (human being) that he makes him to smoke now from a cold smoke, because he couldn't kill him enough with a warm smoke. You can only breathe so deep with fire. Have you been to a sauna and you take a deep breath and it starts to burn after that? So *Shaytan* asks, "How am I going to get to my *dhuriya*, progeny, deeper into that *insaan*? I'll make him smoke something cold." So the e-cigarette is a cold vapour to take the *shayateen* deeper into the body. The *sheesha* has 100 cigarettes in every puff, to completely kill and destroy the lungs so that you destroy the heart and the blood of that *insaan.*

FIRST MAKE *HAJJ* TO YOUR HEART

Allah ﷻ wants that to purify ourselves, purify your being. Make your first *Hajj* within your heart. Govern all your organs so that they are perfected and purified and that *Shaytan* is repelled from your being. Only at that time Allah ﷻ grants sincerity and the heart is lit and the moon is shining, which means their galaxy is lit with energy. Any deficiency within their organs, their sun will clean it, the sun within their heart; the energy that Allah ﷻ is depositing will begin to clean all the organs and everything of their being. At that time Allah ﷻ begins to grant the inheritance of the Heavens. Then the *Hajj* of *Iman* is towards the reality of Prophet ﷺ.

Subhana rabbika rabil 'izzati 'ama yasifoon, Wa salamun 'alal mursaleen wal hamdulillahi rabbil 'alameen. Bi hurmati Muhammadil Mustafa wa bi siratil Suratil Fatiha.

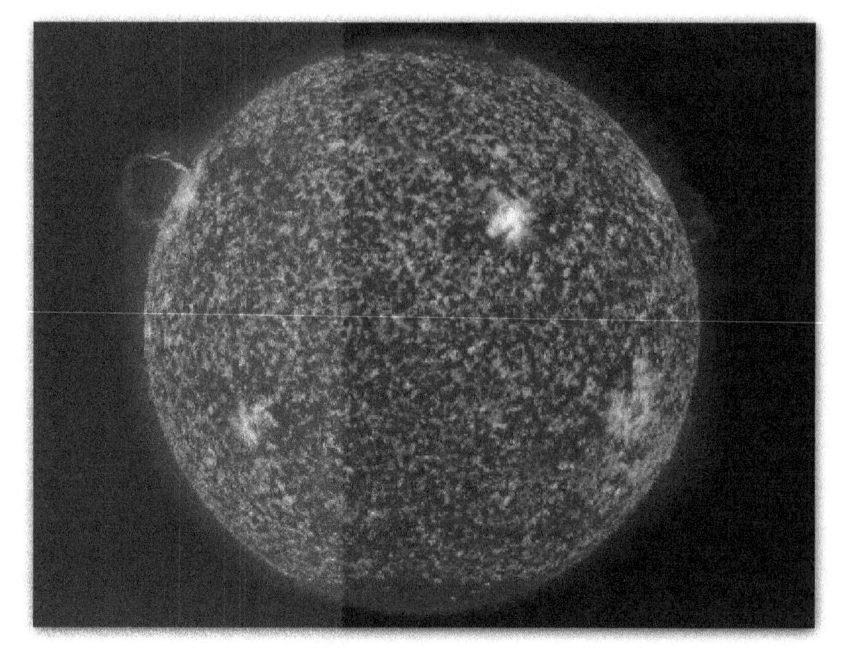

THE SECRET

RED GIANT STAR

وَإِن تَجْهَرْ بِالْقَوْلِ فَإِنَّهُ يَعْلَمُ السِّرَّ وَأَخْفَى (٧)

20:7 – "Wa in tajhar bil qawli fa-innaHu yalamus Sirra wa Akhfa." (Surah Taha)

"If you pronounce the word aloud, (it is no matter): for verily He knows what is secret and what is yet more hidden." (Surah Taha, 20:7)

اِتَّقُوْا فِرَاسَةَ الْمُؤْمِنْ، فَإِنَّهُ يَنْظُرُ بِنُوْرِ اللهِ

"Ittaqo firasatal Mumine, fa innahu yanzuru be Nurillahi."

"Beware [be conscious]of the firasah of the believer, for he sees with the light of Allah." Prophet Muhammad ﷺ (Tirmidhi)

SECOND LEVEL THE SECRET

STATION OF *SIR* سِر

SPIRITUAL VISION

The Station of *Sir* (Secret) is symbolized by the Red Giant Star that is 100 to 1000 times larger and 2,000 to 1 million times more luminous than our Sun. This is the state of *Ruhaniya* (Spirituality), where *Iman* (Faith) is developed. Perfection of faith is to hear and believe, not to see and believe. When one closes the eyes to the material world, through *Tafakkur* (contemplation) and spiritual connection, the spiritual vision, *Firasah* will begin to open.

Realities of the Second Level of the Heart The Secret

State: ***Ruhaniya* (Spiritual)**

Sense: **Seeing**

Stage of Star Formation: **Red Giant Star**

Colour: **Red**

Season: **Fall**

Archangel: **Sayyidina Mikhail (Michael)** عليه السلام

Prophet: **Sayyidina Nuh (Noah)** عليه السلام

Companion: **Sayyidina Umar Farooq** عليه السلام

Pillar of Islam: ***Salah* (Prayer)**

Salat (Prayer time): ***Isha* (Night)**

Dhikr: ***Alhamdulillah* (Praise be to Allah)**

Seek Support: ***Ya Sahib* (O Owner) – *Shuhada* (Those Who Witness /Martyrs)**

6th Sense: **Spiritual Vision (*Firasah*)**

HIGHLIGHTS OF THE STATION OF *SIR* (SECRET)

- Reality of *Firasah* - Vision of the Believer
- Eyes are windows to the soul
- Close the physical eyes and See with the Eyes of the Heart
- *Tafakkur* (Contemplation) opens the spiritual vision
- Focus on Spiritual seeing instead of physical seeing
- Archangel Mikhail عليه السلام assists with the struggle in the way of Allah عز و جل
- Physical sustenance is based on heavenly sustenance
- Prophet Nuh (Noah) عليه السلام - Build your Soul
- *Safinatul Nejat* (Ship of Safety) - Salvation from the flood of ignorance
- Build your faith, face the testing and difficulties
- Sayyidina Umar Farooq عليه السلام - Who distinguishes between truth and falsehood
- Sayyidina Umar عليه السلام Brings the *Haqq* (truth) to destroy the falsehood
- Stand up against the falsehood within yourself
- Build a good character
- *Salah* – Pray as if you see Allah عز و جل at the *Maqam al Ihsan* (Station of Moral Excellence)

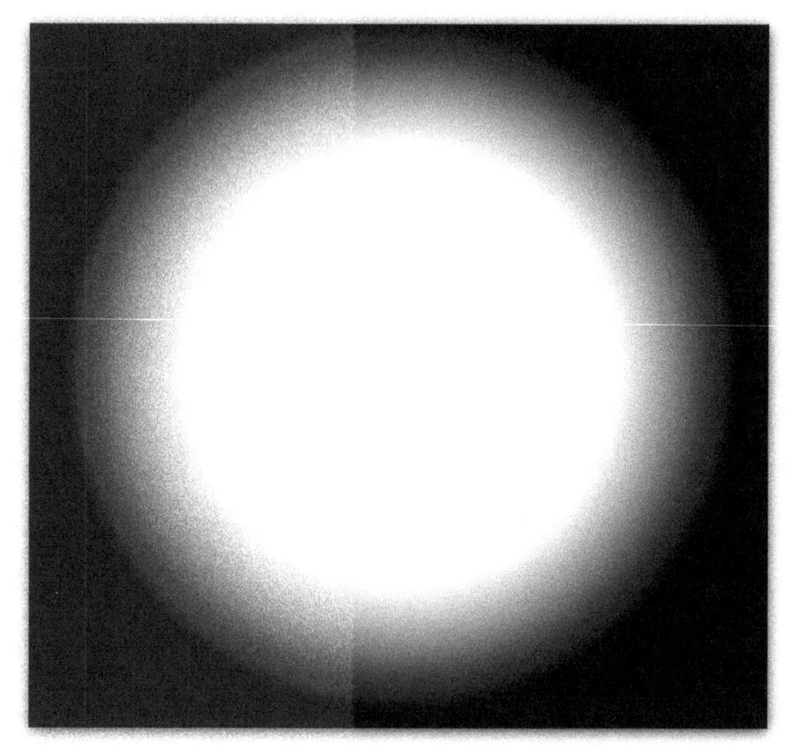

The Secret of the Secret

White Dwarf Star/ The Moon – *Maqam al Fardani*

قُلْ أَنزَلَهُ الَّذِي يَعْلَمُ السِّرَّ فِي السَّمَاوَاتِ وَالْأَرْضِ ۚ إِنَّهُ كَانَ غَفُورًا رَّحِيمًا (٦)

25:6 – "Qul anzalahu alladhee ya'lamus Sirra fis Samawati wal Ardi, innaHu kana Ghaforan Raheema." (Surah Al-Furqan)

Say, [O Muhammad], "It [Qur'an] has been sent down by Him who knows [every] Secret within the heavens and the earth. Indeed, He is ever Forgiving and Merciful." (The Criterian, 25:6)

THIRD LEVEL THE SECRET OF THE SECRET

STATION OF *SIRR E SIR* سر السر

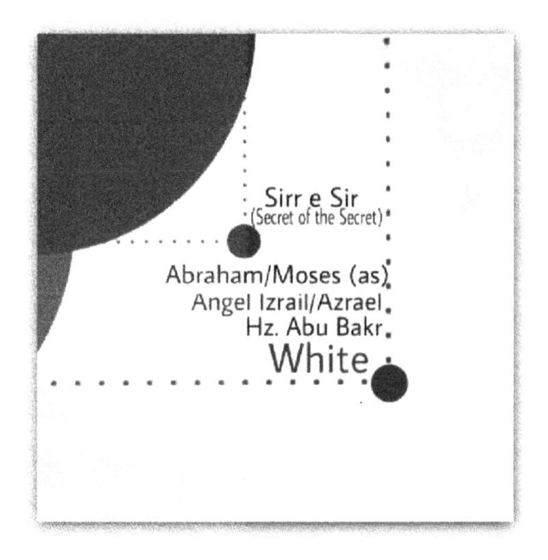

SOUL'S SUBTLETY

The Station of Secret of the Secret *(Sirr e Sir)* is symbolized by the Moon, that represents the spiritual station of *Maqam al Fardani.* In the process of the Star Formation, it is represented by the White Dwarf Star. It is what remains of the Red Giant Star, after it passes Nebula [*Nabiullah* (Prophet of Allah), the Most Hidden (*Akhfa)*]. It is a very small white star with, which is the size of the earth, but has a mass of the Sun.

When you are given heavenly knowledge (*Ilm al Yaqeen*) at the Station of the Heart, and you begin to use spiritual vision *(Ayn al Yaqeen*), at the Station of the Secret, it becomes the Truth of Certainty (*Haqq al Yaqeen*). Spiritual hearing and seeing produces the Truth of Certainty and leads to Soul's subtlety. You enter into the World of Light, *Alam al Mithal.* This is the way of the Spiritual Perfection (*Mithaliya Arwah*).

Realities of the Third Level of the Heart The Secret of the Secret

State: ***Mithaliya Arwah* (Spiritual Perfection)**

Sense: **Touch**

Stage of Star Formation: **White Dwarf Star/the Moon**

Colour: **White**

Season: **Winter**

Archangel: **Sayyidina Izrail (Azrael)** عليه السلام

Prophets: **Sayyidina Ibrahim (Abraham)** عليه السلام **and Sayyidina Musa (Moses)** عليه السلام

Companion: **Abu Bakr as-Siddiq** عليه السلام

Pillar of Islam: ***Zakat* (Charity)**

Salat (Prayer Time): ***Zuhr* (Noon)**

Dhikr: ***La ilaha ilallah* (There is no God but Allah)**

Seek Support: ***Ya Siddiq* (O Truthful) - *Siddiqeen* (Truthful)**

6th Sense: **Subtlety of the Soul**

HIGHLIGHTS OF THE STATION OF *SIRR E SIR* (SECRET OF THE SECRET)

- How to reach the Truth of Certainty (*Haqq al Ya'qeen*)
- Hearing and Seeing lead to becoming subtle nature
- Importance of *Tafakkur* (Contemplation/Meditation)
- Close your eyes to *dunya* (material world)
- Sayyidina Izrail عليه السلام - let your worldly desires die
- Sayyidina Ibrahim عليه السلام - Let the divine fire burn your falsehood and bad characteristics
- Sayyidina Ibrahim عليه السلام - teaches to control the fire of Anger
- Sayyidina Musa عليه السلام - blessed with Hearing and speaking to his Lord – two essential attributes of knowledge
- Sayyidina Musa عليه السلام - turn the Fire of anger into the Fire of Divine Love
- Sayyidina Abu Bakr عليه السلام - Perfection of *Iman* (Faith), Love Prophet صلى الله عليه وسلم more than you love yourself
- Sayyidina Abu Bakr عليه السلام gave everything to Prophet صلى الله عليه وسلم
- *Zakat* and Purification – Give up your bad characteristics
- Winter - Everything dies and stays frozen like *barzakh*
- Enter and Exit from the gate of *Siddiq* (truthful) *(Qur'an 17:80)*

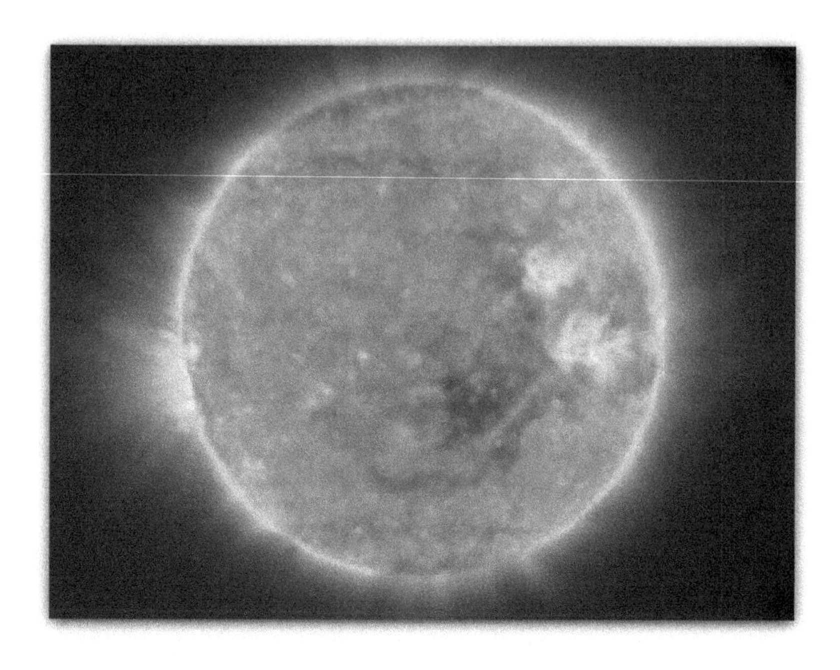

The Hidden

Green Pulsar Star

إِذْ نَادَىٰ رَبَّهُۥ نِدَآءً خَفِيًّا ٣

19:3 – "Idh nada rabbahu nida an khafiya." (Surah Maryam)

"Behold! He cried to his Lord in secret." (Mary, 19:3)

FOURTH LEVEL THE HIDDEN

STATION OF *KHAFA* خفاء

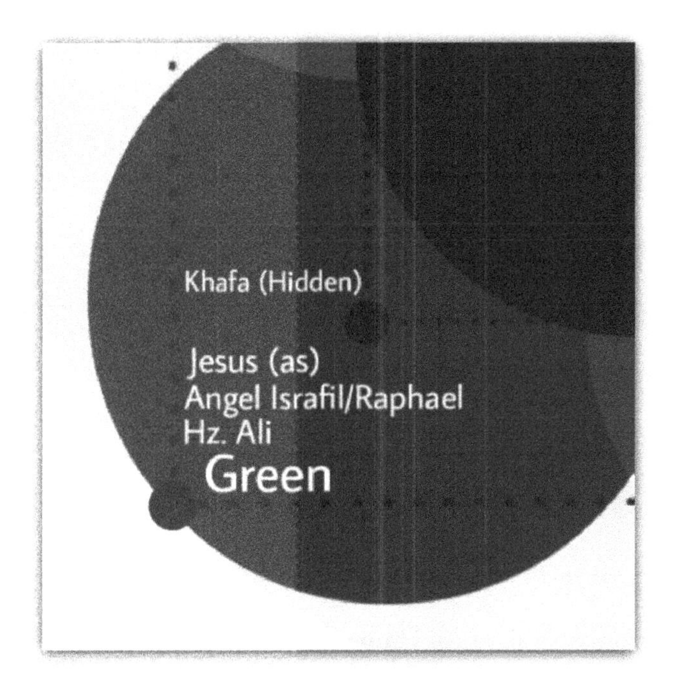

PHYSICAL PERFECTION

The Station of the *Khafa* (Hidden) is symbolized by the Green Pulsar – Neutron Star. These stars are produced when a supernova explodes. Neutron stars are very dense with a mass of three times the Sun but a diameter of only 20 km. This is the state of *Jismiya* (Physical Perfection) and the reality of *Insan Kamil* (Perfected Being). The Soul's perfection will perfect the Physicality, allowing you to reach to Physical Perfection. In this station the sense of smell opens which is the Angelic reality. You become more sensitive and begin to smell energy of the people around you. This level is represented by Green light and spring that is the reality of resurrection. The soul prepares for ascension towards the heavens and to the Divinely Presence *(Sultanan Naseera)*.

Realities of the Fourth Level of the Heart The Hidden

State: ***Jismiya* (Physical Perfection)**

Sense: **Smell**

Stage of Star Formation: **Green Pulsar – Neutron Star**

Color: **Green**

Season: **Spring**

Archangel: **Sayyidina Israfil (Raphael)** عليه السلام

Prophet: **Sayyidina Isa (Jesus)** عليه السلام

Companion: **Sayyidina Ali Haidar** عليه السلام

Pillar of Islam: ***Sawm* (Fasting) in *Ramadan***

Salat (Daily Prayer): ***Asr* (Afternoon) – Before Sunset**

Dhikr: ***Allahu Akbar* (God is Great)**

Seek Support: ***Ya Rasul* (O Messenger) – *Nabiyeen* (Prophets)**

6th Sense: **Spiritual Smell – Angelic Realm**

HIGHLIGHTS OF THE STATION OF THE *KHAFA* (HIDDEN):

- Station of *Khafa* (Hidden) represents resurrection
- Physical perfection and *Insan Kamil* (Perfected Being)
- Archangel Israfil عليه السلام takes us to the gate of *Siddiq* (Truthful)
- How to Approach the *Sultanan Naseera* (Victorious King)
- Sayyidina Muhammad صلى الله عليه وسلم, the Victorious King, is Master of Annihilation
- Sayyidina Isa (Jesus) عليه السلام teaches to leave the physicality and focus on the Soul
- Prophet صلى الله عليه وسلم is the City of Knowledge and Sayyidina Ali عليه السلام is the door to it
- Imam Ali عليه السلام - *Asadullahi Ghalib* (Victorious Lion of Allah) – Reality of *Zulfiqar* and Sacrifice
- Imam Ali عليه السلام leads by example - He lay in bed ready to be sacrificed
- *Ahlul Bayt* carried that example of Sacrifice in *Karbala*
- When Physical desires are down, Soul can connect back to its origin
- *Ramadan* - Fast and abstain with all senses

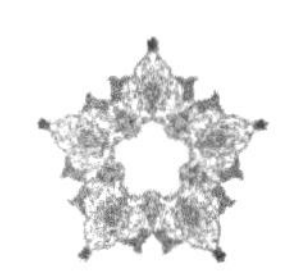

THE MOST HIDDEN

BLACK HOLE - ANNIHILATION

وَإِن تَجْهَرْ بِالْقَوْلِ فَإِنَّهُ يَعْلَمُ السِّرَّ وَأَخْفَى (٧)

20:7 – "Wa in tajhar bil qawli fa-innaHu yalamus Sirra wa Akhfa." (Surah Taha)

"If you pronounce the word aloud, (it is no matter): for verily He knows what is secret and what is yet more hidden." (Surah Taha, 20:7)

FIFTH LEVEL
THE MOST HIDDEN
STATION OF *AKHFA* أخفاء

THE ESSENCE

The Station of the *Akhfa* (Most Hidden) is symbolized by the black hole. The black hole is believed to form from a massive star at the end of its life time. The gravitational pull in a black hole is so great that nothing can escape from it, not even light. That is why people cannot see it. Black is the colour of the Station of the Most Hidden. Black colour absorbs all colours and it represents *Fana* (Annihilation). Once you perfect the hearing, seeing, feeling, and smell, the sense of taste begins to open. The sense of taste is the highest sense. This is where you can taste the heavenly realities. This is the state of *Dhatiya* (Essence) and the reality of going back to our origin in the world of light.

REALITIES OF THE FIFTH LEVEL OF THE HEART THE MOST HIDDEN

State: ***Dhatiya* (Essence)**

Sense: **Taste**

Stage of Star Formation: **Black Hole**

Colour: **Black**

Archangel: **Sayyidina Malik** عليه السلام

Prophet: **Sayyidina Muhammad** صلى الله عليه وسلم

Pillar of Islam: ***Hajj* (Pilgrimage to *Ka'bah*) in *Makkah***

Salat (Prayer time): ***Fajr* (Morning) – Dawn, before Sunrise**

Dhikr: ***La Hawla wa la Quwwata illa billahil 'Ali ul 'Azeem* (There is no Support and no Power except in Allah)**

Seek Support: ***Ya Allah*** يا الله

6th Sense: **Spiritual Taste**

HIGHLIGHTS OF THE STATION OF THE *AKHFA* (MOST HIDDEN):

- Station of *Akhfa* is the Muhammadan Reality
- State of the *Dhatiya*, the Essence - Our Soul's origin
- Archangel Malik عليه السلام oversees other Archangels
- We are created from one soul and going back to it *(Qur'an, 31:28)*
- Everything is Created from *Nur Muhammad* صلى الله عليه وسلم
- Reaching the Presence of *Sultanan Naseera* (Victorious King) صلى الله عليه وسلم
- Sayyidina Muhammad صلى الله عليه وسلم was raised to the Divine Presence, in the Night of Ascension (*Isra wal Mi'raj*)
- There is no Support or Power except in Allah عز وجل and His Rasul صلى الله عليه وسلم (*La hawla wa la Quwwata illa billah*)
- Black absorbs all colours and represents *Fana* (Annihilation)
- Prophet Muhammad صلى الله عليه وسلم is the Master of Annihilation
- Hazrat Bilal's رضي الله عنه Reality - Station of Oneness *(Maqam al Ahadiya)*
- Be Nothing and go back to the Ocean of your Origin

ANGELS AND THE LEVELS OF THE HEART

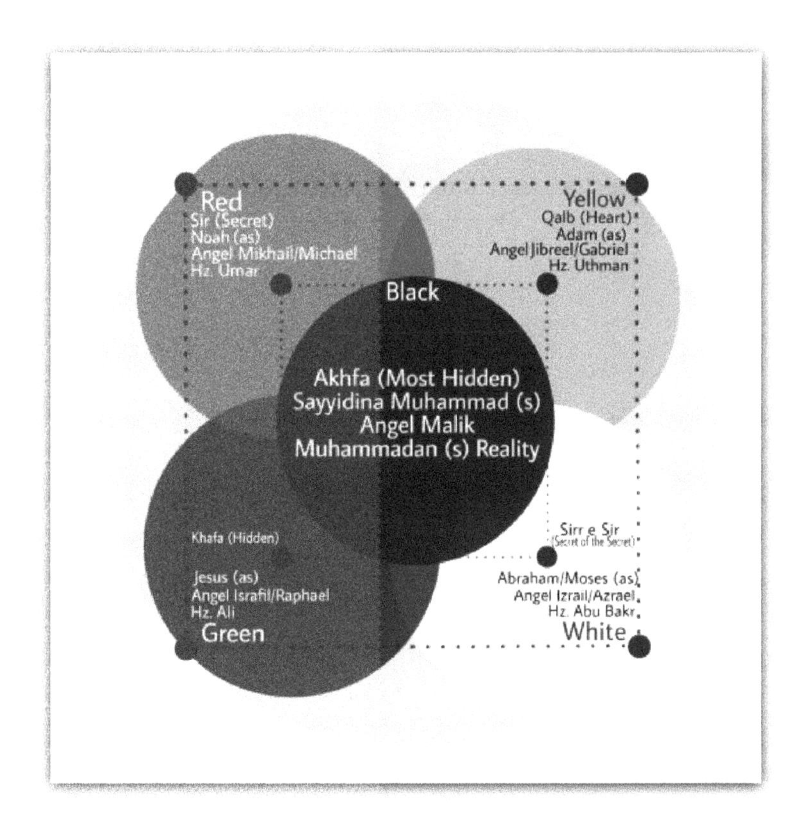

EVERYTHING IS CREATED FROM *NUR MUHAMMAD* ﷺ

Prophet ﷺ said, "I was a Prophet before Adam was between clay and water," before there was *Bayt al Ma'mur*, before there was *Arsh ar Rahman,* before anything was created.

كُنْتُ نَبِيًّا وَآدَمُ بَيْنَ الْمَاءِ وَالطِّينِ

"Kuntu Nabiyan wa Adama baynal Maa e wat Teen."

"I was a Prophet and Adam was between clay and water."
(Prophet Muhammad ﷺ*)*

قَال :يَا جَابِرُ ، إِنَّ اللهَ خَلَقَ قَبْلَ الأَشْيَاءِ نُورُ نَبِيِّكَ مِنْ نُورِهِ ، فَجَعَلَ ذَلِكَ النُّورِ يَدُورُ بِالْقُدْرَةِ حَيْثُ شَاءَ اللهُ ، وَلَمْ يَكُنْ فِي ذَلِكَ الْوَقْتِ لَوْحٌ وَلا قَلَمٌ ، وَلا جَنَّةٌ وَلا نَارٌ ، وَلا مَلَكٌ، ولا سَمَاءٌ وَلا أَرْضٌ ، وَلا شَمْسٌ وَلا قَمَرٌ، وَلا إِنْسٌ وَلا جِنٌّ.

"Ya Jabir, in Allah khalaqa qablal Ashiya e Nooro Nabiyika min Noorehi. Faj'ala dhalikan Noore yadoro bil Qudrati haithu sha Allahlu, wa lam yakun fi dhalikal waqti lawhun wa la qalamun, wa la jannatun wa la Narun, wa la Mulkun, wa la samaun wa la ardun, wa la shamsun wa la qamarun, wa la insun wa la jinnun."

"He (Prophet Muhammad ﷺ said: "O Jabir, the first thing Allah created was the light of your Prophet from His (Allah's) light, and that light remained (lit. "turned") in the midst of His Power for as long as He wished, and at that time, there was no Tablet and no Pen, and no Paradise and no Fire, and no angel, and no heaven or an earth, and no Sun and no Moon, and No Human being and no jinn."

ANGELS ARE THE PURIFIED MUHAMMADAN LIGHT

We want to talk about the reality of the *Malaika* (angels) and the understanding of the *lataif* (energy points). It means that the servant who is opening their heart and making the *tafakkur* (contemplation), then there must be a reality within themselves.

Nur Muhammad ﷺ is the Light of all Creation. Every angel is from the light of Sayyidina Muhammad ﷺ. Now begin to think *Malaika* (angels) are *Muhammadan* lights; they come from the light of Prophet ﷺ. They are owned by Sayyidina Muhammad ﷺ.

اللَّـهُ نُورُ السَّمَاوَاتِ وَالْأَرْضِ ۚ مَثَلُ نُورِهِ كَمِشْكَاةٍ فِيهَا مِصْبَاحٌ ۖ الْمِصْبَاحُ فِي زُجَاجَةٍ ۖ الزُّجَاجَةُ كَأَنَّهَا كَوْكَبٌ دُرِّيٌّ ... يَكَادُ زَيْتُهَا يُضِيءُ وَلَوْ لَمْ تَمْسَسْهُ نَارٌ ۚ نُّورٌ عَلَىٰ نُورٍ ۗ ... ٣٥

24:35 – "Allahu noorus samawati wal ardi. mathalu noorehi kamishkatin feeha misbahun, almisbahu fee zujajatin, azzujajatu kaannaha kawkabun durriyyun ... yakadu zaytuha yudeeo wa law lam tamsashu naarun. noorun 'ala noorin..." (Surah An-Noor)

"Allah is the Light of the heavens and the earth. The Parable of His Light is as if there were a Niche and within it a Lamp: the Lamp enclosed in Glass: the glass as it were a brilliant star: ... though fire scarce touched it: Light upon Light!."
(The Light, 24:35)

So Allah ﷻ wants us to know that these angels are representing the purified lights of Prophet ﷺ. Every angel that comes into existence is coming from *Nur Muhammad* ﷺ.

EVERY ANGEL HAS A UNIQUE PRAISING UPON PROPHET ﷺ

Allah ﷻ says, *innallaha wa Malaikatahu yusaloon `alan nabi* ﷺ

إِنَّ اللَّهَ وَمَلَائِكَتَهُ يُصَلُّونَ عَلَى النَّبِيِّ يَا أَيُّهَا الَّذِينَ آمَنُوا صَلُّوا عَلَيْهِ وَسَلِّمُوا تَسْلِيماً

33:56 – "InnAllaha wa Malaikatahu yusalluna 'alan Nabiyi yaa ayyuhal ladhina aamanu sallu 'alayhi wa sallimu taslima." (Surat Al-Ahzab)

"Allah and His angels send blessings upon the Prophet [Muhammad ﷺ]: O you that believe! Send your blessings upon him, and salute him with all respect." (The Combined Forces, 33:56)

Its power is from the *Dhikr* (remembrance) of Allah ﷻ. The angels, as they come into existence, Allah ﷻ gives them a unique *salawat* to praise upon Prophet ﷺ. Because Allah ﷻ described that, verily Myself and every angel that comes into existence, send blessings upon him ﷺ. As soon as an angel comes into existence, it is given its own unique *salawat* and praising upon Sayyidina Muhammad ﷺ as its source of energy. By that praise and by that *dhikr*, it has been given its power. And every praise has '*allahumma* اللّٰهُمَّ' because it praises Allah الله ﷻ and then mentions the secret of *humma* هُمَّ. *Allah humma* اللّٰهُمَّ الله هُمَّ, Allah ﷻ keeps the *meem* م within the *humma* as a tremendous secret of realities.

ARCHANGELS: JIBREEL عليه السلام, MIKHAIL عليه السلام, IZRAIL عليه السلام, ISRAFIL عليه السلام, MALIK عليه السلام

1. Archangel Jibreel (Gabriel) عليه السلام at the Station of *Qalb* (Heart)

He Teaches Heavenly Knowledge

Sayyidina Jibreel عليه السلام and the reality of Sayyidina Jibreel عليه السلام has to do with the first station of the *Qalb* (Heart). It has to do with Sayyidina Jibreel عليه السلام continuously bringing the Message of Allah عز و جل. It means that when the servant is contemplating and asking to open their heart, they are opening the reality of their soul.

Sayyidina Jibreel عليه السلام brings you guidance. He can't bring you *wahi* (revelation), because *wahi* is only for Sayyidina Muhammad صلى الله عليه وسلم. But continuous teachings and knowledges must be coming to *Bani Adam* (children of Adam عليه السلام, from the order of Prophet صلى الله عليه وسلم.

So for Sayyidina Jibreel عليه السلام to come and go, come and go, come and go, why should he do that? If the servant is opening within themselves their heart and their reality, it means that the light of Sayyidina Jibreel عليه السلام begins to occupy within their soul because it is all *Nur Muhammad* صلى الله عليه وسلم.

Archangel Jibreel عليه السلام is Responsible for Heavenly Knowledge

It means then the servant is opening the heart and asking to be dressed by the heart, that Sayyidina Jibreel عليه السلام and the light of Sayyidina Jibreel عليه السلام must be present within that saint, within that person who is trying to open that reality. That light of Sayyidina Jibreel عليه السلام is responsible for bringing knowledge from Prophet صلى الله عليه وسلم to that servant. Not revelation as revelation is only for Sayyidina Muhammad صلى الله عليه وسلم and there is no more revelation as Prophet صلى الله عليه وسلم is the *khatim (ur risala)*, the Seal of all Messengership.

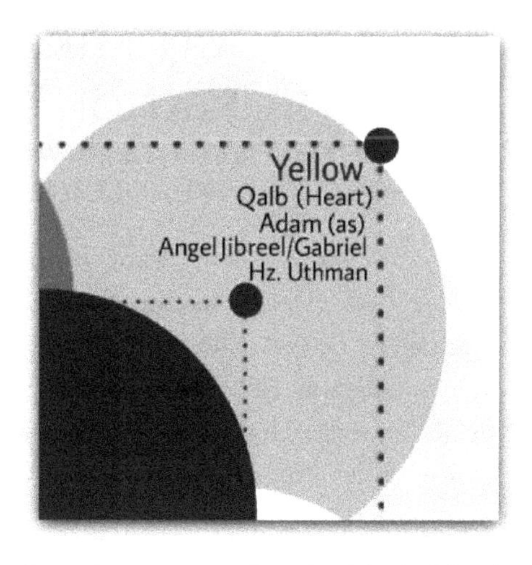

It means every knowledge that is coming in the station of the *Qalb* (Heart), must be coming with Sayyidina Jibreel عليه السلام. The lights of Sayyidina Jibreel عليه السلام must be encompassing that servant's heart and dressing them and blessing them.

Then if you go from *Qalb* (Heart) to Station of *Sir* (Secret), then Sayyidina Mikhail عليه السلام is at the Second Station. As soon as the shaykh (spiritual guide) begins to open for that student the power and the reality of their soul, these are all the heavenly supports that are coming upon their soul.

Angelic Lights Open Upon the Soul

When Allah عز و جل wants to open for the servant, what are they talking about? What is going to open? It means it is going to open with angelic lights upon your soul.

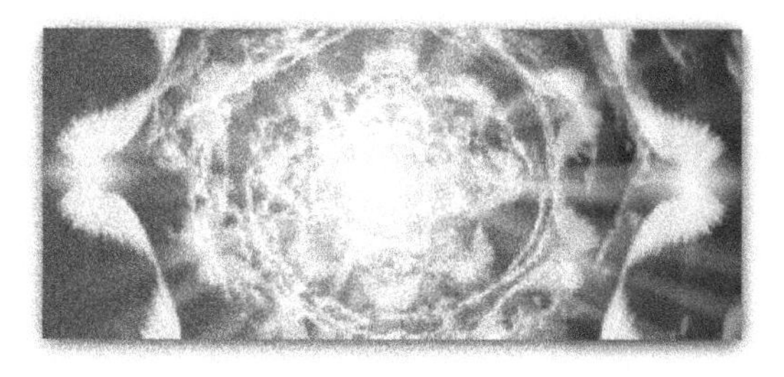

If the light of Sayyidina Jibreel عليه السلام comes and deposits upon your soul, it is an office within your soul of all knowledges. It means every reality that Prophet صلى الله عليه وسلم wants to open, will be opening through that light. Sayyidina Jibreel عليه السلام will be bringing these lights and knowledges upon the soul.

2. Archangel Mikhail (Michael) عليه السلام at the Station of *Sir* (Secret)

He Teaches to Struggle in the Way of Allah عز وجل

When *Awliyaullah* (saints) want to open for the student, from the first station *Qalb* (Heart) to the Second Station, *Sir* (Secret) and it is symbolized by red. The *Sir* (Secret) is then the power to struggle and fight in the way of Allah عز وجل; not fighting against people but fighting against the self. That is, how to fight against my bad character, my bad desire, all the things that are making me to be distant from Allah عز وجل.

It means then the support of Sayyidina Mikhail عليه السلام must come upon that servant. Prophet صلى الله عليه وسلم gives the *isharat*, and guidance, that the light of Sayyidina Mikhael عليه السلام must come into the servant's heart and begin to occupy their soul. That to mix that light upon the light of their soul and support them in their struggle for Allah عز وجل. It means to constantly take the *haqq* (truth) and come against falsehood, and verily falsehood is always perishing.

وَ قُلْ جَآءَالْحَقُّ وَزَهَقَ الْبَٰطِلُ، إِنَّ الْبَٰطِلَ كَانَ زَهُوقًا

17:81 – Wa qul jaa alhaqqu wa zahaqal baatil, innal batila kana zahooqa." (Surah Al-Isra)

"And say, "Truth has come, and falsehood has perished. Indeed falsehood, [by its nature], is ever perishing/ bound to perish." (The Night Journey, 17:81)

The struggle of that servant is going to be supported by Sayyidina Mikhail عليه السلام. That is why Sayyidina Mikhail عليه السلام is symbolized with war; he is the angel of war. When Allah عز وجل describes, "*jundum minas samaa*," "To whom do the armies belong this Day?"

هُوَ الَّذِي أَنزَلَ السَّكِينَةَ فِي قُلُوبِ الْمُؤْمِنِينَ لِيَزْدَادُوا إِيمَانًا مَّعَ إِيمَانِهِمْ ۗ وَلِلَّـهِ جُنُودُ السَّمَاوَاتِ وَالْأَرْضِ ۚ وَكَانَ اللَّـهُ عَلِيمًا حَكِيمًا (٤)

48:4 – "Huwa alladhee anzalas sakeenata fee quloobi almumineena liyazdadoo Imanan ma'a Imanihim, wa lillahi junodu asSamawati wal ardi, wa kana Allahu 'Aleeman Hakeema." (Surah Al-Fath)

"It is He who sent down tranquility into the hearts of the believers, that they would increase faith in their [present level of] faith. And to Allah belong the Forces/soldiers of the heavens and the earth, and Allah is All Knowing and Wise." (The Victory, 48:4)

It means the armies of the Heavens and the angels that are coming for the support, from Allah عزّ وجلّ. The greatest support for the believer is that Allah عزّ وجلّ sends the angels. That your *jihad* and struggle is not against people but against the devil that is within, that is blocking us from every reality and the greatness of what Allah عزّ وجلّ wanted.

عن جابر قال قدم على رسول الله صلى الله عليه وسلم قوم غزاة فقال صلى الله عليه وسلم قدمتم خير مقدم من جهاد الأصغر إلى جهاد الأكبر قيل وما قال مجاهدة العبد هواه وهذا فيه ضعف

"An Jabir qala, 'qadam 'ala Rasulullah (saws) qawm ghazata faqala Sallallahu Alayhi was Salaam: " Qadamtum khaira muqadem min jihadil Asghar ila Jihadil Akbar." Qeela "wa ma?" Qala "Mujahidatal 'Abd hawahu wa hadha fi D'af."

Jabir ﷺ *narrated: 'Some warriors came to the Holy Prophet. He (Muhammad* ﷺ*) said to them, "Welcome back, you came from minor Jihad to the greater one."*
It was asked, "What is that Oh Prophet of Allah?"
He ﷺ *replied, "One's fight against his mundane will/ desires."*
(Bahaqi Kitaab ul Zuhd-al-Kabir)

It means the order comes and the light of Sayyidina Mikhail عليه السلام begins to occupy the soul and begins to give that soul a defense on how to fight and struggle against bad character, bad desires and bad wants, so that Allah عز و جل can be pleased with that servant.

Archangel Mikhail عليه السلام is in Charge of Heavenly Sustenance

As a result of that struggle, and the servant entering into that struggle, Sayyidina Mikhael عليه السلام begins to open, that as a result of your struggles, I am also in charge of your sustenance. Every sustenance that is going to be coming upon this Earth and upon *Bani Adam*, upon this Creation, Allah عز و جل that authority is given to Sayyidina Mikhail عليه السلام.

It means that *tafakkur* (contemplation), and the way of *tafakkur* is the gate of all realities. For the person who is not making *tafakkur* what do they anticipate to open? So the way of opening is to come into this *baab*, into this door, come into the heart where Allah عز و جل says, "I am not in Heaven and I am not on Earth but I am in the heart of My believer."

مَا وَسِعَنِيْ سَمَائِيْ ولا اَرْضِيْ وَلَكِنْ وَسِعَنِيْ قَلْبِ عَبْدِيْ اَلْمُؤْمِنْ

"Maa wasi`anee Samayee, wa la ardee, laakin wasi'anee qalbi 'Abdee al Mu'min."

"Neither My Heavens nor My Earth can contain Me, but the heart of my Believing Servant." (Hadith Qudsi conveyed by Prophet Muhammad ﷺ*)*

Allah's ﷻ only believer who arrived upon Earth is Sayyidina Muhammad ﷺ. The only believer which Allah ﷻ looks to.

Allah ﷻ is giving us an *isharat*, and a direction, to come into the heart, that My Divinely Presence and everything you understood of My Divinely Presence will be inside that heart.

So then Sayyidina Mikhail عليه السلام begins to inspire I am in charge of sustenance. That if you are going to struggle in Allah's Way, I am going to bring from your heavenly sustenance upon your body. If I begin to dress you and bless you from your heavenly sustenance, everything of your heavenly sustenance will begin to affect your physical sustenance.

Physical Sustenance is Based on the Heavenly Sustenance

Your physical sustenance is based on your heavenly sustenance. What Allah ﷻ wants to give to your soul, if it begins to dress your body, it blesses everything that you do in life. It opens the reality of your physical sustenance on this Earth. If Allah ﷻ has *rida* (satisfaction), and is happy with the servant, He is giving that servant from His heavenly sustenance, and everything in the material world will begin to flow towards that servant.

If Allah ﷻ is not happy with the servant, no matter how much they run after *dunya* (material world), *dunya* runs fast away from them because *dunya* is scared of Allah ﷻ. If Allah ﷻ is not happy with that servant, *dunya* is scared of Allah's ﷻ anger. But when Allah ﷻ is happy with the servant, He loves that servant. And the servant is entering in a way, in a struggle against their bad characters, and asking, *yaa Rabbi* (o my lord), I want to open from the *Qalb* (Heart), I want to open from the *Sir* (Secret).

TAKE THE WAY OF *TAFAKKUR* (CONTEMPLATION)

The servant asks, I want to take the way of *tafakkur* (contemplation), I want to be in the way of nothingness, make my *nazar* under the *nazar (gaze)* of *Awliyaullah (saints)*, because Allah ﷻ said, *ati ullah ar Rasula wa ulul amri minkum.*

يأَيُّهَا الَّذِينَ آمَنُوا أَطِيعُوااللَّه وَأَطِيعُواْلرَّسُول وَأُوْلِي الْأَمْرِ مِنْكُمْ...

4:59 – "Ya ayyu hal ladheena amanooAtiullaha, wa atiur Rasola, wa Ulil amre minkum…" (Surah An-Nisa)

"O You who have believed, Obey Allah, Obey the Messenger, and those in authority among you…" (The Women, 4:59)

I want to be under the *nazar* (gaze) *of ulul amr* (saints) because they are under the *nazar* of Prophet ﷺ and Prophet ﷺ is under the *nazar* of Allah ﷻ. That I don't want to be with them once a year for a week, but every moment I want to be with them and under their *nazar.*

Then take the training on how to be under their *nazar* and to take a *hisaab*, an accounting of ourselves. That as soon as I am making *tafakkur*, I am asking that, *yaa Rabbi*, let me be amongst those whom You love. That their light to be in front of me and dress me, that the *fa'iz* (downpouring blessing) to be blessing me. Then they begin to train how to be nothing, how to be nothing.

If that light begins to dress that servant, then all the struggles begin. That red is also symbolic of Sayyidina Mahdi عليه السلام. That red is symbolic of Sayyidina Umar Farooq عليه السلام, the second *Khalifa* (Viceroy) of Prophet Muhammad صلى الله عليه وسلم. Every reality can be understood at these *lataif* and how to open these realities. It means in all of these Levels of the Heart are an eternal understanding.

So Sayyidina Mikhael عليه السلام is coming and teaching if you are going to struggle and you want our support struggling against your bad character, then begin to struggle with yourself, which is the greatest struggle. As a result, Allah عز وجل will begin to change the sustenance of that servant to be from their heavenly sustenance.

The Power of the Pen Changes Your Reality

The fastest way that they change the sustenance of the servant is by writing the knowledges of the Heaven. "*Alama bil qalam.*" It means it is the best way, which is changing the reality of that servant.

الَّذِي عَلَّمَ بِالْقَلَمِ (٤)

96:4 – "Alladhee 'allama bil Qalam." (Surah Al-Alaq)

"Who taught by the pen." (The Clot, 96:4)

Awliyaullah (saints) say that Allah عز وجل is going to change your reality by the power of that *qalam* (pen). So how is this *qalam* going to change my reality and change the sustenance upon my soul? It is very easy because the *qalam* that is writing now is only the angels, *Kiraman Katibin* (Nobel Scribes). The angels who write the good and the angel who write the bad (actions) of the servant. If all the writings are the good and the bad of the servant, the *kitaab* (book) that the person carries is not yet a noble *kitaab.*

وَإِنَّ عَلَيْكُمْ لَحَافِظِينَ (١٠) كِرَامًا كَاتِبِينَ (١١)

82:10-11 – "Wa inna 'alaikum lahafizeen. (10) Kiraman katibeen." (11) (Surah Al-Infitar)

"But verily over you (are appointed angels) to protect you. (10) Kind, Nobel and honourable- recording/ Writing down (your deeds) (11)" (The Cleaving, 82:10-11)

Writing Heavenly Knowledge Raises Your Honour

They come into our lives and teach the secret of *Surah Al-Iqra* (96th chapter of holy Qur'an), that Allah ﷻ is going to raise your honour and grant you from Divinely realities by the power of the *qalam*. So then the people of *haqqaiq* (realities) and students of the *haqqaiq* begin to write the lectures of their teachers because everything they are writinfg is a *Muhammadan* reality. Everything they are writing is from the secrets of the Heavens. These are not the secrets of *dunya* (material world).

When you are writing from the secrets of Heavens these are the treasures of the Divinely Presence. Allah ﷻ describes that, "I am going to honour you with that pen, I am going to teach you that which you knew not."

اقْرَأْ وَرَبُّكَ الْأَكْرَمُ (٣) الَّذِي عَلَّمَ بِالْقَلَمِ (٤) عَلَّمَ الْإِنسَانَ مَا لَمْ يَعْلَمْ (٥)

96:3-5 – "Iqra, wa rabbukal akram.(3) Alladhee 'allama bil Qalam. (4) 'Allamal insana ma lam ya'lam." (5) (Surah Al-Alaq)

"Recite, and your Lord is the most Generous (3) Who taught by the pen. (4) Taught man that which he knew not."(5)(The Clot, 96:3-5)

MAKE YOUR *KITAAB* (BOOK) AN HONOURED BOOK

So by writing these realities this *kitaab* is now changing from what I did good and what I did bad.

I had toast, I had orange juice, I prayed, I missed my prayer, I did this. That is all that is in the *kitaab* (book). As soon as you start to write the *haqqaiq* (realities), and write the realities of Prophet ﷺ, this *kitaab* now becomes from the realities of Sayyidina Muhammad ﷺ. That *kitaab* becomes a very honoured *kitaab*. Allah ﷻ says that is not a normal *kitaab* (book) anymore. These are carrying the lights and the realities of My Most Beloved Creation, and begin to dress that servant with their Paradise realities because of the honour and the love that Allah ﷻ has for Prophet ﷺ.

We have said many times that when you watch the movies of kingdoms, all movies of majestic kings, they say even when the stamp of the king moved into a village, everybody showed respect because it represented the *malik*, the *sultan* (king). Then what do you think of the *sultanate* of Allah ﷻ, the *sultanate* (kingdom) of Sayyidina Muhammad ﷺ?

قُلِ اللَّهُمَّ مَالِكَ الْمُلْكِ تُؤْتِي الْمُلْكَ مَنْ تَشَاءُ وَتَنْزِعُ الْمُلْكَ مِمَّنْ تَشَاءُ، وَتُعِزُّ مَنْ تَشَاءُ وَتُذِلُّ مَنْ تَشَاءُ بِيَدِكَ الْخَيْرُ ... (سُوْرَةُ آلِ عِمْرَان ٣:٢٦)

3:26 – "Qulillahumma Malikul mulki, tu'til mulka man tashaau wa tanzi'ul mulka mimman tasha'u, wa tu'izzu man tasha'u, wa tudhillu man tasha'u, bi yadikal khayr…." (Surah Ali-Imran)

"Say: O Allah, Master of the Kingdom, You give the Kingdom to whom You will, and You Take away the Kingdom from whom You will, You honor whom You will and You humble whom You will; in Your hand is [all] the good…" (Family of Imran, 3:26*)*

CHANGE YOUR SUSTENANCE BY WRITING HEAVENLY KNOWLEDGE

These books [Shaykh is pointing at his shoulders referring to angels who write our deeds] become filled with the realities and *haqqaiq* of Sayyidina Muhammad ﷺ. That servant is no longer a normal servant; everything must be changed for that servant. Every reality must be changed for that servant. As a result Allah ﷻ begins to change the sustenance; that is no longer a regular car but rather that is like a Ferrari. It requires a completely different fuel. Feed that servant from his Paradise realities.

It means everything about the servant can begin to change because of the honour that it is now carrying of these realities; where Allah ﷻ says, whom We gave a wisdom, We gave a tremendous gift. Why? Because these are the love and *haqqaiq* of Paradises realities.

يُؤْتِي الْحِكْمَةَ مَن يَشَاءُ ۚ وَمَن يُؤْتَ الْحِكْمَةَ فَقَدْ أُوتِيَ خَيْرًا كَثِيرًا ۗ وَمَا يَذَّكَّرُ إِلَّا أُولُو الْأَلْبَابِ (٢٦٩)

2:269 – "Yu'til Hikmata mai yasha o; wa mai yutal Hikmata faqad otiya khairan kaseeraa; wa maa yazzakkaru illaa ulul albaab." (Surat Al-Baqarah)

"He gives wisdom to whom He wills, and whoever has been given wisdom has certainly been given much good. And none will remember except those of understanding." (The Cow, 2:269)

Sayyidina Mikhail عليه السلام begins to teach, you want to struggle in the way, you want your *rizq* to be changed, you want to receive your heavenly sustenance, then begin to write these realities. Begin to change your *kitaab* from just your good and bad actions to the noble realities of Sayyidina Muhammad ﷺ.

3. Archangel Izrail (Azrael) عليه السلام at the Station of *Sirr e Sir* (Secret of the Secret)

Enter from the Gate of *Siddiq* to the Presence of the King

Then we get to the two gates that enter at the bottom of the *lataif* which are from the *Sirr e Sir* (Secret of the Secret) and then the *Khafa* (Hidden). Allah عز وجل says in *Surah Al-Isra,* Verse 80, that this is the gate of the *Siddiq*, the *Maqaa as-Siddiq*.

وَقُل رَّبِّ أَدْخِلْنِي مُدْخَلَ صِدْقٍ وَأَخْرِجْنِي مُخْرَجَ صِدْقٍ وَاجْعَل لِّي مِن لَّدُنكَ سُلْطَانًا نَّصِيرًا ٨٠

17:80 – "Wa qul Rabbi adkhelni mudkhala Sidqin wa akhrejni mukhraja Sidqin, waj'al li min ladunka Sultanan NaSeera." (Surah Al-Isra)

Say: "O my Lord! Let my entry be by the Gate of Truth and Honour, and likewise my exit by the Gate of Truth and Honour; and grant me from Your Presence an authority [Sultan/King] to aid (me)."
(The Night Journey, 17:80)

Yaa Rabbi (O my lord), let me enter from the gate of the *Siddiq*, the trustworthy honoured gate, to exit from the gate of the *Siddiq* to the *Sultanan Naseera*, into the presence of the *sultan*. So then they translate the *sultan* as 'an authority'; why don't they just translate *sultan* as *sultan*? It means let me to enter the presence of the *sultan* (king). It means this gate of the *Siddiq*, this gate is into the presence of the honoured *sultan*, which is the presence of the *Sultanan Naseera*, and is the presence of Sayyidina Muhammad ﷺ.

SAYYIDINA IZRAIL عليه السلام TEACHES, LEAVE THE WORLD IN A HONOURED WAY

We are asking, *yaa Rabbi,* with these realities You are opening, that for Sayyidina Jibreel عليه السلام to dress the soul, and Sayyidina Mikhail عليه السلام is dressing, and these servants are supported by these angelic realities. They take from these angelic realities. It means they take from Sayyidina Jibreel عليه السلام the knowledges that are being bestowed upon the soul. They take the support from Sayyidina Mikhail عليه السلام to struggle in the way of Allah عز وجل and to dress their sustenance and bless their sustenance.

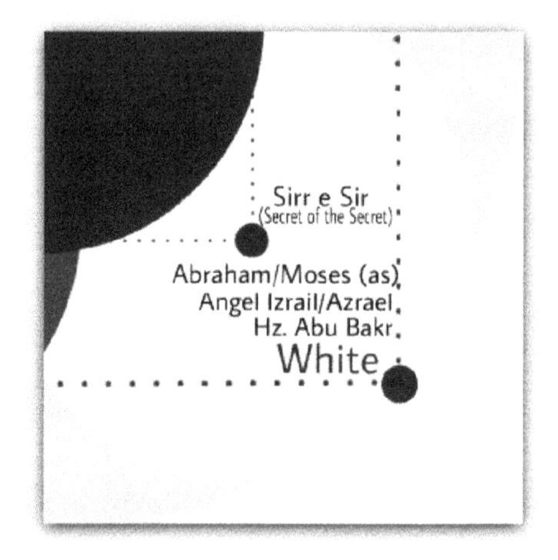

Then comes Sayyidina Izrail عليه السلام at the station of *Sirr e Sir* and is coming to teach you how to die. That I have to come to teach you to go through the gate of the *Siddiq;* it means to leave this *dunya* (material world) with a way that Allah عز وجل gave to you, to leave this way in a noble and honoured way. Don't wait for Allah عز وجل to come and call you back in a condition that you don't know what condition you are in, but *mawt qabl al-mawt* (dead before dead).

DEATH IS COMING – DON'T HOLD TIGHT TO THE WORLD

That if you want our way, we will come, Prophet صلى الله عليه وسلم will send us (angels) to teach you that at every moment not to be attached to this world. Every test will begin to come to you so that you don't hold the world like this (tight fisted). Oh, I am not going to change, this is what I want. No, no this world has to be like a string for you, if they pull it, it falls out of your hand, that there is no attachment. That is through Sayyidina Izrail عليه السلام.

Sayyidina Izrail ﷺ begins to come to the servant and keeps teaching, that death is coming, death is coming, lose the taste of this *dunya*, *hub ad-dunya* (love of material world). And direct yourself to the *hub* of *akhirah* and to the love of *akhirah* (hereafter), which is to the love of Sayyidina Muhammad ﷺ.

LEAVE FROM THE GATE OF *SIDDIQ* (TRUTHFUL)

Then Sayyidina Izrail ﷺ begins to open the secret of *ayat al-kareem*, that how, *yaa Rabbi*, constantly reciting, *yaa Rabbi*, let me leave from the gate of the *Siddiq*.

وَقُل رَّبِّ أَدْخِلْنِي مُدْخَلَ صِدْقٍ وَأَخْرِجْنِي مُخْرَجَ صِدْقٍ وَاجْعَل لِّي مِن لَّدُنكَ سُلْطَانًا نَّصِيرًا ٨٠

17:80 – "Wa qul Rabbi adkhelni mudkhala Sidqin wa akhrejni mukhraja Sidqin, waj'al li min ladunka Sultanan NaSeera." (Surah Al-Isra)

Say: "O my Lord! Let my entry be by the Gate of Truth and Honour, and likewise my exit by the Gate of Truth and Honour; and grant me from Your Presence an authority [a King] to aid (me)." (The Night Journey, 17:80)

THE SOUL COMES OUT IN *TAFAKKUR* (MEDITATION)

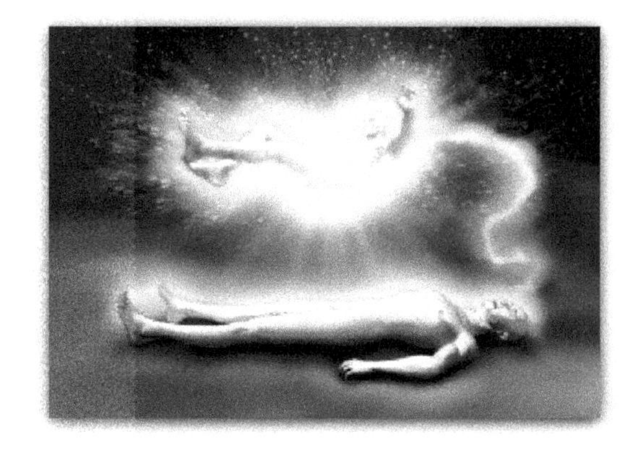

It means he begins to teach you how to crush the form and then the soul begins to come out. You feel it in the contemplation; when you begin to train in contemplation that you are entering into a state of death. You begin to meditate and make *tafakkur* and breathe listening to *salawat*

and you don't even move. You are just breathing as if you are entering into a state of death, where the energy is dropping, energy is dropping and you feel your soul is coming out.

The Biggest Struggle is to Let Your Desires Die

That is where Sayyidina Izrail عليه السلام has to come and train the servant that, die; that every desire you have, let it die. Every hope and want you have, let it die. All that you want is Allah's Will. What you wanted for this world, leave it. What you hoped for in this world, leave it. It means surrender yourself to the will of Allah عزَّ وجلَّ. That becomes the biggest struggle, biggest battle; that you knew I had many thoughts, had many wants, had many desires for myself, all of which may be different from what Allah عزَّ وجلَّ wants. Sayyidina Izrail عليه السلام comes to assist that servant to let it go, let it go, let it perish, let everything to perish. Everything perishes except the will of Allah عزَّ وجلَّ.

When the servant can enter into that state, understanding the testing at that state, they say "uh...I give up." That is the guide who comes into their life. Every time they are depressed and sad and upset, the purpose of the guide is to coordinate, that what you are feeling is correct, it is what Allah عزَّ وجلَّ wants you to feel. That just give it up, your desire give it up. What Allah عزَّ وجلَّ has in store for you is far greater, what Allah عزَّ وجلَّ has in store for you is far better. What Allah عزَّ وجلَّ wants for you is only the best. What you want for yourself may not be good for you.

So then they enter a deep struggle with themselves and many become bi-polar, where they are happy and then they are sad, happy and then sad, happy and then sad. Why? Because this is the battle, no, no I want this, no, no I can't have it. No, no I want to have this, no, no I can't have it. Sayyidina Izrail عليه السلام is coming to teach *mawt* (dead), let everything go; eventually with difficulty you feel yourself moving into that presence.

Difficulties Come, So You Will Run to Allah ﷻ

That opens the secret of every *mushkilat* and difficulty. Without difficulty the servant becomes too comfortable within their physicality; they are building right here on Earth a Paradise within themselves. So the reality of every difficulty, that *Awliya* (saints) are teaching us, difficulty is coming, tests are coming, why? To begin to crack you. As soon as difficulty comes, you find your *tafakkur* so powerful. As soon as you cry and you are sad and upset about something, your *tafakkur* becomes very powerful because of your love for Allah ﷻ, so you run into His Divinely Presence and that is the secret of *zalzala* (earthquake).

Like *Zalzala* (Earthquake) – Body Has to Be Crushed, For the Soul to Come Out

Allah ﷻ describes *zalzala* (earthquake) that when We crush something there must be something hidden inside that wants to come out; if I don't crush it, it doesn't come out.

إِذَا زُلْزِلَتِ الْأَرْضُ زِلْزَالَهَا (١) وَأَخْرَجَتِ الْأَرْضُ أَثْقَالَهَا (٢)

99:1-2 – "Izaa zulzilatil ardu zil zaalaha. (1) Wa akhrajatil ardu athqaalaha (2)" (Surah Al-Zalzalah)

"When the earth is shaken with its [final] earthquake. (1) And the earth discharges its burdens (2)" (The Shaking, 99:1-2)

Just like the womb the baby has to come out, the baby can't sit there for five years, at a certain point the reality has to be born. So when the servant is struggling Allah عزَّ وجلَّ is reminding, then *Malaika* (angels) are reminding, *Awliyaullah* are reminding, that Allah عزَّ وجلَّ wants to bring the reality of the soul out.

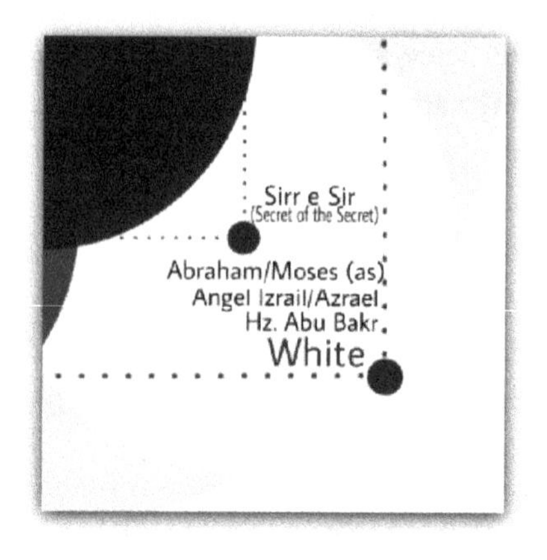

So Sayyidina Izrail عليه السلام comes to teach the servant how to have your desires die. Sayyidina Izrail عليه السلام represents death and that is the white, the station of *Sirr e Sir* (Secret of the Secret). That is why you are buried in a white fabric. That is why you make *Hajj* in this white fabric. Why? It symbolizes nothing, be nothing, don't make yourself to be different from other people.

4. Archangel Israfil (Raphael) عليه السلام at the Station of *Khafa* (Hidden)

He Teaches How to Enter to the Presence of *Sultanan Naseera*

Sayyidina Israfil عليه السلام comes and says, "Come now I will take you to the *baab as-Siddiq* into the presence of the *Sultanan Naseera (Victorious King).*"

وَاجْعَل لِّي مِن لَّدُنكَ سُلْطَانًا نَّصِيرًا ٨٠...

17:80 – "…waj'al li min ladunka Sultanan NaSeera." (Surah Al-Isra)

"...and grant me from Your Presence a King to aid (me)."
(The Night Journey, 17:80)

Sayyidina Israfil عليه السلام comes into our soul and into our reality and shows I am going to teach you how to rise into the Divinely Presence. That as you are learning how to be nothing, how to be nothing, and how to bring your soul out, I will teach you the realities of how to take you into the presence of the *Sultanan Naseera.*

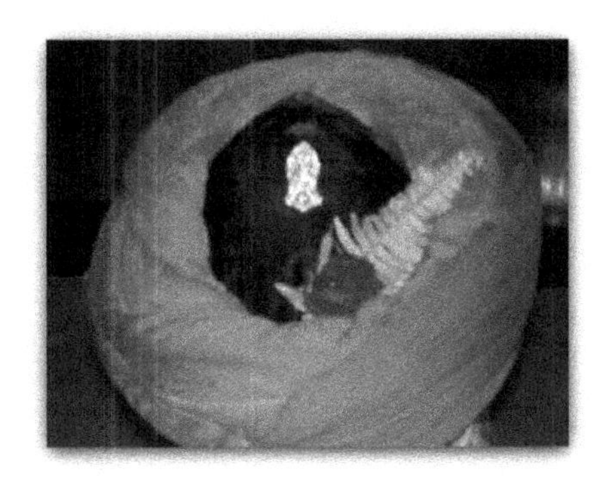

It means Sayyidina Israfil عليه السلام teaches how to perfect your character, how to annihilate yourself, annihilate your character. How when we are going to go into the presence of *Sultanan Naseera* (Victorious King), not to raise your head, be nothing. Don't ask for anything, don't dare look into the eyes of Prophet صلى الله عليه وسلم but keep your head upon the floor, that keep your head upon his holy feet. That is why *Awliyaullah* wear a turban with a sandal mark; that is why they wear the button of the holy sandal of Prophet صلى الله عليه وسلم.

It means that Sayyidina Israfil عليه السلام teaches the protocol of how to enter into that presence; be nothing, be nothing and enter into the presence of that *sultan* who is great and whom Allah عز وجل loves beyond imagination. You can't do anything in the presence of Prophet ﷺ because now you are coming to the master of annihilation.

SAYYIDINA MUHAMMAD ﷺ IS THE MASTER OF ANNIHILATION

Prophet ﷺ is the master of annihilating, that anything other than what Allah عزّ وجلّ wants, Prophet ﷺ will annihilate. So then the servant comes as completely nothing that, *yaa Sayyidi, Yaa Rasul Kareem* (O' generous Messenger), let my head just to be at your feet. Tell me what Allah عزّ وجلّ wants for me, not to lift myself or to think anything, just to be dust under your feet. And they carry the sandal as a reminder upon themselves. You carry it upon your body, upon your head that I want to be nothing.

As Sayyidina Adam عليه السلام bowed down to the light of Sayyidina Muhammad ﷺ we take ourselves to that same understanding. Bowing is not for worship; that is only for Allah عزّ وجلّ. This is *sajdatil ihtiraam* (bowing out of respect) that you are in the presence of someone whom Allah عزّ وجلّ has a magnificent love for, and out of respect. That I am not the one to look at your divinely and blessed face. I am not one to expect anything, *Yaa Sayyidi, yaa Rasul Kareem, Ya Habibul 'Azeem,* just keep me at your threshold, just have pity upon my poor being, dress me from your *nazar*, dress me from your blessings, lift me from my difficulties.

WHEN YOU ARE OPPRESSOR TO YOURSELF, GO TO PROPHET ﷺ

Then the love of Prophet ﷺ comes and begins to enter that reality *Sultanan Naseera.* It means Allah عزّ وجلّ wants to know who signed-off for you, because when the servant is an oppressor to themselves they have to come to you, *yaa Sayyidi, yaa Rasulullah.*

وَلَوْ أَنَّهُمْ إِذ ظَّلَمُوا أَنفُسَهُمْ جَاءُوكَ فَاسْتَغْفَرُوا اللَّـهَ وَاسْتَغْفَرَ لَهُمُ الرَّسُولُ لَوَجَدُوا اللَّـهَ تَوَّابًا رَّحِيمًا ٦٤

4:64 – "...Wa law annahum idh dhalamoo anfusahum jaooka fastaghfaro Allaha wastaghfara lahumur Rasolu lawajado Allaha tawwaban raheema." (Surah An-Nisa)

"...And if, when they had wronged [were oppressor to] themselves, they had but come to you (saws) and asked forgiveness of Allah, and asked forgiveness of the messenger, they would have found Allah Forgiving, Merciful." (The Women, 4:64)

You see all of Qur'an is describing this. This is that *ayat* (verse) opening, they have to come to you and ask My forgiveness, then they have to ask your forgiveness. Then Allah عز وجل describes, then I am forgiving. Why are they coming to Me directly? Why are they asking Me when they didn't come to you?

It means this whole reality is this understanding, that you are coming to perfect your character. Sayyidina Israfil عليه السلام is teaching that you want the real repentance, the real reality of what Allah عز وجل wants, then go into the presence of Prophet ﷺ as nothing and don't claim to be anything. Ask to be dressed from his *nazar* (gaze), dressed and blessed from his light, so that Sayyidina Muhammad ﷺ signs your paper.

That *Sultanan Naseera*, (Victorious King), somebody signed off for you, that, "We know you, we authorized you, we have our *nazar* upon you. You are being dressed by Sayyidina Jibreel عليه السلام, Sayyidina Mikhail عليه السلام, Sayyidina Izrail عليه السلام, Sayyidina Israfil عليه السلام and Sayyidina Malik عليه السلام."

5. Archangel Malik عليه السلام at the Station of *Akhfa* (Most Hidden)

He Guards Your Heavenly Reality

It means the point at the Station of *Akhfa* is the guardian of *jahannam* (hellfire), Sayyidina Malik عليه السلام. Sayyidina Malik عليه السلام is the guardian of Paradise. Your Paradise has no value if Sayyidina Malik عليه السلام is not guarding it because then every *Shaytan* will enter into that Paradise and flip it upside down. They begin to teach that we are entering into the presence of Prophet صلى الله عليه وسلم and they introduce to you Sayyidina Malik عليه السلام and the *Zabaniya*, the guardians of *jahannam*.

Sayyidina Malik عليه السلام has to sign off for you that this is what *Sultanan Naseera*, Prophet صلى الله عليه وسلم wants for you. That our *nazar* is on you; we are watching you, that anything coming from the Heavens coming towards you, we are responsible for guarding you. That this light of Allah عز و جل, this light of Prophet صلى الله عليه وسلم, this light of *Awliyaullah* (saints) must be protected and guarded.

So it means they introduce at that time to Sayyidina Malik عليه السلام and Sayyidina Malik عليه السلام begins to support *Awliyaullah* with the *Zabaniya*. They have the ability to make a *du'a* (supplication) and bring the fires of *jahannam* onto this Earth. One *Awliyaullah* can flip the entire Earth upside down. There are 124,000 of them on this Earth. It is unimaginable when Allah عز و جل gives. It means that for any knowledge to open upon a saint, that first Allah عز و جل must have the flags of guardianship, they must be guarded people, otherwise whatever Allah عز و جل opens for that person will be stolen by *Shaytan*.

So it means first Allah عز و جل will assign that Sayyidina Malik عليه السلام and whom are under the authority of Sayyidina Malik عليه السلام, to guard that one. To guard that one's soul with all they have been dressed from Paradise and Sayyidina Muhammad صلى الله عليه وسلم says, your duty is to guard them. They have a flag and in old times many would draw them with a dragon. In old time drawings they were dragons. So their image is like a dragon and there must be a dragon supporting that *wali* (saint). As a result that fire comes from them as a support.

It means that Paradise reality is now going to walk onto this Earth, it is not going to be without Allah's عزَّ وجلَّ protection. Allah's عزَّ وجلَّ protection is Sayyidina Malik عليه السلام. As you are guarding the Paradises, guard that servant. That fire and that light are guarding them, so that every reality and knowledge that is coming out is a knowledge that is protected. This is a gift from Prophet صلى الله عليه وسلم to servants who are moving to open the realities.

Subhana rabbika rabil 'izzati 'ama yasifoon, Wa salamun 'alal mursaleen wal hamdulillahi rabbil 'alameen. Bi hurmati Muhammadil Mustafa wa bi siratil Suratil Fatiha.

ANGELS – PART 2
SUPPORTING THE SOUL

ARCHANGELS JIBREEL عليه السلام, MIKHAIL عليه السلام, IZRAIL عليه السلام, ISRAFIL عليه السلام, MALIK عليه السلام

There are so many different levels and realities of the Levels of the Heart. If you take just the angelic reality of the *lataif*, that at the first station, the *Qalb* (Heart) is Sayyidina Jibreel عليه السلام and the next station *Sir* (Secret) is Sayyidina Mikhail عليه السلام, then Sayyidina Izrail عليه السلام at the station of *Sirr e Sir* (Secret of the Secret), then Sayyidina Israfil عليه السلام at *Khafa* (Hidden), and Sayyidina Malik عليه السلام is at the innermost, the center, station of *Akhfa* (Most Hidden).

It means it begins to teach that the angels have a reality for us. We are asking for the eternal heart to open. We are asking for the Divinely Lights to open, then everything in Creation has a secret for us; so many things will be linked to this hour glass movement. Once we begin to study it, we can see from the *Qalb* to the *Sir* to *Sirr e Sir* to *Khafa* and *Akhfa*.

1. ARCHANGEL JIBREEL (GABRIEL) عليه السلام AT THE STATION OF *QALB* (HEART)

HE DEPOSITS THE LIGHT OF KNOWLEDGE IN THE HEART

وَعَلَّمَ آدَمَ الْأَسْمَاءَ كُلَّهَا... ٣١

2:31 – "Wa 'allama Adamal Asma a kullaha,..." (Surah Al-Baqarah)

"And He taught Adam the names of all things ..." (The Cow, 2:31)

Just at the level of *Malaika* (angels). Then Sayyidina Jibreel عليه السلام comes and teaches in the yellow light those are secrets from Sayyidina Jibreel عليه السلام and the secret of knowledge and why he was responsible for bringing prophecy to all the prophets.

They begin to teach in the world of light, that in the initial stages, he's coming and going, coming and going, but if you are reaching a station of sincerity then why to come and go? Because you can understand from the world of light, it is no longer a physical world; when you stand there and I stand here, we have two separate presences.

In the world of light, with the angels, the light comes into the reality of your soul, the beginning and ends of these lights are no longer known; light melts into each other. Then Sayyidina Jibreel عليه السلام begins to deposit his lights upon your soul. The more light he deposits, the more light he deposits, it's like an agency opens within the soul for Divinely Knowledges.

It is no longer necessary for him to keep travelling; he merely opens an agency within your soul and begins to deposit, like what they call in agriculture as grafting. He puts a little bit of that light and it begins to multiply, begins to move within the reality, as long as we are keeping the soul purified and clean.

2. Archangel Mikhail (Michael) عليه السلام at the Station of *Sir* (Secret)

وَ قُلْ جَآءَالْحَقُّ وَزَهَقَ الْبَطِلُ، إِنَّ الْبَطِلَ كَانَ زَهُوقًا

17:81 – "Wa qul jaa alhaqqu wa zahaqal baatil, innal batila kana zahooqa." (Surah Al-Isra)

"And say, "Truth has come, and falsehood has perished. Indeed falsehood, [by its nature], is ever perishing/ bound to perish." (The Night Journey, 17:81)

Truth and Falsehood Cannot Occupy the Same Space

Qul jaa al haqq wa zahaqal batil means "truth and falsehood cannot occupy the same space". So once Allah ﷻ grants sincerity, and the soul is trying to purify; it can't keep doing good and then bad, good and then bad, this light will leave; it can't occupy that same space.

So why Allah ﷻ asks for it to be sincere is that through sincerity and contemplation, they begin to open the channel. When they begin the channel of connection, that channel will begin to guide that, don't do that, do this, and make your connection. These are the channels, these are lights and energies, and these are the *isharat* (signs), where Allah ﷻ makes them to be *mahfuz* (guarded), because now the connection of the soul is open.

Then Sayyidina Jibreel عليه السلام comes and begins to deposit light. This is the light of knowledge. These are the lights of the reality that begin to open within the servant's heart. Sayyidina Mikhail عليه السلام comes and begins to teach, and each has an infinite understanding of knowledge.

Sayyidina Mikhail عليه السلام Assists Us With Our Struggle

Sayyidina Mikhail عليه السلام begins to come at the station of *Sir*, the Secret (second station), and says, "I am the angel of war and the angel of sustenance." It means that every article when you read about the levels of the heart, from the heavenly teachings, it begins to open its understanding. It means that red, blood, and war, so we have to struggle against our bad characteristics. Sayyidina Mikhail عليه السلام comes with his angelic lights and begins to assist us in our struggle.

Sayyidina Mikhail ﷺ Sustains the Soul From Its Paradise Reality

Sayyidina Mikhail ﷺ also begins to describe, "I am in charge of sustenance. That anywhere on this Creation, I am the one distributing its sustenance." But more important than the physical sustenance is the spiritual sustenance. He begins to teach that I am responsible for your soul's sustenance.

...وَتَرْزُقُ مَنْ تَشَآءُ بِغَيْرِ حِسَابٍ (٣:٢٧)

3:27 – "... wa tarzuqu man tasha'u bi ghayri hisab." (Surah Al-Imran)

"...And You give provision to whom You will without measure [unlimited]." (Family of Imran, 3:27)

If I am coming and going, coming and going, then you are making that connection. The shaykh (spiritual guide) merely gets permission from Allah ﷻ, *atiullah ati ar-rasula wa ulul amri minkum.* The *ulul amr* (saints) are granted permission and Sayyidina Mikhail ﷺ begins to dress the soul.

...يااَيُّهَا الَّذِينَ آمَنُوا أَطِيعُوااللهَ وَأَطِيعُواالرَّسُولَ وَأُوْلِي الأَمْرِ مِنْكُمْ

4:59 – "Ya ayyu hal ladheena amanooAtiullaha, wa atiur Rasola, wa Ulil amre minkum..." (Surah An-Nisa)

"O You who have believed, Obey Allah, Obey the Messenger, and those in authority among you..." (The Women, 4:59)

Sayyidina Mikhail ﷺ begins to put that light into the soul. That your sustenance, I am now in your soul, I am with you. It means I am now going to control the sustenance that is coming to you. You are going to eat from your Paradise realities. You are going to drink from your Paradise realities. We are going to sustain you from your Paradise realities. Our agency, our office, is already open within your soul. That is what it means to be dressed with angelic lights.

The angels are the ones coming and supporting and everything is essential. It means, for knowledge to open in the soul, Sayyidina Jibreel's عليه السلام lights must be there. Otherwise they are speaking from their head and from books they read. When somebody speaks from the book they read written by professors at school you immediately pass out because it is from the head, head to head. What they (*awliya*/saints) are talking and teaching and give permission to teach is from the level of the soul, energy from the soul.

The angel begins to come and say that, "I am going to deposit that light; my agency is within your soul, whatever sustenance Allah عز و جل wants that agency is there. What do you need, you will receive from your Paradise reality. My light will assist you in your struggle against yourself and your demons." That light begins to emanate within the soul.

3. Archangel Izrail (Azrael) عليه السلام at the Station of *Sirr e Sir* (Secret of the Secret)

وَقُل رَّبِّ أَدْخِلْنِي مُدْخَلَ صِدْقٍ وَأَخْرِجْنِي مُخْرَجَ صِدْقٍ... ٨٠

17:80 – "Wa qul Rabbi adkhelni mudkhala Sidqin wa akhrejni mukhraja Sidqin …" (Surah Al-Isra)

Say: "O my Lord! Let my entry be by the Gate of Truth and Honour, and likewise my exit by the Gate of Truth and Honour…"
(The Night Journey, 17:80)

SAYYIDINA IZRAIL ﷺ TEACHES TO ENTER THE STATION OF *"MAWT QABL MAWT"*

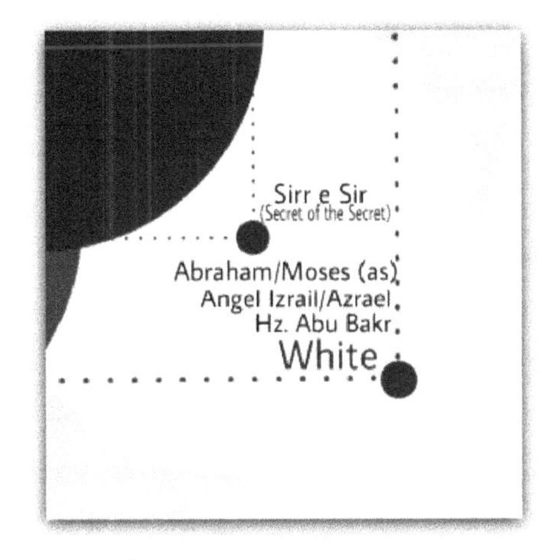

Then Sayyidina Izrail ﷺ, at the *Sirr e Sir* (third station), comes and begins to teach that if you are truly contemplating and meditating, you are now entering the *maqam* of *mawt qablal mawt* (station of death before death).

The station of 'death before death' means so much of this light is coming from your Paradise reality. If it is coming into your body you are not from this Earth any more. Your contract has been flipped because what comes to this physical body is a very small drop of the soul.

THE PHYSICAL BODY HAS A DROP OF THE SOUL FROM PARADISE

The size and age and magnificence of the soul are not something that can be imagined. If you could imagine it, in one time they may show you with your soul standing and the whole Earth fits within the palm of your hand. The size and magnitude of the soul is something unimaginable.

What Allah ﷻ gives for us to play within *dunya* (material world) is a drop, not so that you ruin it. You have not received the trust and received your inheritance, the *amanat*, and they are not going to let us destroy what Allah ﷻ has entrusted. But they begin to teach that when you are bringing this much light onto your soul, you are able to connect with your master and the master is sending from his light, sending from the light of Prophet, sending from Allah's عز و جل Divinely Decree. Because you are obeying, *atiullah ati ar-rasula wa ulul amri minkum.*

يٰأَيُّهَا الَّذِينَ آمَنُوا أَطِيعُوااللهَ وَأَطِيعُواْالرَّسُولَ وَأُوْلِي الأَمْرِ مِنْكُمْ

4:59 – "Ya ayyu hal ladheena amanooAtiullaha, wa atiur Rasola, wa Ulil amre minkum..." (Surah An-Nisa)

"O You who have believed, Obey Allah, Obey the Messenger, and those in authority among you... " (The Women, 4:59)

It means like a telescope, it is reaching you, the *ulul amr* (saints) are sending you lights from where? From the obedience of Prophet صلى الله عليه وسلم and Prophet صلى الله عليه وسلم is sending from where? The obedience of the Divinely Presence, and begins to send these lights.

Sayyidina Izrail عليه السلام begins to describe you are dying; you are more dead than alive in this world. Your desires for this world are no longer and you walk amongst people but you are not from them. We are going to teach you how to die before you die.

THE *DHIKR* OF *KALIMA TAWHID* AND REVIVING THE SOUL

They have a *dhikr* for shutting the heart and reviving it. Mawlana Shaykh's teaching and guides teach in *khalwa*, seclusion, the *dhikr*:

Laa ilaaha ilAllah, laa ilaaha ilAllah (There is no God but Allah) they focus *laa ilaaha ilAllah* on their *lataif* and the body will shut. They enter into a state of death and can revive with *Muhammadun Rasulullah* (Prophet Muhammad صلى الله عليه وسلم is the Messenger of Allah). *Laa ilaha ilAllah, laa ilaha ilAllah, laa ilaha ilAllah,* die, and *Muhammadun Rasulullah,* come back.

Sayyidina Izrail عليه السلام begins to teach that with that light you are going to be taught how to leave your body. It is essential at that gate because Allah عزّ وجلّ describes that you have to go from the gate of the *Siddiq* and return from the gate of the *Siddiq*.

وَقُل رَّبِّ أَدْخِلْنِي مُدْخَلَ صِدْقٍ وَأَخْرِجْنِي مُخْرَجَ صِدْقٍ وَاجْعَل لِّي مِن لَّدُنكَ سُلْطَانًا نَّصِيرًا ٨٠

17:80 – "Wa qul Rabbi adkhelni mudkhala Sidqin wa akhrejni mukhraja Sidqin waj'al li min ladunka Sultanan NaSeera." (Surah Al-Isra)

Say: "O my Lord! Let my entry be by the Gate of Truth and Honour, and likewise my exit by the Gate of Truth and Honour; and grant me from Thy Presence an authority [a King] to aid (me)." (The Night Journey, 17:80)

It means two noble gates, you have to open and purify. They can't let you just send the body out. It means it has to be a very noble and clean sending; come back very noble and clean, not to contaminate, and not to dirty anything in the presence of *Sultanan Naseera.* It means go from the gate of the *Siddiq*, enter from the gate of the *Siddiq* to the *Sultanan Naseera*, an authorized *sultan.*

4. Archangel Israfil (Raphael) عليه السلام at the Station of *Khafa* (Hidden)

تُوْلِجُ اللَّيْلَ فِي النَّهَارِ وَتُوْلِجُ النَهَارَ فِي اللَّيْلِ، وَتُخْرِجُ الْحَيَّ مِنَ الْمَيِّتِ وَتُخْرِجُ الْمَيِّتَ مِنَ الْحَيِّ، وَتَرْزُقُ مَنْ تَشَآءُ بِغَيْرِ حِسَابٍ .(سُوْرَةُ آلِ عِمْرَان ٢٧:٣

3:27 – "Tulijul layla fin nahari, wa tuliju nahara fil layl, wa tukhrijul hayya minal mayyiti, wa tukhrijul mayyita minal hayy, wa tarzuqu man tasha'u bi ghayri hisab." (Surah Al-Imran)

"You make the night to enter into the day and You make the day to enter into the night, You bring the living out of the dead and You bring the dead out of the living, And You give provision to whom You will without measure [unlimited]." (Family of Imran, 3:27)

Sayyidina Israfil عليه السلام Teaches How to Resurrect to the Divinely Presence

Sayyidina Israfil عليه السلام begins to teach us if he (Sayyidina Izrail عليه السلام) is teaching you death, I will teach you to resurrect. That once the station of death is coming, I teach you how to resurrect your soul into the Divinely Presence.

Bring the Kingdom of Allah عز وجل in Your Heart

For all of that, if you look at this (diagram) this was the drawing of castles in old England. Look at the old castles; they had the main palace for the king and four towers for protection. Four towers because it was a symbol of the Heavenly Kingdom. In old movies you see the king's palace and four towers and surrounding the palace was a moat for the protection of the palace. You couldn't get to the palace unless a little *sirat al-mustaqeem*, a little bridge came, because in the moat there were crocodiles to eat you. They made all the palaces with that reality.

Allah ﷻ says, why do you think this is *ajeeb* (strange), you saw it in all your movies. Because We said Thy Kingdom come My Will be done on Earth as it is in Heaven. It means in your heart, "Make My Heavenly Kingdom, My angels will come." These are the archangels and under them millions and billions of angels. It is not something that can be numbered of that support, but what we need are the archangels who come to fortify and make Allah's ﷻ Kingdom within the heart.

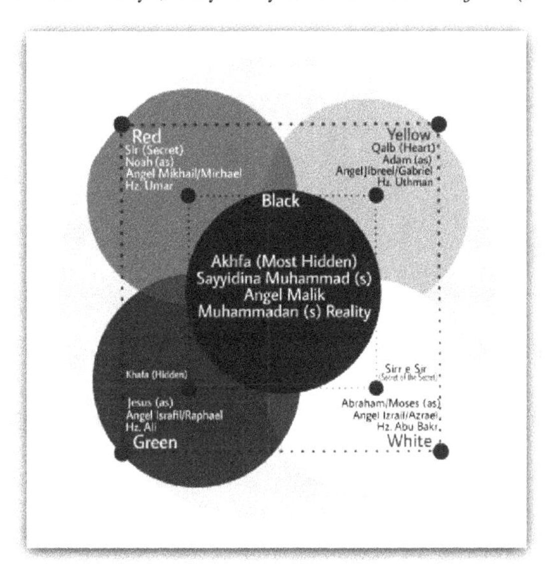

Heart of Sayyidina Muhammad ﷺ is the Ark of the Covenant

The heart of Sayyidina Muhammad ﷺ is the Ark of the Covenant. There are other people who are in search of an Ark so they can be granted a victory in battle. They are hoping to find and take that Ark. They also want to take the stones and the Tablets of Nabi Musa عليه السلام, thinking with that Ark they are going to be granted victory. That was an artificial Ark until the arrival of Sayyidina Muhammad ﷺ.

The Ark means the vessel of the covenant, and is the holy heart, the covenant of Allah ﷻ; nothing in Heavens and Earth can contain it except the heart of the believer.

مَا وَسِعَنِيْ لا سَمَائِيْ ولا اَرْضِيْ وَلَكِنْ وَسِعَنِيْ قَلْبِ عَبْدِيْ اَلْمُؤمِنْ

"Maa wasi`anee la Samayee, wa la ardee, laakin wasi'anee qalbi 'Abdee al Mu'min."

"Neither My Heavens nor My Earth can contain Me, but the heart of my Believing Servant." (Hadith Qudsi conveyed by Prophet Muhammad ﷺ)

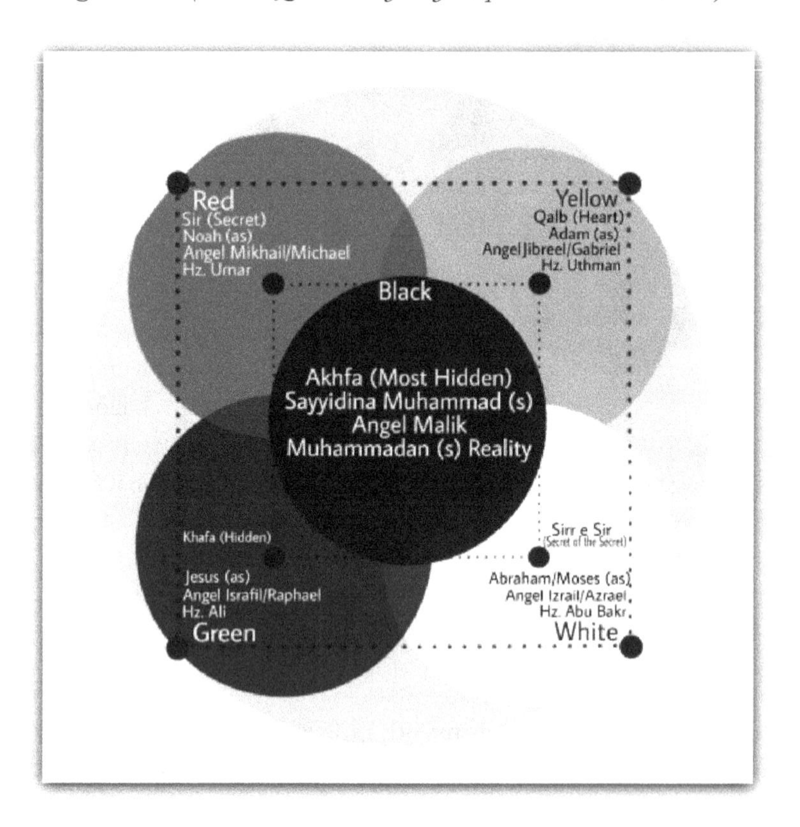

Allah's عزّ وجلّ holy covenant had to arrive with the seal of Sayyidina Muhammad ﷺ. From that point on the heart of the believer is the covenant of Allah عزّ وجلّ. It is carried by the archangels, Sayyidina Jibreel عليه السلام on one side, Sayyidina Mikhail عليه السلام on the other side, Sayyidina Izrail عليه السلام and Sayyidina Israfil عليه السلام are carrying the soul. They are carrying that reality.

5. Archangel Malik عليه السلام at the Station of *Akhfa* (Most Hidden)

إِنَّا أَعْطَيْنَاكَ الْكَوْثَرَ (١) فَصَلِّ لِرَبِّكَ وَانْحَرْ (٢) إِنَّ شَانِئَكَ هُوَ الْأَبْتَرُ (٣)

108:1-3 – "Inna 'atayna kal kawthar. (1) Fasali li rabbika wanhar.(2) Inna shani-aka huwal abtar. (3)" (Surah Al-Kawthar)

"To thee (O Muhammad) we have granted the Fount (of Abundance). (1) So pray to your Lord and Sacrifice.(2) Indeed, your enemy is the one cut off." (The Abundance, 108:1-3)

Sayyidina Malik عليه السلام at the Center is the Enforcer

In the center of its (heart's) authority and power is Sayyidina Malik عليه السلام. Sayyidina Malik عليه السلام means he brings the enforcement of *jahannam* (hellfire) onto that soul. The greatness of our Paradise is based on its protection.

إِنَّ شَانِئَكَ هُوَ الْأَبْتَرُ (٣)

108:3 – "Inna shani-aka huwal abtar. (3)" (Surah Al-Kawthar)

"Indeed, your enemy is the one cut off." (The Abundance, 108:3)

They are showing now about the Heavenly Kingdom and how it operates. Now we understand, for all of the levels of the heart to be operating, from *Qalb* (Heart) to *Khafa* (Hidden), there must be an essential enforcer; there must be a Pentagon, and a NSA (National Security Agency).

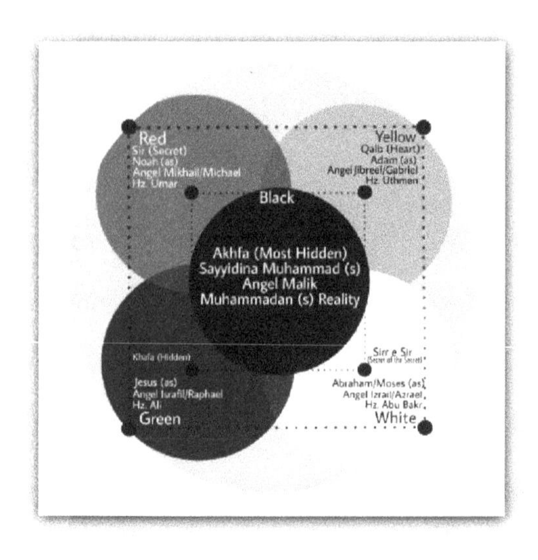

There must be a power that is at the center of it, otherwise how do you know that this angel at the Station of *Qalb* (Heart) or at the *Sir* (Secret), is working correctly? How do they know that this angel at the *Sirr e Sir* and *Khafa* is working correctly? Why? Because *amrullah*, the order of Allah عزّ وجلّ, comes directly to Sayyidina Malik عليه السلام and immediately dispatches to other angels. "*Yaa* Jibreel, did you do what you were told? *Yaa* Mikhail, did you do what you were told? Sayyidina Izrail and Sayyidina Israfil, did you do what you were told?"

It means the center of authority and center of power, and the enforcer is Sayyidina Malik عليه السلام. Allah عزّ وجلّ is saying for these lights and these realities to open upon the soul, he must be protected because *Shaytan* is going to go after him.

To Open the Heart, We Need *Salaam* (Peace) From *Rabbi Raheem* – The Merciful Lord

They say these realities can't open and these dressings can't come until Allah ﷻ gives "*salamun qawlan mir rabbir rahim*", because this is *Yaseen* ﷺ, this is the heart of Prophet ﷺ. This is the heart of Holy Qur'an, this is the heart of Sayyidina Muhammad ﷺ. For this to open, Allah ﷻ has to grant *salaamun qawlan mir rabbir raheem*, a word of peace from *Rabbir Raheem* (Merciful Lord).

سَلَامٌ قَوْلًا مِّن رَّبٍّ رَّحِيمٍ (٥٨)

36:58 – "Salamun qawlam mir Rabbir Raheem." (Surah Yaseen)

"Peace, a word from a Merciful Lord." (Yaseen, 36:58)

When Allah ﷻ grants *salaam* (peace), it means all the angels are trying to run after that servant to be of service, because Allah ﷻ has granted His kiss of love that I am *rida*, I am satisfied. Prophet ﷺ grants, I am satisfied, all the Heavenly Kingdom come to support. With that there must be a power, there must be an authority, and there must be a protection.

Power of *Awliyaullah* on Earth and Support of Sayyidina Malik عليه السلام

Sayyidina Malik عليه السلام brings his flag of protection over that servant and says, "I am now giving to you all my *zabaniyati*, that you merely request and these *zabaniyati* will be unleashed upon Earth." The dragons of

Hellfire will be released upon Earth. If they give permission to one *wali* (saint), imagine the *sultan* of *Awliya* (king of saints) what they have?

When they talk about that they are not scared, when people came to Mawlana Shaykh and described black magic, he was laughing. For us it is very scary because *Shaytan* can cause a lot of problems, but you are talking about the masters of this reality. At their disposal Allah عزّ وجلّ has given them an authority of Sayyidina Malik عليه السلام.

That merely make your request, they are taught a *dhikr*, and when they begin to make that *dhikr* to make their connection and begin to ask, an infinite number of angels of *jahannam* can begin to enter with a fire and fierceness that nothing can be imagined. Do you think that there is a *Shaytan* that would try to stand against them? If they are one or two or five or six, an infinite number coming from Divinely Presence, that they merely look and they are devoured and taken away into pits of difficulty that cannot be imagined.

It means there must be an authority, there must be a flag from *Siffatul Qahhar* (The Subduer), and Allah's عزّ وجلّ *Qadr* and power must be upon them. Sayyidina Malik عليه السلام must be an authorized light upon them.

AHLUL BAYT AND HOLY COMPANIONS AT THE LEVELS OF THE HEART

It is not a coincidence that that light is black and it represents a reality of the *Ahl al-Bayt*, the reality of Prophet صلى الله عليه وسلم, and the reality of annihilation. It is for all that light to be opened, for all that reality to be opened. Then these are the realities of annihilation. This was just the understanding from Mawlana Shaykh's teaching for the angelic reality. Everything has an understanding in these *lataif* and Levels of the Heart.

There must also be from *Ashab Nabi*, the Companions of Sayyidina Muhammad صلى الله عليه وسلم. Sayyidina Uthman عليه السلام at the Station of *Qalb* (Heart), Sayyidina Umar عليه السلام at the Station of *Sir* (Secret). Sayyidina Abu Bakr as-Siddiq عليه السلام is at *Sirr e Sir* (Secret of the Secret). Sayyidina Ali عليه السلام at the Station of *Khafa* (Hidden) and Sayyidina wa Mawlana Muhammad صلى الله عليه وسلم at the center, the *Akhfa* (Most Hidden)

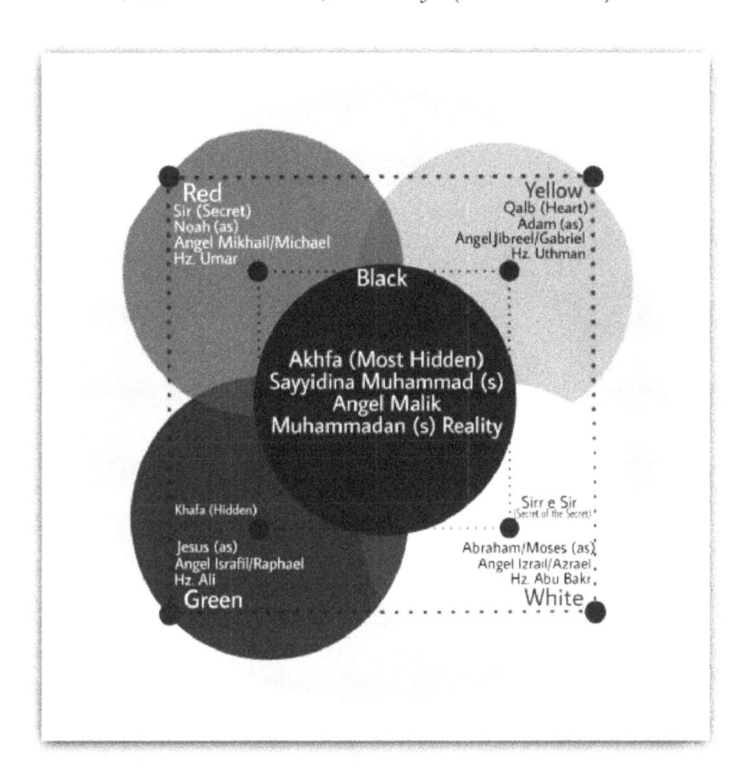

There must be from the *Ahlul Bayt*, the holy Family of Sayyidina Muhammad صلى الله عليه وسلم. Imam Hassan عليه السلام at the Station of *Qalb* (Heart), Imam Hussain عليه السلام at the *Sir* (Secret). Sayyidatina Fatima Zahra عليه السلام is at the *Sirr e Sir* (Secret of the Secret) and Sayyidina Ali عليه السلام is at the Station of *Khafa* (Hidden). Sayyidina Muhammad صلى الله عليه وسلم is at the Station of *Akhfa* (Most Hidden)

There must be *Dhikr* for each level: *Subhan Allahi* at the Station of *Qalb* (Heart), *wa Alhamdulillah* at the Station of *Sir* (Secret), *wa Laa ilaha ilAllah* at the Station of *Sirr e Sir* (Secret of the Secret), *Allahu Akbar* at the Station of *Khafa* (Hidden), *wa la hawla wa laa quwwata illa billa hil 'Aliyyil 'Azheem* at the Station of *Akhfa* (Most Hidden).

CONNECT WITH THE SHAYKH – HE REFLECTS THE LIGHTS OF THE HEART

It means that in every reality and every depth of the *lataif* there is an understanding. Once we begin to want to study it and focus on these lights, the shaykh merely begins to open that reflection. When we see ourselves in that yellow light and study the understandings of the *Qalb* already having made a connection with Mawlana Shaykh.

We see ourselves in that yellow saying, "*Sayyidi,* dress us from the light of the *Qalb,*" and begin to see a light from his heart emanating like a projection TV. This is also like the old style projection television. He will send a yellow light, a yellow light, a yellow light, why? Because this is now the ocean of *ilm* (knowledge) dressing the self. They begin to send a red light, they begin to send the white light, they begin to send the green light, and they begin to send the black light of annihilation.

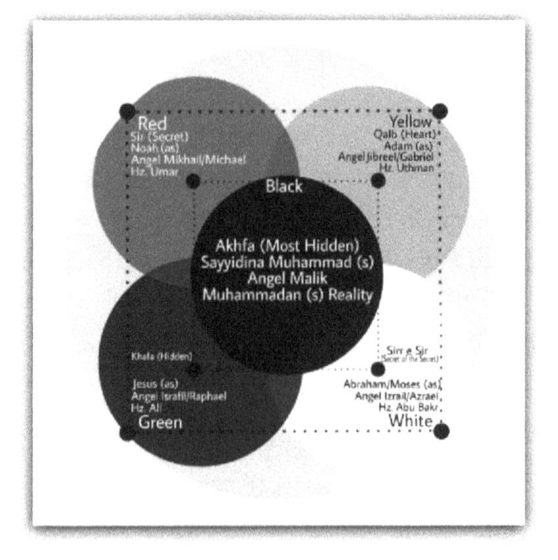

It means we have to want it, and study it, connect and meditate, and ask now to enter within it. But it is not something that you read from the outside. Don't do any meditation and hope that you are going to gain an understanding of it. This is of an infinite capacity that must dress the soul and the reality of the soul because now you are talking about *qalbun mu'min baytullah* (the Heart of the Believer is the House of Allah). This is the house of Allah ﷻ. It has no beginning and no end, infinite in its capacity and very difficult to enter in.

Subhana rabbika rabil 'izzati 'ama yasifoon, Wa salamun 'alal mursaleen wal hamdulillahi rabbil 'alameen. Bi hurmati Muhammadil Mustafa wa bi siratil Suratil Fatiha.

PROPHETS AND THE LEVELS OF THE HEART

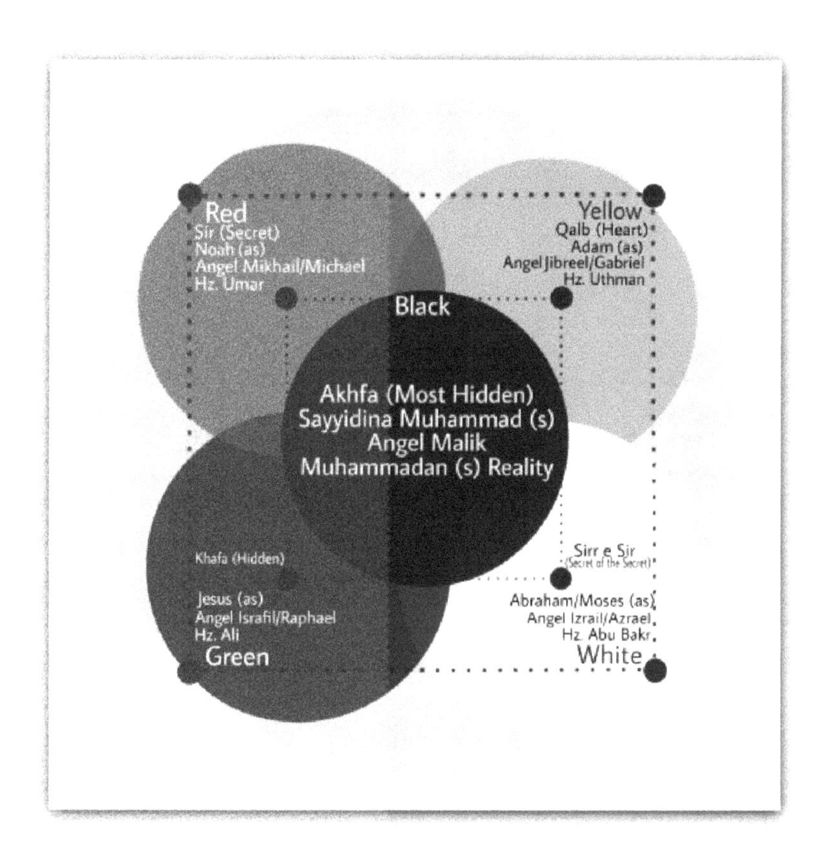

YOUR HEART NEEDS THE LOVE OF ALL PROPHETS

In the understanding of the Levels of the Heart, the prophets have an eternal message; the angels have an eternal message which means it solves everything. What people are fighting over religions, Prophet ﷺ is teaching that your heart needs all of the prophets. You are incomplete without the love of all the prophets. The levels and the reality in which Allah عز وجل wants to bestow upon your heart, you need their love. Only with their love, they begin to convey into the heart what's needed; otherwise how they are going to teach you if you don't love them? It's impossible. They are not forced by Allah عز وجل. So it means that you be with whom you love, the *Hadith* of Prophet ﷺ.

الْمَرْءُ مَعَ مَنْ أَحَب

Qala Rasulullah ﷺ: "Almar o, ma'a man ahab."

Prophet Muhammad ﷺ said: "One is with those whom he loves."

So Sayyidina Muhammad ﷺ was teaching expand your love, especially, love all the prophets; they have an immense message for the completion of your reality to be *kamil* (perfected).

The Eternal Message of the Prophets

The guides teach that every Prophet has an eternal message. They have a message of their physical presence for their physical community but God has no time. Allah عزوجل has no time, what does He care about the physical. Allah عزوجل is eternal in a timeless reality, timeless dimension. Allah عزوجل is even beyond that; *astaghfirullah*, you can't even say Allah عزوجل is timeless. But what Allah عزوجل wants from us, of the souls, is timeless. There is time, timeless, then timelessness. It means it's even *fana* in the *fana*; it's annihilated even in its annihilation.

Heart of Sayyidina Muhammad ﷺ – The Real Covenant of Allah عزوجل

Alhamdulillah, Allah عزوجل granted us to be from the nation of Sayyidina Muhammad ﷺ, to be dressed and blessed with unimaginable realities, unimaginable blessings. *Alhamdulillah* (praise be to Allah), it's the nation of all realities. It means for every other nation that came, it was an imitated reality holding the place for Sayyidina Muhammad ﷺ. It means that Nabi Musa عليه السلام, the Ark of the Covenant, was a placeholder, a contract, a box in which to hold the contract and carried by the angels, which means it was a placeholder for the reality of the Covenant. The Ark of the Covenant and the reality of the Ark of the Covenant is the holy heart; that Allah's عزوجل Covenant and contract is upon the *qalb* and *"qalb al mu'min baytullah."*

قَلْبَ الْمُؤْمِنْ بَيْتُ الرَّبْ

"Qalb al mu'min baytur rabb."

"The heart of the believer is the House of the Lord." (Hadith Qudsi)

By the arrival of Sayyidina Muhammad ﷺ, the reality of that contract comes to light. The reality of its power and its realities come to light by the appearance of Sayyidina Muhammad ﷺ. It means every imitated reality becomes nothing in the face of what Allah's عزّ وجلّ *Haqq* (truth), and *Nabi al Kareem, Habib ul 'Azeem* (the Generous Prophet, the Beloved of the Most High), appears and brings every reality into its existence.

It means the real Ark of the Covenant is the heart. The angels that carry the heart and the realities that are placed within the heart and the secrets that are written upon the heart is the Covenant of Allah عزّ وجلّ. This is the covenant in which Prophet ﷺ wants us to seek. Our whole path of realities is based on the *qalb* (heart), based on how to open the layers of the heart, the realities and the lights of the heart. And by opening those lights and those realities of the heart, Allah's عزّ وجلّ Contract becomes live, becomes active.

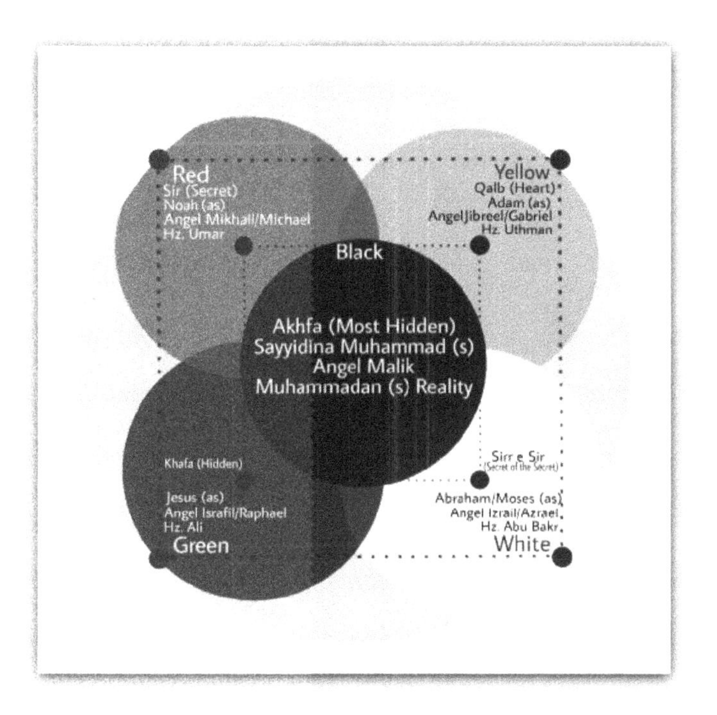

SAYYIDINA ADAM عليه السلام AT THE STATION OF *QALB* قلب (HEART)

ACCESS THE DIVINELY KNOWLEDGE WRITTEN ON YOUR SOUL

At the Station of *Qalb* (First Station – Heart), Sayyidina Adam عليه السلام comes and teaches, *isma kullaha* (all the names). He says, 'I represent the knowledge that the Divine has bestowed upon humanity.'

وَعَلَّمَ آدَمَ الْأَسْمَاءَ كُلَّهَا...٣١

2:31 – "Wa 'allama Adamal Asma a kullaha…" (Surah Al-Baqarah)

"And He taught Adam the names of all things …" (The Cow, 2:31)

ALLAH ﷻ HONOURED THE CHILDREN OF ADAM

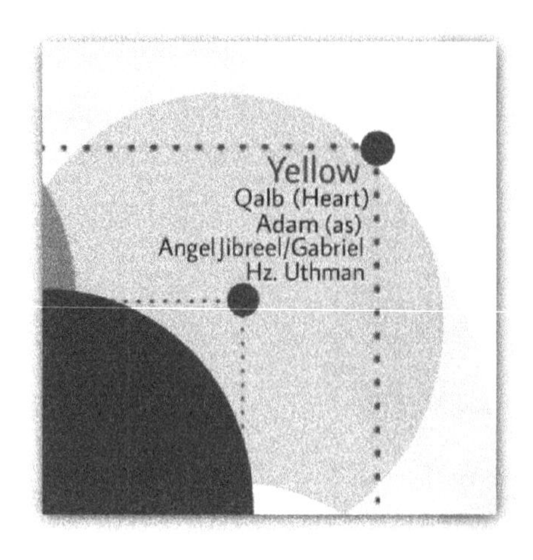

It means from the level of the *Qalb* (heart), and the understanding of Sayyidina Adam عليه السلام, that, *"Wa laqad karamna Bani Adam."*

وَلَقَدْ كَرَّمْنَا بَنِي آدَمَ...

17:70 – "Wa laqad karramna bani adama…" (Surah Al-Isra)

"We have certainly honored the children of Adam…" (The Night Journey, 17:70)

It means that every prophet has a time message and a timeless message, as Allah ﷻ has no time. That what Allah ﷻ wanted from Sayyidina Adam عليه السلام and for the people of Sayyidina Adam عليه السلام is one thing. What He wants eternally for *Bani Adam* (Children of Adam) and the nation under the flag of Sayyidina Adam عليه السلام, is an eternal message; that the level of the *Qalb* (heart) - the First Station, and the opening of that heart has to do with the understanding of Sayyidina Adam عليه السلام.

Allah ﷻ gave us a tremendous *barakah*, blessing, and a tremendous reality that, 'You are not a monkey that has evolved but you are from My Paradise creation. You are in the image of My Divinely Presence; you are in the image of My *Khalifa*, My viceroy and that all trust and all realities have been placed upon your soul. That My angels bow down to the knowledge that you have.'

وَإِذْ قُلْنَا لِلْمَلَائِكَةِ اسْجُدُوا لِآدَمَ فَسَجَدُوا... (٣٤)

2:34 – "Wa idh qulna lilMalaikati osjudo li Adama fasajado…" (Surah Al-Baqarah)

"And [mention] when We said to the angels, "Bow Down to Adam"; so they prostrated…" (The Cow, 2:34)

SAYYIDINA ADAM ﷺ WAS TAUGHT ALL THE REALITIES *'ISMA KULLAHA'*

Sayyidina Adam ﷺ begins to teach because the Adamic dress has to dress us. Each prophet wants to dress us from their perfection. As soon as you focus on that, Sayyidina Adam's ﷺ light begins to come and dress from that light, that we have been taught knowledge. Our soul is the master CD that God has taught everything, *"Alam al-Qur'an, khalaq al-insaan."*

عَلَّمَ الْقُرْآنَ (٢) خَلَقَ الْإِنسَانَ (٣)

55:2-3 – "Allamal Qur'an. Khalaqal Insaan." (Surah Ar-Rahman)

"It is He Who has taught the Qur'an. (2) He has created Man. (3)" (The Beneficent, 55:2-3)

ONLY THE PERFECTED LIGHT CAN READ THE DIVINELY KNOWLEDGE

All knowledges have been bestowed upon the soul. Why is it that you cannot read it, you cannot bring it out? Because we have to go back to light. When the light is perfected, the device is perfected; it begins to be able to read. The message is already burned upon the soul. All the information is burned upon the soul.

All technology today is based on light. Those technologies are teaching us about our soul. This soul is the CD, not the fake one that Toshiba made. The real CD is the one that Allah ﷻ made on the souls; 'I put all its knowledges onto that soul.'

It's not something small, that *"isma kullaha" (Holy Qur'an, 2:31)* that I have taught; I have taught your forefathers and your reality, *dhurriyah* (progeny), all of its realities. *"Alam al Qur'an, khalaq al insaan." (Holy Qur'an, 55:2-3)* that all these realities, all these blessings are upon you. It means seek your *Qalb* (heart) and move into the *Lataif al Qalb*, the Levels of the Heart, and the understanding of the Heart.

At the station of *Qalb* is, *"Wa laqad karamna Bani Adam." (Holy Qur'an, 17:70)* and the *'isma kullaha' (Holy Qur'an, 2:31)*; and that, 'We have taught him all the names'.

SAYYIDINA NUH (NOAH) عليه السلام AT THE STATION OF *SIR* سر (SECRET)

BUILD YOUR FAITH AND SOUL THROUGH TESTS

Then from the First Station of *Qalb* (Heart), they move us to the Second Station of *Sir* (Secret). We go from Sayyidina Adam عليه السلام to Sayyidina Nuh (Noah) عليه السلام. Sayyidina Nuh عليه السلام is directly connected to Sayyidina Mikhail عليه السلام and the rain and floods. It is

directly connected to the struggle of the soul, that if you want to open up your soul, you have to struggle.

Then Sayyidina Nuh عليه السلام comes and says, 'You have to struggle. Your ship that you have to build is the soul; this is the ark, this is the ship of safety that will open the soul towards his destination.' So he teaches that you have to open this reality, you have to struggle in God's way. That will perfect your soul.

Sayyidina Nuh عليه السلام comes into our lives and begins to teach that everybody has a ship, everybody has a soul and that soul has to be built. The soul has to be perfected and the *amal* (good deed) of the soul is the *nurul iman* (light of faith).

وَاصْنَعِ الْفُلْكَ بِأَعْيُنِنَا وَوَحْيِنَا وَلَا تُخَاطِبْنِي فِي الَّذِينَ ظَلَمُوا ۚ إِنَّهُم مُّغْرَقُونَ (٣٧)وَيَصْنَعُ الْفُلْكَ وَكُلَّمَا مَرَّ عَلَيْهِ مَلَأٌ مِّن قَوْمِهِ سَخِرُوا مِنْهُ ۚ ...(٣٨)

11:37-38 – "Wa sna'i alfulka bi a'yunina wa wahyina wa la tukhaTibnee fil ladheena Zhalamo, innahum mughraqon. (37) Wa yasna'u alfulka wa kullama marra 'alayhi malaon min qawmihi sakhiro minhu, … (38)" (Surah Hud)

"And construct the Ark/ship under Our observation and Our inspiration, and do not address Me concerning those who have wronged; indeed, they are [to be] drowned. (37) And he constructed the Ark, and whenever an assembly of the Chiefs/eminent of his people passed by him, they ridiculed him…"
(Prophet Hud, 11:37-38)

It means that when you build a ship and nobody understands why you are building it. It means that in our testing and in our lives, your family comes and says, 'Why do you look like this? Why do you pray like this? Why do you have to do like this? What is this? What is that?' All of that is a sign that what I need to do is that I have to build my ship regardless of every *jahal* and every ignorant that is coming around to stop me.

TESTING MAKES YOU STRONG

Everybody has a ship that has to be built and every building of a ship requires tremendous amount of testing, *imtihan*. All the tests in life, it is the light of that soul and it is the strength of that soul. A soul that has not been tested, a body that has not been tested, it's very fragile. Allah ﷻ describes its frailty like a flower that grows on a rock. A flower that grows on a rock, it may look and it may appear as something beautiful; but the first rain washes that flower away because its roots are not deep into the soil.

It means every reality of the soul and *iman* (faith) is that we are going to be tested. We are going to be put through difficulties; we are going to be squeezed. We are going to be put through all different types of conditions to see how deep the roots can grow. When the roots grow deep, the soul is strong and firm like a firm ship. It is like a ship built out of steel, that nothing can take it; not a rock in the sea, not an ice, nothing in the sea can come against that ship. And the soul knows its way back to Allah ﷻ. That is the *lataif* of the *Sir* (Secret).

It means they open for us the understanding of these *lataifs* (levels of the heart). Each of the prophets comes to teach us from what Allah ﷻ wants from *'atiullah, ati ar-Rasul wa ulul amri minkum.'*

يَاأَيُّهَا الَّذِينَ آمَنُوا أَطِيعُوااللهَ وَأَطِيعُواالرَّسُولَ وَأُوْلِي الأَمْرِ مِنْكُمْ

4:59 – "Ya ayyu hal ladheena amanoo Atiullaha wa atiur Rasola wa Ulil amre minkum…" (Surah An-Nisa)

"O You who have believed, Obey Allah, Obey the Messenger, and those in authority among you…" (The Women, 4:59)

Atiullah (Obey Allah), is what Allah ﷻ wants of timeless realities. *Atee ar Rasul* (Obey the Messenger) is from Prophet ﷺ, in *darajats* (levels) of lights that he inspires within the prophets that, 'Teach my nation from your eternal reality. That their *risalat* and their prophecy is under the prophecy of Sayyidina Muhammad ﷺ. They are agents of Sayyidina Muhammad ﷺ. He ﷺ begins to teach from *Atee ar Rasul* that, 'Teach them from what Allah ﷻ wanted from you and what you have of a timeless reality. That my *ulul amr* (saints) will come into their lives and begin to bring about that reality.'

The Body Complains But the Soul is Happy and Wants to Be Free

The perfection of faith is our way that you have to build your faith. At every moment, build your faith by giving, by donating, by serving, by doing everything that you find difficult with yourself but your soul loves it. It means that in life, any type of difficulty that you feel that your body is having a difficulty with that is from your ego. But anything of difficulty makes the soul to be happy because the soul is a prisoner within the body. The soul wants the body to be finished and gone so that its reality can come through. So any difficulty, any argument, any *waswas* (whispering of Satan), any complaint that we have of the *badani* (physicality) is from the *nafs* (ego). The soul, it wants all of that problem on the body. The soul keeps saying, 'Put more problems on the body and get rid of this body, so that I can be free and bring out

the light and the majesty and the power in which Allah عزَّ وَجلَّ has dressed us.'

The soul knows its reality, knows its wings and is ready to fly from the Oceans of Divinely Light. The soul says, 'You are wasting your time with this physical body of yours, that goes nowhere, sees nothing, hears nothing, feels nothing and is only lost in the desires of *dunya.*'

It means that at the Station of *Sir* (the Secret), it is *"Qul jaa al haqq wa zahaqal baatil."*

وَ قُلْ جَآءَالْحَقُّ وَزَهَقَ الْبَطِلُ، إِنَّ الْبَطِلَ كَانَ زَهُوقًا

17:81 – "Wa qul jaa alhaqqu wa zahaqal baatil, innal batila kana zahooqa." (Surah Al-Isra)

"And say, Truth has come, and falsehood has perished. Indeed falsehood, [by its nature], is ever perishing/ bound to perish." (The Night Journey, 17:81)

SAYYIDINA IBRAHIM (ABRAHAM) عليه السلام AND SAYYIDINA MUSA (MOSES) عليه السلام AT THE STATION OF *SIRR E SIR* سرالسر (SECRET OF THE SECRET)

REALITY OF THE DIVINE FIRE

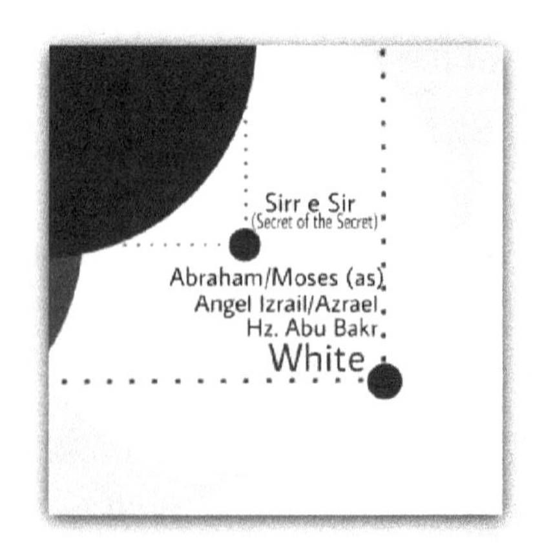

They begin to teach as soon as you pass this station of death, the *Akhfa* (Most Hidden) – Fifth Station, who is waiting for us at the Third Station, in *Sirr e Sir* (the Secret of the Secret)? In this world and the reality of white, and the reality of now opening the soul, is Sayyidina Ibrahim عليه السلام and Nabi Musa عليه السلام.

SAYYIDINA IBRAHIM (ABRAHAM) عليه السلام TEACHES TO BRING DOWN THE FIRE OF ANGER

Sayyidina Ibrahim عليه السلام, from *maqam Sirr e Sir* (Station of Secret of the Secret), from *Lataif Sirr e Sir* begins to open, from the oceans of light. Sayyidina Ibrahim عليه السلام begins to teach those testings and those fires. They are the way towards the Divine reality, that that Divine reality, *"Qul ya naru kuni bardan wa salaman."*

قُلْنَا يَا نَارُ كُونِي بَرْدًا وَسَلَامًا عَلَىٰ إِبْرَاهِيمَ (٦٩)

21:69 – "Qulna ya Naaru, kuni Bardan wa Salaman 'ala Ibrahim." (Surah Al-Anbiya)

"We said, "O fire, be cool and Peaceful upon Abraham." (The Prophets, 21:69)

At the station of *Qalb*, was, *"Wa laqad karamna Bani Adam." (Holy Qur'an, 17:70)* and the *'isma kullaha' (Holy Qur'an, 2:31)*; and that, 'We have taught him all the names'. At the Station of *Sirr e Sir* (Secret of the Secret), it is *"Qul ya naru kuni bardan wa salaaman 'ala Ibrahim." (Holy Qur'an, 21:69)*

THE FIRE OF DIVINELY PRESENCE BURNS ALL IMPURITIES

'Qul ya naru' means that that *naru* (fire) has a huge reality, that Allah's عز وجل Divinely Presence is a fire, and nothing, nothing can move into that fire without being burned. The more we carry of physicality and of our own desires, the more that burning is going to hurt, like a moth drawn to the flame. It only

burns that which is not from itself, that which is not from the fire and that which is not from the light. It means it burns the impurities to bring it into its Divinely Presence.

It means that we are going to move into that fire of Allah ﷻ and everything is going to move into that fire. What someone deems to be *jahannam* (hellfire) may be somebody else's paradise. It's only *jahannam* if you have brought a lot of garbage with you; if you have done a lot of things wrong. If your entire desire is opposite of what Allah ﷻ wants, you view everything to be a *jahannam.*

They begin to teach us that that fire within us, if it's based on *ghadab* (anger), it's going to keep a distance from that reality. The *ghadab* has to be contained, the *ghadab* and the anger has to be brought down so that not to engulf you and lose yourself and become a flame for *Shaytan* (Satan), but to become the flame for *Rahman* (The Most Compassionate) and for *muhabbah* (love). Because every time we become angry then the fire is burning at the wrong direction.

Control and Contain the Fire of Anger

The two prophets are teaching us, because to be from the *khalil* (intimate friend) and the intimacy of Allah ﷻ as were Sayyidina Ibrahim عليه السلام and Nabi Musa عليه السلام. Both prophets are within the *maqam Sirr e Sir*, the Station of Secret of the Secrets, which is the opening of the Divinely Lights and the understanding of *'naru'* (fire).

Sayyidina Ibrahim عليه السلام and the importance of fire and struggling, *"Qul ya naaru."* It means that when I am struggling in Allah's ﷻ way, all of the world will throw fire onto you. Everything will try to stop you from reaching your destination. You can't let that fire come and make you to burn and become angry at people.

You have to be able to contain that fire. When you begin to contain that fire, *"Qul ya nahru kulli bardan wa salaaman 'ala Ibrahim."*

قُلْنَا يَا نَارُ كُونِي بَرْدًا وَسَلَامًا عَلَىٰ إِبْرَاهِيمَ (٦٩)

21:69 – "Qulna ya Naaru, kuni Bardan wa Salaman 'ala Ibrahim." (Surah al-Anbiya)

"We said, "O fire, be cool and Peaceful upon Abraham." (The Prophets, 21:69)

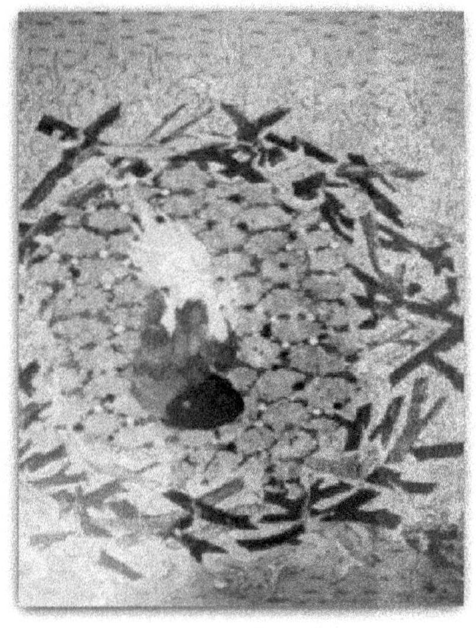

Each of the prophets comes to guide with an eternal message that your life is filled with that fire. If they throw you into that fire and you become angry, you are no different than a volcano and you have lost everything. But take, take the testing, take the difficulties. That with *dhikr*, with practices, with washing, begin to use your practices of washing and *wudu* (always be in state of *wudu* (ablution)). The importance of constantly washing, constantly bathing is to reduce that fire. If we reduce that fire, it becomes the fire of love and they hand us over to Sayyidina Musa عليه السلام.

They tried to throw Sayyidina Ibrahim عليه السلام into the fire of Nimrod. They said, 'Throw!' and he went into the fire and it was cool and peaceful. It means that, that control to open up the reality of the soul; this is now in the perfection of the soul.

The sense that is opening that reality in the station of *Sirr e Sir*, is the touch, they have the sense of touch. It means that this soul is now very *lataif*, very subtle. From hearing at the Station of *Qalb* (Heart), to seeing at the Station of *Sir* (Secret), and now is the touch, which is touching from the level of the soul. Sayyidina Ibrahim عليه السلام saying that you can control your senses, control your anger, control all that fire.

And you begin to bring it into your heart, begin to forgive, and begin to use your practices of washing and *wudu* (ablution).

THE PEACE AND COOLNESS IS FROM PROPHET MUHAMMAD ﷺ

The guides teach us, that fire, we are going to move into that fire. We are going to walk into that reality and Allah ﷻ is going to burn everything other than that Divinely Light. Every impurity is going to come off into that fire. It is going to be cool and peaceful for the believers because they will be dressed with the *Muhammadan* light. They will be blessed with that prophetic light of safety, *"Qul ya naru kuni bardan wa salaaman,"*

قُلْنَا يَا نَارُ كُونِي بَرْدًا وَسَلَامًا عَلَىٰ إِبْرَاهِيمَ (٦٩)

21:69 – "Qulna ya Naaru, kuni Bardan wa Salaman 'ala Ibrahim." (Surah Al-Anbiya)

"We said, "O fire, be cool and Peaceful upon Abraham." (The Prophets, 21:69)

The *'bardan wa salaaman'* (coolness and peace) is the light of Sayyidina Muhammad ﷺ. That if you begin to dress the servant with that prophetic light, it merely enters into these fires into that Divinely Presence. Guides begin to teach us that as you are moving into that light, everything of impurity is going to be washed away and cleansed out and brought into that Divinely Light so that the intimacy can begin to open.

Sayyidina Musa (Moses) عليه السلام Teaches to Turn the Fire of Anger Into Divine's Love

Sayyidina Ibrahim عليه السلام begins to show that if that light and that fire begins to burn, Nabi Musa عليه السلام is right next to him and begins to take us. Sayyidina Musa عليه السلام says, 'Yeah, that is the fire in which I saw Allah. I saw Allah as a burning bush.'

فَلَمَّا أَتَاهَا نُودِيَ مِن شَاطِئِ الْوَادِ الْأَيْمَنِ فِي الْبُقْعَةِ الْمُبَارَكَةِ مِنَ الشَّجَرَةِ أَن يَا مُوسَىٰ إِنِّي أَنَا اللَّـهُ رَبُّ الْعَالَمِينَ (٣٠)

28:30 – "Falammaaa ataahaa noodiya min shaati'il waadil aimani fil buq'atil muubaarakati minash shajarati ai yaa Moosaaa inneee Anal laahu Rabbul 'aalameen." (Surah Al-Qasas)

"But when he came to it (fire), he was called from the right side of the valley in a blessed spot - from the tree, "O Moses, indeed I am Allah, Lord of the worlds." (The Stories, 28:30)

Why? Allah عز و جل is not a bush but you see God in the condition that you are in. We said before, if you are angry, you see God as angry; if you are vengeful, you see God as vengeful; if you are lustful, you think that God is lustful. It means every condition we are in, we see God in that condition.

They perfect us; no, no, you must see and be in the condition of yearning a divine love, in which you are burning to be close to the Divine Presence. That you are seeking a warmth and guidance from the Divine Presence.

Allah ﷻ begins to appear as the Source of the One, as the Source of guidance that, 'Come into My love, come into My yearning, and I begin to dress you from these realities.' These are an eternal dress that the prophets are teaching.

Bring the Fire of Divine Love in the Heart

Sayyidina Musa عليه السلام, is teaching us that when you burn away that fire of anger it becomes the fire of Divine love. It means now is opening a sacred heart. That what burns within the person is the love of the Divinely Presence. Have patience with all creation, patience with all difficulties. Always ask that, "Don't let me to burn on the outside and to be angered by everybody. But, allow and teach me how to bring that as a fire within my being, as a fire for my engine to approach your Divinely Presence." Nabi Musa عليه السلام comes and teaches that fire will become the fire of love that gives and grants the *yaqeen* (certainty) to begin to hear.

We are not going to hear like Sayyidina Musa عليه السلام; these are from *Ulul Azam* (High Station Prophets). But what you will begin to hear with Divine love is you will hear your own consciousness, the lower conscious within the heart connecting to the higher conscious within the heavens. There is a portion of the soul that is always in Divinely Presence, like a satellite wanting to communicate to us but blocked by the ego and the bad character. When this fire is controlled and bad characteristics are controlled, this consciousness begins to open and the servant begins to hear themselves and hear their coordinates, hear what the Divinely Presence wants for us.

Sayyidina Musa عليه السلام begins to come to us and teaches that when the *yaqeen* (certainty) within your heart and the yearning and the fire within your heart, matches your *yaqeen* and yearning for Divinely Love, the intimacy with the Divinely Presence can begin to open. Where the intimacy of being able to speak with the One whom you love, and hear the One whom you love. But, it is going to be required that that *ghadab* (anger) be brought down and that *nur ul iman* (light of faith) to be brought up, and the lights of Divinely Presence to be dressed upon us.

SAYYIDINA ISA (JESUS) عليه السلام AT THE STATION OF *KHAFA* خفاء (HIDDEN)

RETURN BACK TO YOUR ORIGIN, TO YOUR SOUL

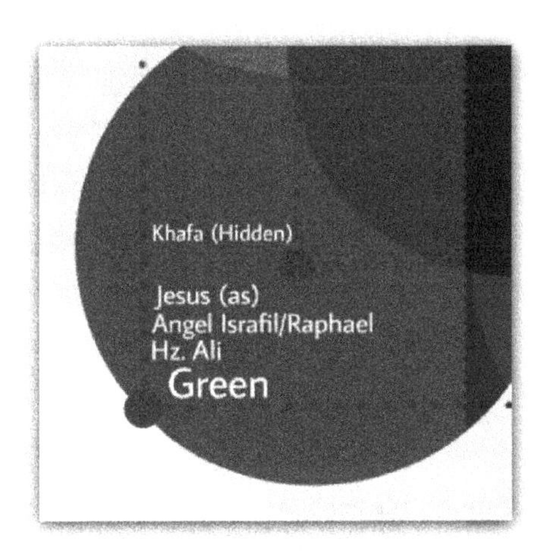

Then they move us to the fourth station, the *Maqam al Khafa* (Station of Hidden). It has to do with the secrets of Sayyidina Isa عليه السلام and it is under the authority of Sayyidina Isa عليه السلام. From this station up, it has to do with that which does not manifest from *dunya* (material world). That means leave your *dunya* because you opened the oceans of lights in the station of *Sirr e Sir* (Secret of the Secret). You have parked and put your body to rest.

Khafa (Hidden) and the secret of the *khafi dhikr*, and the *Naqshbandi dhikr* is the *khafi dhikr* (silent remembrance). It means that the power of the *dhikr* and the *muraqabah* (spiritual connection) and the *tafakkur* (contemplation), where not even the tongue moves in its *dhikr*. The *dhikr* that we do in public is a *dhikr* to catch people. The *khafi dhikr* is that you make your *dhikr* completely silent and devoid of even movement of the tongue, so that the body reaches a state of death. Your *dhikr* is inside the heart. That even if the tongue moves it makes the faculty of the body to be present.

Resurrect Your Reality Back to the Divinely Presence

Then they take us to the resurrection at the Station of *Khafa* (Hidden). That if you are truly dying and the condition of your heart is on fire with that Divine love, then they take us to Sayyidina Isa عليه السلام. It means that one foot off the earth because now, the station of death is there. If the station of death is there, Sayyidina Isa عليه السلام is the resurrected one. He comes and begins to teach that now, lift off because I had to be lifted from the ground.

That is why each of the prophets, their specialty is that although this world wants to come against you and try to crucify you, they have no permission. That's why it is unacceptable to say Jesus عليه السلام was crucified. Otherwise how could he have that much blessing and *Shaytan* was able to crucify him? Allah عز و جل said, 'No. I made his enemy to look like him, Judas.' Immediately Judas had the face of Sayyidina Isa عليه السلام and they grabbed him and Allah عز و جل raised Sayyidina Isa (Jesus) عليه السلام. Why? Because this is an important station.

You are talking about the station of reviving, the station of resurrecting. And every season there is a resurrection. Allah عز و جل says, 'You will be resurrected. If your body is entering that state of death and you have that yearning within your heart, We merely begin to teach your soul how to go back into its origin and lift it to its origin.'

مَّا خَلْقُكُمْ وَلَا بَعْثُكُمْ إِلَّا كَنَفْسٍ وَاحِدَةٍ إِنَّ اللَّهَ سَمِيعٌ بَصِيرٌ

31:28 – "Ma khalqukum wala ba`thukum illa kanafsin wahidatin inn Allaha Samee'un Baseer." (Surah Al-Luqman)

"Your creation and your resurrection will not be but as that of a single soul. Indeed, Allah is Hearing and Seeing." (Luqman, 31:28)

That's why when they changed the face of Judas to Sayyidina Isa عليه السلام, the Companions didn't recognize him. So when they came and Sayyidina Isa عليه السلام said, 'You are going to deny me three times.' Not that they denied Sayyidina Isa عليه السلام – how could 11 Companions not know who their master is? But what they wanted us to think is when they brought Judas and they said, 'Do you know who he is?' They said, 'No we don't know who he is,' because he is not their master. It was Judas that they are looking at, so of course they are going to deny him. They didn't deny Sayyidina Isa عليه السلام.

This station is from Mawlana Shaykh's secrets, that this station is a very important station, to be resurrected, resurrected into the presence of the heavenly kingdom, whose authority is Sayyidina Muhammad صلى الله عليه وسلم.

Sayyidina Isa عليه السلام comes into our lives and begins to teach us that leave the body, leave the characteristics of the body and resurrect your reality back to the Divinely Presence.

Spring Showers Resurrect the Nature

The sign of resurrection is around everywhere. For those who give up hope, Allah عز و جل says, 'Look, I show you My Signs upon the horizon and within yourself.'

سَنُرِيهِمْ آيَاتِنَا فِي الْآفَاقِ وَفِي أَنفُسِهِمْ حَتَّىٰ يَتَبَيَّنَ لَهُمْ أَنَّهُ الْحَقُّ ۗ ... ٥٣

41:53 – "Sanureehim ayatina fil afaqi wa fee anfusihim hatta yatabayyana lahum annahu alHaqqu …" (Surah Al-Isra)

"We will show them Our signs in the horizons and within themselves until it becomes clear to them that it is the truth..." (The Night Journey, 41:53)

Every season, we see that in winter, everything dies. A special rain comes in April and these are rains of resurrection. As soon as the April shower comes, there is a secret within that water of life; it hits the plants and hits the trees, and that which was dead comes back to life. Allah ﷻ is saying, 'Look, at your every day and every place on this earth, there is something dying and I'm bringing it back to life. That which you can see with your eyes, that it dies and it comes back, it dies and it comes back, it dies and it comes back, and you can die and I can bring you back.'

يُخْرِجُ الْحَيَّ مِنَ الْمَيِّتِ وَيُخْرِجُ الْمَيِّتَ مِنَ الْحَيِّ وَيُحْيِي الْأَرْضَ بَعْدَ مَوْتِهَا ۚ وَكَذَٰلِكَ تُخْرَجُونَ (١٩)

30:19 – "Yukhrijul hayya minal mayiti wa yukhrijul mayyita minal hayyi, wa yuhyee al arda ba'da mawtiha wa kadhalika tukhrajon." (Surah Ar-Rum)

"It is He Who brings out the living from the dead, and brings out the dead from the living, and Who revives the earth and Gives it life after it is dead: and thus will you be brought out (from the dead/Resurrected)." (The Romans, 30:19)

It means your desires and bad characters will die. We will take a path of continuously fighting ourselves, bring our self down and let that which is eternal to be resurrected from ourselves. Let our soul to be free from ourselves and move into Divinely Presence. Allah ﷻ shows that sign of eternity all around us.

The Sun is the Greatest Sign of Eternity

The greatest sign of eternity on this earth for us to see is the reality of the sun. The sun has been there for every prophet. Nabi Musa عليه السلام saw that sun; Sayyidina Sulaiman عليه السلام saw that sun; Sayyidina Adam عليه السلام witnessed the same sun. It represents eternity; it represents the light; it represents reality. We begin to understand then to open these 'Levels of the Heart' and open these *lataif*, open these realities; imagine then that sun. Allah عز وجل says, 'The light is always eternal. Seek and move yourself towards that which is eternal. Seek the light of eternity.'

The Power and Benefits of the Sun

It means then the heart when it opens it becomes a sun and becomes a sun which is a real sun from Divinely Presence. The sun of this *dunya* is an imitated sun, with all its power, with all its *qudra*, it is an imitated sun. From that imitated sun, it's required that we study, what do you take from that sun? You take your breath from that sun. With that sun hits the green plants, you have oxygen. With that *shams* (sun), you have the ability to breathe. With that sun, you have the ability to see. With that sun, you have the ability to grow; it sends nourishment and its photons nourish your being.

It means Allah's عز وجل teaching, 'I show you My Signs within yourself and upon the horizon.' The one inside yourself is far greater and much more difficult to understand.

سَنُرِيهِمْ آيَاتِنَا فِي الْآفَاقِ وَفِي أَنفُسِهِمْ حَتَّىٰ يَتَبَيَّنَ لَهُمْ أَنَّهُ الْحَقُّ ۗ أَوَلَمْ يَكْفِ بِرَبِّكَ
أَنَّهُ عَلَىٰ كُلِّ شَيْءٍ شَهِيدٌ (٥٣)

41:53 – "Sanureehim ayatina fil afaqi wa fee anfusihim hatta yatabayyana lahum annahu alhaqqu, awa lam yakfi bi Rabbika annahoo 'alaa kulli shai-in Shaheed." (Surah Al-Isra)

"We will show them Our signs in the horizons and within themselves until it becomes clear to them that it is the truth, is it not enough that your Lord Witnesses all things?" (The Night Journey, 41:53)

That *awliyaullah* (saints) and pious people that are higher than scientists, because they know the *haqqaiq* and the realities. They begin to teach us that study the Sun. How much comes from this imitated sun for your existence on this earth? Imagine now the real suns of Allah عَزَّ وَجَلَّ, the real souls that have light. You can't say that is a *shirk* (partnership with Allah) because this sun is nourishing you by *Izzatullah* (Allah's Honour/Power). No doubt, Allah عَزَّ وَجَلَّ is above everything, but teaching from creation, that sun is giving you breath. Yes, Allah عَزَّ وَجَلَّ is giving you breath, but if that sun doesn't shine and those plants don't release oxygen, you are dead. Allah عَزَّ وَجَلَّ is by cause and effect. Allah عَزَّ وَجَلَّ created that cause and effect. If no oxygen, you are dead. So from creation you are taking your existence.

So 'no mind' people, they say, 'Oh, that is *shirk* (partnering with Allah).' What is *shirk*? You have no mind! Allah عَزَّ وَجَلَّ is showing that in the *dunya*, you are relying upon that sun for breath. Yes, Allah عَزَّ وَجَلَّ is giving the breath, Allah عَزَّ وَجَلَّ is giving the power to the sun, for that sun to shine, to give that photosynthesis and to release oxygen for you to breathe. If He put you in an environment and in another planet that has no sunshine; there is no breath, you die in a second. That is why they go with all their space uniforms and they go under the ocean with their equipment. If Allah عَزَّ وَجَلَّ wanted you to breathe there, He would have let you to breathe but you don't and you die.

That sun provides an exact spectrum of light that reaches your eyes and gives you the ability to see, not higher and not lower. Out of the entire spectrum being released from the light of the sun, a very small portion of it is enough for your eyes to pick up and have eyesight. No sun, no eyesight, no breath, no life, no food.

AWLIYA (SAINTS) ARE THE REAL SUN WITH MUHAMMADAN LIGHT

Allah ﷻ says, 'If the imitated sun is responsible for that, imagine the suns that Allah ﷻ has of realities,' which means the souls of *awliyaullah* (saints). The suns in which their lights and their souls are, *"Alam al-Qur'an, khalaq al-insan."*

عَلَّمَ الْقُرْآنَ (٢) خَلَقَ الْإِنسَانَ (٣)

55:2-3 – "Allamal Qur'an. Khalaqal Insaan." (Surah Ar-Rahman)

"It is He Who has taught the Qur'an. (2) He has created Man. (3)" (The Beneficent, 55:2-3)

That *awliya's* lights are from the lights of *haqqaiq* and reality. That by means of their light and by means of their conveyance, you are breathing. By means of their light, you are seeing. By means of your light and their light, your souls are rejuvenating. And none of it is *shirk* because Allah ﷻ described all of that in the *shams* (sun). And the *shams* is an imitated light.

It means the souls of the *Arifeen* (Gnostics) and the souls of reality that are coming from the light and the reality of Sayyidina Muhammad ﷺ, that everything is in need of *Nur ul-Muhammad* ﷺ. Every *qudra* and every power is reaching from its reality; every breath is reaching from its reality. Every creation is receiving from that reality as the imitated sun that we see within our galaxy. Every galaxy has its own sun.

Allah ﷻ describes, 'That sun, you are in need of it, so pay your respects to it. Be like an earth and a moon and circumambulate around it.' And that becomes the example in our life, that the human and *insaan* have a big ego and bad characteristics. Allah ﷻ shows a sign upon the horizon; you see this planet that has no ego and it circumambulates the sun, it doesn't circumambulate Allah ﷻ. Again, because people have no mind, they say, 'Oh what are you talking about?' The planet circumambulates the light; circumambulates and shows thankfulness for what it's receiving.

Every planet is circumambulating and every moon is showing its perfection. The moon knows exactly where it's taking its light; it circumambulates that light and it transmits. The *nur* (light) of the *qamar* (moon) is the reflection of the *shams* (sun).

So then they teach us if the planets are doing that, imagine the people of reality. They know where their light is coming from and they circumambulate that light. They don't take their face off that light for a moment. It means their whole love and their whole reality is to reach to the presence of Sayyidina Muhammad ﷺ. They circumambulate the light of Sayyidina Muhammad ﷺ and they wish only, '*Ya Rabbi*, to make us to be a perfect moon, in which all of our own bad desires drop, all of our own characteristics drop, and to be a reflection of realities and perfection.' The guides teach us then, in our lives, that every *wali*

(saint) is a sun. Orbit them, perfect your character and reflect their realities.

Reality of Stars and the Levels of the Heart

We pray that Allah عزّ وجلّ open these realities because the *lataif* of the *Qalb* is the secret of being a star. The Prophet صلى الله عليه وسلم described that, 'Follow any of my Companions. They are stars on a dark night.'

أَصْحَابِيْ كَالنُّجُـــومْ بِأَيْهِمْ اَقْتَدَيْتِمْ اَهْتَدَيْتِمْ

"Ashabi kan Nujoom, bi ayyihim aqta daytum ahta daytum."

'My companions are like stars. Follow any one of them and you will be guided." (Prophet Muhammad صلى الله عليه وسلم)

It means the reality of a *najm*, the reality of a star, is that it has no mass but it transmits and emits a light. Allah عزّ وجلّ describes a light that is just coming from itself, *"nurun 'ala nur* (Light upon Light)". It means that lose the physicality and lose the understanding of the form and enter into a timeless reality, an eternal reality and enter into the realities of the star and the eternity and the reality of eternity, *inshaAllah.*

The station of *Khafa* is a very important station, to be resurrected into the presence of the heavenly kingdom, whose authority is Sayyidina Muhammad صلى الله عليه وسلم.

SAYYIDINA MUHAMMAD ﷺ AT THE STATION OF *AKHFA* أخفاء (MOST HIDDEN)

The *Akhfa* أخفاء (Most Hidden) is the fifth station of the heart. There is a reality on all the *lataif* and all the levels of the heart are taking us to the centre-most, *Akhfa* (Most Hidden) reality, which is under the authority of Sayyidina Muhammad ﷺ. Prophet ﷺ comes into our life for the perfection of all the *lataifs*, all Levels of the Heart, for the perfection of submission, and for the perfection of taking us into the Divinely Presence.

Akhfa (Most Hidden) is of the Divinely Presence and it is black because it is a station of annihilation. The colour black is black because it absorbs all colours and gives no colour back. When you enter into the ocean of annihilation, it is to enter into the oceans of nothingness.

SACRIFICE AND BE OF SERVICE

Sayyidina Muhammad ﷺ begins to teach us the path of annihilation, annihilate yourself, annihilate yourself. We are, and this is, *"Inna a'tayna kal Kawthar."*

إِنَّا أَعْطَيْنَاكَ الْكَوْثَرَ (١) فَصَلِّ لِرَبِّكَ وَانْحَرْ (٢) إِنَّ شَانِئَكَ هُوَ الْأَبْتَرُ (٣)

108:1-3 – "Inna 'atayna kal kawthar.(1) Fasali li rabbika wanhar. (2) Inna shani-aka huwal abtar. (3)" (Surah Al-Kawthar)

"To thee (O Muhammad) we have granted the Fount (of Abundance). (1) So pray to your Lord and Sacrifice. (2) Indeed, your enemy is the one cut off." (3) (The Abundance, 108:1-3)

These levels of the heart are the oceans of *Kawthar* (Abundance). "*Fasalli li rabbika wanhar*" *(Holy Qur'an 108:2)*. Pray unto your Lord and take a life of sacrifice. Sacrifice your desires, sacrifice your wants and in the end you are going to sacrifice your body. Everybody leaves and dies from this earth.

كُلُّ نَفْسٍ ذَائِقَةُ الْمَوْتِ ۗ وَنَبْلُوكُم بِالشَّرِّ وَالْخَيْرِ فِتْنَةً ۖ وَإِلَيْنَا تُرْجَعُونَ

21:35 – "Kullu nafsin dhayiqatul Mawti, wa nablokum bish sharri wal khayri fitnatan, wa ilayna turja'oon." (Surah Al-Anbiya)

"Every soul shall have a taste of death and We test you by evil and by good, by way of trial, to Us you must return." (The Prophets, 21:35)

That sacrifice is what Allah ﷻ wants; sacrifice, pray unto your Lord and open the reality of annihilation. Live a life of service; live a life beyond living for ourselves. Live a life trying to serve the Divine and serve the Prophetic reality and serve *Ulul amri minkum* (Saints).

Subhana rabbika rabil 'izzati 'ama yasifoon, Wa salamun 'alal mursaleen wal hamdulillahi rabbil 'alameen. Bi hurmati Muhammadil Mustafa wa bi siratil Suratil Fatiha.

COMPANIONS OF SAYYIDINA MUHAMMAD صلى الله عليه وسلم AND THE LEVELS OF THE HEART

SAYYIDINA UTHMAN عليه السلام, SAYYIDINA UMAR عليه السلام, SAYYIDINA ABU BAKR AS-SIDDIQ عليه السلام, AND SAYYIDINA ALI عليه السلام

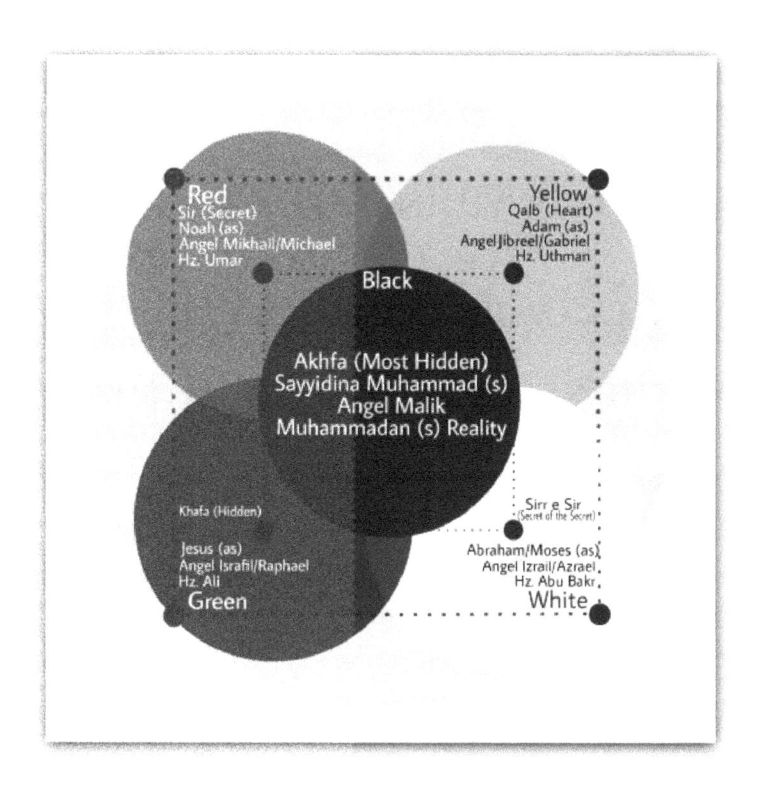

KHULAFA E RASHIDEEN (RIGHTLY GUIDED VICEROY) OF SAYYIDINA MUHAMMAD ﷺ

Once we begin to study the *Khulafa e Rashideen* (Rightly Guided Viceroy), all of them have an eternal message. Sayyidina Uthman عليه السلام is at the first Station of *Qalb* (Heart), Sayyidina Umar عليه السلام at the second Station of *Sir* (Secret), Sayyidina Abu Bakr as-Siddiq عليه السلام at the third Station of *Sirr e Sir* (Secret of the Secret) and Sayyidina Ali عليه السلام is at the fourth Station of *Khafa* (Hidden). Sayyidina wa Mawlana Muhammad ﷺ is at the center, the *Akhfa* (Most Hidden).

It means that without the completion of love, the soul and the heart are not opening. That is why it's not acceptable to not accept, as the heart won't open and the reality of the heart can't open. They are teaching you that the position of these *Sahabi* (Companions) is an eternal reality of the soul. It is not just random names and random people Allah عزَّ وجلَّ put together.

1. SAYYIDINA UTHMAN عليه السلام *JAMI'UL QUR'AN* (THE COMPILER OF HOLY QUR'AN)

AT THE STATION OF *QALB* قلب (HEART)

وَعَلَّمَ آدَمَ الْأَسْمَاءَ كُلَّهَا... ٣١

2:31 – Wa 'allama Adamal Asma a kullaha,..." (Surah al Baqarah)

"And He taught Adam the names of all things ..." (The Cow, 2:31)

At this level of the *Qalb* (Heart), Sayyidina Uthman عليه السلام is responsible for knowledge. He is the compiler of Holy Qur'an which means no Sayyidina Uthman عليه السلام, no compiled Qur'an. We have for ourselves a compiled Qur'an. And all the *tashkil*, all the notes of it, all its secret encodings, were added by Sayyidina Uthman عليه السلام. It's unimaginable because each dot, each *nuqt*, each *waw* (*damma*), each line of it is an immense secret. He encoded everything by the order of Prophet صلى الله عليه وسلم. It means the station of knowledge and that reality begins to open.

الرَّحْمَٰنُ (١) عَلَّمَ الْقُرْآنَ (٢) خَلَقَ الْإِنسَانَ (٣)

55:1-3 – "Ar Rahmaan. 'Allamal Qur'an. Khalaqal Insaan." (Surah Ar-Rahman)

"The Most Merciful. (1) It is He Who has taught the Qur'an. (2) He has created Man. (3)" (The Beneficent, 55: 1-3)

2. Sayyidina Umar Farooq عليه السلام Farooq (Who Differentiates Truth from Falsehood)

At the Station of the *Sir* سر (Secret)

Then, Sayyidina Umar Farooq عليه السلام is at the second station of *Sir* (Secret). It is not a coincidence that he is at the station of war and the station of struggle. The nation was not standing up for itself until Prophet ﷺ asked from Allah ﷻ, 'Send me one of Umar' – why? Because *"Qul jaa al haqq wa zahaqal batil"*. It means the *ayat* in *Qur'an Shareef* (Noble Qur'an) is at that level, *"Qul jaa al-haqq."*

وَ قُلْ جَآءَالْحَقُّ وَزَهَقَ الْبَطِلُ، إِنَّ الْبَطِلَ كَانَ زَهُوقًا

17:81 – "Wa qul jaa alhaqqu wa zahaqal baatil, innal batila kana zahooqa." (Surah Al-Isra)

"And say, "Truth has come, and falsehood has perished. Indeed falsehood, [by its nature], is ever perishing/ bound to perish." (The Night Journey, 17:81)

There are certain *ayats* (verses) that always are on these levels such as "*Isma kulla,*" *"And He taught Adam the names of all things …" (Holy Qur'an, 2:31)*

وَعَلَّمَ آدَمَ الْأَسْمَاءَ كُلَّهَا...٣١

2:31 – Wa 'allama Adamal Asma a kullaha,…" (Surah Al-Baqarah)

"And He taught Adam the names of all things …" (The Cow, 2:31)

So you see that's why Mawlana Shaykh is always reciting certain *ayats* (verses), always, always, always, because this is in regards to the levels of the heart and the reality of the heart, *"Qul jaa al-haqq wa zahaq al-batil," "Truth has come, and falsehood has perished."*

The one who is representing that struggle and the way of struggle was Sayyidina Umar عليه السلام. The Prophet ﷺ described that, 'If there was a prophet after me, it would be Sayyidina Umar.'

Sayyidina Umar ﷺ Says Come Against Your Own Bad Character

Sayyidina Umar ﷺ must come to perfect our soul and that you have to struggle for what is correct. Don't stay silent to oppression, not the oppression outside but within.

Now *amr bil ma'roof*, they are lying. They want to go and correct everybody but not correct themselves. They say *amr bil ma'roof* and then they slap you. And they could be a thief and a crook and have all sorts of unimaginable characteristics. That *ayat* (verse) and that understanding was for ourselves.

وَلْتَكُن مِّنكُمْ أُمَّةٌ يَدْعُونَ إِلَى الْخَيْرِ وَيَأْمُرُونَ بِالْمَعْرُوفِ وَيَنْهَوْنَ عَنِ الْمُنكَرِ ۚ وَأُولَـٰئِكَ هُمُ الْمُفْلِحُونَ (١٠٤)

3:104 – "Waltakun minkum Ummatun yad'oona ilal khayri wa yamurona bil ma'roofi wa yanhawna 'anil munkari, wa olayika humul muflihoon." (Surah Al-Imran)

"And let there be [arising] from you a nation inviting to [all that is] good, enjoining what is right and forbidding what is wrong, and those will be the successful." (The Family of Imran, 3:104)

The *amr bil maroof* is about yourself to come against oppression in yourself and come against your own bad character. Destroy everything within you that's bad, before you can possibly judge anyone else. Otherwise you stand the risk of Allah's ﷻ severe punishment.

Don't Judge Allah's ﷻ Creation

Allah ﷻ says, 'How you judge My creation and you didn't judge yourself? You didn't fix all of your own wrongdoings.' That's why *awliyaullah* (saints) come into our lives and they teach us to be humble. Don't see anything wrong with anyone. See only what's wrong with ourselves.

It means that Sayyidina Umar عليه السلام is coming and his light must be dressing. Again when he is in the world of souls he comes, and Prophet ﷺ asks Sayyidina Umar عليه السلام, 'Go to this beloved servant and dress them from what Allah's عز و جل dressed you.'

When you read about the *Sahabi* (Companions) or *awliyaullah* (saints) that, they say 'If you mention me, I dress you from my secrets.' What does that mean? That they sit and speak some words to you? This is the world of light, which means you have to begin to think outside the box! Don't think physical that they come and they are going to recite. What do they have to recite for?

Companions Dress You With Their Light

You are in the world of light. They merely sit in the presence of your soul and their light dresses your light. You won't know its beginning and its end because two light bulbs go on. When their colour comes, their dress comes; it comes fully loaded, their light intermingles and dresses your soul. It dresses your soul with what? With the ability to struggle, with the ability to stand up for truth, with the ability to come against oppression, internal oppression before you can go against external oppression.

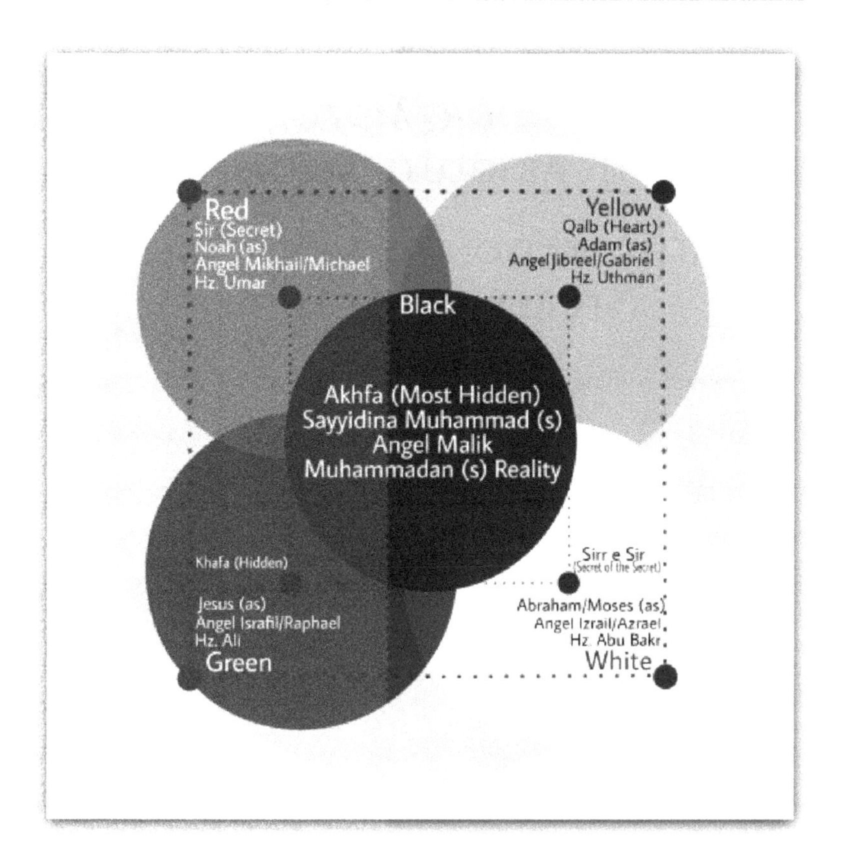

Then all of them are connected to Sayyidina Muhammad ﷺ. All of them are connected to the center and all of them are receiving that power and that light like Sayyidina Malik عليه السلام. It means the authority from the central power is in charge of all four directions that are all four powers. That reality of Prophet ﷺ holds them together and is dressing them eternally; then they are dressing and passing through that light.

3. Sayyidina Abu Bakr as-Siddiq عليه السلام *Siddiq Mutlaq* (The Absolute Truthful)

At the Station of *Sirr e Sir* سر السر (Secret of the Secret)

Now we are coming into the world of light and the Perfection of the Soul (*Mithaliya al Arwah*), the *Sirr e Sir*. The Station of *Sirr e Sir* (the Secret of the Secret) is where *Naqshbandiya* starts and it is with Sayyidina Abu Bakr as-Siddiq عليه السلام. All other *tariqas* (Islamic spiritual paths), they have from *Qalb* (Heart) to the *Sir* (Secret), first and second station of the heart. And at the level of the *Sir* (Second Station), they understood that

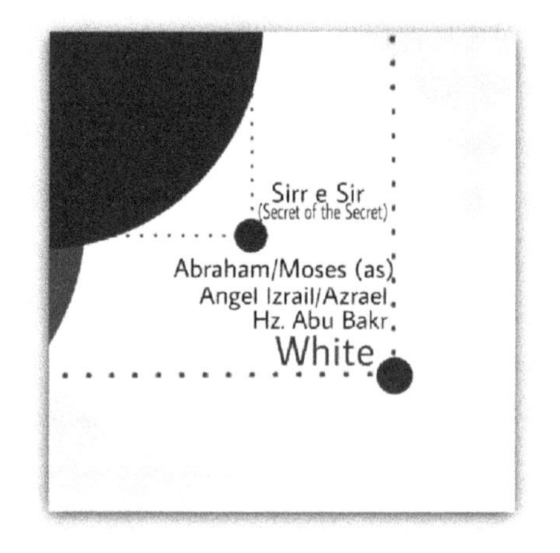

Prophet ﷺ is the *Sultan* (King) of this entire universe. But to go into the dimensions and these realities, *Naqshbandiya* starts because their inheritance is with Sayyidina Abu Bakr as-Siddiq عليه السلام.

Sayyidina Abu Bakr عليه السلام Teaches Perfection of *Iman* (Faith), Love Prophet ﷺ More Than Yourself

They begin to teach us Sayyidina Abu Bakr as-Siddiq عليه السلام is the *siddiqiya* relationship in the perfection of character. He gave everything to Prophet ﷺ, to establish that Prophet ﷺ would say to the

whole of creation, 'You have to love me more than you love yourself.'

لاَ يُؤْمِنُ أَحَدُكُمْ حَتَّى أَكُونَ أَحَبَّ إِلَيْهِ مِنْ وَالِدِهِ وَوَلَدِهِ وَالنَّاسِ أَجْمَعِينَ

Qala Rasulullah ﷺ*: "La yuminu ahadukum hatta akona ahabba ilayhi min walidihi wa waladihi wan Nasi ajma'yeen."*

"None of you will have faith till he loves me more than his father, his children and all mankind." (Prophet Muhammad ﷺ*)*

That is *iman* (faith) because that dialogue is between Sayyidina Umar عليه السلام, Sayyidina Abu Bakr عليه السلام and Sayyidina Muhammad ﷺ. It means, 'You have to love me', you have to give everything for Prophet ﷺ and love Prophet ﷺ more than you love yourself – that is faith.

Perfection of the Soul – Enter as a *Siddiq* and Leave as a *Siddiq* (Truthful)

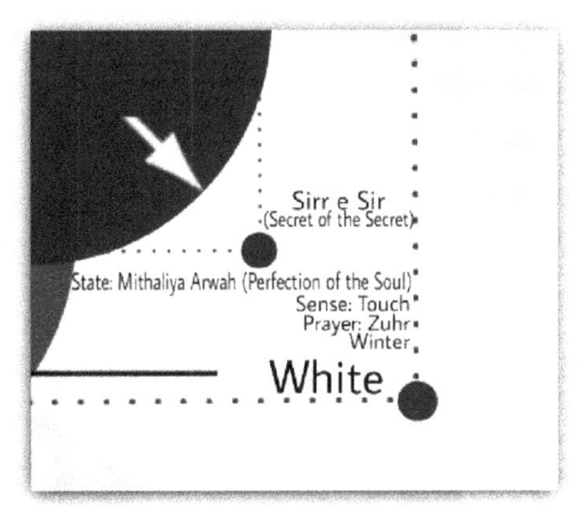

That is why the station of light, the station is the white light; is the *Sirr e Sir* (Secret of the Secret) and now the Perfection of the Soul (*Mithaliya al Arwah*). Sayyidina Abu Bakr as-Siddiq عليه السلام comes and teaches to be a *siddiq* (truthful), to be an upholding and righteous servant of the Divinely Presence. That, they granted you knowledge, they granted you struggle; now I'm going to come and perfect your character, that you sacrifice yourself entirely for Prophet ﷺ.

Sayyidina Abu Bakr as-Siddiq عليه السلام teaches to enter from the gate of *Siddiq* and leave from the Gate of the *Siddiq,* to enter as a truthful servant, to be purified and have good character. Also to leave as a truthful servant, as the only way to enter to the presence of that king, the *Sultanun Naseera* (Prophet ﷺ) is as a truthful servant.

وَقُل رَّبِّ أَدْخِلْنِي مُدْخَلَ صِدْقٍ وَأَخْرِجْنِي مُخْرَجَ صِدْقٍ وَاجْعَل لِّي مِن لَّدُنكَ سُلْطَانًا نَّصِيرًا ٨٠

17:80 – "Wa qul Rabbi adkhelni mudkhala Sidqin wa akhrejni mukhraja Sidqin waj'al li min ladunka Sultanan NaSeera." (Surah Al-Isra)

Say: "O my Lord! Let my entry be by the Gate of Truth and Honour, and likewise my exit by the Gate of Truth and Honour; and grant me from Thy Presence an authority [a King] to aid (me)." (The Night Journey, 17:80)

4. Sayyidina Ali عليه السلام *Asadullahi Ghalib* (The Victorious Lion of Allah عز وجل)

At the Station of *Khafa* خفاء (Hidden)

Then they hand us over to Sayyidina Ali عليه السلام. It means the one who is the master of fighting. The victorious lion of Allah عز وجل, *Asadullahi Ghalib*, teaches us that now you are coming, because we are the owners of the *Kawthar* (Heavenly Fountain of Abundance). All of them are drinking from it, but he wants to take us to the prophetic inheritance and the family inheritance.

All of this *Lataif al Qalb*, Levels of the Heart, is a *siddiqiya* inheritance but Imam Ali عليه السلام is coming and teaching to come into this reality. We are the owners of the *Kawthar, "a'tayna kal Kawthar,"* 'we are granted the Fountain of Abundance' but, I'm going to show you, *"fa salli li rabbika*...Pray onto your Lord ..."

إِنَّا أَعْطَيْنَاكَ الْكَوْثَرَ (١) فَصَلِّ لِرَبِّكَ...

108:1-2 – "Inna 'atayna kal kawthar. (1) Fasali li rabbika..." (2) (Surah Al-Kawthar)

"To thee (O Muhammad) we have granted the Fount (of Abundance). (1) So pray to your Lord..." (2) (The Abundance, 108:1-2)

Pray unto your Lord, Lordship and the reality of the kingdom; pray to Allah ﷻ and acknowledge all of this authority. Acknowledge the authority of Sayyidina Muhammad ﷺ, the superior authority of all the Companions, the angels, the *Ahlul Bayt*; (family of Sayyidina Muhammad ﷺ) and acknowledge all of them.

Sayyidina Ali عليه السلام Teaches to Sacrifice Yourself

Imam Ali عليه السلام says, I'll show you how to live a life of sacrificing yourself, where you put your head on the table to be a *zabiha*.

Now, you see people bringing other people's heads on the table and they say they are going to purify them for Allah ﷻ. The Holy Companions say, 'No, no, you purify yourself for Allah. Come to us; we show you to put your head on the table.'

Then you look at the lives of pious people and how much they took *adhab* (torture) and *bala* (affliction) from people and how much they suffered at the hands of people. Look at Abu Yazid al Bistami ق (6th Shaykh of the Naqshbandi Golden Chain) and how many rocks they threw at him. How many curses they throw at pious people and how much difficulty they throw on pious people. Why? *"Fa salli li rabbika wanhar"*, they prayed unto their Lord and they sacrificed.

إِنَّا أَعْطَيْنَاكَ الْكَوْثَرَ (١) فَصَلِّ لِرَبِّكَ وَانْحَرْ (٢)

108:1-2 – "Inna 'atayna kal kawthar. (1) Fasali li rabbika wanhar" (2) (Surah Al-Kawthar)

"To thee (O Muhammad) we have granted the Fount (of Abundance). (1) So pray to your Lord…" (2) (The Abundance, 108:1-2)

They knew that when difficulty comes that they intercede for humanity. They intercede because they are trying to re-enact the reality that Sayyidina Ali عليه السلام wants. That is my brother, Sayyidina Abu Bakr as-Siddiq عليه السلام, who perfected your *siddiqiya* and truthfulness and that you gave everything for Prophet ﷺ. Come to me, and I'm going to show you now how to sacrifice yourself and stay quiet. When you sacrifice yourself, it means you are serving this *malik*; you are serving this king; you are serving this reality, Sayyidina Muhammad ﷺ at the station, *Akhfa* (Most Hidden).

IMAM ALI عليه السلام LEADS BY EXAMPLE

HE LAY IN BED READY TO BE SACRIFICED FOR PROPHET ﷺ

How do we understand that sacrifice is in the opening of *Muharram* (First lunar month). Prophet ﷺ wants to establish the City of Lights and he is preparing now to move towards *Madinatul Munawarrah* and two very important events take place.

One is representing the reality of *Ahlul Bayt* and Imam Ali عليه السلام. He said, "*Sayyidi yaa Rasulullah* (My master, O' Messenger of Allah), they are coming to kill you. Let us take our role as your Family and we lie within your bed and let us to be sacrificed." *Fasalli li rabbika wanhar*, because these are *Ahlul Kawthar* means this is all *Muharram*.

فَصَلِّ لِرَبِّكَ وَانْحَرْ (٢)

108:2 – "Fasali li rabbika wanhar" (2) (Surah Al-Kawthar)

"So pray to your Lord and sacrifice" (The Abundance, 108:2)

Imam Ali عليه السلام is coming and saying, "We are from *Ahlul Kawthar*, *fasalli li rabbika wanhar*, We prayed unto our Lord and we are ready to sacrifice ourselves and we lie within the bed. Take your place and your position, establish your kingdom on Earth, establish the City of Lights which Allah عز و جل wants you to establish. Take your complete *Siddiq*, your *Khalil*, your friend and Companion," which means the perfection of your character.

Then Sayyidina Ali عليه السلام is lying in bed, taking the place of Sayyidina Muhammad صلى الله عليه وسلم so that Prophet صلى الله عليه وسلم can escape and move towards *Madinatul Munawwarah*. This was all in the first ten days of *Muharram*. Before entering into the city on *Ashura* (10th of *Muharram*), Prophet صلى الله عليه وسلم stayed in the Holy Cave with Sayyidina Abu Bakr as-Siddiq عليه السلام. It means then the importance of *Naqshbandiya til Aliya*, and how it carries that reality.

THERE IS NO MISTAKE ABOUT THE FIRST *KHALIFA*

Sayyidina Ali عليه السلام is representing, "I am hidden and that is our place, the Family's place," because these are the Moons (the Twelve Imams representing the 12 months). This is a perfection of the Moon that is happening on the first month. So in the first month is the first physical *Khalifa* and the face of the Nation are the *Khulafa ir Rashideen wal Mahdieen* (The Rightly Guided and Most Perfected Muhammadan Guides). The first of them is Sayyidina Abu Bakr as-Siddiq عليه السلام.

There is no mistake. There is no confusion because in the beginning of *Muharram*, Imam Ali عليه السلام is describing, "No, no, I wasn't going to go and Sayyidina Abu Bakr عليه السلام was supposed to stay behind." From that time Sayyidina Abu Bakr as-Siddiq عليه السلام was to go, he is the face of this reality, and he must accompany Sayyidina Muhammad صلى الله عليه وسلم. Imam

Ali عليه السلام is saying, "My position is to be hidden. We sacrifice ourselves for that reality and we carry the Family secret of Sayyidina Muhammad ﷺ."

They begin to teach there is 'no mistake' there is 'no confusion'. Anyone who believes there was a mistake, they are coming against Allah عز وجل. Allah عز وجل wrote everything perfectly. They are all in *tasleem* (submission) and they begin to show the highest level of reality. We know the reality and our position was to sacrifice.

So Imam Ali عليه السلام leads a life of sacrifice. As soon as he lay himself to represent Sayyidina Muhammad ﷺ, when they came to kill, Allah عز وجل didn't allow even a hair of Sayyidina Ali عليه السلام to be touched. What happened? He was released and Sayyidina Ali عليه السلام went into *Madinatul Munawwarah* (City of Light).

Ahlul Bayt (The Holy Family) Sacrificed Themselves to Intercede For Us

Imam Hussain عليه السلام is the *Sayyidi Shuhada* (Master of the Martyrs)

Imam Ali عليه السلام shows by example through his beloved sons; all of them were *shaheed* (martyred). Imam Hassan عليه السلام is *shaheed* and Imam Hussain عليه السلام, is the *sayyid shuhada* (master of the martyrs). It means that the master of this *maqam* (station), to witness this reality, is Imam Hussain عليه السلام. The guides come and teach that these are the owners of the *Kawthar*. *"Fa salli li rabbika wanhar."*

فَصَلِّ لِرَبِّكَ وَانْحَرْ (٢)

108:2 – "Fasali li rabbika wanhar" (2) (Surah Al-Kawthar)

"So pray to your Lord and sacrifice." (The Abundance, 108:2)

They sacrificed and obliterated their physicality. Because of this station of annihilation and *fana*, Imam Hussain عليه السلام is showing through Sayyidina Ali عليه السلام that we not only obliterate spiritually, but we obliterated physically. They said 72 plus the whole body of Imam Hussain عليه السلام were shredded into the desert; their bodies were shredded. They decapitated his holy body.

They teach that this is sacrifice! Not that they came and annihilated and obliterated entire towns and villages and went from village to village and slaughtered everybody. They said, 'No, we go and allow ourselves to be slaughtered, so that we can intercede. We can show Prophet صلى الله عليه وسلم, who was saying *'Ummati, ummati, ummati'*, *Ya Rasulullah* صلى الله عليه وسلم, we came to serve and uphold, that you are Allah's عز وجل *rahmah* (mercy), that we are not here as oppressors on this earth, but we are *rahmah*.'

وَمَا أَرْسَلْنَاكَ إِلَّا رَحْمَةً لِّلْعَالَمِينَ ١٠٧

21:107 – "Wa maa arsalnaka illa Rahmatan lil'alameen." (Surah Al-Anbiya)

"And We have not sent you, [O Muhammad], except as a mercy to the worlds." (The Prophets, 21:107)

They lead by example, an example that nobody can follow. But they show us that this is your hero. That serve, not by hurting and abusing people but by taking their hurt and their abuse and by carrying their burdens and their difficulties. Stay silent so that you can take these bags into the presence of Prophet صلى الله عليه وسلم.

5. Sayyidina wa Mawlana Muhammad ﷺ – The Best of Creation at the Station of *Akhfa* أخفاء (Most Hidden)

إِنَّ شَانِئَكَ هُوَ الْأَبْتَرُ (٣)

108:3 – "Inna shani-aka huwal abtar." (Surah Al-Kawthar)

"Indeed, your enemy is the one cut off." (The Abundance, 108:3)

Allah ﷻ says, *"Inna shani-aka huwal abtar."* If you can reach to this destination of Prophet ﷺ, the station of *Akhfa* (Most Hidden), Allah ﷻ says, 'I will obliterate all your opponents.' It means 'I grant you My *Rida* and Satisfaction. I grant you annihilation; this is the station of the master of annihilation.'

Why is it black – because there's no more manifestation. Prophet ﷺ is the lord of annihilation, the master of annihilation, where he teaches you how to annihilate. He ﷺ even annihilates you within your annihilation that you no longer manifest a light, because he is going to take you into the innermost secret of Allah's ﷻ Divinely Presence. To witness, not to be One, because there is no oneness with Allah's ﷻ Divinely Presence, but to witness. To witness what Allah عزَّ وجلَّ wants our souls to witness but, you can't have an existence in Divinely Presence.

Prophet صلى الله عليه وسلم, like a black hole, teaches you to be nothing and that even your somethingness will vanish in that black light. That is why it's black because nothing manifests back. The lord of annihilation, the lord of that reality, the master of that reality is Sayyidina Muhammad صلى الله عليه وسلم. It means that all this reality into the ocean, without the love of the Companions, that this ocean can't be achieved.

Subhana rabbika rabil 'izzati 'ama yasifoon, Wa salamun 'alal mursaleen wal hamdulillahi rabbil 'alameen. Bi hurmati Muhammadil Mustafa wa bi siratil Suratil Fatiha.

COMPANIONS – PART 2 CLEAN YOUR HEART BEFORE YOU ADVISE PEOPLE

Eternal Reality of Sayyidina Uthman عليه السلام, Sayyidina Umar عليه السلام, Sayyidina Abu Bakr عليه السلام, and Sayyidina Ali عليه السلام

وَقَالُوا الْحَمْدُ لِلَّـهِ الَّذِي هَدَانَا لِهَـٰذَا وَمَا كُنَّا لِنَهْتَدِيَ لَوْلَا أَنْ هَدَانَا اللَّـهُ ۖ لَقَدْ جَاءَتْ رُسُلُ رَبِّنَا بِالْحَقِّ ...(٤٣)

7:43 – "…wa qalo Alhamdulillahi al ladhee hadana lihadha wa ma kunna linahtadiya lawla an hadana Allahu, laqad jaa at Rusulu Rabbina bil Haqqi…" (Surah Al-A'raf)

"… And they will say, "Praise be to Allah, who has guided us to this [joy and happiness]; and we would never have been guided if Allah had not guided us. Certainly the messengers of our Lord had come with the truth…" (The Heights 7:43)

If Allah ﷻ is not guiding, there is no guidance. It means that every *ni'mat*, every blessing, we owe to our Creator for infinite *Rahmah* and Mercy upon our souls. That we take a path in which we try to negate our self and to be nothing. That Allah's ﷻ Oceans of everything, Allah's ﷻ *Rahmah* and Mercy be upon us.

Seek That Which is Eternal, the World of Light

It is important always to remind myself and remind everyone, that this path of realities is based on *malakut* (heavens), based on the world of light and the supremacy of the world of light. That the world of light, when you take a path, will clarify everything and the world of form is an abode of *fitna*, is the abode of confusion and difficulty. If you take your path of only the world of form, you find yourself in every type of *fitna*, in every type of difficulty, in every type of confusion. What Allah ﷻ wants for us, and what Prophet ﷺ wants for us, and they inspired us to take these *turuqs* (spiritual paths), to take the hand of these perfected and *kamil* guides. That, seek the *malakut* (heavens), seek that which is eternal. Seek the light.

وَ قُلْ جَآءَالْحَقُّ وَزَهَقَ الْبَطِلُ، إِنَّ الْبَطِلَ كَانَ زَهُوقًا

17:81 – "Wa qul jaa alhaqqu wa zahaqal baatil, innal batila kana zahooqa." (Surah Al-Isra)

"And say, "Truth has come, and falsehood has perished. Indeed falsehood, [by its nature], is ever perishing/ bound to perish." (The Night Journey, 17:81)

If you take a path in your life in which you seek the light. Not speak of it but take the path of it. There are people who talk a philosophy, but that is not this place. It's not only you talk the talk, but you have to walk the walk. You have to take a life in which you are moving towards that *malakut* (heavens). It means that in the way of reaching the heaven realities, everything from the world of form has to be brought down. Everything about the importance of the world of form has to be brought down. Like a dust, all that is existing is an illusion and you bring its form down and to reveal its reality.

So it means that when we took a path of reality and lights, it saves us from every confusion and it illuminates the heart towards every reality. We have said before that if we understand, in the levels of the heart when we are taking a path towards the heart, there are *lataifs* of the heart. There are subtle energies and realities that are dressing the heart. *Awliyaullah* (saints) come and teach because this was the Ark of the Covenant.

Heart of Sayyidina Muhammad ﷺ is the Ark of the Covenant

The Ark of the Covenant, for Nabi Musa عليه السلام was a box with Allah's عز وجل Holy Words. It was the placeholder until the *Khatim* and the Seal of Perfection arrives upon the earth, being Sayyidina Muhammad ﷺ. That Prophet ﷺ is the

Covenant of Allah ﷻ. It means the *Muhammadan* heart contains the Covenant of Allah ﷻ and they are not in need of carrying a box around because you are carrying Allah ﷻ around, *"Qalb al-mu'min baytullah."*

مَا وَسِعَنِيْ لَا سَمَائِيْ ولا أَرْضِيْ وَلَكِنْ وَسِعَنِيْ قَلْبِ عَبْدِيْ اَلْمُؤْمِنْ

"Maa wasi`anee laa Samayee, wa la ardee, laakin wasi'anee qalbi 'Abdee al Mu'min."

"Neither My Heavens nor My Earth can contain Me, but the heart of my Believing Servant." (Hadith Qudsi conveyed by Prophet Muhammad ﷺ)

قَلْبَ الْمُؤْمِنْ بَيْتُ الرَّبْ

"Qalb al mu'min baytur rabb."

"The heart of the believer is the House of the Lord." (Hadith Qudsi)

Allah ﷻ wants for those who are seeking a reality that, 'I open My Presence within your heart and that your heart carries My Covenant and My Contract.' So then open your heart, purify your heart, and perfect your heart.

Spiritual Guides Teach *Tazkiyah* (Purification) in *Zawiyas*

Then all the *tazkiyah* (purification), all the training that the *zawiyas* have is different than the *masjid.* We have said it many times, no disrespect, they are of a different reality. That the *zawiyas* have a *masjid* for praying, but they also have *mashaikh* (spiritual guides), who are the teachers of the *tazkiyah* (purification). They come and they teach all these characteristics that are required to open that heart, and that you can't find everywhere.

So it means they carry a *khusos*, they carry a specific recipe from Allah عزَّ وَجَلَّ given to Prophet ﷺ, Prophet ﷺ has given it to the Companions; and the Companions, through their tree, have given it out into the *tariqas* (Islamic spiritual paths). It means that recipe of *akhlaq* (manners) and character is to clean the heart, to perfect the *akhlaq*.

Seal Your Mouth, Your Opinion is Contaminated

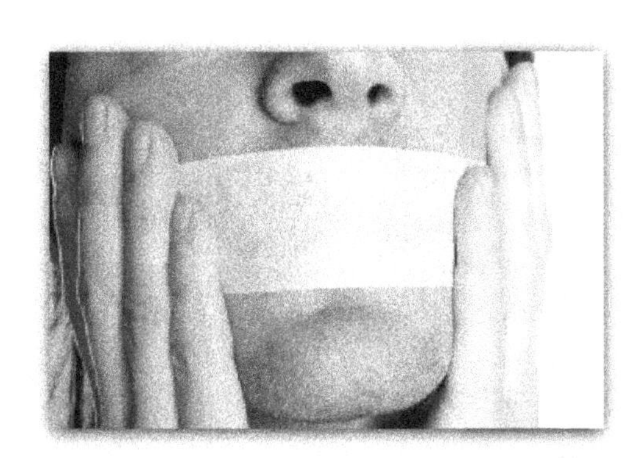

When they teach that don't talk, don't show yourself. Don't put your opinion into anything, because that opinion may be contaminated. When you take a way of *tazkiyah* (purification), they teach you, first thing to do is put a rock in your mouth. Put a rock in your mouth because everything coming from your mouth has to be held, to be observed. That when you are a patient coming to a doctor's office (*Zawiya)*, stay quiet, because you want to share. But what is in your heart may not be from the realities that Allah عزَّ وَجَلَّ wants you to be shared.

So it means that the *turuqs* (spiritual paths), they have a tremendous amount of discipline. They know from what knowledges they are going to teach, what practices they are going to give, that they are going to focus an energy upon the heart. If you want that energy to come into the heart, then seal your mouth because your mouth is going to give everything away. The character that you contain within your mouth will reveal everything. It means then every sickness is going to come.

SAYYIDINA ABU BAKR ﷺ CARRIED A STONE IN HIS MOUTH FOR 7 YEARS

Sayyidina Abu Bakr as-Siddiq ﷺ for 7 years carried a stone within his holy mouth. Not because he is in need of that and anything bad was coming but, as an *isharat*, as an example for us. What Allah ﷻ was dressing him was of immense realities. This was not a regular stone, these were the diamonds of power, seven of which are on this earth, that *awliyaullah* (saints) face that reality to take a *barakah* (blessing) from.

It means that carrying that reality of (putting a stone in the mouth) as an example for us in life. That if you cannot contain the tongue and hold the tongue, Allah ﷻ says, 'What's in your heart is far worse.' If you think that what's coming from your lips is difficult, imagine the immensity of the *nifaq* (hypocrisy) that is coming out of the heart.

So the way of *tazkiyah*, they are teaching is you put a cap. If you can put a cap on what is coming from your mouth, like a fire, that every *ghadab*, every anger, every incorrect understanding is coming from that mouth. If you are able to contain the mouth, control the mouth, then you can begin the *tazkiyah* of the heart. If you can't control the mouth what is the purpose of the *tazkiyah* (purification) of the heart because this is like a volcano. If it is coming out of your mouth out of control, then imagine the immensity of the fire because the way is based on how much you can control.

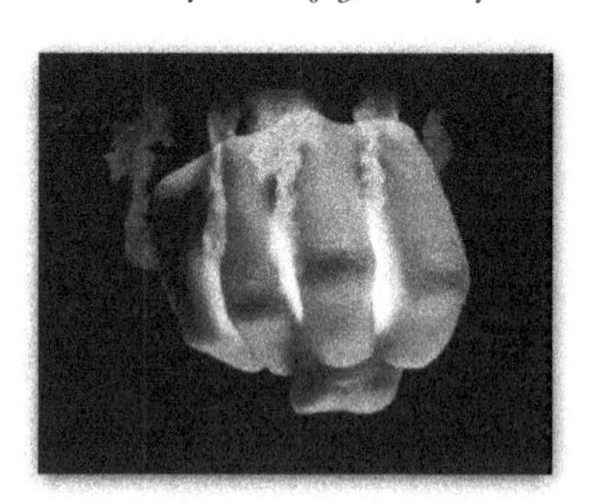

When You Let Aggression Out, It Gains More Power

Some Western philosophy is, 'No, let it out. When you are feeling aggressive, get a pillow with your friend and beat each other with a pillow.' But you are letting an aggression out to gain more power. You are letting a bad character out to gain more power.

What Allah ﷻ wants for us, and the way of *tazkiyah,* is to suffocate it. Suffocate that bad character, so that it receives no oxygen. Anything that you are able to suffocate, suffocate, suffocate, means hold that fire; don't let that fire to come out. They say for 40 days, if you can handle and control a bad characteristic, Allah ﷻ gives you supremacy over it. It means He gives you an ability to control that characteristic. So it means the *tazkiyah* then comes to wash and perfect the heart.

You Need to Love All the Companions of Prophet ﷺ

In the understanding of the levels of the heart is the Companions, because they have an eternal message. What people are fighting over, Prophet ﷺ is teaching that your heart needs all of the companions. You need the love of all companions, to achieve the realities Allah ﷻ wants to give your heart. They dress you with their realities and lights, if you love them. Otherwise how they are going to teach you, if you don't love them? So the *Hadith* of Prophet ﷺ is that you will be with whom you love. The Companions of Prophet ﷺ, they carry a reality that makes the believer to be *kamil* (perfected).

Holy Companions and the Levels of the Heart

1. Sayyidina Uthman عليه السلام – First Station, *Qalb* (Heart)
2. Sayyidina Umar Farooq عليه السلام – Second Station, *Sir* (Secret)
3. Sayyidina Abu Bakr as-Siddiq عليه السلام – Third Station, *Sirr e Sir* (Secret of the Secret)
4. Sayyidina Ali عليه السلام – Fourth Station, *Khafa* (Hidden) and
5. Sayyidina Muhammad ﷺ – Fifth Station, *Akhfa* (Most Hidden)

Allah's عز وجل *Salaam* and Blessing is Already Upon Holy Companions

We said at the *lataif* of the *Qalb* (Heart), which is the station of knowledge, is Sayyidina Uthman al Ghani عليه السلام, *Jami'ul Qur'an al Majeed* (The Compiler of Holy Qur'an). Without the love of Sayyidina Uthman عليه السلام – if Allah's عز وجل *Salaam* (Peace) is not upon Sayyidina Uthman عليه السلام, then who's His *Salaam* upon? Some people come and correct, 'Why you say *'alayhis salaam*?' Doesn't Allah عز وجل say, "*Salaamun qawlam mir Rabir Raheem?*" Allah عز وجل says "*Salaamun hiya hatta matla al fajr?*"

سَلَامٌ قَوْلًا مِّن رَّبٍّ رَّحِيمٍ (٥٨)

36:58 – "Salamun qawlam mir Rabbir Raheem." (Surah Yaseen)

"Peace," a word from a Merciful Lord." (Yaseen, 36:58)

سَلَامٌ هِيَ حَتَّىٰ مَطْلَعِ الْفَجْرِ (٥)

97:5 – "Salamun, hiya hatta matla'il Fajr." (Surah Al-Qadr)

"Peace it is until the emergence of dawn." (The Power, 97:5)

Allah عزَّ وجلَّ, throughout Holy Qur'an, is saying, 'I'm going to give you *salaam*'. If He is not giving the *salaams* to Holy Companions, goodness, we are all in *jahannam* (hellfire). It means that the *salaam* is most definitely upon them, Allah's عزَّ وجلَّ love is upon them, Allah's عزَّ وجلَّ reality is dressed upon their divinely souls.

1. Sayyidina Uthman عليه السلام *Jami'ul Qur'an* (The Compiler of Holy Qur'an)

at the Station of *Qalb* قلب (Heart)

The *Jami'ul Qur'an* عليه السلام is coming and teaching us, 'I am the compiler of Holy Qur'an.' That's not something small. You hear these things and you pass it. It means that in the time of Prophet صلى الله عليه وسلم there was no manifested *kitaab* (book). So then what the reality of the soul of Sayyidina Uthman عليه السلام comes to give?

Sayyidina Uthman عليه السلام Teaches the Coding and Secrets of Holy Qur'an

Sayyidina Uthman عليه السلام comes and says that, 'I was given the responsibility from Allah عزَّ وجلَّ, by Prophet صلى الله عليه وسلم, to compile these papers into the *Kitaab* (book). And not only that, but I was given all of its secrets to give the *tashkilat* (short vowels).' You say *tashkilat* in Arabic - yeah the *waw* وُ, *fatha* بَ, *kasra* بِ, *dammah* بُ, all these notes over each letter). All of those (short vowels) are the coding of the *huroof* (letters). The *tashkilat* means that every *huroof* has a code, right?

If that *huroof* has a *waw* وُ *(damma)*, *awliyaullah* (saints) come and teach you that *waw* is from the oceans of *Wadood* (the Most Loving). That *huroof* and the *Sir* and the secret of that *huroof* is carrying from Allah's ﷻ Oceans of *Wadood* and opening a reality within that letter, within that word.

What Allah ﷻ gave to Sayyidina Uthman عليه السلام, to bring how many hundreds of thousands of letters, to bring the whole of Qur'an, put it into a *Kitaab* and then make all the *tashkilats*, all the codings superficially; they say, 'No this was for non-Arabs to read.' No! This was his secret of encoding all of its *haqqaiqs* (realities). So it's immense; immense!

Without the love of Sayyidina Uthman عليه السلام there is no dress upon the soul, no openings of the lights of Holy Qur'an because Prophet ﷺ said, 'You'll be with whom you love.'

الْمَرْءُ مَعَ مَنْ أَحَب

Qala Rasulullah ﷺ: "Almar o, ma'a man ahab."

Prophet Muhammad ﷺ said: "One is with those whom he loves."

So when the *turuq* come and teach, keep their love, keep their respect. Keep asking, '*Ya Rabbi*, as You granted, from their lights, grant to my lights. *Ya* Sayyidina Uthman عليه السلام, please dress me from your lights; dress me from *Jami'ul Qur'an.* What Allah ﷻ dressed upon you, send the oceans of those lights upon my heart.'

From *malakut* (heavens), they are teaching that connect with the *malakut* and remember the world of light. Don't be distracted by the world of form; it's so temporary and this physical body is going into a grave and will dissolve. The soul, when it makes a soul connection, means that's when all those lights are being conveyed.

They begin to teach by making that connection, by keeping that love, by making that respect, those lights of Holy Qur'an from the Holy Companion will dress you. Because if you love whom Allah عزّ وجلّ loves, love whom Sayyidina Muhammad صلى الله عليه وسلم loves, now the conveyance begins to come into the heart.

So at the *lataif* of the *Qalb* is the station of knowledge. That means the *madad* and the support of Sayyidina Uthman عليه السلام must be upon the heart; the love and the respect must be upon the heart and he begins to give the coding.

ALLAH عزّ وجلّ GAVE HIGHER RANK TO THE CHILDREN OF ADAM THAN ANGELS

It means in *darajat* (rank), who is above? The Companions are and then the angels. *Malaika* (angels) are below the rank of the souls, *insaan* (human being), *"Wa laqad karamna Bani Adam."*

وَلَقَدْ كَرَّمْنَا بَنِي آدَمَ...

17:70 – "Wa laqad karramna bani adama..." (Surah Al-Isra)

"And We have certainly honored the children of Adam..."
(The Night Journey, 17:70)

The angels are to support the souls. The souls whom Allah ﷻ blessed and dressed, the angels, they are serving them. It means that Sayyidina Uthman عليه السلام begins to give that *nazar* (gaze), then Sayyidina Jibreel عليه السلام begins to send that light upon the heart of the believer and all knowledges begin to convey from that *Lataif al Qalb* (Heart), the First station.

2. Sayyidina Umar Farooq عليه السلام The One Who Differentiates Truth From Falsehood

At the Station of *Sir* سر (Secret)

At the *Lataif as Sir* (Secret), the Second Station, is the reality of the struggle. Then Sayyidina Umar al-Farooq عليه السلام is at that station. *"Qul jaa al-haqq wa zahaq al-baatil."*

وَ قُلْ جَآءَالْحَقُّ وَزَهَقَ الْبَطِلُ، إِنَّ الْبَطِلَ كَانَ زَهُوقًا

17:81 – "Wa qul jaa alhaqqu wa zahaqal baatil, innal batila kana zahooqa." (Surah Al-Isra)

"And say, "Truth has come, and falsehood has perished. Indeed falsehood, [by its nature], is ever perishing/ bound to perish." (The Night Journey, 17:81)

Sayyidina Umar ﷺ Puts the Light of *Haqq* (Truth) in the Heart, to Oppose Falsehood

If not for the love of Sayyidina Umar al-Farooq ﷺ, that reality of struggling in Allah's ﷻ way, won't dress the believer. It means have the love and the respect for the Holy Companion, he begins to send from his station. That, 'I am in charge of putting that light of *haqq* (truth) within you, that you stand for the truth, that you oppose every falsehood. That don't let in the falsehood. Truth and falsehood don't come together, they don't even mix.' That's why the people of falsehood, they don't even come into the proximity of the people of the truth.

Perfect Yourself Before you Advise People on Right and Wrong

Sayyidina Umar ﷺ begins to inspire within your heart, to struggle in Allah's ﷻ way. Struggle in Allah's ﷻ way, with all the falsehood that the believer carries within themself, not the falsehood of other people. Because they come and say, *'Nahi wal munkar'* (Forbid what is wrong).

وَلْتَكُن مِّنكُمْ أُمَّةٌ يَدْعُونَ إِلَى الْخَيْرِ وَيَأْمُرُونَ بِالْمَعْرُوفِ وَيَنْهَوْنَ عَنِ الْمُنكَرِ ۚ وَأُولَـٰئِكَ هُمُ الْمُفْلِحُونَ (١٠٤)

3:104 – "Waltakun minkum Ummatun yad'oona ilal khayri wa yamurona bil ma'roofi wa yanhawna 'anil munkari, wa olayika humul muflihoon." (Surah Al-Imran)

"And let there be [arising] from you a nation inviting to [all that is] good, enjoining what is right and forbidding what is wrong, and those will be the successful." (Family of Imran, 3:104)

They say, 'No, no, you have to say what is wrong.' Say, 'No, you are incorrect. You have a misunderstanding of that *ayat* (verse) of Qur'an.' How can you correct someone who is wrong, when you are still doing something wrong. You are a hypocrite. Allah ﷻ doesn't want the advice of a hypocrite.

Allah ﷻ wants the advice of somebody who is correct in their belief, correct in their practices. That they struggled against themself, they destroyed all their bad characteristics, and they are continuing to destroy their bad characteristics; the advice of that one has a weight with Allah ﷻ.

It means then, when you struggle against yourself, struggle against yourself, the light of *haqq* (truth) begins to come. Many times they quote, 'No, no, you should tell people when they are doing something wrong.' Not if you are doing something wrong. Not if you are in every bad characteristic, you are cheating, you are not praying, you are barely fasting, every kind of corruption and wrongdoing; and you feel that it's necessary for you to open your mouth and correct things. That is a *munafiq* (hypocrite). That, *tariqas* (spiritual paths) come and teach be careful of that characteristic. That is not something that Allah ﷻ likes at all. That is why the stone was mentioned at the beginning; keep the stone in your mouth.

Allah ﷻ is Not Going to Ask You About Other People's Actions

Before you advise people, the greatest advice is to advise yourself. Why you are advising anyone; why you are telling anyone? That is why when you go to the other places, everybody has an opinion. '*Akhi* (brother) come up; *akhi* go back. Move your feet here, move your feet there.' Are you crazy? Is Allah ﷻ going to ask you about *salah* (prayer) or Allah ﷻ is going to ask you about what you did last night, what you are thinking about right now in your *salah*? Why are you worried about where my feet are? Anybody who doesn't take a path of *tazkiyah* and purification [would do that].

The shaykhs come and teach you if you are going to take this path, busy yourself only with yourself. Don't talk to a single person about anything they are doing wrong, until you perfected everything about yourself. Because you have a grave and Allah ﷻ is going to ask you about your grave, not your neighbor's grave and not your children's graves. You can't say, 'I gave; they don't have to give. I did, I prayed; they don't have to pray.' They are going to have *azab* (punishment) in their grave. It means every person takes care of themselves, worry about themselves, purify yourself, perfect yourself.

That becomes your biggest difficulty in life. Everywhere you go, 'Oh how am I going to stay quiet? How am I going to keep myself silent and how am I not going to make a comment? How am I not going to try to break anyone's heart? How am I going to have the best of manners. When I come to visit somebody, I'm a guest of them in their home. How can you enter somebody's home and make a comment? It's *tark al adab*; it's against every *adab* (manners). It's against all; it shows all the bad manners and bad characteristics.

Fix Your Character Before Focusing on Minor Issues

That's why the *tazkiyah* (purification). That's why the *shuyukh* (guides) take a path of *tazkiyah* and they teach their students, perfect yourself. Busy yourself only with yourself and bring yourself to a state of perfection. Those that don't take a path of *tazkiyah*, their *tazkiyah* is every issue that you can't even imagine; because they don't want to clean themselves.

So they want to go round and tell people, 'There's marshmallow in this.' You say, 'What?' 'There is marshmallow. Shaykh, these beans are not *halal*.' The other one we get is gelatin! 'The credit card is *haram* (forbidden)! Don't take house mortgage.' This is their *tazkiyah*. They don't want to fix themself. They want to be distracted by things that Allah's ﷻ going to find very insignificant in relationship to your character.

You think Allah's ﷻ going to ask you, 'Did you pay your Citibank credit card? Wait right here.' Or does He have something more significant to ask you? Why did you cheat and steal? Why, when somebody gave you something, you stole it and you didn't return it. Why do you beat your children and beat your wife, or beat your husband? Why do you have such an aggressive character? There are many more significant characteristics that you should be worried about, the least of which is your Citibank credit card.

If you fixed all of your character and your *akhlaq*, in which you feel confident that Allah ﷻ is not going to ask you, 'That you are praying and going to work, and cheating everybody.' We watched the videos. Now in their country, they are selling them dog meat, pig meat, rat meat, and saying it's *halal* beef. What happened to *tazkiyah*? What happened to the nation in *Hijaz* (Saudi Arabia)? All over the world they are doing that. They think it's not a big deal. They take some dogs and sell them as a *halal* meat. Then they come and tell you, those same people, 'No *riba*!' (charging interest). Hmmm, you think Allah ﷻ is going to ask you about the *riba*, or that you took dog meat and sold it as *halal* for people?

It means you can see what a corruption *Shaytan* (Satan) brought upon the people. They focused on all of these minor issues and they no way want to go towards the greater issue. The way of *tazkiyah* (purification) is that you don't speak about anything. Don't worry about what's in the can of beans. If it says pork and pork feet and pork nose, don't eat it. But busy yourself perfecting yourself. Take away all your bad characteristics. If you go somewhere and you see something incorrect, stay silent. Stay silent and correct yourself. Prophet ﷺ taught that, 'Find 70 excuses for your brother.' He never said one of them was to go out and insult him and embarrass him in front of people.

When You Perfect Yourself, Allah ﷻ Gives You Knowledge With Wisdom

So it means they come into our life and begin to teach, Sayyidina Umar al Farooq ؓ is teaching, struggle against yourself, take all the bad characteristics of yourself. Reach a state of perfection. Then with a perfected character, when you advise people, they feel it from your heart to their heart and Allah ﷻ gives you, *ilm al la dunni wa hikmati bis Saliheen* (Heavenly Knowledge and the Wisdom of the Pious Ones). Without the two, you are very dangerous. You can be given an *ilm* (knowledge) but no *hikmah* (wisdom). No *hikmah* means you destroy everything, you harm everything, you insult everyone.

When Allah ﷻ gives a knowledge, he also has to give a *hikmah* (wisdom) on how to use that knowledge, so that you can teach without anybody being insulted. There is never anyone's name mentioned here. Somebody may come after, 'Shaykh, were you talking about me?' I say, 'No, I wasn't talking about you.' You don't name people; you are not here to insult and to harm and to hurt people. This is a *nisah* and an advice only for myself. You can't go back to my shaykh and say, 'He talked bad about me.' I never mentioned anyone's name; I'm never thinking about any one person. I'm thinking and reminding only to myself. That's, "*Qul jaa al Haqq wa zahaqal baatil.*"

وَ قُلْ جَآءَالْحَقُّ وَزَهَقَ الْبَطِلُ، إِنَّ الْبَطِلَ كَانَ زَهُوقًا

17:81 – "Wa qul jaa alhaqqu wa zahaqal baatil, innal batila kana zahooqa." (Surah Al-Isra)

"And say, "Truth has come, and falsehood has perished. Indeed falsehood, [by its nature], is ever perishing/ bound to perish." (The Night Journey, 17:81)

It means bring the *haqq* in your life and push away every falsehood. Reach a state of perfection. They begin then to send us to Sayyidina Abu Bakr as-Siddiq عليه السلام.

3. SAYYIDINA ABU BAKR SIDDIQ عليه السلام *SIDDIQ MUTLAQ* (THE ABSOLUTE TRUTHFUL)

AT THE STATION OF *SIRR E SIR* سرالسر (SECRET OF THE SECRET)

Sayyidina Abu Bakr as-Siddiq عليه السلام begins to perfect the character, that, 'When my two Companions dressed you, then Prophet صلى الله عليه وسلم is sending you to me to perfect your character. Give everything in the way and in the love of Sayyidina Muhammad صلى الله عليه وسلم because what was the focus of Sayyidina Abu Bakr as-Siddiq عليه السلام was the stations of *iman* (faith).

SAYYIDINA ABU BAKR عليه السلام TEACHES GIVE EVERYTHING FOR THE LOVE OF SAYYIDINA MUHAMMAD صلى الله عليه وسلم

When Prophet صلى الله عليه وسلم said, 'We have a struggle. Bring me everything.' Sayyidina Abu Bakr as-Siddiq عليه السلام brought everything. Everything of his life, he put at the feet of Prophet صلى الله عليه وسلم, and Prophet صلى الله عليه وسلم asked, '*Ya* Abu Bakr, what did you leave for your family?' He said, [Allah and His Messenger صلى الله عليه وسلم.]

'La ilaha illallah, Muhammadun Rasulullah ﷺ.'

Naqshbandiyya is inheriting that reality, our father Sayyidina Abu Bakr as-Siddiq (as), the *tariq e siddiqiya.* It means it's coming from the heart of Sayyidina Abu Bakr as-Siddiq (as) teaching that, make your life, that everything to be at the threshold of Sayyidina Muhammad ﷺ. As they taught you these knowledges and they are going to pour into your heart. Sayyidina Umar al-Farooq (as) is going to support you with your struggle so that you always choose *haqq* (truth) and leave the falsehood of *Shaytan.*

Perfection of *Iman* (Faith) is to Love Sayyidina Muhammad ﷺ More Than Yourself

Now that you are in my hands, I teach you how to love Sayyidina Muhammad ﷺ more than you love yourself.

لاَ يُؤْمِنُ أَحَدُكُمْ حَتَّى أَكُونَ أَحَبَّ إِلَيْهِ مِنْ وَالِدِهِ وَوَلَدِهِ وَالنَّاسِ أَجْمَعِينَ

"La yuminu ahadukum hatta akona ahabba ilayhi min walidihi wa waladihi wan Nasi ajma'yeen."

"None of you will have faith till he loves me more than his father, his children and all mankind." (Prophet Muhammad ﷺ)

I pour within your heart the *siddiqiyya* love for Prophet ﷺ in which, '*Ya Sayyidi, ya RasulAllah, labbaik* (I am here at your service). I'm hearing Allah's (AJ) call in my heart for the love of you and I'm coming with everything. I have everything on the table in your presence; what is it that you want?'

People of the Spiritual Path Dedicate Their Lives to *Da'wah* (Invite)

That's why you find only in the *turuqs* (spiritual path), they live a life of selflessness. Only the *turuqs*, they dedicate themselves entirely for *da'wah* (invitation). That everything Allah (AJ) gives to them is a means of *da'wah* (to invite). Every sustenance Allah عز وجل gives to them is to put out websites, articles, magazines, papers, media, television – why? Because they want the world to have love for Sayyidina Muhammad صلى الله عليه وسلم. Everyone else, they want to do something part-time; they want to come just the Friday and go.

HAVE CONSCIOUSNESS AND ACCOMPANY THE TRUTHFUL SERVANTS

But the guides are inheriting from Sayyidina Abu Bakr as-Siddiq عليه السلام, where Allah عز وجل says, *"Ittaqullah wa kullum as-sadiqeen."*

يَا أَيُّهَا الَّذِينَ آمَنُوا اتَّقُوا اللَّهَ وَكُونُوا مَعَ الصَّادِقِينَ ١١٩

9:119 – "Ya ayyuhal ladheena amano ittaqollaha wa kono ma'as sadiqeen." (Surah At-Tawba)

"O you who have believed, have consciousness of Allah and be with those who are truthful/pious (in words and deed)." (The Repentance, 9:119)

They are going to teach, have an immense *taqwa*, immense consciousness; understand yourself. Pray all night and day crying that, '*Ya Rabbi*, don't let me to be a *munafiq* (hypocrite). Don't let me to say something to people and I know I'm not doing it myself.' At night they begin to cry. They cry in their *salah* that, '*Ya Rabbi*, I know You are going to have a problem with me. If You call me to judgment, what am I going to answer to You? *Ya Rabbi*, grant me Your *Najat*, grant me Your Salvation, grant me Your Light'.

The guides are teaching have a *taqwa* (consciousness). If you have a *taqwa*, then keep the company of these truthful servants, so then you love them. Look left and right of you in life and see, are you keeping the company of truthful servants or do you keep the company of crooks and thieves, and hope that you will be raised amongst the *siddiqeen* (truthful)? That's why, they tell the children, 'Show me your friends and I'll tell you a little bit about yourself.' Why? Allah عز وجل can't tell the same thing? Allah says, 'I can see who you're hanging out with all the time.' You are not going to be from *siddiqeen* or *sadiq*, you arc not going to be truthful.

Make your life that you eat, you drink, you pray with Allah's عز وجل truthful servants, truthful in deed and in character, not just the title they give themselves. That their deeds are truthful and their character is truthful.

This is Sayyidina Abu Bakr As-Siddiq عليه السلام teaching for us, if you look left and right in your life that you are with truthful, pious people. You should be raised at the table of pious people, that when you take your last breath, you will be at that table that you spent your life in that association.

4. Sayyidina Ali عليه السلام The Gate to the City of Muhammadan Knowledge

At the Station of *Khafa* خفاء (Hidden)

Then, Sayyidina Abu Bakr as-Siddiq عليه السلام takes us then to the hands of Imam Ali عليه السلام. Imam Ali عليه السلام says, 'Now you are entering *Madina*, the City of Knowledge, and I am the one who takes care of the *baab* (Gate).'

قَالَ رَسُولَ اللَّهِ صلى الله عليه وسلم "انا مدينة العلم و علي بابها"

Qala Rasulallah صلى الله عليه وسلم*: "Ana madinatul-ilmin wa `Aliyun baabuha."*

"I am city of knowledge and `Ali is the door." (Prophet Muhammad صلى الله عليه وسلم*)*

That city of knowledge is the *Kawthar* of Sayyidina Muhammad ﷺ. All the *Sahabi*, they are around Prophet ﷺ, Prophet ﷺ is the center, he is the nucleus, the *Akhfa* (Most Hidden). The Companions are all surrounding to perfect the character to take you now to the presence of Prophet ﷺ.

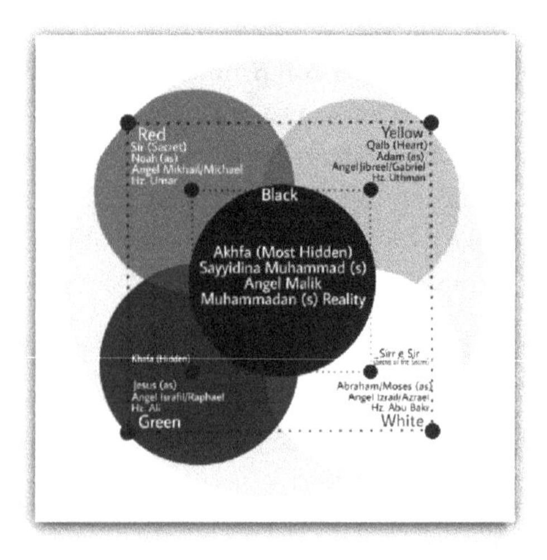

IMAM ALI عليه السلام TEACHES TO SACRIFICE YOUR BAD CHARACTER

Now you are at the *baab* of the one who's going to teach you. *"Inna a'tayna kal Kauthar; fa salli li-Rabbika wanhar."*

إِنَّا أَعْطَيْنَاكَ الْكَوْثَرَ (١) فَصَلِّ لِرَبِّكَ وَانْحَرْ (٢)

108:1-2 – Inna 'atayna kal kawthar. (1) Fasali li rabbika wanhar" (2) (Surah Al-Kawthar)

"To thee (O Muhammad) we have granted the Fount (of Abundance). (1) So pray to your Lord…" (2) (The Abundance, 108:1-2)

Imam Ali عليه السلام teaches you, pray unto your Lord and live a life of sacrifice, because he stands with the *Zulfiqar* (name of the sword of Imam Ali's عليه السلام). That, you want to enter into this *baab*, and you want to enter into the presence of Prophet ﷺ, live a life in which you sacrifice. Sacrifice your bad character, sacrifice all that Allah عز وجل has given to you; put it all and be nothing, put it all and be nothing. He comes and teaches the way of annihilation that, annihilate all your bad character. If people are not willing to give up one bad characteristic and then they say that, 'We are, we are *Muhsen* (perfected).' They are coming and teaching, no, that put all these bad characteristics and sacrifice them.

Big Struggle is Between the Head and the Heart

They teach put everything away for that love and we take you into that presence. But they teach that this head can't go into that presence. If you are going to come with your mind into that reality, it will never open. Leave your mind for your

business on how to do your accounting or whatever your *rizq* and sustenance; that head is only for that. The reality is based on the heart and they begin to teach what we have talked about before; the head is going to fight the heart. The head is occupied by *Shaytan*. *"Qalb al-mu'min baytullah."*

قَلْبَ الْمُؤْمِنْ بَيْتُ الرَّبْ

"Qalb al mu'min baytur rabb."

"The heart of the believer is the House of the Lord." (Hadith Qudsi)

Allah عَزَّ وَجَلَّ says, 'Don't listen to that *Shaytan*; he is not going to understand how to get into the House of *Ar-Rahman* (The Most Compassionate).' It means everything at that time they are teaching, the head is going to continuously battle you, continuously battle you. The head is continuously saying things that, 'No, no, no; don't do this, don't do that, don't do this.' Then the believers belief and struggle is between what their head is trying to think and what Allah عَزَّ وَجَلَّ is pouring within the heart. Because they say, 'You want to come to this *Kawthar,*' but that head is going to block you. The head is going to give every doubt; every *waswas* (whispering) comes to the head.

So that becomes the great struggle, that to negate the head, the first *dhikr* for all the *turuqs*, *La ilaha illallah* (there is no God but Allah) [from *La* to head, *ilaha* to right of chest, then *ilAllah* to left of chest]. *La ilaha illallah* [again from head, to right of chest, then to left of chest] which means don't use the head. The light comes, *illallah* to left of chest, which means all light into the heart, there is nothing but Allah عز وجل.

We pray that Allah عز وجل open more and more understanding for us.

Subhana rabbika rabil 'izzati 'ama yasifoon, Wa salamun 'alal mursaleen wal hamdulillahi rabbil 'alameen. Bi hurmati Muhammadil Mustafa wa bi siratil Suratil Fatiha.

COMPANIONS – PART 3
SAYYIDINA ABU BAKR AS-SIDDIQ عليه السلام AND SAYYIDINA ALI عليه السلام

WHERE THE TWO RIVERS MEET

NABI MUSA'S عليه السلام ARK OF COVENANT WAS A PLACEHOLDER FOR SAYYIDINA MUHAMMAD صلى الله عليه وسلم

Alhamdulillah, from the *lataif* of the heart and these are from the secret of the Ark of the Covenant. Everything was an imitation for the arrival of Sayyidina Muhammad صلى الله عليه وسلم. The Ark of the Covenant for Nabi Musa عليه السلام was a box in which the Tablets of the Torah were put in that and that box was so holy it was carried by the angels.

The box and the Ark of the Covenant is merely a placeholder for the real Covenant by the arrival of the *khatim*, the Seal of Creation, the Seal of Prophecy, the Seal of all Realities, who brought upon his heart the true Covenant of Allah عز و جل, the *Ahd.* That Covenant is the perfection in which Allah ﷻ wants to dress His Creation, that gift can't be given until Sayyidina Muhammad ﷺ arrives to give that gift. There is an *adab* (manners). You can't go into the party, into the celebration without the host. It means Allah's ﷻ making all this Creation for the love of Sayyidina Muhammad ﷺ.

PROPHET MUHAMMAD'S ﷺ HEART IS THE ARK OF THE COVENANT

It means the *Muhammadan* Heart and the realities that Prophet ﷺ was bringing upon this *dunya* from Paradise realities, is the Ark of the Covenant. That is why Allah ﷻ says, for the Nation of Muhammad ﷺ, *qalbun mu'min baytullah* (Heart of the believer is the house of Allah).

قَلْبَ الْمُؤْمِنْ بَيْتُ الرَّبْ

"Qalb al mu'min baytur rabb."

"The heart of the believer is the House of the Lord." (Hadith Qudsi)

If you purify and cleanse your heart, it will be My House. It means My Divinely Presence, My Kingdom will be in your heart. This is why 'Thy Kingdom come Thy Will be done.' Every *kitaab* (book) is bringing the same Message that My Kingdom is coming, My Will be done on Earth as it is in Heaven. The will of

Allah ﷻ to manifest within the heart of the believer, means then every *nazar* (gaze), every perfection, every way, is based on how to open the heart.

ALLAH'S ﷻ PEACE IS DEFINITELY UPON THE COMPANIONS

From the realities of the *Khulafa e Rashideen al Mahdiyeen* (The Perfected and Most Guided Viceroy of Sayyidina Muhammad ﷺ); Sayyidina Uthman al Ghani عليه السلام, Sayyidina Umar Farooq عليه السلام, Sayyidina Abu Bakr as-Siddiq عليه السلام and Sayyidina Imam Ali عليه السلام.

Alayhi 's-salaam عليه السلام, Peace be upon him, means that most definitely Allah's ﷻ *Salaam* and love and Divine Mercy is emanating upon them, is dressing upon them. That if we understood or even move towards the understanding that the archangels and all the angels are in service to *Bani Adam* (Children of Prophet Adam).

وَإِذْ قُلْنَا لِلْمَلَائِكَةِ اسْجُدُوا لِآدَمَ فَسَجَدُوا... (٣٤)

2:34 – "Wa idh qulna lilMalaikati osjudo li Adama fasajado..."
(Surah Al-Baqarah)

"And [mention] when We said to the angels, "Bow Down to Adam"; so they prostrated..." (The Cow, 2:34)

وَلَقَدْ كَرَّمْنَا بَنِي آدَمَ...

17:70 – "Wa laqad karramna bani adama..." (Surah Al-Isra)

"And We have certainly honored the children of Adam..."
(The Night Journey, 17:70)

The greatest of *Bani Adam* is Sayyidina Muhammad ﷺ and the prophets and the Companions, and the angels serve that reality.

Sayyidina Uthman عليه السلام
Jami'ul Qur'an
(The Compiler of Holy Qur'an)

At the Station of *Qalb* قلب (Heart)

Sayyidina Uthman عليه السلام, *Jami'ul Qur'an* (the compiler of Holy Qur'an) is at the *Lataif* of the *Qalb* (Heart), the First station of Heart. The station of *Qalb*, which is under the authority of Sayyidina Jibreel (Gabriel) عليه السلام because he is bringing *wahi* (revelation), bringing knowledges. *Qalb* is the *lataif* of knowledge, which means he is in service to Sayyidina Uthman عليه السلام. The *darajat* (rank) of Sayyidina Uthman عليه السلام can't be imagined. The holy Companion is receiving from Prophet صلى الله عليه وسلم and is giving to the angels what needs to be sent out, because there is *ihtiram*, respect, and *darajat* (rank).

That Allah عز وجل brought Sayyidina Adam عليه السلام and taught *isma kulaha* and the angels were to bow down and show their respect for the greatest for this *uloom* (knowledges) and light that poured into the heart of Sayyidina Adam عليه السلام from Sayyidina Muhammad صلى الله عليه وسلم.

وَعَلَّمَ آدَمَ الْأَسْمَاءَ كُلَّهَا... ٣١

2:31 – "Wa 'allama Adamal Asma a kullaha..." (Surah Al-Baqarah)

"And He taught Adam the names of all things..." (The Cow, 2:31)

SAYYIDINA ABU BAKR SIDDIQ عليه السلام
SIDDIQ MUTLAQ
(THE ABSOLUTE TRUTHFUL)

AT THE STATION OF *SIRR E SIR* سرالسر
(SECRET OF THE SECRET)

It means that the whole reality, from the Companions, Sayyidina Uthman عليه السلام was the *Jami'ul Qur'an* (compiler of the Holy Qur'an). Sayyidina Umar Farooq عليه السلام was to come and bring the light of struggle within the heart of the believer. That Sayyidina Abu Bakr as-Siddiq عليه السلام was to bring the perfection of love, and the character, that you have to be because that *Maqam Sirr e Sir* is by the example of the moon. Your life has to be like the moon that follows the sun. Sayyidina Muhammad صلى الله عليه وسلم is the Sun.

THE LIGHT OF THE UNIVERSE IS FROM THE MUHAMMADAN SUN

Prophet صلى الله عليه وسلم is Allah's عز وجل Divinely Lights, the soul of Prophet صلى الله عليه وسلم is an ancient source of all realities. *Laa sharik* (No partner with Allah), you can never say, "It is from Allah عز وجل," because Allah عز وجل has no partner. You cannot be from Allah عز وجل, you cannot be like Allah عز وجل, you cannot be in any proximity with Allah عز وجل, He is the Creator. So it means all these realities are in the reality of Creation.

Then that light that is emanating throughout this entire universe is the *Muhammadan* Sun, the *Muhammadan Shams, Shams al Islam, Shams al-Ma'rifah* (Gnosticism); every reality is emanating from that.

Sayyidina Abu Bakr ؓ Teaches, Be the Moon and Accept the Testing

Sayyidina Abu Bakr as-Siddiq ؓ is coming into our life and teaching that be like the moon; you see the moon and you see the surface of the moon, it has taken a tremendous beating. The surface has been under significant testing. It has been crushed and crushed and crushed so that it reflects the reality of the sun. It is not trying to be a 'source of light' because it is showing the best of *adab* (manner).

Negate Yourself – Don't Attribute Anything to Yourself

Don't think you have anything, don't think you have any light, don't think it is anything from you, Negate you, and take 'you' out of the equation. The difference between us and *Fir'aun* (Pharaoh) is that *Fir'aun* was claiming everything to himself *ananiyya*, I have power, and I have authority. When you hear these people talk on television everything is, 'I', 'I', 'I'. "I did this, I did that, I am like this, I am like that." They attribute everything to the ego, to themselves. The guides are coming from the *haqqaiq* (realities) and teaching completely opposite. Whatever light is shining upon you is not from you, you are merely the reflection.

Sayyidina Abu Bakr as-Siddiq عليه السلام comes to perfect the *Siddiqiya* character that be nothing, be nothing. You see the moon, it has no cities, no villages, no towns but a whole lot of asteroids that hit the surface of the moon. There are lots of holes, lots of difficulty, lots of bombarding, lots of bombarding on the moon. So then the bombardment was what? To take out any type of bad characteristic. So then this way is like the way of the *Ashab al Kahf* (Seven Sleepers of the Cave).

Be Like the Dog of *Ashab al Kahf* (Seven Sleepers of the Cave)

The *Ashab al Kahf* (Seven Sleepers of the Cave), and all these *qisas* (stories), again these are examples that will be found within the Nation of Sayyidina Muhammad صلى الله عليه وسلم. That be like *Ashab al Kahf* (Seven Sleepers), you want to come into the cave, the cave of all realities, then take your beating. You cannot say, "No, *yaa Rabbi,* I want to come, but I also want to be like *Ashab al Kahf.* I want to be one of Your great chosen ones." That is going to be difficult.

Better to think, *yaa Rabbi,* let me be like the dog. The dog of *Ashab al Kahf* took a tremendous beating. *Awliya* (saints) come into our life and teach that Allah عز وجل gives such a mercy. If you say *Ashab al Kahf* many people say, "Shaykh I am never going to be like that, I am not that type of character, I am not going to reach to those heights. I don't have the time to do all of that." Allah's عز وجل infinite mercy is that yes, we should all think like that, none of us are going to be like that, none of us are worthy of that reality. But Allah's عز وجل *Rahmah* (mercy) is that do you see the character of the dog? How the dog in Islam is *najis*, dirty for us, but Allah عز وجل allowed that dirty dog into Paradise, why? Because when he followed the *Ashab al Kahf* the dog was inspired; I will follow you, and it followed.

They kept throwing rocks at him. This is our testing. They were throwing rocks at the dog, "Go away, we are going to *khalwa* (seclusion)." We are running from *Shaytan* and we are going into the cave that Allah عز وجل will dress us from His Mercy; you are going to give us away and they began to throw more rocks at the dog. Allah عز وجل gave the dog a tongue. At that moment the dog stood up on his two legs and said, "Whatever you throw of rocks I am not stopping. I am going to follow you to guard your cave so that you go in and do Allah's work, my great joy will be to just guard the cave in which you are in."

Then they realized this is coming from Allah عز وجل. A dog doesn't talk to you and definitely doesn't show that I am going to be of service to you. The gift that Allah عز وجل dressed upon that dog was the *hayba* of the whole cave. Whatever He was giving as a gift inside for *Ashab al Kahf*; Allah عز وجل was emphasizing that the dog was dressed with such a *hayba* - *Hayba* is a dress of *jalaali* (majestic emanations). That he was dressed with such a *jalaali tajalli* upon the dog that people merely came near the cave and they were frightened, and they left. It means Allah's عز وجل *rida* (satisfaction) dressed that reality.

وَتَحْسَبُهُمْ أَيْقَاظًا وَهُمْ رُقُودٌ ۚ وَنُقَلِّبُهُمْ ذَاتَ الْيَمِينِ وَذَاتَ الشِّمَالِ ۖ وَكَلْبُهُم بَاسِطٌ ذِرَاعَيْهِ بِالْوَصِيدِ ۚ لَوِ اطَّلَعْتَ عَلَيْهِمْ لَوَلَّيْتَ مِنْهُمْ فِرَارًا وَلَمُلِئْتَ مِنْهُمْ رُعْبًا (١٨)

18:18 – "Wa tahsabuhum ayqaazanw wa hum ruqod; wa nuqallibuhum dhatal yameeni wa dhatash shimali, wa kalbuhum baasitun dhiraa'ayhi bilwaseed; lawit tala'ta 'alaihim la wallaita minhum firaaran wa lamuli'ta minhum ru'baa." (Surah Al-Kahf)

"And you would think them awake, while they were asleep. And We turned them to the right and to the left, while their dog stretched his forelegs at the entrance. If

you had looked at them, you would have turned from them in flight and been filled by them with terror." (The Cave, 18:18)

DON'T RESIST THE TESTING AND TAME THE EGO

Awliyaullah (saints) come into our life and say, "This is an opening for us, this is a door for all people to be brought into Allah's *Rahmah*, for Allah ﷻ to dress them with *tajalli* (manifestations) and bless them with *tajalli*." If you are not going to accomplish all these things, at least you can support and accompany those who are trying to. By means of that support, by means of accompanying, by means of taking the rocks.

It means this path is not going to be easy. There are going to be many rocks from your family, from people you know, from all directions, from people you don't know. Even probably from the *Ashab al Kahf* (guides). They are going to throw testing, they are going to throw rocks, and our life is to do what? To do nothing, to say nothing, never to fight back, never to answer back. Then you are *wahshi*, you are wild. If you are wild then they throw you out. They don't like anything wild. They want something that is tamed.

TESTING IS NECESSARY TO SHOW YOUR TRUE CHARACTER

So that the testing comes to show the character of the self. That you want to accompany us, you can't be wild or as soon as we go into the cave you are going to eat us. When you are tame it means you have been tested, you have been tested, you have been tested, and your character is what Allah ﷻ wants. Allah ﷻ wants softness. You will be tested at work, you will be tested at home, you will be tested

on the street. You will not only be tested in here, wherever you go the character has to be consistent.

If you don't pass the test, it only escalates because Allah's عزَّ وَجَلَّ Will will be done. If you don't pass the test, then they become *shadeed* (intensified). Allah عزَّ وَجَلَّ begins to shake the servant with all sorts of difficulties. Because you can't say, "I am only nice on the carpet in spiritual association, but I am obnoxious everywhere else on this Earth." You are going to be tested severely, because Allah عزَّ وَجَلَّ loves you. If you find yourself here (spiritual association), Allah عزَّ وَجَلَّ loves you, and Allah's عزَّ وَجَلَّ Will will be done.

GIVE UP YOUR BAD CHARACTER FOR THE LOVE OF PROPHET ﷺ

Sayyidina Abu Bakr as-Siddiq عليه السلام will come and teach that give everything for Prophet ﷺ and the most you can give is to give all your (bad) character. I am giving everything for Prophet ﷺ. *Yaa Rabbi,* I don't want these bad characteristics. I want a life in which I am trying to serve Sayyidina Muhammad ﷺ; I can't serve him with all my *nifaaq* (hypocrisy), with all my bad character, with all my craziness.

There are people now all over the internet pretending they serve Prophet ﷺ, *Ashaab an-Nabi* ﷺ, *Ahlul Bayt an-Nabi* ﷺ and every day they are crazier than the next. The guides say you are a clown and making a fool of yourself. You don't represent them; you represent the wildness and craziness of your ego. This is not their way.

Their way is that they took a beating, they took a beating, and they took a beating, until the character was nothing, nothing. They were severely humiliated in life, until the character showed nothing. When there is nothing then Allah عزَّ وَجَلَّ says, "This one is tame. This one is *aarom* (quiet), this one is house worthy, a house pet. He is no longer *wahshi*, he is no longer a wild barn animal." The character is tamed, no matter what we do of difficulty; it always comes the same sweetness that one can be bestowed.

Sayyidina Abu Bakr عليه السلام is teaching that "Give everything of yourself. Don't say, "No, I am going to keep some of these bad things for myself, to go defend myself against the world." Give everything for the love of Prophet صلى الله عليه وسلم.

IMAM ALI عليه السلام - THE GATE TO THE CITY OF MUHAMMADAN KNOWLEDGE

Then we were handed into the hand of Imam Ali عليه السلام. Prophet صلى الله عليه وسلم described that these *Sahabi* (Companions) are now going to bring you to the City of Knowledge. It means I am the city of all realities, I am the *Kawthar. Ataina kal kawthar,* Allah عز و جل says, "I gave you the *Kawthar.*"

THE REALITY OF THE *KAWTHAR*, THE FOUNTAIN OF ABUNDANCE

إِنَّا أَعْطَيْنَاكَ الْكَوْثَرَ (١)

108:1 – Inna 'atayna kal kawthar." (Surah Al-Kawthar)

"To thee (O Muhammad) we have granted the Fount (of Abundance)." (The Abundance, 108:1)

All our *mashaykh* (guides) come and describe the *Kawthar* is from the oceans of *katheer* (abundance); it has no beginning, no end. Allah عز و جل describes, I have given you everything. If all the trees were pens and all the oceans were ink, these words, these realities that I have given, will never be finished.

This is the description of the *Kawthar* and it was given to Prophet ﷺ and this is the City of Knowledge that we are trying to enter and he describes that Imam Ali عليه السلام is at the gate.

قَالَ رَسُولَ اللَّهِ صلى الله عليه وسلم "انا مدينة العلم و علي بابها

Qala Rasulallah ﷺ: *"ana madinatul-ilmin wa `Aliyun baabuha."*

"I am city of knowledge and `Ali is the door." (Prophet Muhammad ﷺ*)*

THE REALITY OF ANNIHILATION - *LAM ALIF* AND *ZULFIQAR*

The owner of the *baab* (door) and from the *Kawthar* is the *laam alif* لا, the 29th letter in the Arabic *huroof*, and 29th is *laa* لا. The 29th cycle of the moon, the 29th day is when the moon disappears. It is the reality of annihilation. That *zulfiqar* was Prophet's ﷺ *Zulfiqar* (sword). That is the reality of Prophet ﷺ, that, "I am the reality of *laa ilaaha illallah Muhammadun Rasulullah* ﷺ (There is no God but Allah, Sayyidina Muhammad ﷺ is the Messenger of Allah. And I am giving you (Imam Ali) that sword as the caretaker of the *baab* (Gate).

They want to come to me, you hit them with "*laa ilaha illallah Muhammadun Rasulullah.*" Because of their Divinely hit, when they hit with a physical reality, Allah عزّ وجلّ opens a spiritual reality. It is Divinely because when they hit and take away that part of *dunya* (material world), Allah عزّ وجلّ exchanges it with *akhirah* (hereafter).

Allah ﷻ Warns in Qur'an, If you Fear, Allah's ﷻ Mercy Will Take Away Difficulty

Even Mawlana Shaykh was saying that, when you read the verses of holy Qur'an that are very severe, very tough, that you begin to cry at night and say, "*Yaa Rabbi*, oh my gosh what am I going to do, if I get into that *ahzab* (punishment)? Who can you call to? If Allah ﷻ calls you to Judgment, there is no angel that can come; there is nothing that can come. Mawlana Shaykh is describing that *azhab* is like a family, when you describe to your children, "Don't do bad things; you are going to run into difficulty."

Allah's *rahmah* (mercy) is so immense, that just by the fear of the *ayat* Allah ﷻ takes away the bad character. He hit you with a fear, that you should have a fear when you read His Words, they are real. If the fear should come to you, Allah's ﷻ *Rahma* will take away the difficulty. If you have no fear, then there is a sword that is waiting for your head. *Ittaqullah*, have a conscious of Allah ﷻ, that it merely comes to you and by means of that fear coming to you I pull it way and I dress you with My *Rahma* and My Mercy.

Sayyidina Musa ﷺ Wanted to See His Lord

Then come to the *laam alif* لا. Everyone wanted the *laam-alif*, Nabi Musa ﷺ asked, "*Yaa Rabbi*, I want to see You."

وَلَمَّا جَاءَ مُوسَىٰ لِمِيقَاتِنَا وَكَلَّمَهُ رَبُّهُ قَالَ رَبِّ أَرِنِي أَنظُرْ إِلَيْكَ ۚ ...(١٤٣)

7:143 – "Wa lamma jaa Musa limeeqatina wa kallamahu Rabbuhu, qala rabbi arinee anzhur ilayka…" (Surah Al-A'raf)

"And when Moses arrived at Our appointed time and his Lord spoke to him, he said, 'My Lord, show me [Yourself] that I may look at You..."
(The Heights, 7:143)

I am only speaking, *yaa Rabbi,* I want to see the reality, not only speak to the reality. So what you are seeking, you can look to the mountain and see if it stays there.

قَالَ لَن تَرَانِي وَلَـٰكِنِ انظُرْ إِلَى الْجَبَلِ فَإِنِ اسْتَقَرَّ مَكَانَهُ فَسَوْفَ تَرَانِي ۚ فَلَمَّا تَجَلَّىٰ رَبُّهُ لِلْجَبَلِ جَعَلَهُ دَكًّا وَخَرَّ مُوسَىٰ صَعِقًا ۚ فَلَمَّا أَفَاقَ قَالَ سُبْحَانَكَ تُبْتُ إِلَيْكَ وَأَنَا أَوَّلُ الْمُؤْمِنِينَ (١٤٣)

7:143 – "...Qala lan taranee wa lakini onzhur ilal jabali fa inistaqarra makanahu, fasawfa taranee, falamma tajalla Rabbuhu lil jabali ja`alahu, dakkan wa kharra Musa sa`iqan, falamma afaqa qala Subhanaka tubtu ilayka wa ana awwalul Mumineen." (Surah Al-A'raf)

"...[Allah] said, "you will not see Me, but look at the mountain; if it should remain in its place, then you will see Me." But when his Lord manifested His glory on the mountain, He made it as dust, and Moses fell unconscious. And when he awoke/recovered his senses, he said, "Glory be to You! to You I turn in repentance, and I am the first of the believers." (The Heights, 7:143)

What did Musa عليه السلام see? He saw 124,000 lights of the prophets and Sayyidina Muhammad صلى الله عليه وسلم in front of him, and he went unconscious. He realized at that moment, "That is the reality I am seeking." From what Nabi Musa عليه السلام witnessed of that reality after that he took *Shahada, ana awal muslimeen,* he declared his *Shahada* to Prophet صلى الله عليه وسلم.

LAAM ALIF لا – WHERE THE TWO RIVERS MEET, THAT'S WHERE SAYYIDINA MUSA عليه السلام WANTED TO REACH

Then Nabi Musa عليه السلام set off for where the two rivers meet.

وَإِذْ قَالَ مُوسَىٰ لِفَتَاهُ لَا أَبْرَحُ حَتَّىٰ أَبْلُغَ مَجْمَعَ الْبَحْرَيْنِ أَوْ أَمْضِيَ حُقُبًا (٦٠)

18:60 – "Wa idh qala Mosa lefatahu laa abrahu hatta ablugha majma'a albahrayni aw amdiya huquba." (Surah Al-Kahf)

"Behold, Moses said to his attendant, "I will not give up until I reach the junction of the two seas or (until) I spend years and years in travel." (The Cave, 18:60)

What rivers? *Laa ilaaha illallah Muhammadun Rasulullah* Where they meet is the *zulfiqar*. The handle of the *zulfiqar* means it holds the reality of *laa ilaha illallah, laa ilaha illallah, hay* (ه) *waw* (و) *Muhammadun Rasulullah*. It is unbroken, it is one sentence. *Laa ilaaha illallah hay* ه *waw* و next to *Muhammadun Rasulullah* صلى الله عليه وسلم.

لا اله الا اللهُ (هو) محمد رسول الله

So all the people of *zulfiqar*, what is their *dhikr*? *Hay*, *waw*, *Hu* (هو), because *Hu* is the great connection between *laa ilaaha illallah* to the *hay*

and the *waw* it connects to *Hu Muhammadun Rasulullah*. It is now a description; it is a reality, a description that *Hu* is pointing to *Muhammadun Rasulullah* ﷺ.

YOU CAN'T ENTER INTO THE *HU* هو WITH YOUR HEAD

Then the one carrying that reality is standing at the gate. Do you want to enter into the *Hu* هو and be dressed by that reality? You can't come with your head. That is why we keep repeating this, but I think some people think it is for somebody else. It means that the whole way is based on that you can't enter that reality with that head.

We went somewhere and somebody greeted us like this, crossing arms over chest holding index fingers up, showing لا. He was a very old man, he went like this لا on his chest. I said *ajeeb* (strange) why is he going like this? I said, okay and I greeted him back like this (imitating him). Later I went home, and asked my guide what is this? The guides said, "This was one of the people of the *zulfiqar*." He is acknowledging there is no head here in this association. So it means they are the people with 'no head'. They are not putting their faith in the head. They use the faculty of their head for their *dunya* and only barely because their heart is so powerful they don't need to think through their head. Low-level people, they think through their head and try to think about everything. Everything they have to analyze through their head. These people and the people of *haqqaiq* are using *qalbun mu'min baytullah*.

قَلْبَ الْمُؤْمِنْ بَيْتُ الرَّبْ

"Qalb al mu'min baytur rabb."

"The heart of the believer is the House of the Lord." *(Hadith Qudsi)*

When you say the shaykh is your *Ka'bah* and your *qibla* (direction of prayer), it means that he is describing a reality, that his heart is the house of Allah ﷻ. Allah's ﷻ Divinely Lights are upon their heart. If Allah ﷻ is in your heart why do you have to use your head?

It is the Light of the Heart That Reflects to the Face

Allah ﷻ is in the heart which means He reflects to the head. What shines from the face is the reality of the light within the heart. If there is no light in the heart, there is nothing shining from the face.

So the whole way is based on building the heart, build the heart, build the good characteristics for all the lights to enter into the heart. That light cannot enter with bad character, with bad desires. Then that light begins to flow into the heart, a clean heart.

Heart is a Vessel That Carries the Divine's Light

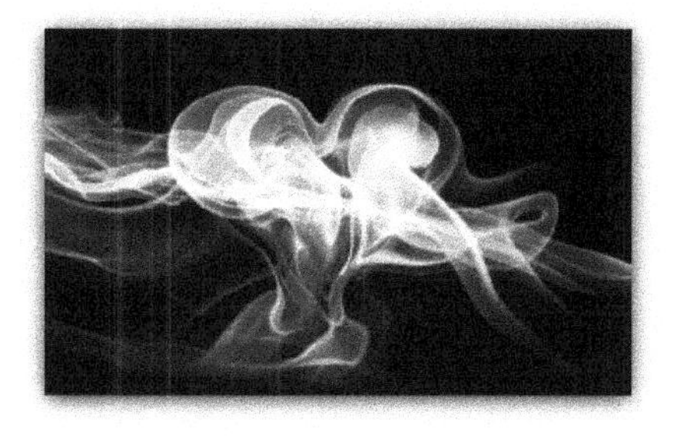

They say the heart is like a vessel to carry Allah's ﷻ Light. Most people's cup (heart) is Styrofoam. If Allah ﷻ poured that light it is like liquid gold, it burns the Styrofoam. It means the heart that has been purified, has been cleansed, has been tested, it becomes something solid, becomes something strong in which Allah ﷻ begins to pour those lights. These are the lights of *iman* (faith), the lights of *Maqaam al Ihsan* (Station of Moral Excellence).

Imam Ali عليه السلام is coming and saying, "That head has to come off. You want to reach to *laa ilaaha illallah*, you are not going to get there with that head." Then we are repeating again, always for myself, that our battle is between the head and the heart. And those who are fortunate enough to be with the shaykh, a shaykh from these oceans of reality, they are not reading a book for you; it is not a philosophy.

You know the poetry of the flute? [Rumi says, the reed pipe is visible, but the pipe-player is hidden]. If you hear somewhere in the middle of nowhere a flute going *oooovv, ooouu*, (sound of flute), you will be astonished right? You will wonder how this flute is making noise. It is just levitating and sound is coming out. No, don't think about the one who is speaking, but the one who is speaking behind them. That they are merely blowing a flute. If you negate yourself to be nothing, you are like a flute for them.

Negate Yourself and Become the Smartphone for *Awliya* (Saints)

The guides say we are going to play you, we are going to play through you, we are going to speak through you, we are going to seek through you, you are our mobile phone. The best of mobile phones, better than a Smartphone, better than the bitten apple that brought us here, better than that other phone that explodes in people's face because it is not working correctly. We can't say the name of label and we don't want to bother the company. Better than all those is Allah's عزَّ وجلَّ phone.

It is the *Hadith*, "I will be the ears in which you hear, I will be the eyes in which you see and through the end..." This is the description of the mobile phone. That negate yourself and these realities will be coming out.

...وَلَا يَزَالُ عَبْدِي يَتَقَرَّبُ إلَيَّ بِالنَّوَافِلِ حَتَّى أُحِبَّهُ، فَإِذَا أَحْبَبْتُهُ كُنْت سَمْعَهُ الَّذِي يَسْمَعُ بِهِ، وَبَصَرَهُ الَّذِي يُبْصِرُ بِهِ، وَيَدَهُ الَّتِي يَبْطِشُ بِهَا، وَرِجْلَهُ الَّتِي يَمْشِي بِهَا، وَلَئِنْ سَأَلَنِي لَأُعْطِيَنَّهُ، وَلَئِنْ اسْتَعَاذَنِي لَأُعِيذَنَّهُ." [رَوَاهُ الْبُخَارِيُّ]

"… wa la yazaalu 'Abdi yataqarrabu ilayya bin nawafile hatta ahebahu, fa idha ahbabtuhu kunta Sam'ahul ladhi yasma'u behi, wa Basarahul ladhi yubsiru behi, wa Yadahul lati yabTeshu beha, wa Rejlahul lati yamshi beha, wa la in sa alani la a'Teyannahu…"

"…My servant continues to draw near to Me with voluntary acts of worship so that I shall love him. When I love him, I am his hearing with which he hears, his seeing with which he sees, his hand with which he strikes and his foot with which he walks. Were he to ask [something] of Me, I would surely give it to him…" (Hadith Qudsi, Sahih al-Bukhari, 81:38:2)

The Interaction With the Shaykh is Important, Not the End Result

Then the whole way of those teachers, if you find one of those as a teacher, their whole specialty is that *zulfiqar*. Their whole specialty is to continuously test you, shut off your head. Why do you want to think with this guidance? Why every time they say something you have to think? You think that meat inside that box of your skull is going to understand anything? Especially with them, the more you think, the more you will be confused, the more they will send all sorts of different confusing signals, because you shouldn't be using your head with them. You should be listening to your heart and listening to their guidance because they are going to go left, they are going to go right. They will go left then go right, until you are assured, and you feel that they are completely confused. No, they are not confused, they are merely confusing you because they want you to shut off, shut off.

A reminder that the goal is not important. Everyone has a goal in which they can interact with the Shaykh. So we said in our own lives, "I want to go buy a house." You come to me and say, "I want to buy a house." Buying a house is not important for us, but your interaction with the shaykh is. He will drive you down "that street." You go and you get frustrated. Then you go and he says, "Maybe it's that street." Then you drive down that way and you get confused. He says, "Maybe it is in Richmond (British Columbia, Canada)." 'Aaah what the heck, this guy doesn't know what he is talking about.' No, he does know what he is talking about. It wasn't to give you the coordinance so that you get the house. It was merely to flip you around, until you stop thinking, until you just enter an ocean of *tasleem* (submission).

How can you get to *tasleem* (submission), if Allah عز و جل doesn't give everyone a unique way, a unique opportunity in which to interact with the shaykh? There is no fixed thing where everybody has to do a fixed thing to understand that reality. But as soon as Allah عز و جل opens an interaction with the shaykh, he is giving you an opportunity. That you are going to be tested now, lose your head, lose the faculty of trying to put your head on his coordinance and trying to understand his coordinance. It is nothing for you to understand. It is only for Allah عز و جل to understand. It is merely to lose the head.

Listen to the Guidance, Don't Doubt It

This *dunya* (material world) is so much about the head, that you think you can use the head to enter Allah's عز و جل Oceans of *Kawthar*. They are standing there with the *zulfiqar*, they say, "The head is still very active. That head keeps thinking about everything." And when you talk to him privately, he will give the shaykh a talk, a *suhbah*, on why he is using his head. That means there is still lots of work to do.

The guides want the reality in which they say, "Walk ten feet then duck." You walk and then duck. Then somebody walks by and asks, "What are you doing?" You say, "I don't know, they said walk ten feet and duck." At that moment *phow*, you see a stick was coming for your head. Other people come and say, "Shaykh doesn't know what he is talking about. I walked ten feet and nothing happened." All of a sudden, ding, something hit you.

AWLIYA (SAINTS) ARE PATIENT, THEY KEEP TESTING UNTIL YOU LISTEN TO GUIDANCE

Our life is a miraculous way, we are on a boat in the middle of an ocean, where Allah ﷻ is blowing, and these are the oceans of faith. How are you going to have faith if you are not going to be tested to be brought into that faith? It means then they keep testing, keep testing, and Mawlana Shaykh would describe I can sit with you ninety years, ninety-nine years until you die. They don't get tired of testing. They don't think you can play around for ten or fifteen years and then you are just going to get it and they will be tired with you. No, no, I will sit with you for ninety-nine years until I put you into the grave. When Allah ﷻ takes your last breath you go into the grave, *Awliya* will meet you in the grave to finally test you there. It means it just keeps repeating, keeps repeating.

HEAR THE GUIDANCE THROUGH YOUR HEART AND SOUL, NOT THE HEAD

So then the ones at the gate are reminding, teach them to take that head away, take their thinking away, and use your heart. They want to open the reality of the heart. The heart has an infinite capacity for Allah's ﷻ Divinely Presence. The brain has a very limited capacity and it's always wrong, its understandings are wrong.

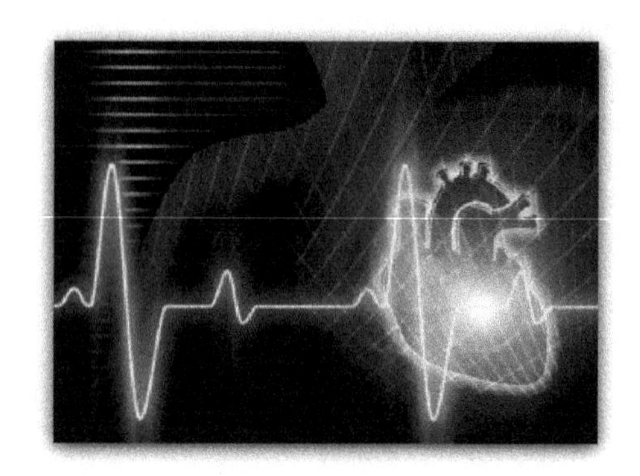

So our whole life is battling with what is being said in the head. What you heard through these two ears, is not the hearing you should have opened, you should have opened the hearing of your soul. Because these two ears when the hearing comes in here, the brain begins to chew on it, grrrrr, and it begins to make a *tafsir* (interpretation). "Maybe the shaykh meant this, maybe the shaykh meant that, maybe I can do like this, maybe I can do like that." Add a few *jinn* and some other crazy things to it and your head is so confused. A confusing person you can't imagine, that is not the hearing.

The hearing they wanted is the hearing through your soul. You build your *tafakkur*, build your contemplation, that when you are in their attendance you are hearing through the ears; more powerful is when you are hearing through your soul. That coordinance is coming to your soul with an understanding, that I understand what they want from me and I am going to try to accomplish it. But you hear through these physical ears, wash it around in our brain with *Shaytan* and your *nafs* (ego), and you have *kale pache*, (soup of the head and legs of sheep). I don't know what is in that. It is definitely not what the shaykh talked about. You just made something crazy in your mind and then you begin to try to do that.

So always a reminder from Imam Ali ﷺ teaching that this head knows nothing from the Divinely Presence, use your head for your work but for the *akhirah* (hereafter) you open the heart. The greatest battle of the believer is between their head and their heart. Every *waswas* (whispering) comes into the heart but follow the guidance that is coming into the heart. The interaction with the shaykh is to make everything upside down, upside down, upside down, so that the servant enters into *tasleem* (submission). I am submitting, you tell me, "Go right," I go right. You tell me, "Go left," I go left. Not that I tell you, "Go left," and you go left and then you get lost and you go and you don't listen to anymore right or left. Everything is about the oceans of *tasleem* and they wait to see how tired you are going to get and they keep going and keep going. It could be years like that.

Subhana rabbika rabil 'izzati 'ama yasifoon, Wa salamun 'alal mursaleen wal hamdulillahi rabbil 'alameen. Bi hurmati Muhammadil Mustafa wa bi siratil Suratil Fatiha.

Reality of *Salah* (Daily Prayer) and the Levels of the Heart

Life and Death in Each Day

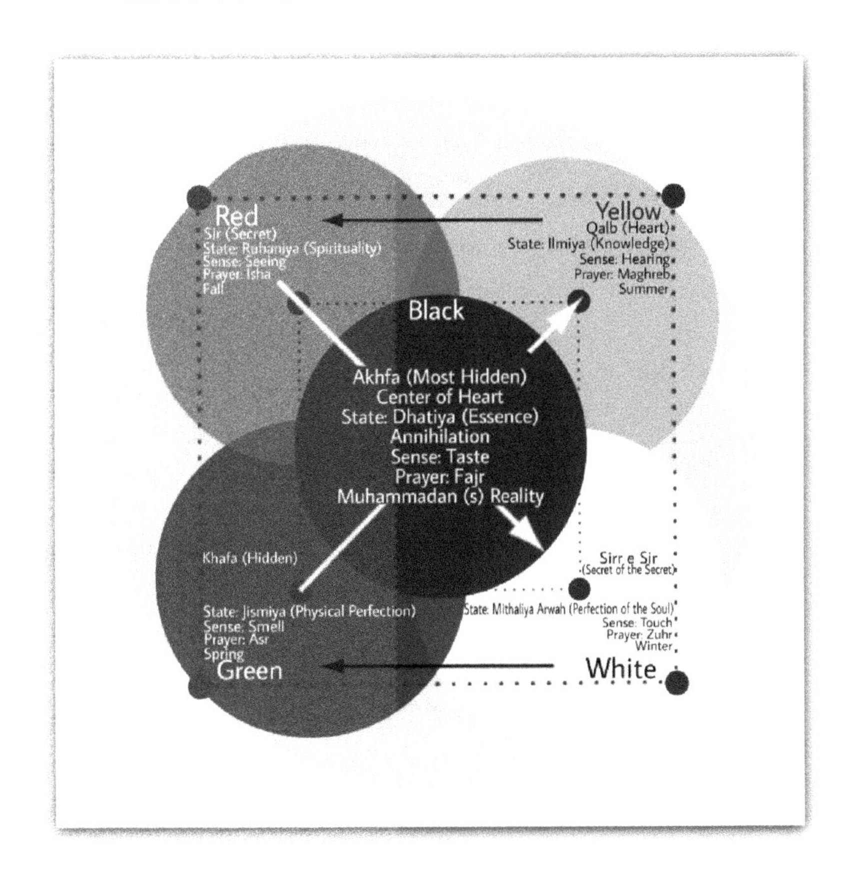

Alhamdulillah (Praise be to Allah), that Allah ﷻ guided us to the love of Sayyidina Muhammad ﷺ and into the hands of *awliyaullah* (saints), and their *uloom* and knowledges to take us towards the *marif'ah*, the realities in which Allah ﷻ wants.

The *salah* (daily prayers) are based on the reality of the levels of the heart. The first station of the heart, *Qalb* (Heart) is the point of entry and the station of knowledges. It means that we go from the Heart *(Qalb),* to the *Sir* (Secret), then it cuts down like an 8, it goes through the black, the *Akhfa* (Most Hidden), the Fifth Station of the heart. That black is like a black hole and the reality of the *Fajr* (morning prayer). It means you are going through that black to the *Sirr e Sir* (Secret of the Secret), which is white. Then you go over to the green, the fourth Station of the *Khafa* (Hidden). From the green, it crosses back through the black, and back to that yellow at Station of the *Qalb* (Heart).

In the understanding of the *salah* and how it relates to the *Lataif* of *Qalb*, the Levels of the Heart. It means that you start from *Salat al Maghrib* at the station of *Qalb (Heart),* left of the chest, to *Salat al-Isha* at the station of *Sir* (Secret), the center of the chest, and then you pass the black, *Salat al-Fajr*, the 5th station – *Akhfa* (Most Hidden), which is a state of death. That's why the morning, *Fajr* prayer, before the sun rises is the most powerful because that is the birth canal of the day.

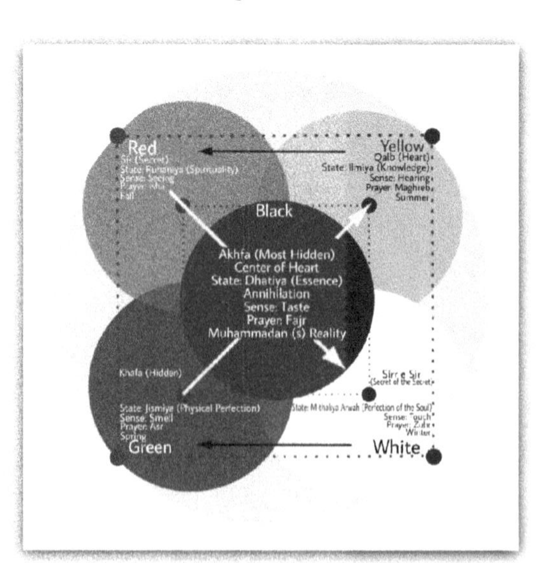

That with our *Maghrib* (evening prayer) it starts and then becomes *Salat al-Isha* (night prayer), the night time, the darkest point of night, and then you pass the black part of *Fajr* (morning prayer).

1. ***Maghrib*** (Evening Prayer) – First Station of *Qalb* (Heart)

2. ***Isha*** (Night Prayer) – Second Station of *Sir* (Secret)

5. ***Fajr*** (Morning Prayer) – Fifth Station of *Akhfa* (Most Hidden)

3. ***Zuhr*** (Noon Prayer) – Third Station of *Sirr e Sir* (Secret of the Secret)

4. ***Asr*** (Afternoon Prayer) – Fourth Station *Khafa* (Hidden)

We Are Spiritual Beings Sent For Physical Experience

Allah عزّ وجلّ wants us to know that we come from the heavens. We are a spiritual creation sent upon earth for the physical experience. That Allah عزّ وجلّ and what Prophet صلى الله عليه وسلم brought for us is a fine line on how *Shaytan* (devil) tries to fool *insaan* (human being). *Shaytan's* cleverness is like a line, that if he can't pass that line on to people, they lose their reality and their understanding.

The Greatness of Allah عزّ وجلّ, greatness of the *deen* and the religion that Prophet صلى الله عليه وسلم brought was a completion for humanity to complete the understanding of themselves. They are in need of all the prophets, the understanding of all the messengers and the love that completes their reality.

1. *MAGHRIB* (EVENING PRAYER) AT THE STATION OF *QALB* قلب (HEART)

OUR JOURNEY BEGINS AT EVENING - AT *MAGHRIB*

What Allah ﷻ wants to know is that our day starts from the night; our day starts from *Salat al-Maghrib. Salat al-Maghrib* is the beginning of our journey because Allah ﷻ wants a reminder within ourselves because as soon as we come to this reality, we begin to keep contemplating, why everything begins at night time? Why are all the celebrations, the night of *Isra wal-Mi'raj* (Journey and Ascension), the Night of Power (*Laylatul Qadr*)? It means that every celebration in this way is based on the *layl* (night), why? Because Allah ﷻ, Prophet (ﷺ), and the *ulul amr*, who are teaching us from their realities, that Allah ﷻ wants us to know that the occasion is there in heavens, not on your *dunya* (material world).

In the world of light, in Heavens, in the *akhirah* (hereafter) and to you it is represented by darkness because it's a dimension in which you can't see. That you are coming from the oceans of the heavens, you are coming from the *malakut* (heavens).

إِنَّا لِلَّـهِ وَإِنَّا إِلَيْهِ رَاجِعُونَ ١٥٦...

2:156 – "...Inna lillahi wa inna ilayhi raji'oon." (Surah Al-Baqarah)

"...Indeed we belong to Allah, and indeed to Him we will return." (The Cow, 2:156)

They are now just understanding that darkness doesn't mean it's void of anything. They found that the universe is actually a tremendous amount of dark matter; there is a tremendous amount of darkness but there is something there that Allah ﷻ has just not illuminated.

It means then the reality for us is that we are from the heavens. That every occasion is starting from the heavens, the *rahmah* (mercy) from the heavens *'wa Tanzila'* and it will come down upon your creation. So then remember you come from the heavens and that you don't come from this *dunya* (earth). Don't forget your origin. So our day starts with that reality of *Maghrib.*

Life Begins at the Womb and It Should Be Counted

It means that we said before, *Shaytan* wants to fool and it's like a string. That when you conceive a child, 9 months it's alive within the womb. The birthday is when? As soon as the baby's born. You bring a cake, and say, 'Happy birthday!' They don't say that; they wait until one year and then say, 'Happy birthday'. Why? Why wait; why *Shaytan* wants that wait? So that you think that baby is not alive in the womb; that that doesn't count as a life. You kill it if you want, *astaghfirullah. Shaytan*, fools people to think, something so simple by waiting 1 year to say, 'Happy birthday'. It is a lie and they start everything with a lie.

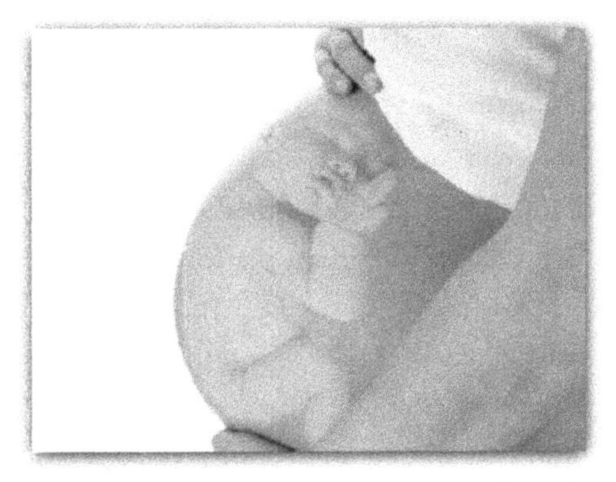

Islam comes to say, 'No, speak the truth. Live a life of truth. Don't base your life off of falsehoods, from one false thing to another false thing.' *Haqq al-Islam* (Truth of Islam) and what Prophet ﷺ brought are realities. That no, no; from the moment that heart moves in, the conception begins, 120 days the soul, like a passenger, comes into the heart of that creation; immediately the heart is beating, life is beginning.

Nine months is 36 weeks; 36 is what? The heart of Qur'an, *Yaseen* ﷺ, 36th chapter of Holy Qur'an. Everything, Allah عز و جل says, 'Everything is perfectly numbered,' but who will understand? The people of *tafakkur* (contemplation).

الَّذِينَ يَذْكُرُونَ اللَّهَ قِيَامًا وَقُعُودًا وَعَلَىٰ جُنُوبِهِمْ وَيَتَفَكَّرُونَ فِي خَلْقِ السَّمَاوَاتِ وَالْأَرْضِ رَبَّنَا مَا خَلَقْتَ هَٰذَا بَاطِلًا سُبْحَانَكَ فَقِنَا عَذَابَ النَّارِ

3:191 – "Alladheena yadhkurona Allaha qiyaman wa qu'odan wa 'ala junobihim, wa yatafakkarona fee khalqis Samawati wal ardi, Rabbana ma khalaqta hadha batilan subhanaka faqina 'adhaban nar." (Surah Al-Imran)

"Who remember Allah while standing or sitting or [lying] on their sides and Contemplate/Meditate the creation in the heavens and the earth, [saying], "Our Lord, You did not create this aimlessly; exalted are You [above such a thing]; then protect us from the punishment of the Fire." (Family of Imran, 3:191)

They slow down and they don't let the fast life to fool them. Everything is contemplation, *tafakkur.* Everything is to take a *hisaab* (an account). '*Ya Rabbi*, 9 months and the power of 9 and the 9 *sultans* and all these realities; and this 9 times 4 becomes 36, the heart of Qur'an, *Yaseen.*' It means there must be a secret coming that is making this creation to come into existence and it's coming from paradise. The light is coming, the soul of the passenger is coming from paradise, coming into the womb; then coming onto this earth and is a reminder for us that this is a sacred existence.

So then our day begins at *Maghrib.* As soon as we go to *Salat al-Maghrib*, we pray *Salat al-Maghrib* and then we have the *Janazat al-Gha'ibeen*, the unseen *janazah.* It is a reminder for us that, *salat al-janazah* (funeral prayer) is not only for all those who passed away, because these are from the *maqam al ihsaan* (station of moral excellence); these are not common people understanding. They want us to understand the *salah* and the reality of *salah* from the stations of perfection. From the station of perfection, the servant is entering back into their origin, because it'll loop around and we catch back that understanding. That these (saints) are the people of *hayat* (ever living) in which they mastered a state of death. As soon as *Salat al-Maghrib* comes it's a reminder for them.

THREE VEILS OF DARKNESS – FROM *MAGHRIB*, TO *ISHA*, TO *FAJR*

خَلَقَكُم مِّن نَّفْسٍ وَاحِدَةٍ ثُمَّ جَعَلَ مِنْهَا زَوْجَهَا وَأَنزَلَ لَكُم مِّنَ الْأَنْعَامِ ثَمَانِيَةَ أَزْوَاجٍ ۚ يَخْلُقُكُمْ فِي بُطُونِ أُمَّهَاتِكُمْ خَلْقًا مِّن بَعْدِ خَلْقٍ فِي ظُلُمَاتٍ ثَلَاثٍ ۚ ذَٰلِكُمُ اللَّهُ رَبُّكُمْ لَهُ الْمُلْكُ ۖ لَا إِلَٰهَ إِلَّا هُوَ ۖ فَأَنَّىٰ تُصْرَفُونَ (٦)

39:6 – "Khalaqakum min nafsin wahidatin thumma ja'ala minha zawjaha, wa anzala lakum minal-an'aami samaani yata azwaaj; yakhuluqukum fee butooni ummahaatikum khalqam mim ba'di khalqin fee zulumaatin salaas; zaalikumul laahu Rabbukum lahul mulk; laaa ilaaha illaa Huwa fa annaa tusrafoon." (Surah Az-Zumar)

"He created you (all) from one soul: then from it, He created its mate, of like nature, and He produced for you from the grazing livestock eight mates. He creates you in the wombs of your mothers, creation after creation, within three darknesses. That is Allah , your Lord; to Him belongs dominion. There is no deity except Him, so how are you averted?" (The Troops, 39:6)

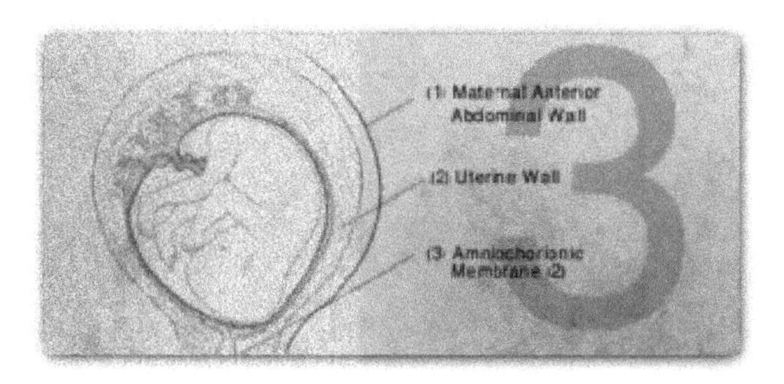

Allah ﷻ described that the child is created in three veils of darkness. It means that the womb has three veils of darkness and this whole understanding is like a *rahem*, is like a womb. That you are going to pass *Maghrib* (evening prayer), *Salat al-Isha* (night prayer) and *Fajr* (early morning) and then you are going to be born. Three veils of darkness; you are going to come from *Maghrib*, to the apex of the world of *malakut* (heavens), which is *Salat al-Isha*, and you are going to be descending through *Salat al-Fajr* into your existence and manifestation.

Then for us, the understanding is that as soon as these servants enter into *Salat al-Maghrib*, it's a reminder for them, a state of death, annihilation. It's a state in which the *akhirah* [points upwards], their *malakut*, that they're asking, '*Ya Rabbi*, we are asking to leave this *dunya* and return us back, *'wa ilaihi turja'oon.'*

فَسُبْحَانَ الَّذِي بِيَدِهِ مَلَكُوتُ كُلِّ شَيْءٍ وَإِلَيْهِ تُرْجَعُونَ (٨٣)

36:83 – "Fasubhanal ladhee biyadihi Malakutu kulli shay in wa ilayhi turja'oon." (Surah Yaseen)

"Therefore Glory be to Him in Whose hand is the [heavenly] dominion/ kingdom of all things, and to Him you will be returned." (Yaseen, 36:83)

That we come from a different reality. We're asking to go back into that reality. That, for them, begins at *Salat al-Maghrib*. As soon as Allah ﷻ darkens the sky, *"layli wan nahar,"* that you are entering into a state of *fana* and annihilation.

تُولِجُ اللَّيْلَ فِي النَّهَارِ وَتُولِجُ النَهارَ فِي اللَّيْلِ، وَتُخْرِجُ الْحَيَّ مِنَ الْمَيِّتِ وَتُخْرِجُ الْمَيِّتَ مِنَ الْحَيِّ، وَتَرْزُقُ مَنْ تَشَآءُ بِغَيْرِ حِسَابٍ .(سُوْرَةُ آلِ عِمْرَان ٣:٢٧

3:27 – "Tulijul layla fin nahari, wa tuliju nahara fil layl, wa tukhrijul hayya minal mayyiti, wa tukhrijul mayyita minal hayy, wa tarzuqu man tasha'u bi ghayri hisab." (Surah Al-Imran)

"You make the night to enter into the day and You make the day to enter into the night, You bring the living out of the dead and You bring the dead out of the living, And You give provision to whom You will without measure [unlimited]." (Family of Imran, 3:27)

Darkness represents annihilation, that Allah ﷻ says, 'You are coming to Me, but don't manifest yourself. Don't manifest from you, from what you acquired from *dunya.* Don't manifest thinking that you're anything. Begin your phase of death in which you are nothing, which you are nothing.' And that, '*Ya Rabbi, "wa ilayhi turja'oon";* [points upwards] let me go back. Let me go back to my reality.'

SALATUL JANAZAT AL-GHA'IBEEN IS PRAYED AT *MAGHRIB*

TO GET RID OF OUR FOUR ENEMIES: MATERIAL WORLD, DESIRES, EGO, AND SATAN, (*DUNYA, HAWA, NAFS,* AND *SHAYTAN*)

Then they ask that pray *Salatul Janazat al-Gha'ibeen* (Funeral Prayer for the Unseen) at the end of your *Salat al-Maghrib* – why? Because these 4 *takbirats* are for the four enemies that have destroyed *insaan* (human being). It means the *nafs* (ego), *dunya* (material world), *hawa* (desires) and *Shaytan* (Satan) are 4 enemies against *insaan*; and they have quartered the reality of the soul. The *nafs*, the wildness of the *nafs*, the *hubb ad-dunya* (love of material world), *hubb al-hawa* and all the physical pleasures, and *Shaytan* (Satan), they have split the soul from what was whole. Because when the soul is whole, it means its realities are reaching to it; it has a tremendous power. And *Shaytan* wants to block all of that so that the soul cannot gain its power.

So the reality of their *Salat al-Janazat al-Gha'ibeen* is that they see themselves on that *janazat*; that everyone should visualize themself on that table of *janazat.* That, '*Ya Rabbi*, it's my funeral prayer, that everybody, *inshaAllah,* gathering tonight for my funeral prayer. With every *takbirat, ya Rabbi*, destroy; destroy my *dunya*, my *hubb ad dunya*, destroy my *hubb al-hawa* and my seeking of my physical pleasures.

Destroy my *nafs* (ego) and destroy the *Shaytan* that continuously is destroying everything I'm trying to do, *ya Rabbi.'*

EVERY *TAKBIR* DESTROYS ONE ENEMY

It means every *Salat al-Maghrib*, they are entering into an intention that only Allah ﷻ, only Allah ﷻ – when they say *'Allahu Akbar'*, like a tremendous lightning and power that come to destroy everything. *Al Muntaqim* (the Avenger), Allah ﷻ says, 'I'm going to avenge you. I'm going to destroy that *Shaytan* and everything he thinks he is doing. I send upon you like a lightning that destroy and finish everything wrong and bring you back into My Perfection. I will make your desire for *dunya* to be destroyed; I destroy your desire for your *hawa*. The *nafs*, I discipline so it becomes your *buraq* and you ride upon it. And *Shaytan* will fear you and run away from you because you become from *mukhliseen*.' *Shaytan* has no business with the *mukhlis* (sincere), but is continuously chasing. It means they enter into an understanding that they are praying their own *janazat*.

2. *ISHA* (NIGHT PRAYER)
AT THE STATION OF *SIR* سر (SECRET)

APEX OF DARKNESS AND SYMBOL OF ANNIHILATION

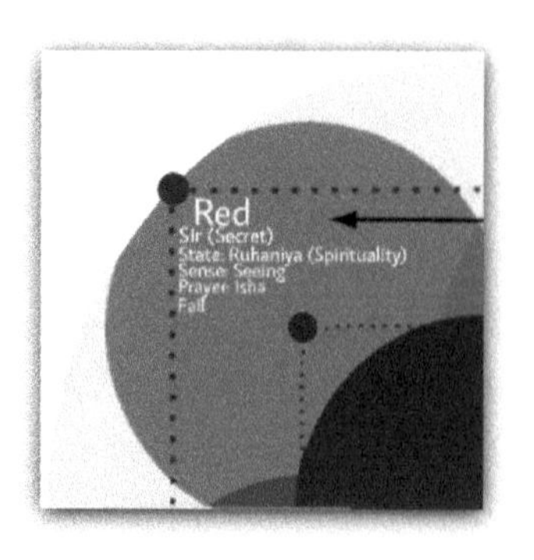

By the time they reach, which means from the *Qalb* (Heart), the first station, then they start to move into the *Sir* (second station). These are the world of light in which the *Sir* (Secret) is symbolic of their *salah* and the reality of their *salah*. It means the *Qalb* (heart) is the station of knowledges. They understood that to reach Allah's ﷻ Divinely Presence is that you have to enter a state of *fana*; you have to annihilate. Why Allah ﷻ gives the symbol of the darkness is a symbol of annihilation; they don't manifest anything. If you are coming to *malakut*, leave your manifestation behind.

SALAT AL-ISHA TO *FAJR* IS THE DOOR TO DIVINELY PRESENCE

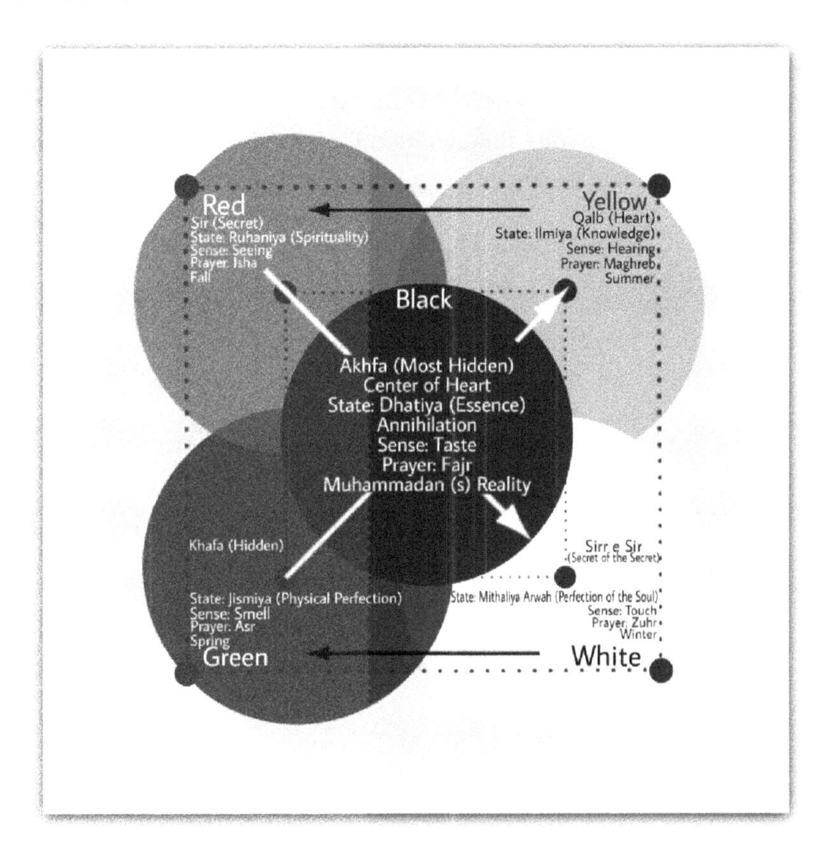

Then *Salat al-Isha*, the *Isha* (night) prayer, is the apex of *malakut* (heavens). It's the height of darkness, when the night is the darkest. For those whom are making *tafakkur* (contemplation), Allah ﷻ is then describing, 'The importance of your *Salat al-Isha* to your *Salat al-Fajr* is going to be your door to My Divinely Presence'; because at the time of *Salat al-Isha* everything is darkened and the servant begins to remember the heavenly kingdom. All the *Tanzil*, all the blessings and the lights begin to manifest upon the servant. That's why all of the holy nights and holy events are at night time. They are taking the dress of all the heavenly manifestations; they come upon the heavens first and then they come towards *dunya* (earth).

It means then the servant is entering into *Salat al-Isha* in a state in which they are losing that existence. They are entering into a state of tranquility and *mawt qabl al-mawt* (death before death). They understood their phase of death because they are asking to return back to Allah ﷻ. As soon as they enter back into *Salat al-Isha*, and *Salat al-Isha* is finishing, they are entering now into *Salat al-Tahajjud.*

Stages of Star Formation and Levels of the Heart

These are important points of energy, that from *Salat al-Isha*, they pass through that black point, that black circle *Akhfa* (Most Hidden) because these are the phases of a sun, these are the *najm*. When Prophet ﷺ described, 'My *Sahabi*, they are stars; any one of them you follow.'

أَصْحَابِيْ كَالنُّجُــومْ بِأَيْهِمْ اَقْتَدَيْتِمْ اَهْتَدَيْتِمْ

"Ashabi kan Nujoom, bi ayyihim aqta daytum ahta daytum."

"My companions are like stars. Follow any one of them and you will be guided." *(Prophet Muhammad ﷺ)*

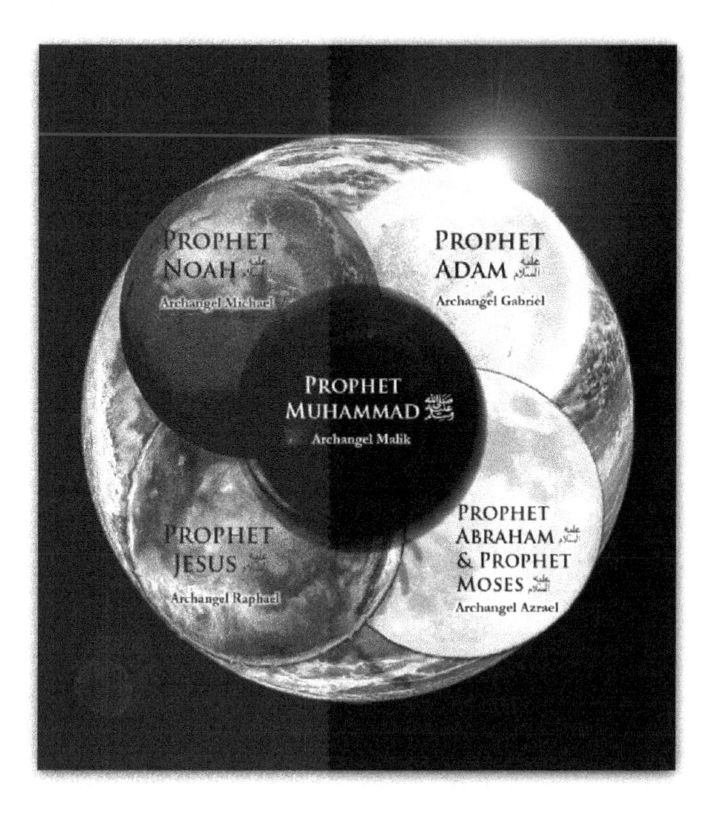

This is a phase of the stars, that you have from this star, The Sun at first station, *Qalb* (Heart) to the Red Giant star at the second station, *Sir* (Secret) to the White Dwarf star at the third station, *Sirr e Sir* (Secret of the Secret), to the Pulsar/Neutron Star at the fourth Station, *Khafa* (Hidden) and then the center, *Akhfa* (Most Hidden), the fifth station. *Akhfa* (Most Hidden), is being like a black hole, which its power is so immense, that it absorbs everything. Nothing escapes the black hole. This is from the reality of Sayyidina Muhammad صلى الله عليه وسلم.

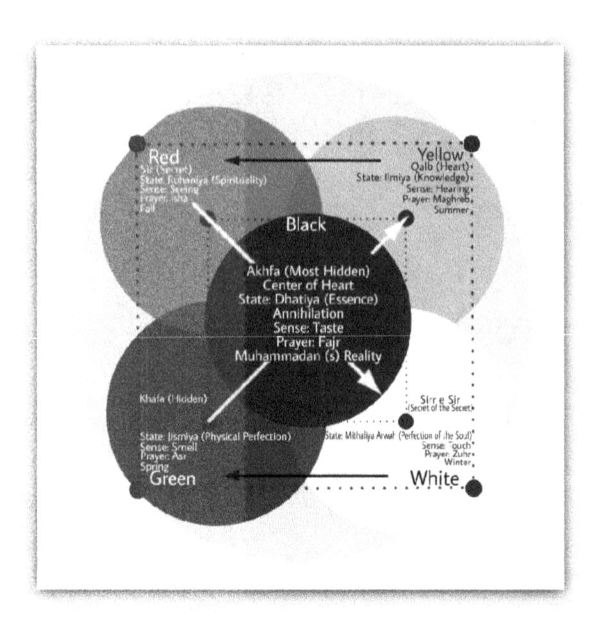

It means Allah ﷻ gave such a dress and such majesty to Prophet ﷺ. That means when the servant is praying from *Salat al-Isha* and moving to *Salat al-Fajr*, what Allah ﷻ wants from them is then wake up, wake up and pray your *Salat al-Tahajjud*. It means this whole phase from *Salat al-Isha* to *Salat al-Fajr*, from station of *Sir* (Secret) to *Akhfa* (Most Hidden) is the womb of the reality.

5. *FAJR* (MORNING PRAYER) AT THE STATION OF *AKHFA* أخفاء (MOST HIDDEN)

YOU ARE BEING BORN IN *FAJR*

That every day has a life and every day has a death. It means from the time of *Maghrib*, that life is coming. The reality of its life is coming, *Salat al-Isha* is dressing it, *Salat al-Fajr* is now the womb; from *Salat al-Fajr* it comes out and now has an existence. You manifest at the *Salat al-Fajr* (morning prayer) and you come into existence again. By night time you died. They go through the phase of death, they move through that; that channel of light and realities.

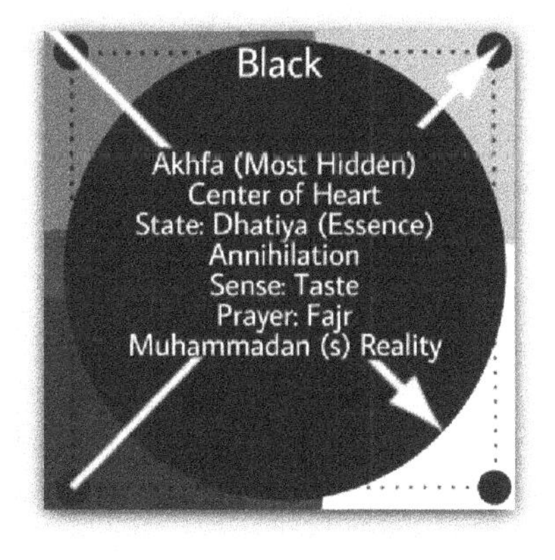

You come through the black of *Fajr* (morning prayer), it shows you its importance because *Fajr* is a state of annihilation; that something is going to be born, something is going to be brought to life and resurrected. That's why the *Fajr* is so powerful, that all the lights that the servant and those servants are taking are that they annihilate themselves in this phase of darkness. They lose their importance, they enter into their *Salat al-Fajr* and Allah ﷻ dresses them from the realities of their paradise.

IN *SALAT AL-FAJR* YOU TAKE FROM PARADISE REALITIES AND KNOWLEDGE

That is why we said in *Surah Al-Qadr* that is the reality, *Salat al-Fajr* is the reality of, *"Salamun hiya hatta matla'il Fajr."*

سَلَامٌ هِيَ حَتَّىٰ مَطْلَعِ الْفَجْرِ ٥

97:5 – "Salamun, hiya hatta matla'il Fajr." (Surah Al-Qadr)

"Peace it is until the emergence of dawn."
(The Power, 97:5)

The *'Salamun'* means Allah ﷻ is dressing them from that reality, blessing them all the way until their *Fajr.* It means that how to take the dress of your paradise reality is only through *Salat al-Fajr;* how to take the knowledges through your paradise reality is through *Salat al-Fajr.* As soon as they pray their *Salat al-Fajr*, Allah ﷻ is dressing the soul with all of its paradise realities.

The center of that *lataif* has to do with the reality of *Fajr*. The *Fajr* (morning prayer), means the birth canal of this life is now going to be born. As soon as the next light is coming out, there is going to be the light of the sun rising. So that white point at that time would be the apex of the sun, which will be *Salat al-Zuhr*. You come through the black of *Fajr*, it shows you its importance because *Fajr* is a state of annihilation; that something is going to be born, something is going to be brought to life and resurrected.

3. *ZUHR* (NOON PRAYER)
AT THE STATION OF *SIRR E SIR* سرالسر
(SECRET OF THE SECRET)

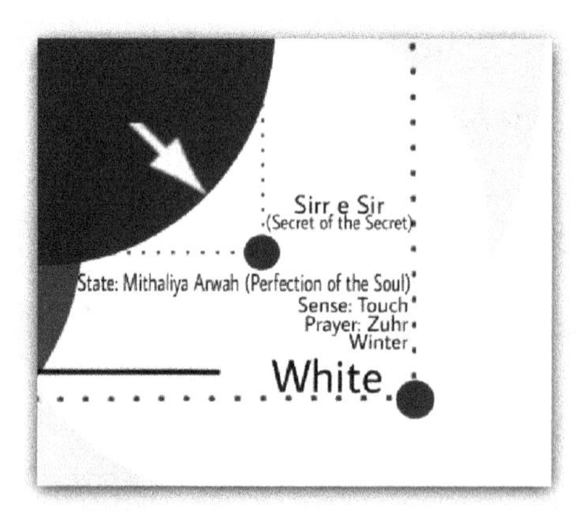

As soon as they leave that *Salat al-Fajr* at *Akhfa*, then the next *salah* that's coming at the Station of *Sirr e Sir* (Secret of the Secret) is *Salat al-Zuhr*. *Zuhr* is actually like a *zuhur* (appearance); it's their manifestation.

RIJALALLAH (MEN OF GOD) DON'T GET DISTRACTED BY BUSINESS OR TRADE

They understood that these are *Rijalallah* (Men of God), where Allah ﷻ described, 'Not trade, nor business distracts them from the remembrance of Allah ﷻ.'

رِجَالٌ لَّا تُلْهِيهِمْ تِجَارَةٌ وَلَا بَيْعٌ عَن ذِكْرِ اللَّـهِ وَإِقَامِ الصَّلَاةِ وَإِيتَاءِ الزَّكَاةِ ۙ يَخَافُونَ يَوْمًا تَتَقَلَّبُ فِيهِ الْقُلُوبُ وَالْأَبْصَارُ (٣٧)

24:37 – "Rijalun la tulheehim tijaratun wa la bay'un 'an Dhikrillahi wa iqamis Salati wa eetayiz Zakati, yakhafona yawman tataqallabu feehi alqulobu wal absar." (Surah An-Nur)

"By men of God (Rijal) whom neither business/ commerce nor sale distracts (them) from the remembrance of Allah and performance of prayer and giving of regular Charity. Their (only) fear is for a Day in which the hearts and eyes will be transformed/ turn about (in a world wholly new)." (The Light, 24:37)

It means they understood that in every moment, there is a life and death; and in every day, there is a life and death. They passed that phase of death to be dressed by their paradise realities. As soon as the day comes up, they are dressed with the reality of that day. They go all the way to *Salat al-Zuhr* (noon prayer). The *Salat al-Zuhr* is their *zuhur*, their manifestation.

ZUHR (NOON) IS SYMBOLIC OF OUR MANIFESTATION IN THE MATERIAL WORLD

Then what Prophet ﷺ described is the most difficult prayer for the believer, is the *Zuhr* prayer because he is busy with business and work.

Why? Because *Zuhr* (noon prayer) is symbolic of our manifestation and our love for *dunya.* The *Shaytan* wants to come and take the servant to make them think that they are going to live in this *dunya* forever, and forgetting that, no, death is coming! Death may come in 5 minutes or in 50 years.

But that servant, from *maqam al ihsaan,* (Station of Moral Excellence) is understanding that, '*Ya Rabbi,* this is my time of manifestation, that I pray my *Salat al-Zuhr* (noon prayer) as to not be conquered by the *dunya.*' It's important and it's tremendously important to show the *nafs* (ego) that, 'No, I'm not conquered by *dunya.*' And that is the one prayer, where everyone wants an excuse to get out of *Salat al-Zuhr.* They ask 'Can I shorten it? Can I pray in my car? Can I do anything?' because of the busy-ness of *dunya.*

Every Day Has a New *Tajalli* (Manifestation) of Allah ﷻ

Then how to conquer that reality is what they are teaching us, because when you understand the reality, it opens an understanding. *Fajr* is not just a time that you are praying in the dark and it's dark and everyone's asleep; you are coming through a birth canal; you are being born that day. Allah ﷻ described, 'Every day, I have a new *tajalli*' (manifestation). It means the one who catches that *tajalli,* as if he is born new that day, not the same *tajalli* that Allah ﷻ dressed him with yesterday. As soon as he enters into that *Fajr,* as soon as he prays his *Salat al-Fajr,* as soon as he comes out, is as if he's been born new that day and dressed with all of its blessing.

Then whatever Allah ﷻ is opening for that servant, He is describing that, 'My *Rijalallah*, no matter business or trade, because all of them are big merchants, all of them are big traders, they are not people who sit on a carpet and do nothing. So all of My *Rijalallah*, not business nor trade divert them from remembrance of Allah ﷻ.' It means they pray that *Salat al-Zuhr* to make sure that they are good with Allah ﷻ. That, '*Ya Rabbi*, we are from *malakut* (heavens) and we understood and servants of the *malakut*; and we are your servants also in the *mulk*,' because *bayna* (between) *Isha* and *Zuhr* is from *malakut* and the *mulk*, from top to bottom. The prayer of *mulk* is your *zuhur*, is your manifestation of *Salat al-Zuhr*.

Our Life is Between *Zuhr* (Noon) and *Asr* (Afternoon) Prayer

Then they understood that in this *mulk*, 'I have to submit to Allah ﷻ, so my *Salat al-Zuhr* is important and my life is *bayna Zuhr wa al 'Asr*.' Again I'm going to die between *Zuhr* and *Asr* (afternoon). So that's all our manifestation because you take, we take life as one day. Don't make too many big plans. You don't know if you have 50 days or 5 years, 50 years. We say, '*Ya Rabbi*, we live day by day. My manifestation, my existence and I put all my importance upon myself; it's only from *Zuhr* to *Asr*.' You are only manifesting from *Salat al-Zuhr* to *Salat al-Asr*.

Then *Zuhr* is the apex of the day. So the afternoon is the apex of your life. From the point of *Zuhr*, now that day is dying.

4. *ASR* (AFTERNOON PRAYER)

AT THE STATION OF *KHAFA* خفاء (HIDDEN)

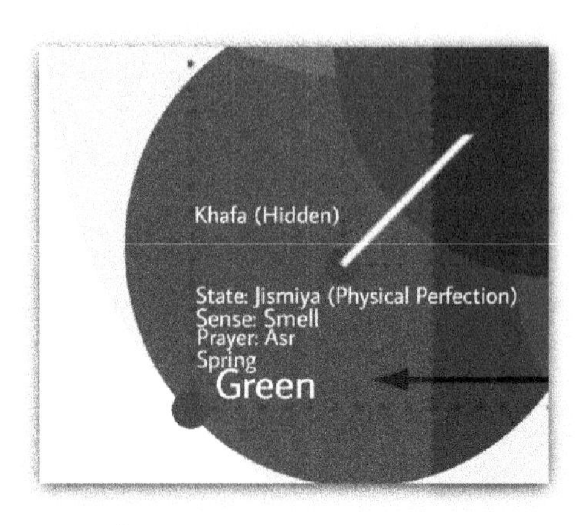

Then it's the *Salat al-Asr*, the midday prayer, around 3:30 pm or 4 o'clock, depending upon the time of the year and which areas you live in. It's a state in remembrance for now the death of that day. So they understood the *mulk* of this *dunya* is all fading until you reach *Salat al-Asr*, and then Allah ﷻ gives you even a *Surah, Surah al-Asr.*

YOU ARE AT THE STATE OF DESCENT AND DYING EVERYDAY

وَالْعَصْرِ (١) إِنَّ الْإِنسَانَ لَفِي خُسْرٍ (٢)

103:1-2 – "Wal 'Asr.(1) Innal insaana lafee khusr.(2)" (Surah Al-'Asr)

"By al 'Asr (the time)! (1) Verily, Mankind is in loss. (2)"
(The Declining Day, 103:1-2)

Allah ﷻ describes in that *Surah* that, *"inal insan lafi khusr."* 'Mankind is in Loss"; you are dying. You are dying; don't think you have too much time. That becomes the understanding that you have to meditate. It doesn't make sense on the tongue, that you actually are born dying; everything about you, from the time Allah ﷻ gave you life because He's describing it. He is describing in *Surah al-Asr* that you are in a state of descent. You are not growing like a tree where, 'I brought you here, you are going to live for 1000 years. From the moment you came and I gave you life, you are dying.' Now you're going to die in 1 day, 50 days, 500 days, 50,000 days; you are going.

And everything within you, as it's growing, it's also dying or all your cells. There are 3 million cells a day die within the body out of your 4 trillion cells. It means we are in a continuous state of where we think we are alive and everything within us is also in a state of death. For the servants whom are trying to reach their reality say, '*Ya Rabbi*, that we are leaving this *mulk* of *dunya* and we entered into *Asr'* (afternoon); and again this day is entering into its *Qiyamah*. Because how are you supposed to prepare for *Qiyamah* (Judgment Day) – 50 years from now? No! Every day has a *Qiyamah*; every day has a death.

As soon as you enter into it, what does Allah ﷻ say? *"Wa tawaa saw bil-haqq wa tawaa saw bil-sabr."*

إِلَّا الَّذِينَ آمَنُوا وَعَمِلُوا الصَّالِحَاتِ وَتَوَاصَوْا بِالْحَقِّ وَتَوَاصَوْا بِالصَّبْرِ (٣)

103:3 – "Illal ladheena aamano wa 'amilos saalihaati, wa tawasaw bil haqqi wa tawasaw bis Sabr (3)." (Surah Al-'Asr)

"Except for those who have believed and done righteous deeds and advised each other to truth and advised each other to patience." (The Declining Day, 103:3)

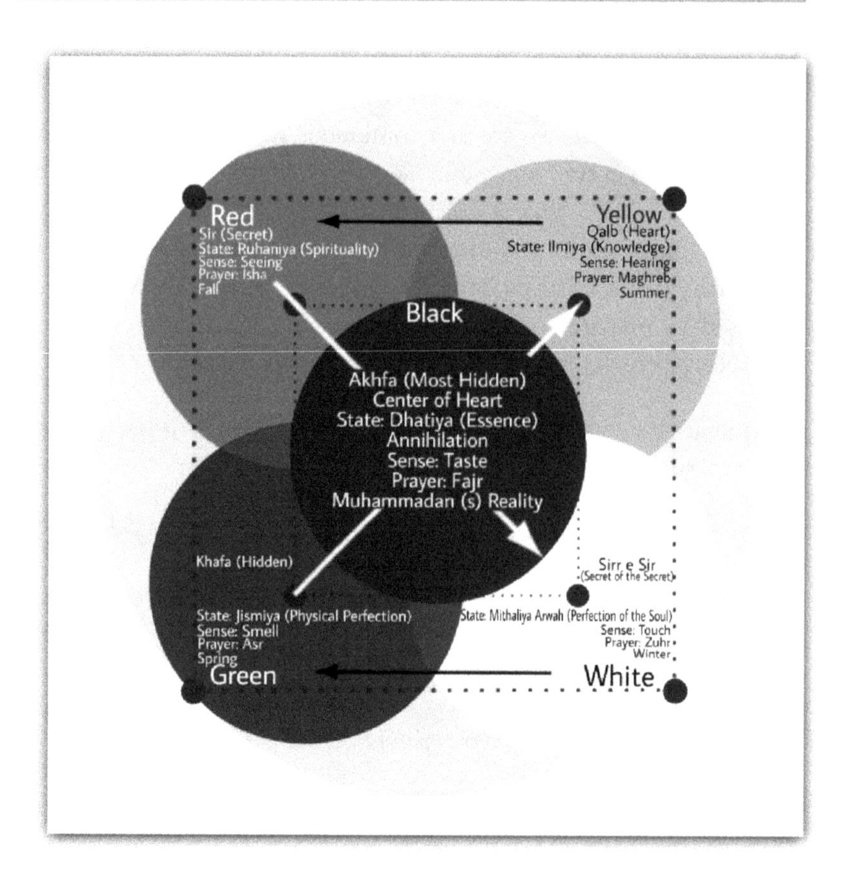

That you are going to enter into this phase of death; your success from your *Salat al-Asr* back to your *Maghrib*, from fourth Station of *Khafa* (Hidden) back to top the first Station of *Qalb* (Heart), which means you are dying now. This phase of life of yours, if you truly understood just 1 day of it. That as soon as you enter into *Salat al-Asr*, all your plans mean nothing. All your hopes mean nothing. It means that you enter into yourself that, '*Ya Rabbi*, whatever I planned, I could be going,' and that everything is leaving.

THIS PATH OF *HAQQ* (TRUTH) IS BASED ON *SABR* (PATIENCE)

Then Allah ﷻ is reminding, 'This path of *haqq* is based on *sabr;* have patience'; that everything in your life is going to be based on *sabr.*

إِلَّا الَّذِينَ آمَنُوا وَعَمِلُوا الصَّالِحَاتِ وَتَوَاصَوْا بِالْحَقِّ وَتَوَاصَوْا بِالصَّبْرِ ٣

103:3 – "Illal ladheena aamano wa 'amilos saalihaati, wa tawasaw bil haqqi wa tawasaw bis Sabr (3)." (Surah Al-'Asr)

"Except for those who have believed and done righteous deeds and advised each other to truth and advised each other to patience." (The Declining Day, 103:3)

The only way to be dressed by *sifat al-sabr*, because when Allah ﷻ dressed those *Ibadullah* (holy servants of Allah) from *sifat al-Sabr* (attribute of Patience). The guides have been dressed from all the attributes, because the last attribute is the most difficult. All the other attributes is *"tawa saw bil haqq"*; Allah ﷻ dress you, dress you, dress but not complete until you have been dressed by *sabr* (patience), that if you're going to be on a path of *haqq*, it has to be based on patience.

The patience comes and *awliya* come and teach you that you are dying, you are dying; from the time you have life, you are truly actually dying. This is the oxymoron of life that we think we have forever. Allah ﷻ says, 'If you really observe yourself, you are actually going down. I gave you a certain amount of breaths, don't waste them. Don't run too much and exercise too much, you lose all your breath. I gave you a numbered amount of breath, a numbered amount of heart beats, and that everything is perfectly numbered.

وَأَحْصَىٰ كُلَّ شَيْءٍ عَدَدًا ٢٨

72:28 – "… wa ahsa kulla shay in 'adada. " (Surah Al-Jinn)

"… has enumerated all things in number. " (The Jinn, 72:2)

FAJR (MORNING) IS THE RISING OF LIFE AND *ASR* (AFTERNOON) IS THE SETTING OF LIFE

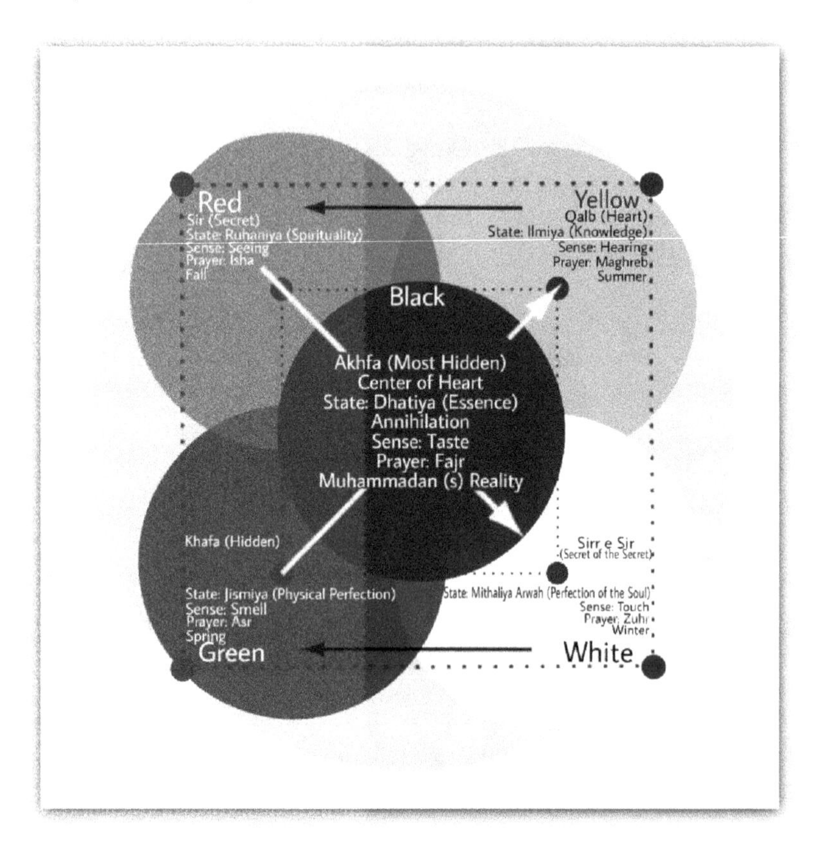

That's why then the two most powerful prayers are going to be the *Fajr* and *Asr*. *Fajr* because the rising of light, the rising of life, and between *Asr* and *Maghrib*, because now that is the setting of life, the setting of that power.

DON'T SLEEP BETWEEN *ASR* AND *MAGHRIB*

These realities, at the 4th Station of *Khafa* (Hidden), means Allah ﷻ says, 'Why don't you look to My Creation to understand the reality better?' Then we look to the birds because they represent angelic realities. Birds are singing at what two times? Your *Asr* is a state of death; you are entering in actual energy of death. That's why Prophet ﷺ said, 'Don't sleep between *Asr* and *Maghrib*; you may go *majnoon* (insane).' Why? There is an energy being changed, a life force means a life is going and a *tajalli* of *Qiyamah* (Judgment Day), *tajalli* of death and *mawt* is coming.

BIRDS SING IN TIME OF *SALAT AL-FAJR* AND *ASR*

Allah ﷻ says, 'Why don't you look to My Creation to understand the reality better?' Then we look to the birds because they represent angelic realities. Birds are singing at what two times?

Fajr and *Asr* are the two times in which the birds and the animals come out and they praise the Divine. They praise at the rising, thanking the Divine for this grace and the beauty of life and the existence that they have. Then they are praising as *Maghrib* is coming, asking for the protection of what darkness brings of difficulty.

PRAY FOR YOUR PROTECTION AT NIGHT

عن جندب بن عبدالله رضي الله عنه قال : قال رسول الله صلى الله عليه وسلم : (مَن صَلَّى الصُّبحَ فَهُوَ فِي ذِمَّةِ اللَّهِ ، فَلا يَطلُبَنَّكُمُ اللهُ مِن ذِمَّتِهِ بِشَيْءٍ فَيُدرِكَهُ فَيَكُبَّهُ فِي نَارِ جَهَنَّمَ) .مسلم (657)

Qala Rasullullah ﷺ: 'Man Salla as Subha fa huwa fi dhimmatillahi, fala yatlubannakum ullahu min dhimmatihi bi shayin,..." (Sahih Muslim)

Prophet Muhammad ﷺ said: "Whoever prays Fajr is under the protection of Allah, so do not fall short with regard to the rights of Allah,..."
(Narrated by Muslim)

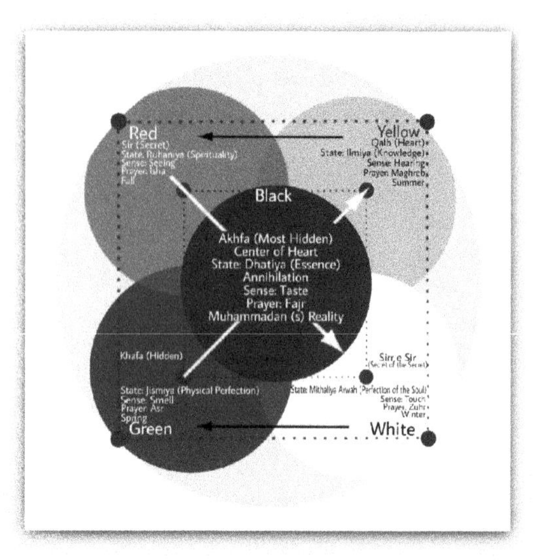

When birds sing at *Fajr*, it is very beatific when you hear it. Sayyidina Abu Bakr as-Siddiq ﷺ said, 'You already missed your *Fajr*. The birds did it before you.' When you hear the birds singing at *Fajr*, they are praising Allah ﷻ with a beatific praise, why? To receive these *tajallis* of Fajr at the Station of *Akhfa* (Most Hidden). They want this manifestation of light because they understood that, 'By *Maghrib* we may be dead, something is going to eat us; we want the manifestation of this day'; and they praise with a beatific praise.

Then go to the same birds at *Salat al-Asr*. And Burnaby (British Columbia, Canada), on the freeway, there are at least 10 thousand birds on that exit, near Willingdon, near BCIT (British Columbia Institute of Technology), right there, 10,000! Wherever there are birds, you hear their *dhikr* of *Maghrib* is not the same praising as it is at *Fajr*. As a result of that *tajalli* of death that is coming, the birds, when they recite at *Maghrib*, it's not a very pleasant sound. It's more like a crowing sound. They are begging Allah ﷻ to be protected. They are begging Allah ﷻ that their death is coming; many will die at

night and some will survive for the day. This is when they have hardship.

Prophet Muhammad ﷺ said, "A group of angels stay with you at night and (another group of) angels by daytime, and both groups gather at the time of the 'Asr and Fajr prayers. Then those angels who have stayed with you overnight, ascend and Allah asks them about you —- and He knows everything about you. 'In what state did you leave My slaves?' The angels reply, 'When we left them, they were praying, and when we reached them they were praying."
(Sahih Bukhari, Book 97, Hadith 56)

THE SAME WORD *ZULUMAT* IS FOR DARKNESS AND OPPRESSION

When the darkness comes, difficulty comes. Darkness by itself is a state of difficulty because you don't have the protection, you don't have the healing, and you don't have the power of lights that are shining. So then all of the creatures come out asking God for protection through the darkness and to survive to the light, until the light rises again, *InshaAllah.*

Allah ﷻ even described night time is *Zulumat*, is every oppression. It means you are at the 4th Station of *Khafa* (Hidden), and move to 5th Station of *Akhfa* (Most Hidden). The servant is entering into a state of oppression as they are dying in that day and that's why you need *"tawaa saw bil-haqq wa tawaa saw bil-sabr."*

That you were an oppressor to yourself that whole day, thinking that you are existing forever. 'My *Salat al-Asr* is a reminder for you, no, this day that you thought is going forever is just now in a phase of death.' And begin to see how everything is going and darkness is coming. And all the plants and the beautiful daylight have gone and now *Zulumat* (darkness) has now again descended upon that servant.

So it means it's a conscious meditation and *tafakkur* of the *salah*, that, '*Ya Rabbi*,' that, '*Salat al-Asr* is coming and I'm entering now back into a phase of death where everything slows down, that all the running of *dunya* has put itself down and I'm entering back into that phase. And then my day and my reality of the heavens again begin at *Maghrib.*'

THE TWO POWERFUL STATIONS: *KHAFA* (HIDDEN) AND THE *AKHFA* (MOST HIDDEN)

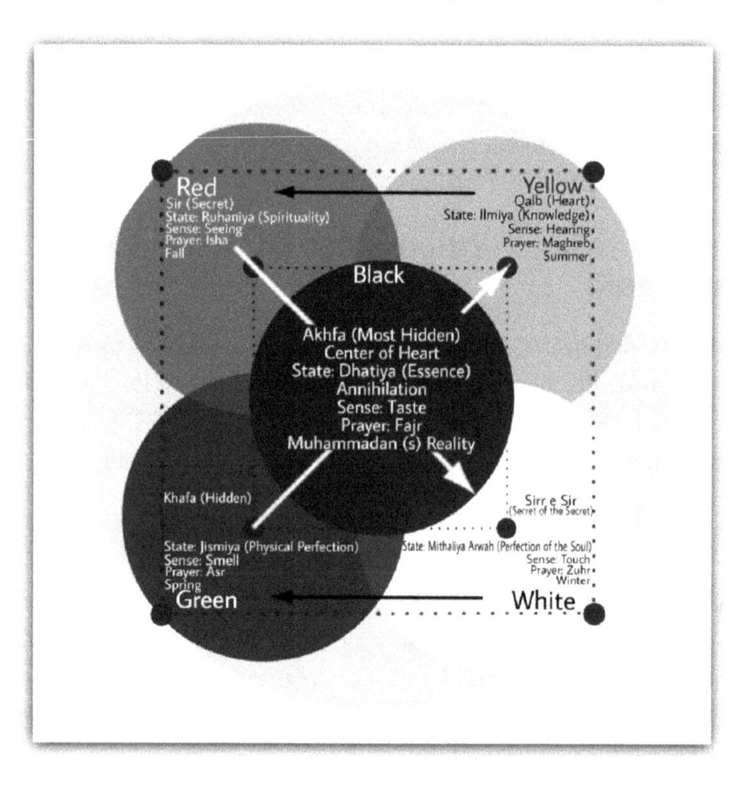

So the two powerful points are the 4th Station *Khafa* (Hidden) and Center point, 5th Station *Akhfa* (Most Hidden). Where the birds are singing is *Salat al-Fajr* because they are coming through this *Fajr*, at *Akhfa*, which is actually *Farij* (opening), it is your salvation. With your *Farij* and your *zuhur*, you are manifesting. From the time you manifest, you are only living until *Asr* and you are dead by *Asr*. Then from *Asr*, it is going to pass a death point, the fifth station of *Akhfa*, to the *Maghrib* the 1st Station, the *Qalb* (Heart), which is the setting of the sun

It means everything is going; the darkness has come again and from *Asr*, you are going back into that ocean of reality because you are passing the *Akhfa tajalli*. Each of these names have a tremendous reality, that that *Fajr* and that *Asr* is passing the *Akhfa* reality. The *Akhfa* reality is a black hole in which it takes everything in and nothing remains and this is the annihilation. That is the station of annihilation in which the servant is to be dressed by annihilation. And these are the servants of *mawt wa qabl al mawt* (death before death).

Subhana rabbika rabil 'izzati 'ama yasifoon, Wa salamun 'alal mursaleen wal hamdulillahi rabbil 'alameen. Bi hurmati Muhammadil Mustafa wa bi siratil Suratil Fatiha.

DHIKR AND THE LEVELS OF THE MUHAMMADAN HEART

1. ***SUBHANALLAH* (GLORY BE TO ALLAH)**
STATION OF *QALB* (HEART)

2. ***ALHAMDULILLAH* (PRAISE BE TO ALLAH)**
STATION OF *SIR* (SECRET)

3. ***LA ILAHA ILALLAH* (THERE IS NO GOD BUT ALLAH)**
STATION OF *SIRR E SIR* (SECRET OF THE SECRET)

4. ***ALLAHU AKBAR* (ALLAH IS GREAT)**
STATION OF *KHAFA* (HIDDEN)

5. ***LA HAWLA WA LA QUWWATA ILLA BILLAH***
(THERE IS NO SUPPORT AND NO POWER EXCEPT IN ALLAH)
STATION OF *AKHFA* (MOST HIDDEN)

يَاأَيُّهَا الَّذِينَ آمَنُوا أَطِيعُوااللَّه وَأَطِيعُوالرَّسُولَ وَأُوْلِي الأَمْرِ مِنْكُمْ

4:59 – "Ya ayyu hal ladheena amanoo Atiullaha wa atiur Rasola wa Ulil amre minkum…" (Surah An-Nisa)

"O You who have believed, Obey Allah, Obey the Messenger, and those in authority among you…" (The Women, 4:59)

As we attempt to draw closer to the heavenly kingdom, to that Divinely Reality where we become more and more aware of our nothingness, that Allah's عزّ وجلّ Greatness is beyond imagination. We pray that Allah عزّ وجلّ grant us His Divinely Forgiveness and Divinely Lights.

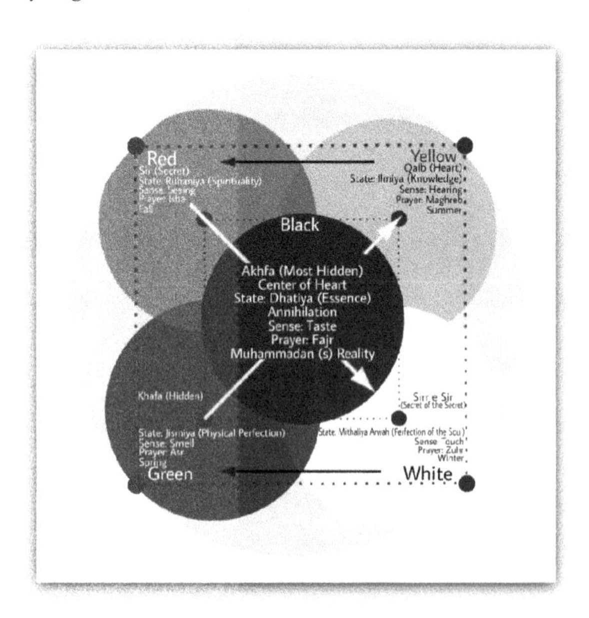

From the understanding of the *Lataif al Qalb* and the levels of the heart, that it moves like an hourglass. For us to understand upon the body; I'm moving from left of the chest, the *Qalb* (Heart), to right of the chest, the *Sir* (Secret), back down to the left of the abdomen at *Sirr e Sir*, (Secret of the Secret), then to the right of the abdomen *Khafa* (Hidden) at the right, and then back to the middle of the abdomen, the *Akhfa* (Most Hidden). Then it starts again at *Qalb* (Heart). So it is like a figure 8 across your chest and it is an eternal hourglass.

LATAIF AL QALB IS ABOUT THE MUHAMMADAN ﷺ HEART

From that reality of the heart in which every reality is within that reality, it is not only understanding and unveiling our heart, because we negate that we are nothing. That, 'My heart is a imitated heart, *ya Rabbi*; I'm not claiming that anything lies within me, but I'm asking to negate myself.' The only heart that counts is the heart of Sayyidina Muhammad ﷺ. This is a *marifah* into the heart of Prophet ﷺ. This has nothing to do with us.

We call it our Levels of the Heart because Allah ﷻ describes, 'I show you My Signs within yourself and upon the horizon.'

سَنُرِيهِمْ آيَاتِنَا فِي الْآفَاقِ وَفِي أَنفُسِهِمْ حَتَّىٰ يَتَبَيَّنَ لَهُمْ أَنَّهُ الْحَقُّ ۗ ... ٥٣

41:53 – "Sanureehim ayatina fil afaqi wa fee anfusihim hatta yatabayyana lahum annahu alhaqqu ..." (Surah Al-Isra)

"We will show them Our signs in the horizons and within themselves until it becomes clear to them that it is the truth..." (The Night Journey, 41:53)

Sometimes the inner self may be something to understand, especially in the way of the *marifah* (Gnosticism), that you focus upon your heart and you realize your heart is but nothing. That, 'I'm nothing, I'm like epsilon, the dot in non-existence.' Then whose heart is counting? It is the heart of Sayyidina Muhammad ﷺ.

Allah عز و جل, 'I'm not in heaven and I'm not on earth; but I'm in the heart of that reality.'

مَا وَسِعَنِيْ سَمَائِيْ ولا اَرْضِيْ وَلَكِنْ وَسِعَنِيْ قَلْبِ عَبْدِيْ اَلْمُؤْمِنْ

"Maa wasi`anee Samayee, wa la ardee, laakin wasi'anee qalbi 'Abdee al Mu'min."

"Neither My Heavens nor My Earth can contain Me, but the heart of my Believing Servant." (Hadith Qudsi conveyed by Prophet Muhammad ﷺ)

There is no place that you are going to die and that you are going to see Allah عز و جل, *la sharik* (Allah has no partner)! When Allah عز و جل has a Divinely Kingdom, has a Kingdom of Light. That Kingdom of Light has a palace of a heart, central command. This understanding of *Lataif al Qalb* is a story in the heart of Sayyidina Muhammad ﷺ. So we teach it from ourselves, but its reality is in the *marif'ah* of Prophet ﷺ.

The *dhikr* is the *SubhanAllah wa Alhamdulillah, La ilaha illallah, Allahu Akbar*, and then at the *Akhfa; la hawla wa la quwwata illa billahil Aliyil 'Azheem*. That how these *dhikrs* and the importance of the reality of that *dhikr* in the Muhammadan heart that we are trying to reflect.

POLISH YOUR HEART FOR THE MUHAMMADAN LIGHT TO REFLECT

It means Prophet ﷺ described that, 'We are a mirror,' that the believer is a mirror to his brother. The greatest mirror in the Divinely Presence is Sayyidina Muhammad ﷺ reflecting all of Allah's عزَّ وجلَّ realities.

المؤمن مرآة المؤمن

"Al mu'min miratal mu'min."

"The believer is the mirror of the believer." (Abu Hurairah)

So when we are trying to understand our heart, we are beginning to realize this is nothing, the real heart that's trying to reflect. So then all of Islam comes to teach then purify your heart, clean your heart – why? When you purify and clean the heart and take away the bad character, *"Qul jaa al-haqq."*

وَ قُلْ جَآءَالْحَقُّ وَزَهَقَ الْبَطِلُ، إِنَّ الْبَطِلَ كَانَ زَهُوقًا

17:81 – "Wa qul jaa alhaqqu wa zahaqal baatil, innal batila kana zahooqa." (Surah Al-Isra)

"And say, "Truth has come, and falsehood has perished. Indeed falsehood, [by its nature], is ever perishing/ bound to perish." (The Night Journey, 17:81)

This *haqq* (truth) of Allah عزّ وجلّ that is reflecting to the *haqq* of Prophet صلى الله عليه وسلم. Prophet صلى الله عليه وسلم is the manifestation of Allah's عزّ وجلّ *Haqq* because you are not going to see Allah's عزّ وجلّ *Haqq*. There is no *sharik* (partner) with Allah عزّ وجلّ.

So the apex of truth is the light of Prophet صلى الله عليه وسلم. For that light of Prophet صلى الله عليه وسلم to reflect, it can't come to something false and it can't come to something dirty. So as we begin to clean and purify, clean and purify the heart, then the *Haqq* of Allah عزّ وجلّ, the *haqq* of Sayyidina Muhammad صلى الله عليه وسلم begins to reflect. So you think it as your heart but in reality you are non-existent. It's the heart that counts; it is the heart of Sayyidina Muhammad صلى الله عليه وسلم.

1. Station of *Qalb* (Heart) - Knowledge

Qalb is the Doorway to the Presence of Prophet صلى الله عليه وسلم - the Owner of Divine Knowledge

So this way of *marif'ah* and the understanding of the *Lataif al Qalb* is the doorway into the presence of Prophet صلى الله عليه وسلم. That's why you can understand the *lataif* in the understanding of the Companions. So we went with the Companions. We said Sayyidina Uthman عليه السلام, *Jami'ul Qur'an*, compiler of Holy Qur'an, is at the station of *Qalb* (Heart), because *Qalb* is the station of knowledge – why? Because knowledge comes to the *qalb*.

Knowledge Without Wisdom is Dangerous

So it means the *qalb* (heart) itself is a door to all knowledge; that knowledge will be deposited into the heart, not into your mind. Anything that you read through your mind is not this knowledge that Allah ﷻ is talking, *"Ittaqullah wa Alimukumullah."*

واتقوا الله وَيُعَلِّمُكُمُ الله والله بِكُلِّ شَيْء عَلِيمٌ...

2:282 – "...Wat taqollaha, wa yu'allimukumullahu, wallahu bi kulli shayin 'Aleem." (Surah Al-Baqarah)

"...And Be conscious of/fear Allah, And Allah teaches you. And Allah is the All Knower of everything." (The Cow, 2:282)

Allah ﷻ says you have to have a consciousness, 'I'm going to teach you'. *'Alama* – 'I'm going to teach you from the heavenly knowledges but I have to bestow upon you a *hikmah* (wisdom). If I give you knowledge without wisdom, you are dangerous. If you lead knowledge with no wisdom, you are dangerous.'

It means Allah ﷻ is going to send it with a balance; so knowledge that counts is what Allah ﷻ wants to send into the heart. So the *qalb* (heart) is the vessel for all knowledge and reality. It is that doorway from our heart that connects into the heart of Prophet ﷺ, and this is, *"Wa laqad karamna."*

وَلَقَدْ كَرَّمْنَا بَنِي آدَمَ...

17:70 – "Wa laqad karramna bani adama..." (Surah Al-Isra)

"And We have certainly honored the children of Adam..."
(The Night Journey, 17:70)

This is when Allah ﷻ is describing, 'I have honoured your creation; I gave you a means in which to reach to the heart of Prophet ﷺ. You have a *qalb*; you have a will, you have a permission to enter your heart.' So Prophet ﷺ described, "Who knows himself will know his *Rabb*."

مَنْ عَرَفَ نَفْسَهُ فَقَدْ عَرَفَ رَبَّهُ

"Man 'arafa nafsahu faqad 'arafa Rabbahu."

"Who knows himself, knows his Lord." (Prophet Muhammad ﷺ)

"Who knows himself will know his *Rabb*". It means 'come through this door; you will begin to learn who Prophet ﷺ is.' The Muhammadan heart is the heart that has all realities.

THE *DHIKR* OF THE MUHAMMADAN HEART AT THE *LATAIF AL QALB*

Then from the *Qalb* (Heart) we go to the *Sir* (Secret), and the *Sir* is the station of prayers, the station of vision. Then to the *Sirr e Sir* (Secret of the Secret), which becomes the station of lights, the station of purity. Then to the *Khafa* (Hidden), which is now the rising into the heavenly dimensions all the way to the *Akhfa* (Most Hidden), which is the Divinely Presence and annihilation.

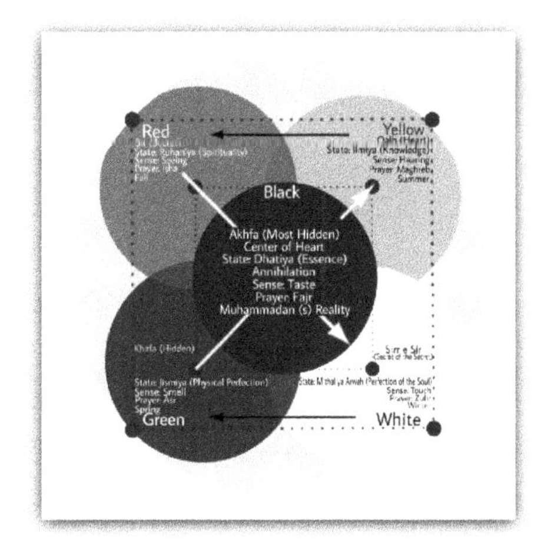

The *dhikr* of '*SubhanAllah*' at *Qalb* (Heart) left side of the chest, '*wa Alhamdulillah*' at *Sir* (Secret) at right side of chest, '*wa La ilaha illallah*' at *Sirr e Sir* (Secret of the Secret) to the left part of abdomen, '*Allahu Akbar*' at *Khafa* (Hidden) to right of abdomen; and to the center *Akhfa*, '*La hawla wa la quwwata illa billahil Aliyil 'Azheem*' (There is no Support and no Power except in Allah, the most high), in the hand of Prophet ﷺ; *hawla and quwwa* (support and power).

PROPHETS AT THE LEVELS OF THE HEART

SAYYIDINA ADAM عليه السلام AT THE STATION OF *QALB* قلب (HEART)

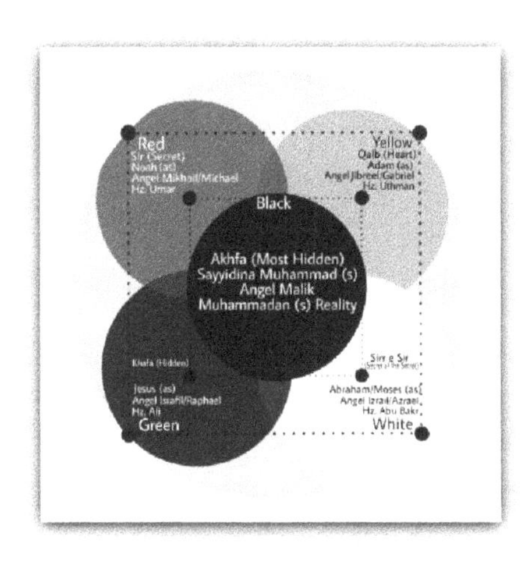

It means then that everything in the Muhammadan way is beginning to teach that Sayyidina Adam عليه السلام is at the station of *Qalb* (Heart). So Prophet ﷺ wants to teach that, 'My heart has the secret of all these messengers because they represented by message.' There is only one messenger of Allah عز و جل; *La ilaha illallah, Muhammadun RasulAllah* ﷺ (There is no God but Allah, Muhammad ﷺ is the

Messenger of Allah. So the message that all the prophets brought was a message from within the secrets of Holy Qur'an; it means all *kitaabs* (holy books) can be found in the reality of Holy Qur'an.

So then Sayyidina Adam ﷵ has a reality in the heart of Prophet ﷺ. Then you go from Sayyidina Adam ﷵ, to Sayyidina Nuh ﷵ, and *Iman* and faith. Then to Sayyidina Ibrahim ﷵ and Sayyidina Musa ﷵ the faculties of faith; now divine hearing, divine seeing is beginning to open. Sayyidina Isa ﷵ, about the *mi'raj* (ascension) and the uplifting towards the heavens, and Sayyidina Muhammad's ﷺ *haqqaiq* and realities in the *Akhfa*, which means now you are entering into that presence.

Importance of Choosing a Teacher and Spiritual Guide

Sayyidina Adam ﷵ was taught all the names:

وَعَلَّمَ آدَمَ الْأَسْمَاءَ كُلَّهَا...٣١

2:31 – "Wa 'allama Adamal Asma a kullaha..." (Surah Al-Baqarah)

"And He taught Adam the names of all things ..." (The Cow, 2:31)

But before Sayyidina Adam ﷵ was created, there was another teacher. There was an *imam* called *Shaytan*. His *uloom* and knowledge was something that he acquired it himself. This is an important understanding, that the *uloom* of *Azazeel* (Satan's name) which he was teaching himself acquiring knowledge. And from *dunya* he was elevating with that knowledge towards the *samaa* (heavens).

That he had learned many things and had prostrated everywhere. They say wherever you walk there is a prostration from *Shaytan*, that he had prostrated in every place of this Earth. His worshiping was very strong. He started to seek his knowledges where he was training himself and he was acquiring those knowledges.

As a result of this knowledge, he was moving towards the Heaven and he would begin to teach the *Malaika* (angels). This is an important understanding, that the *Malaika* were impressed by the knowledge that *Shaytan* had. At that time he was not (yet) *Shaytan* (Satan), he was a *jinn*. He had acquired a tremendous amount of knowledge and the *Malaika* (angels) were learning from his knowledge.

Angels Learned Bad Characteristics From *Shaytan*

But what happened in this whole event with the creation of Sayyidina Adam عليه السلام, is that the *Malaika* (angels), as a result of studying from *Shaytan*, began to acquire the characteristics of *Shaytan*, where they had *shak* (doubt). Because when Allah عز وجل was going to create the form of Sayyidina Adam عليه السلام, the *Malaika* (angels) came and questioned. Where *Malaika* (angels) are not supposed to have any questions, *sami`na wa ata`na*, they hear and they obey. They came and heard and said, "What is this Creation that You are going to create? They will create a bloodshed on Earth?"

وَإِذْ قَالَ رَبُّكَ لِلْمَلاَئِكَةِ إِنِّي جَاعِلٌ فِي الأَرْضِ خَلِيفَةً قَالُواْ أَتَجْعَلُ فِيهَا مَن يُفْسِدُ فِيهَا
وَيَسْفِكُ الدِّمَاء وَنَحْنُ نُسَبِّحُ بِحَمْدِكَ وَنُقَدِّسُ لَكَ قَالَ إِنِّي أَعْلَمُ مَا لاَ تَعْلَمُونَ

2:30 – "Wa idh qala rabbuka lilmalayekati innee ja'ilun fil ardi khaleefatan, qaloo ataj'alu feeha man yufsidu feeha wa yasfikud dima a wa nahnu nusabbihu bihamdika wa nuqaddisu laka, qala innee a'lamu ma la ta'lamoon."
(Surah Al-Baqarah)

"And [mention, O Muhammad], when your Lord said to the angels, "Indeed, I will make upon the earth a Representative/ successive authority." They [angels] said, "Will You place upon it one who causes corruption therein and sheds blood,

while we declare Your praise and sanctify You?" Allah said, "Indeed, I know that which you do not know." (The Cow, 2:30)

Be Careful Who You Pick as a Teacher and an *Imam* (Leader)

It means they had *shak*, they had doubt. Who did they get that *shak* (doubt) from? From their teacher. That is why Allah ﷻ is warning, 'I am going to raise you with your *imam* (leader),' because your *imam* is dressing you with his character.

يَوْمَ نَدْعُو كُلَّ أُنَاسٍ بِإِمَامِهِمْ ۖ فَمَنْ أُوتِيَ كِتَابَهُ بِيَمِينِهِ فَأُولَـٰئِكَ يَقْرَءُونَ كِتَابَهُمْ وَلَا يُظْلَمُونَ فَتِيلًا (٧١)

17:71 – "Yawma nad'oo kulla onasin bi imamihim ..." (Surah Al Isra)

"[Mention, O Muhammad], the Day We will call forth All Human Beings with their imam [Guides/Records]..." (The Night Journey, 17:71)

The *Imam* is dressing you with his *akhlaq* (manners). He is not only dressing you from his *uloom*, his knowledge because the knowledge, maybe everybody has a certain level, but the characters and the manners are going to be dressed upon that person. Are you going to be a rude person with the knowledge that you have? If that *imam* is rude he will teach you how to be rude. If that *imam* is vulgar and harsh, then he will teach the *jama'ah* (community) to be vulgar and harsh. He is multiplying his character wherever he goes.

It means for us it is a tremendous warning and a tremendous understanding. That not only knowledge is being conveyed to me, but more importantly it is the character because I watch the character. I watch how he is acting, how he is talking and how he is interacting with people. Does he think that people are below him, and that there are other people above him? Or does he think he is the lowest and that he is here to serve Allah's عزَّ وجلَّ Creation? Not to judge them! The first of *usool* (jurisprudence) is not to judge, Not to be *sharik* (partner with Allah). This is the biggest *shirk*, to come sit and judge Allah's عزَّ وجلَّ Creation. Allah عزَّ وجلَّ created that creation; we are here merely to be a *khadim*, a servant of Allah عزَّ وجلَّ, *inshaAllah,* if He accepts us.

1. *SUBHANALLAH* (GLORY BE TO ALLAH) IS THE *DHIKR* AT STATION OF THE *QALB* (HEART)

They begin to teach that when *Shaytan* is teaching *Malaika*, the angels begin to have doubt and *shak*. And when Allah عزَّ وجلَّ had enough, He knows His Creation and what *Shaytan* is doing. He knows the *uloom* (knowledges) with which *Shaytan* is raising himself with. Allah عزَّ وجلَّ says I am going to show his *uloom* in one shot. In one test I am going to send him and it will show his entire knowledge that had no *yaqeen* (certainty), it was just empty knowledge. If he had *yaqeen* he would have known the light that is within Sayyidina Adam عليه السلام.

PROPHECY OF SAYYIDINA MUHAMMAD ﷺ IS ANCIENT

As soon as Allah عزَّ وجلَّ brought the creation of Sayyidina Adam عليه السلام, put into him from that breath; that was what breath? It was from *Nur Muhammad* ﷺ, where the *Hadith* of Prophet ﷺ said, I was a *Rasul* before Adam was between clay and water.

كُنْتُ نَبِيًّا وَآدَمُ بَيْنَ الْمَاءِ وَالطِّينِ

"Kuntu Nabiyan wa Adama baynal Maa e wat Teen."

"I was a Prophet and Adam was between clay and water."
(Prophet Muhammad ﷺ)

The *risalat* (Prophecy) of Sayyidina Muhammad ﷺ was first, was *qadeem* (ancient). That nobody talks to Allah عزوجل, they talk to *Rasulullah* (Messenger of Allah) ﷺ. That *nur*, that light Allah عزوجل says, "I am going to bring it and put it into the *Khalifah* (Viceroy)."

That *Khalifah* (Viceroy) is going to be the supreme *Khalifah*, he is going to be the *mu'allim* (teacher), because this is the light of Sayyidina Muhammad ﷺ coming in. As soon as the light entered into Sayyidina Adam عليه السلام, *Allama isma kullaha.*

وَعَلَّمَ آدَمَ الْأَسْمَاءَ كُلَّهَا ثُمَّ عَرَضَهُمْ عَلَى الْمَلَائِكَةِ فَقَالَ أَنبِئُونِي بِأَسْمَاءِ هَٰؤُلَاءِ إِن كُنتُمْ صَادِقِينَ (٣١)

2:31 – "Wa 'allama Adamal Asma a kullaha, thumma 'aradahum 'alal Malaikati faqala anbioonee bi asma i haola e in kuntum sadiqeen." (Surah Al-Baqarah)

"And He taught Adam the names – all of them. Then He showed them to the angels and said, "Inform Me of the names of these, if you are truthful." (The Cow, 2:31)

Allama isma kullaha, means that light *"allamal qur'an khalaqal insaan"* is already filled with the light and knowledges of Sayyidina Muhammad ﷺ, because he was a *Rasul* before, so Allah عزوجل had already taught *allamal Qur'an, khalaqal insaan*, all the knowledge to Prophet Muhammad ﷺ.

عَلَّمَ الْقُرْآنَ (٢) خَلَقَ الْإِنسَانَ (٣)

55:2-3 – "Allamal Qur'an. Khalaqal Insaan." (Surah Ar-Rahman)

"It is He Who has taught the Qur'an. (2) He has created Man. (3)"
(The Beneficent, 55:2-3)

So *Nur Muhammadi* went into Sayyidina Adam عليه السلام. Immediately *Malaika* (angels) saw that light and they went into *sujood* (prostration). The knowledge and the light, the blessing of this light, they understood that its reality is from a *hijab* (veil) that they don't have access to. That is why on *Isra wal Mi`raj* Sayyidina Jibreel عليه السلام said, "We have a *hadd* (boundary), we don't go beyond the *hadd* (limit) or we become non-existent."

قَالُوا سُبْحَانَكَ لَا عِلْمَ لَنَا إِلَّا مَا عَلَّمْتَنَا ۖ إِنَّكَ أَنتَ الْعَلِيمُ الْحَكِيمُ (٣٢)

2:32 – "Qalo subhanaka la 'ilma lana illa ma 'allamtana, innaka antal 'Aleemul Hakeem. (32)" (Surah Al-Baqarah)

"They said, "Exalted are You; we have no knowledge except what You have taught us. Indeed, it is You who is the Knowing, the Wise." (The Cow, 2:32)

They saw that light from the *had* coming into Sayyidina Adam عليه السلام. That light gave all the knowledge, *Uloom al-Awwaleen wal Akhireen.* And *Malaika* understood, this is *Allama*, this knowledge Allah عزَّ وجلَّ had conveyed; *allama* is from Allah عزَّ وجلَّ to the servant.

SAYYIDINA ADAM عليه السلام WAS A VESSEL TO BRING *NUR MUHAMMADI* TO EARTH

So it means then what does the *Surah Al-Baqarah* (Verse 31 and 32) describe.

وَعَلَّمَ آدَمَ الْأَسْمَاءَ كُلَّهَا ثُمَّ عَرَضَهُمْ عَلَى الْمَلَائِكَةِ فَقَالَ أَنبِئُونِي بِأَسْمَاءِ هَٰؤُلَاءِ إِن كُنتُمْ صَادِقِينَ (٣١)

2:31 – "Wa 'allama Adamal Asma a kullaha, thumma 'aradahum 'alal Malaikati faqala anbioonee bi asma i haola e in kuntum sadiqeen."
(Surah Al-Baqarah)

"And He taught Adam the names – all of them. Then He showed them to the angels and said, "Inform Me of the names of these, if you are truthful."
(The Cow, 2:31)

Isma kullaha means this was the dialogue in the understanding of this door that's opening, that when Allah عز وجل created Sayyidina Adam عليه السلام, and said, 'Now this is a vehicle in which I am going to bring My Realities onto this world of form.'

...وَإِذْ قَالَ رَبُّكَ لِلْمَلَائِكَةِ إِنِّي جَاعِلٌ فِي الأَرْضِ خَلِيفَةً

2:30 – "Wa idh qala rabbuka lil Malaikati innee ja'ilun fil ardi khaleefatan, ..." (Surah Al-Baqarah)

"And [mention, O Muhammad], when your Lord said to the angels, "Indeed, I will make upon the earth a Representative/successive authority..."
(The Cow, 2:30)

The physicality of Sayyidina Adam عليه السلام was created for the *mulk* (earth), to bring the realities of *malakut* (heavens). It was just a stopping in *malakut* to go down to where – the *mulk*, and was bringing the *haqqaiq* (realities) and the lights that Allah عز وجل had not exposed yet.

So it means then now, what we are understanding *Isma kullaha*, this is the *baab* (door) of knowledge. Where Allah عز وجل says, 'You want *Isma kullaha*, you want all the realities', that Sayyidina Adam عليه السلام is merely a vehicle or vessel that contained; he is bringing all the realities of Sayyidina Muhammad صلى الله عليه وسلم.

Angels Bowed Down to the Light They Saw in Sayyidina Adam ﷺ

Nur ul Muhammadi is the light that dressed Sayyidina Adam ﷺ, that the angels were in awe of that light that they had not seen but they know that it came from behind a veil of the Divinely Presence. As a result of the *ihtiram* (respect), they made *sujood* (prostration). They bowed down for the *ihtiram* and the respect of that light, which they knew it to be from Divinely Presence.

وَإِذْ قُلْنَا لِلْمَلَائِكَةِ اسْجُدُوا لِآدَمَ فَسَجَدُوا... (٣٤)

2:34 – "Wa idh qulna lilMalaikati osjudo li Adama fasajado…" (Surah Al-Baqarah)

"And [mention] when We said to the angels, "Bow Down to Adam"; so they prostrated …" (The Cow, 2:34)

Then this opening of knowledge from Sayyidina Adam ﷺ is inspiring within the heart that you want *Isma kullaha*, that the angels were astonished by this knowledge.

Angels Said, "Glory Be to You"; We Only Know What You Taught Us

Then the next verse of *Surah Al-Baqarah*, 2:32 is, Say *Subhanallah* (Glory be to Allah).

قَالُوا سُبْحَانَكَ لَا عِلْمَ لَنَا إِلَّا مَا عَلَّمْتَنَا ۖ إِنَّكَ أَنتَ الْعَلِيمُ الْحَكِيمُ (٣٢)

2:32 – "Qalo subhanaka la 'ilma lana illa ma 'allamtana, innaka antal 'Aleemul Hakeem." (Surah Al-Baqarah)

"They said, "Exalted are You; we have no knowledge except what You have taught us. Indeed, it is You who is the Knowing, the Wise." (The Cow, 2:32)

That is what Allah عزّ وجلّ is saying, *"Qalu subhanaka,"*- 'Glorify Me' because this knowledge that I bestowed, Allah عزّ وجلّ wants to show, 'You want this knowledge' because the angels and everything in *malakut* want knowledge; they want realities, they are fed realities. What they were being fed was nowhere in proximity to that knowledge because this is now from the deep *haqqaiqs* of Sayyidina Muhammad ﷺ that is coming.

Prophet Muhammad ﷺ is the Eternal Messenger of Allah عزّ وجلّ

The creation of Sayyidina Adam عليه السلام was to bring these realities because *"Wa ma arsalnaka rahmatan lil-'aalameen."*

وَمَا أَرْسَلْنَاكَ إِلَّا رَحْمَةً لِّلْعَالَمِينَ ١٠٧

21:107 – "Wa maa arsalnaka illa Rahmatan lil'alameen." (Surah Al-Anbiya)

"And We have not sent you, [O Muhammad], except as a mercy to the worlds." (The Prophets, 21:107)

'I only created Adam so that your light would be known to creation' and that's why Prophet ﷺ clarified in the *Hadith Al-Jabr, "An awal khalqillah"*- 'I am the first that Allah عزّ وجلّ created before Adam was between clay and water.'

كُنْتُ نَبِيًّا وَآدَمُ بَيْنَ الْمَاءِ وَالطِّينِ

"Kuntu Nabiyan wa Adama baynal Maa e wat Teen."

"I was a Prophet and Adam was between clay and water."
(Prophet Muhammad ﷺ)

So RasulAllah ﷺ has always been; it's eternal. *Rasul* (messenger), 'I'm the one who speaks for Allah عز وجل. I speak throughout the heavens. I teach throughout the heavens'. The *Rasul* teaches; Allah عز وجل teaches the *Rasul* ﷺ, not teaching the *insaan* (human being). Nobody can carry the Speech of Allah عز وجل. The *Rasul* ﷺ is eternally created to deliver the message of Allah عز وجل.

SUBHANALLAH – GLORIFY ALLAH عز وجل AT EVERY MOMENT OF YOUR LIFE

Then (Allah) is clarifying that you want this, you want these realities? Allah عز وجل is saying, 'Say *Subhanallah.*' It means that *maqam* of *Subhan* is then they become the angels, 'I want to bring these *uloom* and the knowledges into the heart,' because now you have to reflect the Divine Presence. You have to reflect the *malakut* and the heavenly lights of heaven that make a life in which you are glorifying Allah عز وجل at every moment of your life. Because now you want to enter into these realities. You cannot enter the reality if you are not making continuous *Subhan* (glorification). If you are not continuously glorifying Allah عز وجل, because the next *maqam* is going to be *hamd* (praise).

So it means Allah's عز وجل *Subhan* is immense which means we can't go deeper. So you live a life of *Subhanallah.* [Some people force you to say '*Subhanallah*', when they speak. No! It's not that.] It is that our life is *Subhanallah.* Everything from Allah عز وجل is *Subhanallah.* The angels are teaching, glorify Allah عز وجل; He wants to be glorified. It's not a life where they ask you, 'Why you have to make *dhikr*?' 'Say, we are the people searching from the world of *malakut.*'

The *malakut* (heavens), the angels and the world of light, their whole

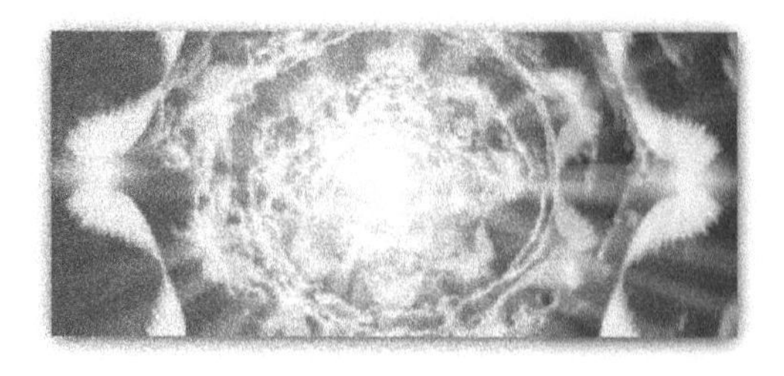

existence is in praising Allah ﷻ, is in glorifying Allah ﷻ. They are not interested in accounting; they are not talking about sports and soccer, and who played this game and who played that game. The angels are coming and saying, 'You want these knowledges, the knowledges that we were astonished at; live a life in which everything is *Subhanallah, Subhanallah.*'

ALLAH ﷻ SHOWED HIS *SUBHAN* (GLORY) TO NABI MUSA عليه السلام

Then Allah ﷻ clarifies that, 'If you want to really glorify Me,' what Nabi Musa عليه السلام asked, 'I want to see you, *ya Rabbi.*' He Says, 'You want to see me? Look to the mountain. I'm going to send My *Subhan*; I'm going to send My Glory onto the mountain. If you could take that, we talk.'

وَلَمَّا جَاءَ مُوسَىٰ لِمِيقَاتِنَا وَكَلَّمَهُ رَبُّهُ قَالَ رَبِّ أَرِنِي أَنظُرْ إِلَيْكَ ۚ قَالَ لَن تَرَانِي وَلَـٰكِنِ انظُرْ إِلَى الْجَبَلِ فَإِنِ اسْتَقَرَّ مَكَانَهُ فَسَوْفَ تَرَانِي ۚ فَلَمَّا تَجَلَّىٰ رَبُّهُ لِلْجَبَلِ جَعَلَهُ دَكًّا وَخَرَّ مُوسَىٰ صَعِقًا ۚ فَلَمَّا أَفَاقَ قَالَ سُبْحَانَكَ تُبْتُ إِلَيْكَ وَأَنَا أَوَّلُ الْمُؤْمِنِينَ (١٤٣)

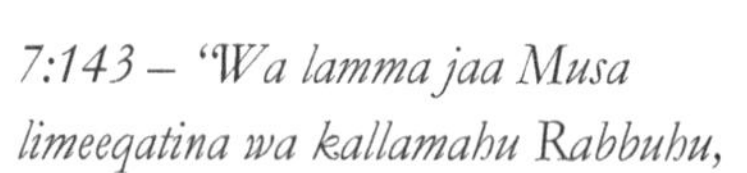

7:143 – "Wa lamma jaa Musa limeeqatina wa kallamahu Rabbuhu, qala rabbi arinee anzhur ilayka, Qala lan taranee wa lakini onzhur ilal jabali fa inistaqarra makanahu, fasawfa taranee, falamma tajalla Rabbuhu lil jabali ja`alahu, dakkan wa kharra Musa sa`iqan, falamma afaqa qala Subhanaka tubtu ilayka wa ana awwalul Mumineen." (Surah Al-A'raf)

"And when Moses arrived at Our appointed time and his Lord spoke to him, he said, 'My Lord, show me [Yourself] that I may look at You."

[Allah] said, "you will not see Me, but look at the mountain; if it should remain in its place, then you will see Me." But when his Lord manifested His glory on the mountain, He made it as dust, and Moses fell unconscious. And when he awoke/recovered his senses, he said, "Glory be to You! to You I turn in repentance, and I am the first of the believers." (The Heights, 7:143)

What was Allah's ﷻ Glory that Nabi Musa ﵇ saw? It was the light of Sayyidina Muhammad ﷺ. 124,000 prophets appeared and Sayyidina Muhammad ﷺ in front and opened a deep reality that Allah's ﷻ Glory is His Creation; and the best of His Creation is Sayyidina Muhammad ﷺ.

So, Allah ﷻ says, 'If you truly love Me and want to glorify Me, don't you see the greatness of what I sent to you? Don't you see the greatness of your life and your existence, as in, all its secrets are coming from Sayyidina Muhammad ﷺ?'

It means then a continuous life of *SubhanAllah, SubhanAllah*; that's why in *Surah Ar-Rahman*, Allah ﷻ said, 'Thank Me for the grapes, the figs, the dates, the grass,' hinting that, 'My Greatest Favour is I gave you Sayyidina Muhammad ﷺ, '*Wa ma arsalnaka rahmatal lil-'aalameen."*

فِيهِمَا فَاكِهَةٌ وَنَخْلٌ وَرُمَّانٌ (٦٨) فَبِأَيِّ آلَاءِ رَبِّكُمَا تُكَذِّبَانِ (٦٩)

55:68-69 – "Feehimaa faakihatunw wa nakhlunw wa rummaan . (68) Fabi ayyi aalaaa'i Rabbikumaa tukazzibaan. (69)." (Surah Ar-Rahman)

'In both of them are fruit and palm trees and pomegranates.(68) So which of the favors of your Lord would you deny? (69)" (The Most Compassionate, 55:68-69)

وَمَا أَرْسَلْنَاكَ إِلَّا رَحْمَةً لِّلْعَالَمِينَ ١٠٧

21:107 – 'Wa maa arsalnaka illa Rahmatan lil'alameen." (Surah Al-Anbiya)

"And We have not sent you, [O Muhammad], except as a mercy to the worlds." (The Prophets, 21:107)

Sayyidina Muhammad ﷺ is an immense treasure of creation. 'I sent that treasure for you. Did you find it? If you found it, glorify Me day and night because I guided you to that reality'.

...وَقَالُوا الْحَمْدُ لِلَّـهِ الَّذِي هَدَانَا لِهَـٰذَا وَمَا كُنَّا لِنَهْتَدِيَ لَوْلَا أَنْ هَدَانَا اللَّـهُ ۖ لَقَدْ جَاءَتْ رُسُلُ رَبِّنَا بِالْحَقِّ ...(٤٣)

7:43 – "...wa qalo Alhamdulillahi al ladhee hadana lihadha wa ma kunna linahtadiya lawla an hadana Allahu, laqad jaa at Rusulu Rabbina bil Haqqi..." (Surah Al-A'raf)

"... And they will say, 'Praise be to Allah, who has guided us to this [joy and happiness]; and we would never have been guided if Allah had not guided us. Certainly the messengers of our Lord had come with the truth..." (The Heights, 7:43)

WHO TAUGHT THE REALITIES TO ALL PROPHETS?

The angels are then teaching glorify, glorify Allah عز وجل so that He can teach you. *'Alama Isma kullaha* (He taught Adam, all the Names) *(Holy Qur'an 2:31).* Who taught the names to Sayyidina Adam عليه السلام is the *Akhfa* (Most Hidden) reality. Where our *mi'raj* (ascension) is going is to presence of Prophet ﷺ. Who taught Sayyidina Adam عليه السلام all the realities – Allah عز وجل? Allah عز وجل says, 'I only speak to Sayyidina Muhammad ﷺ; there is nothing that can contain My *Qaf.* And Allah عز وجل says in Qur'an, *'Qaf, wal-Qur'an al-Majeed."*

ق ۚ وَالْقُرْآنِ الْمَجِيدِ ١

50:1– "Qaf, wal Qur'anil Majeed." (Surah Qaf)

"Qaf. By the honored Qur'an." (Qaf, 50:1)

'Nobody can contain My Qur'an. So when I speak it is Qur'an'. Nabi Musa عليه السلام doesn't have Qur'an; Sayyidina Isa عليه السلام doesn't have Qur'an; Sayyidina Nuh عليه السلام has no Qur'an. None of them can contain that *Qaf.*

So who they spoke to was that *Hadith* of Prophet صلى الله عليه وسلم, 'I was the *Rasul.* I am the *Rasul*; I am the Messenger of Allah عزّ وجلّ. In the world of light, my soul has always been teaching them, has always been talking to them. They know it, they don't know it; they are behind a veil.'

It means then all those realities of *Akhfa* (Fifth Station) were teaching Sayyidina Adam عليه السلام in the *qalb* (heart), in the *Lataif al Qalb* (First Station). It means that, 'You want *Isma kullaha*, the one who taught me all realities is about to teach you'.

Prophet Muhammad صلى الله عليه وسلم Was Taught By Immense Power

Allah عزّ وجلّ describes the reality of Prophet صلى الله عليه وسلم, that he was taught by someone *Shadeed al-Quwwa*, in *Surah An-Najm. Surah An-Najm* is Allah عزّ وجلّ describing Prophet's صلى الله عليه وسلم reality.

وَالنَّجْمِ إِذَا هَوَىٰ (١) مَا ضَلَّ صَاحِبُكُمْ وَمَا غَوَىٰ (٢) وَمَا يَنطِقُ عَنِ الْهَوَىٰ (٣)
إِنْ هُوَ إِلَّا وَحْيٌ يُوحَىٰ (٤) عَلَّمَهُ شَدِيدُ الْقُوَىٰ (٥) ذُو مِرَّةٍ فَاسْتَوَىٰ (٦)

53:1-6 – "Wan Najmi idha hawa. (1) Ma dalla sahibukum wa ma ghawa. (2) Wa ma yantiqu 'anil hawa. (3) In huwa illa wahyun yooha. (4) 'Allamahu shadeedul Quwa.(5) Dho mirratin fastawa. (6)" (Surah An-Najm)

"By the star when it descends. (1) Your companion [Muhammad] has not strayed, nor has he erred. (2) Nor does he speak from [his own] desire. (3) It is not but a revelation revealed.(4) He was taught by one Mighty in Power. (5) One of soundness. And he rose to [his] true form. (6)" (The Star, 53:1-6)

He is one whom has been taught by *Shadeed al-Quwwa.* Is Allah عزّ وجلّ describing Himself, as the Creator, 'I'm the One of Immense Power. This companion of yours has been taught by My Reality. You have been taught by his reality'. This is *ihtiram* and respect, that Allah عزّ وجلّ *Shadeed al-Quwwa* doesn't teach you, teach you Sayyidina Muhammad صلى الله عليه وسلم. We are taught by Prophet صلى الله عليه وسلم, not even by Prophet صلى الله عليه وسلم, but by *ulul amr* (saints); *"Atiullah atee ar-rasul wa oolul amirn minkum."*

...يٰأَيُّهَا الَّذِينَ آمَنُوا أَطِيعُوااللَّهَ وَأَطِيعُواالرَّسُولَ وَأُوْلِي الْأَمْرِ مِنْكُمْ

4:59 – "Ya ayyu hal ladheena amanoo Atiullaha, wa atiur Rasola, wa Ulil amre minkum…" (Surah An-Nisa)

"O You who have believed, Obey Allah, Obey the Messenger, and those in authority among you…" (The Women, 4:59)

So it means that, *SubhanAllah,* a life of *SubhanAllah,* glorify Allah عزّ وجلّ *Awliyaullah* (saints) come into our life that glorify Allah عزّ وجلّ for everything but most of all, for sending us to Prophet صلى الله عليه وسلم, for having the love of Sayyidina Muhammad صلى الله عليه وسلم.

If You Want Paradise, Why Don't You Come to Circles of Paradise *(Dhikr)?*

Abu Razeen عليه السلام, a companion of Prophet صلى الله عليه وسلم, narrates that Rasulullah صلى الله عليه وسلم said, "I will show you such a thing which will strengthen you in your *deen* thereby causing you to succeed in both worlds; hold fast to the gatherings of *dhikr* and when you are in privacy, continue to engage in *dhikr*."

Then you know why *Milad an Nabi* صلى الله عليه وسلم (Celebration of birth of Prophet Muhammad صلى الله عليه وسلم), is so important; the *mehfils* (associations) are so important, and the circles and the *halaqas* of *dhikr* are so important. If everybody loves paradise, how come they are not coming to the circles of paradise? They are sitting at home on the couch and having popcorn.

Ibn Umar عليه السلام reported that the Prophet صلى الله عليه وسلم said, "When you pass by the gardens of Paradise, avail yourselves of them." The Companions asked, "What are the gardens of Paradise, O Messenger of Allah?"

He replied, "The circles of *dhikr*. There are roaming angels of Allah عز وجل who go about looking for the circles of *dhikr*, and when they find them they surround them closely. They call each other and encompass them in layers until the first heaven – the location of which is in Allah's عز وجل knowledge.

So then the people who run to the circle of paradise, they must really love to be in paradise. Allah عز وجل exhibits, 'Your life in this *dunya* was always in My circles of paradise. Imagine your life in My *akhirah* (hereafter).' If in the *dunya* you were always in the circle of paradise, imagine your *akhirah* reality. Then you know what Allah ﷻ is dressing from a *ni'mat* (blessing).

2. *ALHAMDULLILAH* (PRAISE BE TO ALLAH) IS THE *DHIKR* AT STATION OF THE *SIR* (SECRET)

SAYYIDINA NUH ﷺ TEACHES BUILD YOUR FAITH AND PRAISE ALLAH ﷻ

Then, they take us to the *Sir* (Secret), the Second Station of the heart. The *Sir* and the secret of faith that Sayyidina Nuh ﷺ comes and says, 'In this *maqam* of *Sir* (secret),' because all the prophets are under Sayyidina Muhammad ﷺ. So Prophet ﷺ is going to teach you about Sayyidina Nuh ﷺ; the ship he was building, this is the *maqam* of faith. You want faith; you want to build your ship? You are going to be tested. None of that is going to benefit you if you are not from the people of *hamd*, *"Alhamdulillahi Rabb al-'Aalameen."*

الْحَمْدُ لِلَّـهِ رَبِّ الْعَالَمِينَ (٢)

1:2 – "Alhamdulillahi Rabb al-'Aalameen." (Surah Al-Fatiha)

"Praise be to Allah, the Cherisher and Sustainer of the worlds."
(The Opener, 1:2)

So it means your whole life is in making *hamd* (praise). Glory was *subhan, 'Subhan al ladhee bi yadihi'*, Allah ﷻ even in *Surah Yaseen.* 'Glory be to the Hand that carries all the *malakut.'*

فَسُبْحَانَ الَّذِي بِيَدِهِ مَلَكُوتُ كُلِّ شَيْءٍ وَإِلَيْهِ تُرْجَعُونَ (٨٣)

36:83 – "Fasubhanal ladhee biyadihi Malakutu kulli shay in wa ilayhi turja'oon." (Surah Yaseen)

"Therefore Glory be to Him in Whose hand is the [heavenly] dominion/ kingdom of all things, and to Him you will be returned." (Yaseen, 36:83)

Then the angels inspire in the *Sir* (Second Station) that come and now live a life of *hamd* (praise). That everything is a *hamd*, every moment of your life, praise Allah ﷻ; *Alhamdulillah*, and that even goes deeper. If you praise Allah ﷻ living a life of continuous praise, continuous praise; so they carry with themselves a *tasbih* to continuously praise Allah ﷻ. You want to be from that reality, you want the *maqam* of *iman* (station of Faith) to begin to open, because now it's all connected; it's like a science course. Praise – make *hamd*.

ALLAH ﷻ GAVE HIS MESSENGER THE NAME OF *MU-HAMD* (MOST PRAISED)

Then Allah ﷻ gives a clue because in case you were deceived by *Shaytan*, 'I made your messenger's name to be *Mu-hamd*'. There is no guessing. The *hamd* is in the name of Sayyidina Muhammad ﷺ. *Meem*, most *hamd*, most praised one in Divinely Presence. *'Innallah wa Malaikatahu yusalloona 'alan-Nabi ﷺ."*

إِنَّ اللَّهَ وَمَلَائِكَتَهُ يُصَلُّونَ عَلَى النَّبِيِّ يَا أَيُّهَا الَّذِينَ آمَنُوا صَلُّوا عَلَيْهِ وَسَلِّمُوا تَسْلِيماً

33:56 – "InnAllaha wa Malaikatahu yusalluna 'alan Nabiyi yaa ayyuhal ladhina aamanu sallu 'alayhi wa sallimu taslima. " (Surah Al-Ahzab)

"Allah and His angels send blessings upon the Prophet [Muhammad ﷺ]: O you that believe! Send your blessings upon him, and salute him with all respect." (The Combined Forces, 33:56)

"Allah and His angels send blessings upon the Prophet (Muhammad ﷺ). The rest Allah عزوجل doesn't care for; 'I don't care if you follow it, you don't follow it'. But the most praise in all of *malakut* (heavens) is the reality of Sayyidina Muhammad ﷺ. Then they even clarify, you want *hamd*, you want to make *hamd*? The best *hamd* is praise upon Sayyidina Muhammad ﷺ because they want to perfect your *aqidah* (belief).

Allah عزوجل Says, Don't Mention Me Without Mentioning Sayyidina Muhammad ﷺ

If you think that you are only going to praise Allah عزوجل, *'Allah, Allah, Allah, Allah, Allah, Allah,'* What is the difference between you and *Shaytan*? *Shaytan* accepted only Allah عزوجل and said, 'I don't care for this Adam and what he is bringing'. Uh-oh, that is big *guhunnah* (sin)! Sayyidina Adam عليه السلام was bringing the light of Sayyidina Muhammad ﷺ. So Allah عزوجل wants to perfect the character, 'Even I'm going to perfect your remembrance. Don't mention Me without mentioning Sayyidina Muhammad ﷺ.

So when you praise upon Sayyidina Muhammad ﷺ, the *salawat* on Prophet ﷺ is what - *Allahumma salli 'ala Sayyidina Muhammad.*

اللَّهُمَّ صَلِّ عَلَى سَيِّدِنَا مُحَمَّدٍ، وَعَلَى آلِ سَيِّدِنَا مُحَمَّدٍ وَ سَلِّمْ

"Allahumma salli 'ala Sayyidina Muhammadin wa 'ala aali Sayyidina Muhammadin wa Sallim."

"O Allah! Send Peace and blessings upon Muhammad and upon the Family of Muhammad ﷺ."

So you said 'Allah', you mentioned *Allahhumma salli 'ala Sayyidina Muhammad* ﷺ *wa 'ala aali Sayyidina Muhammad* ﷺ. So even the *hamd* the angels will come to perfect. Not only praise upon Allah ﷻ, but Allah ﷻ wants your praise to be perfected. Don't be rude to His Messenger. *"Qul inni kuntum tuhibbunallah fatta bi'ooni yuhibbukumulla."*

قُلْ إِنْ كُنْتُمْ تُحِبُّوْنَ اللَّـهَ فَاتَّبِعُوْنِي يُحْبِبْكُمُ اللَّـهُ وَيَغْفِرْ لَكُمْ ذُنُوْبَكُمْ ۗ وَاللَّـهُ غَفُورٌ رَّحِيمٌ ٣١

3:31 – "Qul in kuntum tuhibbon Allaha fattabi'oni, yuhbibkumUllahu wa yaghfir lakum dhunobakum wallahu Ghaforur Raheem." (Surah Al-Imran)

"Say, [O Muhammad], "If you should love Allah, then follow me, [so] Allah will love you and forgive you your sins. And Allah is Forgiving and Merciful." (Family of Imran, 3:31)

Allah ﷻ says, 'You want My Love, follow Prophet ﷺ'. How you can follow Prophet ﷺ if you are not continuously making *salawat* on Prophet ﷺ? That is the *hamd* of the most *hamd* of all the *malakut*!

Allah ﷻ Gave You a Heart to Make *Mi'raj* (Ascension) to the Heart of Prophet ﷺ

So they begin to perfect, because now you are on a *mi'raj* (ascension) into the heart of Prophet ﷺ. You came through the door and you glorified that, *'Ya Rabbi, Subhanaka allahumma, ya Rabbi'* (Glory be to you o my Lord). Why now these treasures are going to open? If you find yourself lucky enough to be brought to the heart of Prophet ﷺ and entering into these gates, *"Wa laqad karamna Bani Adam."*

وَلَقَدْ كَرَّمْنَا بَنِي آدَمَ...

17:70 – "Wa laqad karramna bani adama..." (Surah Al-Isra)

"And We have certainly honored the children of Adam..."
(The Night Journey, 17:70)

Allah ﷻ gave you a heart to make your *mi'raj*, to make your *buraq* into the heart of Prophet ﷺ. So now in *"Alhamdulillahi Rabbil 'Alameen" (Holy Qur'an, 1:2), Alhamdulillah,* every praise Allah ﷻ is going to be teaching that, 'Keep praising upon Me, praise upon Me, praise upon Sayyidina Muhammad ﷺ.'

الْحَمْدُ لِلَّـهِ رَبِّ الْعَالَمِينَ (٢)

1:2 – "Alhamdulillahi Rabb al-'Aalameen." (Surah Al-Fatiha)

"Praise be to Allah, the Cherisher and Sustainer of the worlds,"
(The Opener, 1:2)

Praising Prophet ﷺ Cleanses Your Praise of Allah ﷻ

The guides clarify the reason, because when you praise upon Allah ﷻ, if *Shaytan* is already in you, that praise goes nowhere. So if *Shaytan* is inside somebody because they wash very good outside but they are not washing the inside and when *Shaytan* is inside somebody, inside their heart, inside their blood, when they praise Allah ﷻ, it has *Shaytan* in it. It has a dirtiness in it. It doesn't rise. That's why nothing opens for them. They have no *maqam al-iman* (station of faith). They make *salah* (daily prayer) and it goes nowhere. *Shaytan* is already inside of them; what that *salah* is going to count? *Shaytan* is already inside! Allah ﷻ knows that, Allah ﷻ says, 'How you are going to praise Me?

You are not from the Perfected one. What we say in *khutbat jummah* is *Hamdan kamileen.*

"Alhamdulillahi Hamd al kamileen, was salatu was salamu 'ala Rasulina Sayyidina Muhammadin wa 'ala Aalhee, was Sahbihee ajma'yeen."

"All praises be to Allah, the praise of those who have been perfected. And peace and blessings be upon our messenger Sayyidina Muhammad ﷺ *and upon all his blessed family, and all his companions."*

Hamdan kamileen (Praise of the Perfected ones). Allah ﷻ is clarifying the *hamd* of the *kamileen*, they are perfected. When they say, 'Allah ﷻ', there is no *Shaytan* inside them. Allah ﷻ, that fragrance that they release, the angels immediately take to Allah ﷻ.

If there is *Shaytan* inside somebody and they say 'Allah', it is coming with a dirty smell; the angels can't approach. They can't approach a dog; imagine a dirty heart.

Prophet ﷺ Has the Secret of Intercession

Then how Allah ﷻ wants that praise to be perfected? Make *salawat* upon Prophet ﷺ; he is going to clean you. As soon as you say, *'Allahumma salli 'ala Sayyidina Muhammad wa 'ala aali Sayyidina Muhammad'*,

اللَّهُمَّ صَلِّ عَلَى سَيِّدِنَا مُحَمَّدٍ، وَعَلَى آلِ سَيِّدِنَا مُحَمَّدٍ وَ سَلِّمْ

"Allahumma salli 'ala Sayyidina Muhammadin wa 'ala aali Sayyidina Muhammadin wa Sallim."

"O Allah! Send Peace and blessings upon Muhammad and upon the Family of Muhammad ﷺ."

That *hamd* of Allah عزّ وجلّ will now be interceded by Prophet ﷺ. Sayyidina Muhammad ﷺ immediately intercedes for that *hamd*, purifies, cleanses it and presents it to Allah عزّ وجلّ pure and purified.

That's why Allah عزّ وجلّ said, 'Don't come to Me alone; maybe you don't know the *Shaytan* has tainted your being'. But as soon as you praise upon Sayyidina Muhammad ﷺ, his existence is the intercession.

Prophet ﷺ Intercedes, Cleanses, and Presents the Praise to Allah عزّ وجلّ

Every prophet was given a secret; he was given the highest secret of all realities – it was the intercession, that any sound, any prayer, any *du'a* that is coming, if Prophet ﷺ moves into it, he begins to purify it, cleanse it and present it to Allah عزّ وجلّ because Allah عزّ وجلّ wants to hear from Prophet , *"Qul inni kuntum tuhibbunallah fattabi'ooni."*

قُلْ إِنْ كُنْتُمْ تُحِبُّوْنَ اللَّـهَ فَاتَّبِعُوْنِي يُحْبِبْكُمُ اللَّـهُ وَيَغْفِرْ لَكُمْ ذُنُوْبَكُمْ ۗ وَاللَّـهُ غَفُورٌ رَّحِيمٌ ٣١

3:31 – "Qul in kuntum tuhibbon Allaha fattabi'oni, yuhbibkumUllahu wa yaghfir lakum dhunobakum wallahu Ghaforur Raheem." (Surah Al-Imran)

"Say, [O Muhammad], "If you should love Allah, then follow me, [so] Allah will love you and forgive you your sins. And Allah is Forgiving and Merciful." (Family of Imran, 3:31)

Ya Rabbi, labbaik! You said *tabi'ooni* (follow). Everything I'm mentioning is through Prophet ﷺ. Allah's promise is what – that 'I'm going to love you. Then I'm *Ghafoor as-Raheem*, I'm going to forgive everything; everything about you'. It means every *hamd* (praise) you make will be purified and sent into Divinely Presence.

Allah ﷻ Makes You Mention Prophet's Name in *Adhaan* and *Salah*

Every *salah* (daily prayer) you make, why in your *salah* is continuously mentioning Sayyidina Muhammad ﷺ? You have to mention Prophet's ﷺ name in the *adhaan* because Allah ﷻ won't even care for you if you don't call the *adhaan* with Prophet's ﷺ name. You say;

أَشْهَدُ أَنْ لَا إِلَٰهَ إِلاَّ الله أَشْهَدُ أَنَّ مُحَمَّدٌ رَسُولُ ٱلله

"Ashhadu an la ilaha illa-lah, ashhadu anna Muhammadan RasulAllah."

"I bear witness that there is no god but Allah, I bear witness that Muhammad is the messenger of Allah."

In the *salah*, before the *salah* is finished, you have to say *'Assalamu alaika ayyu han Nabi'* (Peace be upon You, O Prophet ﷺ) in present tense; this means you are facing Prophet ﷺ in the *salah* and Allah ﷻ has you making *salah* in the name of Sayyidina Ahmad احمد عليه السلام. You have a *Alif* ا, a *Ha* ح, a *Meem* م and a *Daal* د. So *Alhamdulillah*, they are describing everything.

Everywhere you look is going to be the signs of Prophet ﷺ. If you use that love of Prophet ﷺ, he will cleanse your *salah*, he will cleanse your *du'a* (supplication), he will cleanse your *dhikr*; everything will be purified because Prophet ﷺ is pure, and he will be taking it up.

كَمَا أَرْسَلْنَا فِيكُمْ رَسُولًا مِّنكُمْ يَتْلُو عَلَيْكُمْ آيَاتِنَا وَيُزَكِّيكُمْ وَيُعَلِّمُكُمُ الْكِتَابَ وَالْحِكْمَةَ وَيُعَلِّمُكُم مَّا لَمْ تَكُونُوا تَعْلَمُونَ (١٥١)

2:151 – "Kama arsalna feekum Rasulam minkum yatlo 'Alaykum ayatina wa yuzakkeekum wa yu'Allimukumul kitaaba walhikmata wa yu'Allimukum ma lam takono ta'Alamon." (Surah Al-Baqarah)

"Just as We have sent among (within) you a messenger from your own, reciting to you Our Signs, and purifying you, and teaching you the Scripture/Book and Wisdom and teaching you New Knowledge, that which you did not know." (The Cow, 2:151)

That's why *Hadith* of Prophet ﷺ that, 'I look to the action of my nation. If it's good, I say *Alhamdulillah* (Praise be to Allah). If it's bad, I intercede for that *amal*.'

قَالَ رَسُولُ اللَّهِ صَلَّى اللهُ عَلَيْهِ وَسَلَّمَ : حَيَاتِي خَيْرٌ لَكُمْ ، تُحَدِّثُونَ وَيُحَدَّثُ لَكُمْ ، فَإِذَا أَنَا مُتُّ كَانَتْ وَفَاتِي خَيْرًا لَكُمْ تُعْرَضُ عَلَيَّ أَعْمَالُكُمْ ، فَإِنْ رَأَيْتُ خَيْرًا حَمِدْتُ اللهَ ، وَإِنْ رَأَيْتُ غَيْرَ ذَلِكَ اسْتَغْفَرْتُ اللهَ لَكُمْ

Qala Rasulullahi ﷺ: "Hayatee khayrun lakum tuhadithona wa yuhdatha lakum, fa idha anaa mutta kaana wafati khayran lakum. Tu'radu `alayya `amalukum, fa in ra`itu khayran hamidtu Allah, wa in ra`aytu ghayra dhalik astaghfartullaha lakum."

"The Messenger of Allah said: 'My life is good for you, as you will relate from me and it will be related to you, and when I die my passing will be better for you. I observe the deeds of my ummah/Nation. If I find good [in it] I thank/praise

Allah, and if I see bad, I ask forgiveness for them/ on their behalf."
(Prophet Muhammad ﷺ)

3. *LA ILAHA ILALLAH* (THERE IS NO GOD BUT ALLAH)
IS THE *DHIKR* AT STATION OF *SIRR E SIR* (SECRET OF THE SECRET)

It means continuously Prophet ﷺ is interceding, cleansing, purifying and bringing to Divinely Presence. So *SubhanAllah* (Glory be to Allah) is at the station of *Qalb* (Heart), *Alhamdulillah* is at Station of *Sir* (Secret); then we can reach into the heart of Prophet ﷺ at *Sirr e Sir* (The Secret of the Secret). The Station of *Sirr e Sir* is where the *Naqshbandiyat al-Aliya* starts their station. They start from the *Sirr e Sir* and they enter into the oceans of *La ilaha illallah.*

It means *La ilaha illallah* (there is no God except Allah), the angel at that *maqam* (station) is beginning to teach the heart that in this *maqam* is complete *tawhid* (oneness). Everything is coming from Allah ﷻ. Everything is coming from Allah ﷻ. When you make *dhikr* of *La ilaha illallah* (there is no God except Allah), that Allah's ﷻ Hand is in everything. [This is what we talked about in *Surah al-Fatiha*: *"Iyyaka na'budu wa iyyaka n'asta'een"*]. What's to be angry with? What's to be disturbed with?

SOUL IS IN SUBMISSION, BUT IT IS HARD TO APPLY THE ORDER IN THE PHYSICAL WORLD

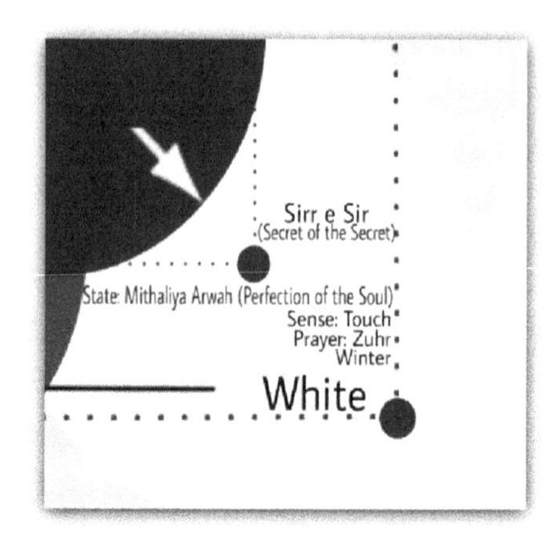

The *Sirr e Sir* (Secret of the Secret), is the *maqam* of light, is the *'alam al mithal*, is the world of *malakut* (heavens). The guides teach that in this world of *malakut*, everything is in submission to Allah عزوجل. This world of *mulk* (earth) is in flux and fighting. It means that if your soul begins to enter into that reality of *La ilaha illallah*, that every decree is coming from Allah عزوجل your soul accepts everything but it doesn't mean when you come back into *mulk* it's going to be easy for you.

The soul says to everything *'Labbaik, labbaik ya Rabb'*; whatever the order been given to you in that association *'Labbaik'* (I am at your Service); whatever Prophet صلى الله عليه وسلم ordered for you *'Labbaik'*. Soul is in complete submission that everything is in submission in *malakut.* Nothing is in disobedience. Then there is deeper into *La ilaha illallah* but you can't say that.

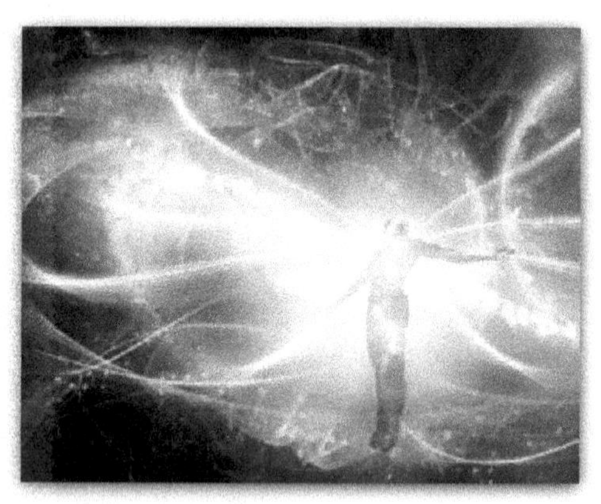

But in *mulk*, as soon as you come back with that order into the world of *mulk*, everything is in confusion because it's very difficult to apply into the world. If in that association they tell you something, in this world it is very difficult to complete it and become a lot of difficulties.

It means the Companions of Prophet ﷺ, whatever they went through, whatever their orders were given in *malakut*, they said *Alhamdulillah*; but when they came into *mulk*, they were all over. Also for *Awliya*; if you have ever accompanied *awliya* and their families, it is the same thing. Whatever was in *malakut*, no problem; you came into *mulk*, we got a problem because the *mulk* is going to be the area of confusion.

Then the guides begin to teach *La ilaha illallah, La ilaha illallah, La ilaha illallah,* there is nothing but Allah عزَّ وجلَّ, nothing but Allah عزَّ وجلَّ, *tasleem* (submit), "*sallu alayhi wa sallimu tasleem.*"

إِنَّ اللَّهَ وَمَلَائِكَتَهُ يُصَلُّونَ عَلَى النَّبِيِّ يَا أَيُّهَا الَّذِينَ آمَنُوا صَلُّوا عَلَيْهِ وَسَلِّمُوا تَسْلِيماً

33:56 – "InnAllaha wa Malaikatahu yusalluna 'alan Nabiyi yaa ayyuhal ladhina aamanu sallu 'alayhi wa sallimu taslima." (Surah Al-Ahzab)

"Allah and His angels send blessings upon the Prophet [Muhammad ﷺ]: O you that believe! Send your blessings upon him, and salute him with all respect [Submit]." (The Combined Forces, 33:56)

They say, 'No shaykh, say *tasleema.*' No, *tasleema* is the beauty that you get only if you are in *tasleem.* You don't have *tasleema*, if you are not in *tasleem* (submission); you have no peace if you are not submitting. Your life will be continuously all over the place.

SAY *LA* لا (NO) TO THE HEAD

Awliya (saints) begin to teach that *haqqaiq* (realities), that *dhikr* of *La ilaha illallah, La ilaha illallah* (there is no God except Allah). That is why they bring the *La* لا to the head, into the head, *ilaha* to right of chest , *ilAllah* to left of chest.

La لا

IlAllah الا الله   Ilaha اله

This head is not understanding *'alam al-mithal.* It means now where we are going into that reality, the head doesn't understand it.

THESE REALITIES ARE NOT FOR EVERYONE

That is why you can't talk to people that are not from that reality. You can't take what you hear here in spiritual associations, and go home to tell, and try to teach your mom and dad. They are not from that reality and you are going to confuse them. You can't teach your cousins or find someone you know, or somebody you don't even know. 'Ah, you want to tell me, you go like this and go like that'. They would tie you up and throw you out.

The guides are going to teach you that these realities are not for everybody. They have to have that; that dress and a permission from Allah ﷻ that had given to them and begin to open that reality of *la* – no head. The head won't understand these realities. If everything you are going to try to debate it and understand it and ask questions, your head will never make it; you will be confused and you walk away. It's not for you.

So then in *La ilaha illallah*, there is a reality on *ilaha illallah*, from right to left of chest; nothing but *Allah, Allah, Allah.* Then they can go deeper into that. We can't say it now because even the *La ilaha iillallah* will go deeper. That the reality of that *lam alif* is what we are trying to achieve.

4. *ALLAHU AKBAR* (ALLAH IS GREAT) IS THE *DHIKR* AT STATION OF *KHAFA* (HIDDEN)

Then they take us to the *Khafa* (Hidden), the fourth station of the heart, and the *dhikr* for the *Khafa* is, *La ilaha illallah*, *Allahu Akbar* (there is no God but Allah, Allah is Great). In the *Khafa* reality is the *dhikr* '*Allahu Akbar*' (Allah is Great), because of the oceans of *tawhid* (oneness).

When they enter into *Allahu Akbar* it is Imam Ali عليه السلام of the Companions at the *Khafa*. That now you are about to enter into the presence of Prophet صلى الله عليه وسلم which is the next stage, *Akhfa* (Most Hidden). You want to go into that presence, then we have a *Zulfiqar*. Because they just taught you in *La ilaha illallah*, this *Zulfiqar* has to come. It has to. That you can't go there with this *aqal* (mind) and head. You can only enter into that presence with this heart - *Allahu Akbar*.

ALLAHU AKBAR WILL DESTROY ALL FALSEHOOD

When they begin to teach the *dhikr* of *Allahu Akbar*, it extinguishes everything. Mawlana Shaykh even was teaching that if you see a fire and if you are in danger, as soon as you scream '*Allahu Akbar!*', Allah Supreme, means '*Izzatullah* can come to reduce that difficulty. When they make *dhikr* of *Allahu Akbar* (Allah is Great), it means, 'Every badness is in me, *ya Rabbi*, and that how *Shaytan* is still trying to attack me, to bother me, to make me to be dirty.' You need Allah's ﷻ *Akbar.*

It means Allah ﷻ comes and begins to destroy every falsehood, every incorrection, everything that *Shaytan* is trying to do. Allah ﷻ is then describing, 'From what you understood of these realities, *Ana al Akbar*; I am still beyond your imaginations.' What you are now about to go into the *Akhfa* (Most Hidden) reality, Allah ﷻ is clarifying, *'Ana Al Akbar'.*

THE *SALAH* (PRAYER) WAS A GIFT TO PROPHET MUHAMMAD ﷺ

It means everything they are going to bestow upon you, the best of character is that you continuously say *'Allahu Akbar'.* Because the *salah* was from who? It was not about us; the *salah* (daily prayer) was not for me and you. The *salah* was for Prophet ﷺ. He was taught that *salah*, a way in which to pray to Allah ﷻ.

So then why at every station of the *salah* was *'Allahu Akbar'*? Because of the respect that, what Prophet ﷺ was seeing of realities, of dresses, of what Allah ﷻ had bestowed upon him, the only word that would be sufficient is *'Allahu Akbar'* (God is Great). But if you don't say it, then it's as if you are becoming proud.

So Prophet is teaching that whatever Allah ﷻ is bestowing upon you, continuously glorify Allah ﷻ with *'Allahu Akbar* (Allah is Great). *Allahu Akbar* that, *'Ya Rabbi,* whatever You bestowed, I'm nothing and You are continuously More Supreme; nothing that I can even ever imagine'. Otherwise you become *Fir'aun* (Pharaoh); you think, 'Oh, what I got is great, I'm so great, I'm great'. But our way is; no, no, no, you deflate so Allah ﷻ gives you more.

SALAH HAS AN *'ALLAHU AKBAR'* FOR EVERY MOVEMENT

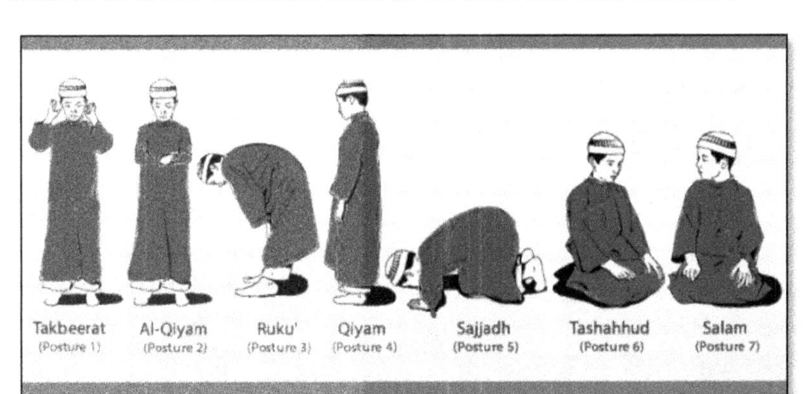

So even the *salah* (daily prayer), which is the *mi'raj* for the believer, its every move is *Akbar* (great), because in every movement there is a *tajalli* (manifestation), and a witnessing. When they are standing, what Allah ﷻ is dressing them through their heart, if they have a vision? For people whose hearts are open, at the *ruku*, what Allah ﷻ is showing them? In their *sajdah*, what Allah ﷻ is showing them? When they make *sajdah*, where are they making *sajdah* (prostration)?

So Prophet ﷺ taught the best of manners to say *'Allahu Akbar'*. Whatever Allah ﷻ is showing your soul's movement into these realities, continuously say *'Allahu Akbar'*, that Allah is More Supreme. And Allah's Answer, *'Ana Al-Akbar'*, I'm even More Supreme than what you can imagine', so that the journey continues eternally.

5. *La Hawla wa la Quwata illa Billah* (There is No Support and No Power, Except in Allah) is the *Dhikr* at Station of *Akhfa* (Most Hidden)

Then from that door, if they are able to teach that no more head, use your heart, you are entering now into that presence of *La hawla wa la quwwata illa bilahil Aliyil 'Azeem* (There is no Support, and no Power, Except in Allah عزوجل. It means who? You are in the presence of Sayyidina Muhammad صلى الله عليه وسلم.

Allah's عزوجل Support and Power is in the Hand of Sayyidina Muhammad صلى الله عليه وسلم

So then Allah's عزوجل *Hawla* and *Quwwa*, you want Allah's عزوجل Power, you want Allah's عزوجل Support, Allah's عزوجل Help, you want all of that majestic light; it is in the hand of Sayyidina Muhammad صلى الله عليه وسلم. So then Allah عزوجل said, "*Innal ladhina yubayyonaka inama yubayion Allah.*"

إِنَّ الَّذِينَ يُبَايِعُونَكَ إِنَّمَا يُبَايِعُونَ اللَّـهَ يَدُ اللَّـهِ فَوْقَ أَيْدِيهِمْ ۚ فَمَن نَّكَثَ فَإِنَّمَا يَنكُثُ عَلَىٰ نَفْسِهِ ۖ وَمَنْ أَوْفَىٰ بِمَا عَاهَدَ عَلَيْهُ اللَّـهَ فَسَيُؤْتِيهِ أَجْرًا عَظِيمًا (١٠)

48:10 – "Innal ladheena yubayi'oonaka innama yubayi'on Allaha yadullahi fawqa aydeehim, faman nakatha fa innama yankuthu 'ala nafsihi, wa man awfa bima 'ahada 'alayhu Allaha fasayu teehi ajran 'azheema." (Surah Al-Fath)

"Indeed, those who give Baya (pledge of allegiance) to you, [O Muhammad] – they are actually giving Baya (pledge of allegiance) to Allah. The hand of Allah is over their hands. So he who breaks his pledge/oath, only breaks it to the

detriment/ Harm of himself. And he whoever fulfills their Covenant (Bayat) that which he has promised Allah – He will grant him a great reward."
(The Victory, 48:10)

'Take the hand of Sayyidina Muhammad ﷺ'. Every *hawla* and every *quwwa* will be reaching to your hand because it's on the hand of Prophet ﷺ. Allah عز و جل is describing 'My Hand is upon the hand of Sayyidina Muhammad ﷺ. You want My Hand in your life, means you want *quwwa*, you want My Power, you want My *Madad*, you want My Support', it's not coming to everyone; it has to have *tawhid*, has to have *La ilaha illallah Muhammadun RasulAllah.*

It's always perfect in *shari'a* (Islamic Jurisprudence). It's the perfection of *shari'a. Tariqa* (Islamic Spiritual Path) never goes outside of *shari'a.* Some people just don't understand *shari'a*, because everything is *tawhid* (oneness). If you don't have and you say everybody can reach to Allah's عز و جل *Quwwa*, it's a free ocean like a Turkish *bazaar*, well how would you have *tawhid*? And why would anybody come to *La ilaha illallah Muhammadun RasulAllah*? Allah عز و جل is saying, 'No, you can never reach *La ilaha illallah* unless you come to *Muhammadun RasulAllah* ﷺ.' This is the perfect in oneness. By taking the hand of Prophet ﷺ you are now reaching Allah's *'Izza; 'Izzatullah, 'izzat ar-Rasul wa 'izzat al-mu'mineen.*

وَلِلَّهِ الْعِزَّةُ وَلِرَسُولِهِ وَلِلْمُؤْمِنِينَ وَلَكِنَّ الْمُنَافِقِينَ لَا يَعْلَمُونَ

63:8 – "…Wa Lillahil 'izzatu wa li Rasuli hi wa lil Mumineena wa lakinnal munafiqeena la y'alamoon." (Surah Al-Munafiqoon)

"…And to Allah belongs [all] honor, and to His messenger, and to the believers, but the hypocrites do not know." (The Hypocrites, 63:8)

Subhana rabbika rabil 'izzati 'ama yasifoon, Wa salamun 'alal mursaleen wal hamdulillahi rabbil 'alameen. Bi hurmati Muhammadil Mustafa wa bi siratil Suratil Fatiha.

SENSES AND THE LEVELS OF THE HEART

CONTROL THE FIVE SENSES TO OPEN THE SOUL

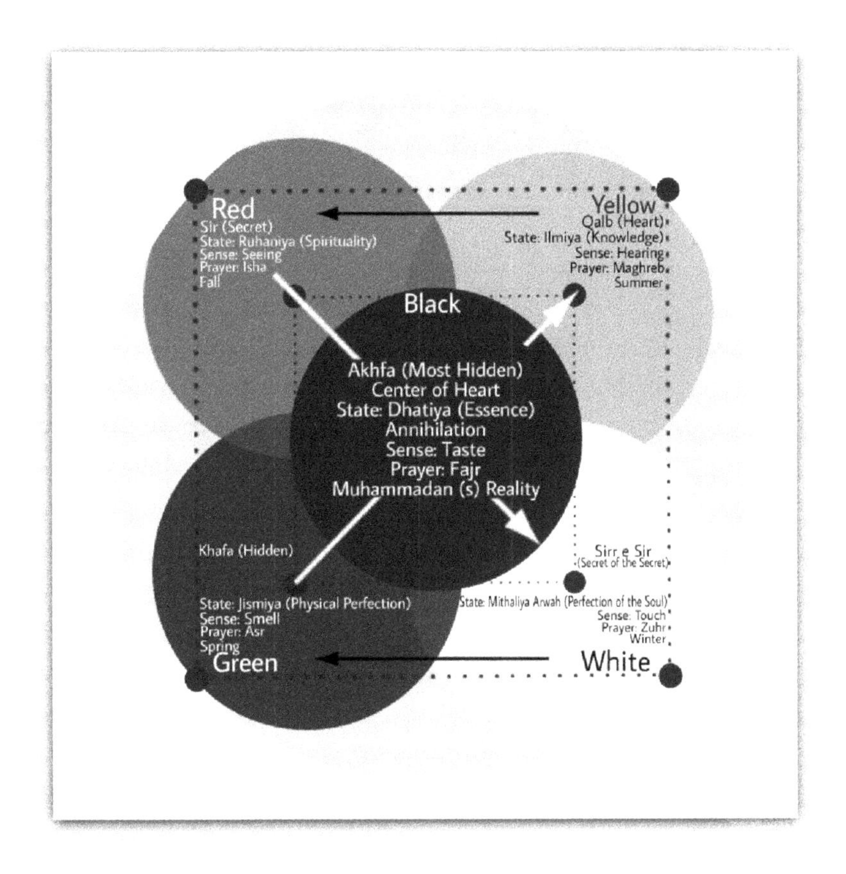

The gift of life is such a precious gift, and what the Divine wants for us is to achieve the reality of this life that was given. Many choose the lower existence and the pursuit of the physical desires. And then there are some whom the Divine inspires within themselves that there is a higher reality. That, by a means of coming into this world, you are to discipline yourself to see the majesty, magnificence and munificence of the Divine soul, the Divine lights, that the Divine has created upon the soul.

Discipline the Physicality to Bring Out the Spiritual Reality

Then the spiritual paths come and begin to teach the reality of the religious orders and the religious understandings. By disciplining your physicality and bringing the physicality and the physical desires down, the guides begin to teach us how to bring out the spiritual reality. As much as we listen to the physical ears and take enjoyment from the physical hearing, spiritual hearing can't open. So guides begin to train that, control what you are hearing and don't let unnecessary sounds occupy the ear because it's going to be a direct effect to the heart.

They begin to teach us, in Sufism, that everything is based on the heart. Even the physiology of the body has an effect onto the heart. This was from the knowledge of the prophets, then inherited by knowledge of *awliyaullah* (saints). That is the inheritance of the Prophet Muhammad ﷺ.

Now in science they know that based on what you hear, aggressive loud noises can actually cause an agitation into the heart. They know that certain sounds, when they are beating and the repetition of that sound, begins to cause a difficulty within the heart.

For all the senses, there is also an inner reality. Maybe we are using only the ears from the outside, but it doesn't mean that we are hearing from the soul.

At the Levels of the Heart, from hearing at station of *Qalb* (Heart) to seeing, that has to do with the station of *Sir* (Secret). Then at station of *Sirr e Sir* (Secret of the Secret) is the sense of touch and subtlety of the soul. The spiritual hearing and seeing produces certainty and leads to the soul's subtlety. Then at the station of *Khafa* you learn about importance of breath. At *Khafa* (Hidden) the sense of smell opens, which is the Angelic reality. Then hearing with reality, begin the seeing of reality, the breathing of reality, the touch, and then opening up the taste of reality at the Station of *Akhfa* (Most Hidden).

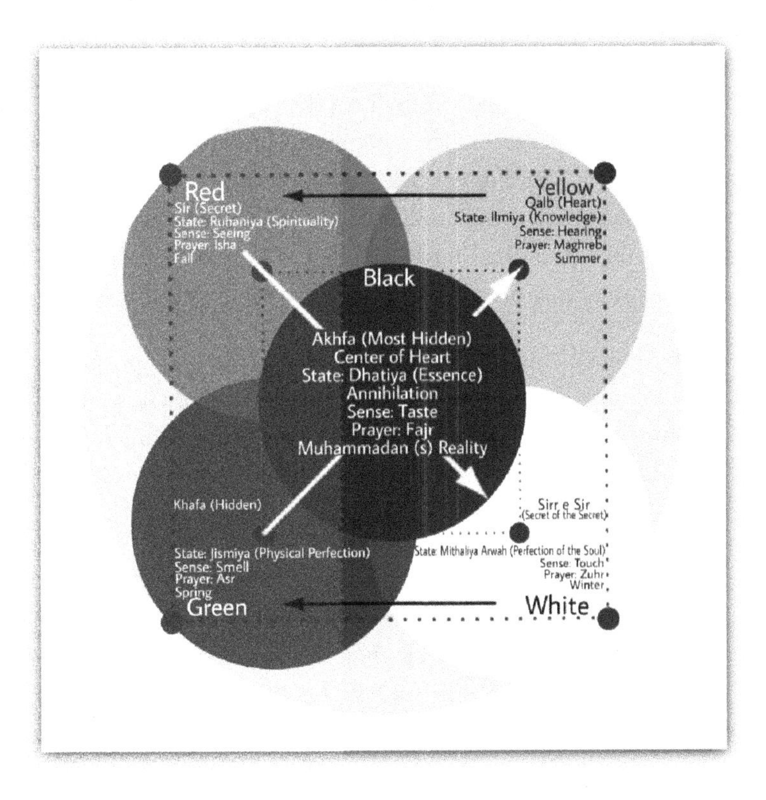

1. Sense of Hearing at the Station of *Qalb* (Heart)

Discipline the Physical Hearing to Open Spiritual Hearing

They begin to teach us that if you want spiritual hearing to open, then begin the disciplining of your physical hearing.

What You Hear of Negative Energies Affects Your Heart

It means all the bad sounds and all the bad gossips and unnecessary noises, those are all *dhikrs* that are coming into the heart. If it's an agitating sound, it has a direct effect into the heart. If it's nasty, then the soul and body will be accountable for what it is hearing. It will be written on and transcribed into the heart. That the negative and the very vile chanting that people listen to, it's moving into the heart.

It's not by coincidence that the negative and the evil ego comes up with this, because the ego and egoism, *Shaytan* and all the negativity, it doesn't want us to reach our reality. It doesn't want us to reach the goal of our existence here because that's not its goal. Its goal is to play and enjoy the physical world.

The soul comes from above, comes from the heavens; there is no up or down. The soul comes from the heavens and returns to the heavens. The ego and bad desires, they stay here. Their only interest is in entertainment and playing. And they know that when the power of the soul comes, they are in trouble and they are going to be burned by the power of the soul.

...إِنَّا لِلَّـهِ وَإِنَّا إِلَيْهِ رَاجِعُونَ

2:156 – "Inna lillahi wa inna ilayhi raji'oon." (Surah Al-Baqarah)

"Indeed we belong to Allah, and indeed to Him we will return."
(The Cow, 2:156)

So at every stop, it says, "Listen to this," and begins to put iPods and music and sounds that will directly darken the heart. Then the fasting of the ears and the beginning of the practices of 'I'm going to listen to spiritual sounds that bring about an enjoyment in my soul, that bring about a pleasure and an energy in my soul.' That those other sounds I will be accountable for. They are a chanting from very negative forces that are being chanted upon and trying to darken the soul.

Knowledge is Directly Connected to Hearing

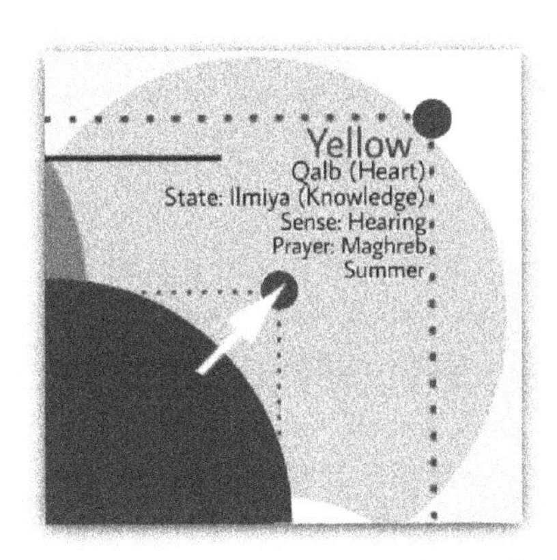

Then the *Qalb* (Heart), is also the station of knowledge. Every knowledge has to enter from where? The hearing. Knowledge is directly connected to hearing, how well you hear, not physical hearing only, it is hearing and obeying.

...سَمِعْنَا وَأَطَعْنَا

2:285 – "...Sam'ina wa ata'na ..." (Surah Al-Baqarah)

"...We hear, and we obey..." (The Cow, 2:285)

Hearing and obeying means it's really absorbing, you act upon what you hear, not just merely hear it through the faculty of the ear. Both hearing has to be there; the physical is the outside and the inner *ka'bah*, the inner reality of the circle has to be hearing.

2. Sense of Seeing
at the Station of *Sir* (Secret)

Control the Physical Eyes to Open the Spiritual Vision

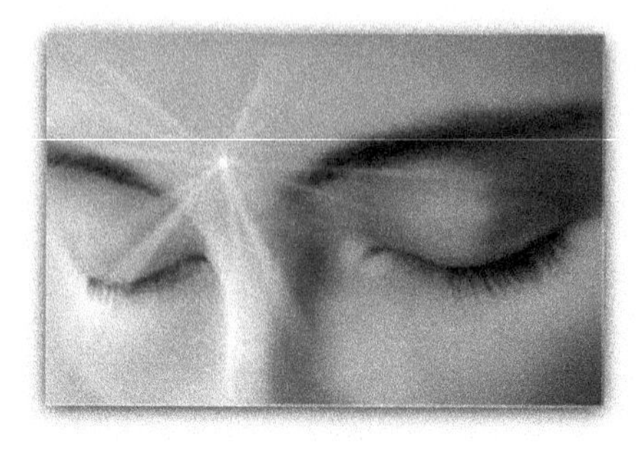

Then they begin to teach to control your eyes. If you want the soul to open, then when you look with your physical eyes and your eyes become hungry and they eat and absorb everything. The guides teach, then keep a path of closing your eyes. The insatiable appetite of the eyes never end. If everything in our lives is based on eyes and what we see we want, it will never end. So then they teach, keep a path in which you keep closing your eyes. That what we are looking for is not through the physical eyes.

Each Sense Has a Dual Nature

As soon as we close each sense, each sense has a dual nature, like the moon. There is a side you see and a side that you don't. You have the outer ear, the physiology of the self, and you have the inner ear. As soon as you close the outer ear, the inner ear becomes more fine-tuned. It means the inner ear begins to hear, not the voices of angels first but the voices of the conscience. The lower conscience locked within us, the higher conscience is in Divinely Presence. The Divinely lights are telling that conscience, "Teach them. He came down to earth and he forgot what he has promised Me." [He or she – doesn't make a difference.]

It means we have a reality always in Divinely Presence. Only a small part of that light was sent into the physicality. So then the higher reality is always trying to communicate with the lower reality that's locked behind the egoism of the body.

Then they begin to teach that as soon as you close your eyes, then your outer vision stops so that the inner vision of the heart can begin. It means that with every abstinence and every fasting, its reality will be born. But as much as we indulge in it, that reality will never be born.

In old times they would go to the shaykh and the shaykh would show a seed. Have you ever seen an avocado seed? It's like a baseball. They take the seed and say, "Look at the seed. Is it ever going to become anything if I just hold it like this?" They would say, "No, it's actually going to be a very hard piece of wood. You can use it for baseball; you can throw it at somebody."

That seed, it can become a tree, which is amazing in itself; that where the sprout comes from that big seed. So then they teach by taking that seed and putting it into the soil and the reality of the soil is the reality of the physicality because we are made from soil.

IMPORTANCE OF *KHALWAH* (SECLUSION) TO SPIRITUAL GROWTH

Allah ﷻ says, "You put your sense back in. Go into your soil; put the seed in." That becomes the concept of seclusion and *khalwah*. We can make seclusion in our daily life just by isolating ourselves at times. Having a discipline that at certain times in which, 'I'm going to isolate, not to see and speak to anyone, and just be with myself; thinking of my reality so that the seed can one day be a tree.'

If it becomes a tree, it can one day bear fruits. Those fruits become eternal gifts upon the soul because people are now benefiting from the fruits of your tree. Versus the Divine teaching that most come into this world with the capability, they have the seed and they leave with the seed. They didn't take the time to plant it. And they become immensely saddened by the reality that is lost, because you show up to the Divine with a seed. It didn't become a tree and it bore no fruit.

So all the discipline of the spiritual order, it is not hocus pocus. It's a very defined science and matches the science that is known in this *dunya*; not their hypothesis that they keep guessing and hope one day that they will be right, but the proven ones.

Then, by abstaining in the hearing, to open real hearing, abstaining in the vision to open the real vision of the soul. What we are seeing is an illusion. All these atoms are moving and none of it is real. As soon as you witness with the soul, the soul can witness what Allah ﷻ wants it to witness.

START THE GREATER STRUGGLE AND CLOSE YOUR EYES TO *DUNYA*

This is also the station of seeing, the sense of seeing. So the only way to begin to see is if you are dying towards the *dunya* life, to the material life. If you are loving the material life, then there is no reason to feel that you are dying towards it, to go towards the spiritual reality. It means that the desires have to be brought down.

That is why Prophet ﷺ was teaching his Companions, "The fights that we were going through, in my physical presence was one thing; but now what is going to be opening is the much greater fight which is the fight against the self."

عن جابر قال قدم على رسول الله صلى الله عليه وسلم قوم غزاة فقال صلى الله عليه وسلم قدمتم خير مقدم من جهاد الأصغر إلى جهاد الأكبر قيل وما قال مجاهدة العبد هواه وهذا فيه ضعف

"An Jabir qala qadam 'ala Rasulullah ﷺ qawm ghazata faqala Sallallahu Alayhi was Salaam: " Qadamtum khaira muqadem min jihadil Asghar ila Jihadil Akbar." Qeela "wa ma?" Qala "Mujahidatal 'Abd hawahu wa hadha fi D'af."

Jabir عليه السلام narrated: 'Some warriors came to the Holy Prophet. He (Muhammad ﷺ said to them: "welcome back, you came from minor Jihad to the greater one."

It was asked, 'what is that Oh Prophet of Allah?" He ﷺ replied: "One's fight against his mundane wills/ desires." (Bahaqi Kitaab ul Zuhd-al-Kabir)

As you begin to lose the desire of *dunya* (material world), more of the seeing and spiritual vision begins to open.

3. Sense of Touch

At the Station of *Sirr e Sir* (Secret of the Secret)

Control the *Hawa* (Physical Desires) to Open Subtlety of the Soul

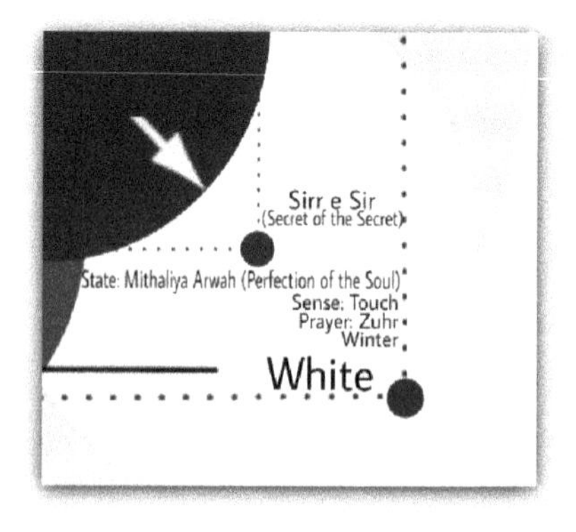

It means they begin to teach from the *Sirr e Sir*. That from hearing, from seeing, is now the sense of touch. For *Sirr e Sir* to open its reality, it has to enter into a state of touch. Come against your *dunya* (material world), your *nafs* (ego), your *hawa* (desires), and *Shaytan*. Come against these enemies of the body, so that you can bring the power of your soul back. The *Sirr e Sir* has to do with *Alam al Mithal* in the World of Light.

Discipline Your Physicality With Hardship

Hawa is the pleasures of your physicality. If you can't control that *hawa* and enter into a state, the *Sirr e Sir* can't open. If you are not able to enter a state in which you put a hardship upon your physicality, the fasting of touch and sensation, you can't control *hawa*.

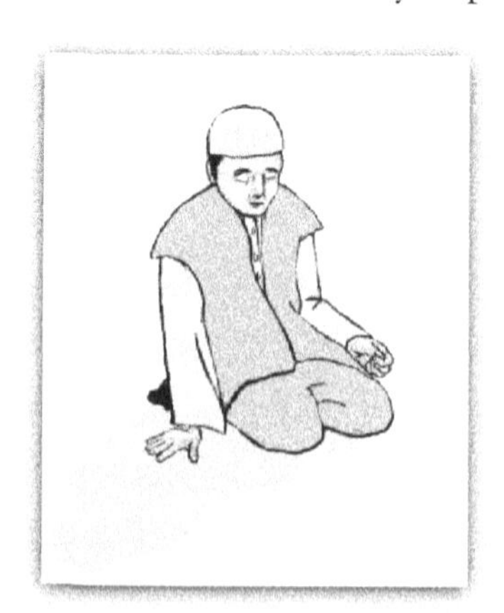

It means they put a hardship upon their physicality. They come and say, "O shaykh this is going to be hard!" That is exactly the prescription. When they sit in a position that increases the difficulty and pain within their contemplation, that is the solution. When we were young we were able to sit all the time upon our knees and have a tremendous amount of pain. Because the pain wouldn't let you sleep, so you would be able to sit for long periods of time in contemplation because the pain just agitates you. It is not about entering a state of complete comfort and sleeping, meditation/*tafakkur* and sleeping are two different understandings.

DON'T SLEEP SO COMFORTABLY THAT YOU MISS *FAJR* PRAYER

Then Prophet ﷺ was teaching even his sleep was through difficulty. Prophet ﷺ slept on a bamboo mat so that the marks from his sleeping were visible to his Companions. They would say, "*Yaa Sayyidi, yaa Rasulul Kareem, yaa Habibul 'Azheem,* (O my master, O the generous Messenger, O the Majestic Beloved of Allah), let us get you something beautiful to sleep, why is it like this." The teaching was that this difficulty allows me to wake up for my *Fajr* (morning prayer).

We know through training that when you put difficulty upon yourself, your sleep is not going to be too deep. So then when people say they can't wake up for *Fajr*, drink a lot of water and sleep on the floor. The water makes you constantly get up to make *wudu* (ablution), what's wrong with that? Get up, make *wudu*, it's *nurun `ala nur* (light upon light). That every time when you wash and make *wudu,* it is light upon light and you will be glowing on the Day of Judgment. They recommend that you take a big bottle of water and drink right before your sleep so that you wash all night long. And train yourself that you don't sleep more than two hours, two hours, two hours; don't go deep into your sleep.

That is different from what this world is teaching you with a Serta mattress, comfortable bed, with all that cushion and pillow top so that you just melt into it and never come out. Then we are amazed that how we cannot (get up) to pray and we can't do anything. But the way of struggling was that they slept on the floor and drank a lot of water. And throughout the night they were struggling with themselves so that the sleep would never be so deep. That way they came against their *hawa*, against their desires and through that then the *Sirr e Sir* can be opened.

4. Sense of Smell
at the Station of *Khafa* (Hidden)

Safeguard Your Breath to Open Sense of Spiritual Smell

Then they begin to teach, control your breath. That makes with your breath the chanting of the Divinely Presence. Your life is based on breath. The extent and the time of your life is based on how many breaths you have. So no need for all the life insurance and all the big plannings. It is better to sit and make *dhikr Hay, Hay, Hay* (The Ever living Living, One of Attributes of Allah ﷻ). That is why they call *Nafas ur Rahmah* – the Breath of Mercy. Because Allah ﷻ is saying, "Before you make big plans and how long you are going to live here, how you're going to spend your money, you still haven't thanked Me for the breath you have. You may have 1 breath left, 10 breaths left, 70,000 breaths left; so make them in My remembrance."

Then you have energized and opened the reality of your breath. So then all the *tariqas* (Islamic spiritual paths), they are all based on breathing, consciousness of the breathing, importance of the breath, and the power that's coming in with the breath. Then when you look to the lungs, you see it is a tree upside down, and that is the tree of life. Before you can reach the lote tree of the furthest boundary, Allah ﷻ says, "Before you can make the external *mi'raj* (ascension), you have to make your internal pilgrimage."

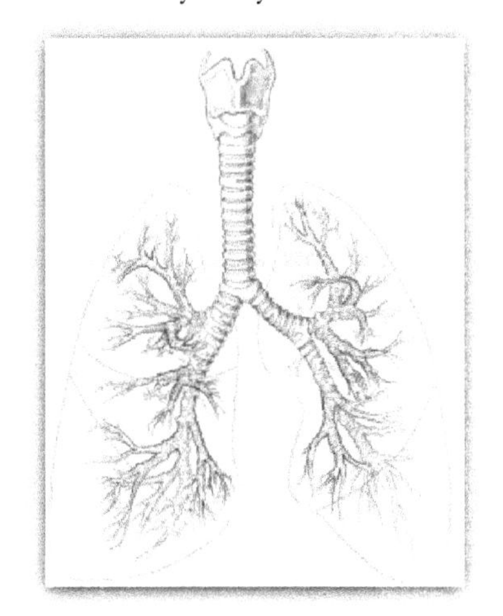

Before you can find that bodi tree and that reality, the Divine says, "It exists within you," the tree that are the lungs. What is happening when we are breathing is that energy and that light is coming in, nourishing the blood and the first place that blood goes is to the heart. It doesn't go to any of the other organs. That breath comes in and stamps the blood. It takes all of the energy it needs from the breath and then that blood goes to the heart.

If the Heart is Pure, the Whole Body is Pure

Then *tariqa* and Sufism says, everything is based on the heart. If the heart is pure, it takes that blood and then stamps it with *Allah*, with the *dhikr* of the Divine, and then moves to 11 essential organs. If the heart is dirty, and the breath coming in contaminated, all the being is going to be then made dirty from all the dirty blood flowing. It means if the reservoir is filthy and filled with *najas* and dirtiness, whatever you pour into it will sicken everything that comes in contact with it.

Then *tariqa* comes and says, that is the reservoir of your entire being. Why you want to focus on your leg and your head and your back and this chakra and that chakra? The main reservoir of your physiology, not hocus pocus, of your physiology, your breath is coming in, going into your lungs, your blood into your heart. If that heart is sick, Prophet ﷺ described from holy *Hadith*, "If one part of you is sick, all of you will be sick;" and said, "that one part is the *qalb* (heart)."

أَلا وَإِنَّ فِى الْجَسَدِ مُضْغَةً إِذَا صَلَحَتْ صَلَحَ الْجَسَدُ كُلُّهُ، وَإِذَا فَسَدَتْ فَسَدَ الْجَسَدُ كُلُّهُ، أَلا وَهِى الْقَلْبُ"

"Ala wa inna fil Jasadi mudghatan idha salahat salahal jasadu kulluho, wa idha fasadat fasadal jasadu kulluho, ala wa heyal Qalb."

"There is a piece of flesh in the body, if it becomes good (reformed) the whole body becomes good but if it gets spoiled the whole body gets spoiled and that is the heart." (Prophet Muhammad ﷺ)

MAKE YOUR HEART THE HOUSE OF ALLAH عز و جل

Then that same part, the heart, if it's purified, the Divine says, "Then I'm not in heavens and I'm not on earth; but I'm in the heart of the one who believes in Me."

"Maa wasi`anee laa Samayee, wa la ardee, laakin wasi'anee qalbi 'Abdee al Mu'min."

"Neither My Heavens nor My Earth can contain Me, but the heart of my Believing Servant." (Hadith Qudsi conveyed by Prophet Muhammad ﷺ)

"Qalb al mu'min baytur rabb."

"The heart of the believer is the House of the Lord." (Hadith Qudsi)

This means *'qalb al mu'min baytullah'*. The Divine's saying that's such an important organ that if you purify it, if you wash it, if you cleanse it, and you circumambulate around it, it will become My Divinely house within your being. It means you will have a *Ka'bah* within your soul, your very own *Ka'bah* that you wash, you clean, you purify and you begin to make your *tawaf* around your heart; because Divinely light is now like rays of sun dressing your heart.

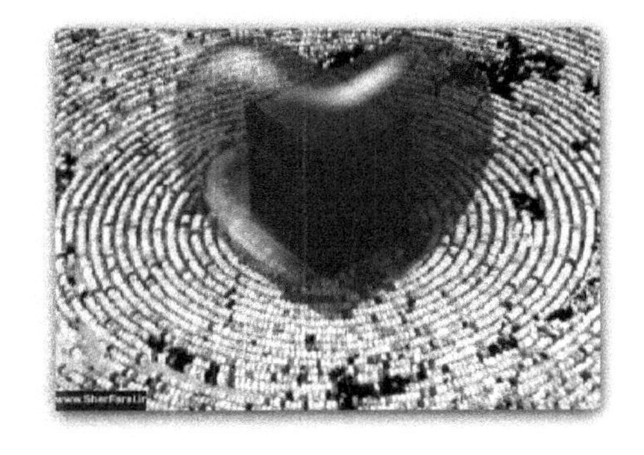

5. SENSE OF TASTE
AT THE STATION OF *AKHFA* (MOST HIDDEN)

WHEN OTHER 4 SENSES OPEN, YOU CAN TASTE THE HEAVENLY REALITIES

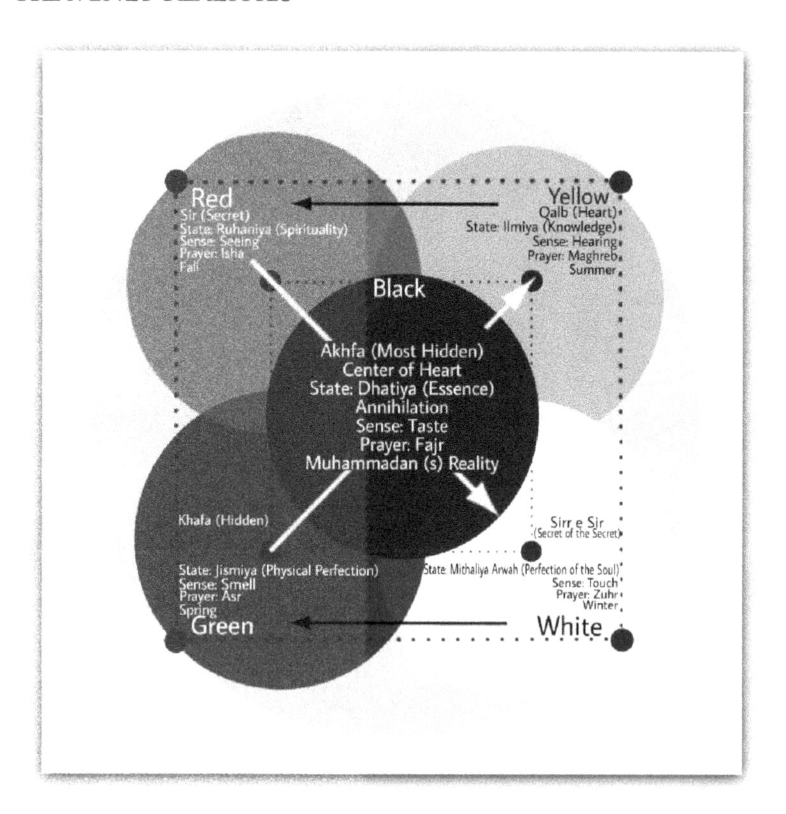

Then hearing with reality, begins the seeing of reality, the breathing of reality, the touch, and then opening up the taste of reality. That if everything is working on the level of the soul, it is now hearing its conscious' orders. Because of the discipline, it can hear what it's supposed to do and it doesn't keep making crazy choices. When we want to see our life, how out of whack we are, it is when we listen to ourselves. How we are always falling short and making very crazy choices and seem to have a very chaotic life.

Then they begin to teach that as you begin to discipline, discipline, discipline, you are hearing now the co-ordinance and those co-ordinance are coming from the Divine. As you are abstaining with your vision and looking for the vision of the soul, your lights are going on and you begin to be inspired within your heart. And the real vision and the real purpose of our being here becomes more and more clear.

'I'm not being sent here to be a doughnut shop'. We have not been sent here to do all these different jobs we do. But once we are inspired and understand what is the reality of the soul, what is the mission and the purpose that we have been sent here. Then I open the ability to hear, to see and to breathe with reality; then I begin to taste the reality.

DHIKR EMPOWERS THE SOUL AS LIGHT HAS NO BOUNDARIES

At the level of the soul then opens the reality of light; and the reality of light is different from the reality of physicality. In the physical world, we see this room with 60 people sitting around doing their best to chant. In the world of light, these are 60 souls and millions of other lights. And as soon as the guides begin their chanting, the energy that begins to dress their souls then begins to dress all the souls.

All those energies, they have no boundaries. We have our boundaries – you can't sit on somebody's lap; he is not going to appreciate it. Physicality has boundaries. But once you begin to open from the reality of the soul, your light is everywhere. And the light of many beings are present because it's a holy association gathering for chanting and *dhikr*.

As soon as the guides begin chanting, there is a fierce Divine light that begins to dress the souls and they begin to wash and cleanse and bathe within that light. Purify themselves, dress from realities that are unimaginable in their dressing.

فِي بُيُوتٍ أَذِنَ اللَّـهُ أَن تُرْفَعَ وَيُذْكَرَ فِيهَا اسْمُهُ يُسَبِّحُ لَهُ فِيهَا بِالْغُدُوِّ وَالْآصَالِ

24:36 – "Fee buyotin adhina Allahu an turfa'a wa yudhkara feeha ismuhu yusabbihu lahu feeha bil ghuduwwi wal asal." (Surah An-Nur)

"(Lit is such a Light) in houses, which Allah hath permitted to be raised to honor; and that His name be mentioned therein: In them He is glorified in the mornings and in the evenings, (again and again)." (The Light, 24:36)

DHIKR ENERGY ENABLES THE SOUL TO FIGHT BACK NEGATIVITY

Then when the chanting and the program ends, those souls go back fully loaded, fully energized, fully dressed with ability to empower themselves and more able to conquer themselves of all the desires we have already talked about.

الَّذِينَ آمَنُوا وَتَطْمَئِنُّ قُلُوبُهُم بِذِكْرِ اللَّـهِ ۗ أَلَا بِذِكْرِ اللَّـهِ تَطْمَئِنُّ الْقُلُوبُ

13:28 – "Alladheena amano wa tatma'innu Qulobu hum bidhikrillahi, ala bidhikrillahi tatma'innul Qulob." (Surah Ar-Ra'd)

"Those who believe, and whose hearts find satisfaction in the remembrance of Allah. for without doubt in the remembrance of Allah do hearts find satisfaction." (The Thunder, 13:28)

But if the soul doesn't take from that energy, it is virtually impossible to come against all the other desires of the body, because the hearing desires are so overwhelmed by negative surroundings. We are talking about 1000 negative sounds versus 1 holy association for a nice sound. We are talking about millions of negative visions and images popping up to us versus sitting and meditating. Most people can't do that for five minutes, versus how many minutes a day you look at negative and horrible images? It means the overwhelming tide of negativity is to darken all the senses.

With energy of *dhikr*, the soul controls five senses and fights back negativity. So then they begin to teach, by these associations, an immense energy is released. The soul becomes loaded with that energy and goes back and now has more ability to fight against its desires. And again, to push down the negative desires so that it can come out, it can come out, it can come out until enough of those associations and the tide flips; where the power of the soul is enough to begin to push down and take control.

Then it has control and abstains from hearing negativity. It has control and abstains from seeing negativity. It has control and abstains from breathing in negativity. And begins to harness the reality of the breath, of pulling every energy out of that breath and igniting it to its reality. And then abstaining with the tongue and not speaking negativity and purifying to represent the reality of the soul.

Ask for the Gift of Faith and Blessings of *Dhikr* Associations

Then *tariqa* comes and spirituality comes with a big reality for the lights and for the reality of the soul. That the biggest gift the Divine can give us, is the gift of faith; that to create that love and that yearning within our heart, to keep coming for *dhikr* and to keep doing what we do. For a day may come when the Divine takes that and we find ourselves not wanting to do and not wanting to go for *dhikr*. It's not our cleverness that not wanting to go and not wanting to do.

اسْتَحْوَذَ عَلَيْهِمُ الشَّيْطَانُ فَأَنسَاهُمْ ذِكْرَ اللَّـهِ ۚ أُولَـٰئِكَ حِزْبُ الشَّيْطَانِ ۚ أَلَا إِنَّ حِزْبَ الشَّيْطَانِ هُمُ الْخَاسِرُونَ

58:19 – "Istahwadha 'alayhimush Shaytanu fa ansahum Dhikra Allahi, Olayika hizbush Shaytani, ala inna hizbash Shaytani humul khasiroon." (Surah Al-Mujadila)

"The Evil One has got the better of them: so he has made them lose the remembrance of Allah. They are the Party of the Evil One. Truly, it is the Party of the Evil One that will perish!" (The Pleading Woman, 58:19)

It is a gift and a *ni'mat* (blessing) from the Divine to go to these associations. It's a gift that somebody gives you a diamond and if you know the value of it, you are constantly thanking God. You asking that, "Don't let that faith to go from me; don't let that love to go from me. Don't let that yearning that you placed into my heart to be taken by the thieves of the heart." And then I find myself cut from that line and cut from that blessing.

So always, always ask that, "Please don't lift that mercy from me and increase my yearning to move towards Your Divinely oceans and to open the reality of the soul."

Subhana rabbika rabil 'izzati 'ama yasifoon, Wa salamun 'alal mursaleen wal hamdulillahi rabbil 'alameen. Bi hurmati Muhammadil Mustafa wa bi siratil Suratil Fatiha.

SENSES OF THE *MUTTAQEEN* (THOSE WITH CONSCIOUSNESS)

THEY TEACH YOU TO FAST WITH ALL FIVE SENSES

اَللهُمَّ اجعَلنِى مِنَ التَّوَّابِينَ وَاجعَلنِى مِنَ المُتَطَهِّرِين

"Allahumma ij'alni Minat Tawwabeena Waj'alni Minal MutaTahireen."

"O Allah, make me to be from those who repent and make me from those who are clean and purified."

These are the associations; *"minat tawwabeen wal mutatahireen* (those who repent and are clean and purified)." That Allah ﷻ granted their Islam to become more real and they ask, *yaa Rabbi,* we are constantly asking and begging Your forgiveness. This is the abode of difficulty and this Earth is the place of difficulty and testing. They are asking Allah's ﷻ infinite forgiveness and that Allah ﷻ send a means in which to be *mutatahireen,* to be purified and cleansed. Allah ﷻ loves those who are clean and constantly trying to clean themselves.

إِنَّ اللهَ يُحِبُّ التَّوَّابِينَ وَيُحِبُّ الْمُتَطَهِّرِينَ...

2:222 – "…inna Allaha yuhibbu attawwabeena wa yuhibbu al Mutatahhireen." (Surah Al-Baqarah)

"…Surely Allah loves those constantly repentant, and He loves those who purify themselves." (The Cow, 2:222)

THE BLESSING AND GIFT OF *RAMADAN*

Alhamdulillah, the greatest gift for Creation is the month of *Ramadan. Alhamdulillah,* Allah ﷻ gave us good life, a long, good health to participate in the fasting of *Ramadan.* We pray that Allah ﷻ gives us that *Rahma,* that Mercy and the secrets of *Ramadan* to be upon us. In the month of *Ramadan,* Allah ﷻ cleans the soul, cleans the ego, dresses the soul, and destroys the ego. It is a month in which *siyaam* (fasting) is a means in which to annihilate the *nafs* (ego), obliterate the *nafs* and adorn the realities that Allah ﷻ wants for us upon the soul. It's a means in which the soul achieves what it has to achieve. That Allah's ﷻ lights come fiercely against the ego to destroy the ego. May Allah ﷻ grant us these lights and grant us these blessings.

From Mawlana Shaykh's teaching, we are asking to inherit from *muttaqeen*, whom Allah ﷻ granted such high levels of consciousness and realities. A reminder is that they are fasting with all of their senses.

THE BEGINNER LEVEL OF FASTING IS TO FAST WITH THE MOUTH

The fast of the beginner (level) is to fast by mouth, abstaining from food for a certain number of hours which seems so difficult but, truly it is not difficult. When these orders were coming for the Companions, they were fiercely engaged in struggles in 130°F – 140°F (50°C – 60°C) temperatures, with very little water and their lips and tongue would crack from dryness. Allah ﷻ now gave us a life of luxury with air conditioners and all sorts of amenities, providing us ease. *Alhamdulillah,* that reward is still coming upon us and dressing us, as a tremendous gift upon the soul.

FAST WITH ALL FIVE SENSES TO OPEN LEVELS OF THE HEART

To understand that, *yaa Rabbi,* we are asking to inherit from Your highest realities, that we are following from the highest level of *Awliyaullah;* they are all *muttaqeen.* Allah ﷻ granted them a high level of *taqwa* (consciousness) upon all their senses. A reminder is that they are fasting with their ears.

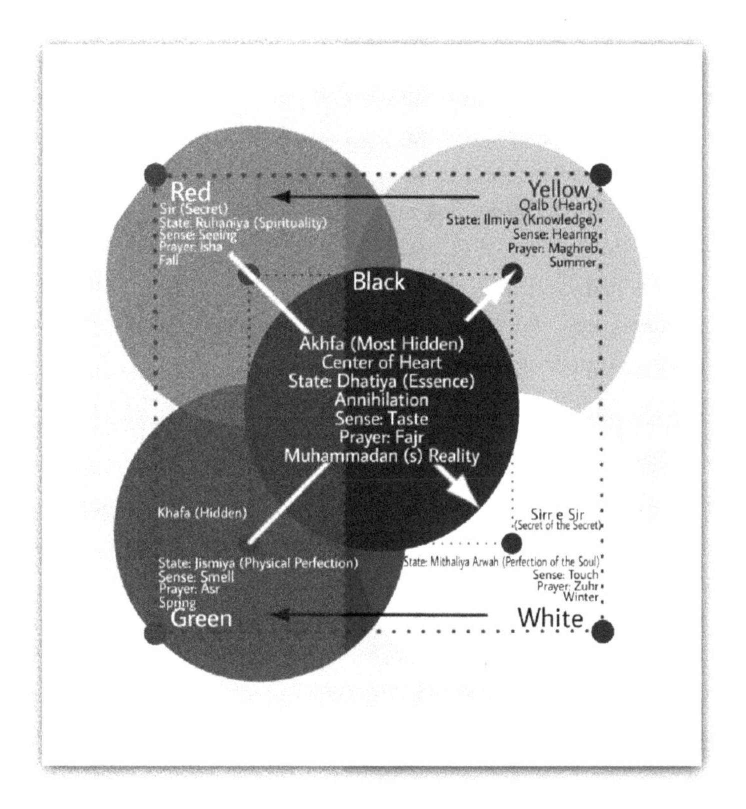

As the holy month of *Ramadan* is opening they are in a continuous fast upon their ears. They understand these senses from the sense of hearing, the sense of seeing, the sense of touch, the sense of smell and the sense of taste. These are correlated with the *lataif* of the heart; from the *Qalb* (Heart), to the *Sir* (Secret), to *Sirr e Sir* (Secret of the

Secret), to *Khafa* (Hidden), and then the *Akhfa* (Most Hidden) of their heart.

1. Sense of Hearing
at the Station of *Qalb* (Heart)

To Open *Qalb's* Secret, Fast with Hearing

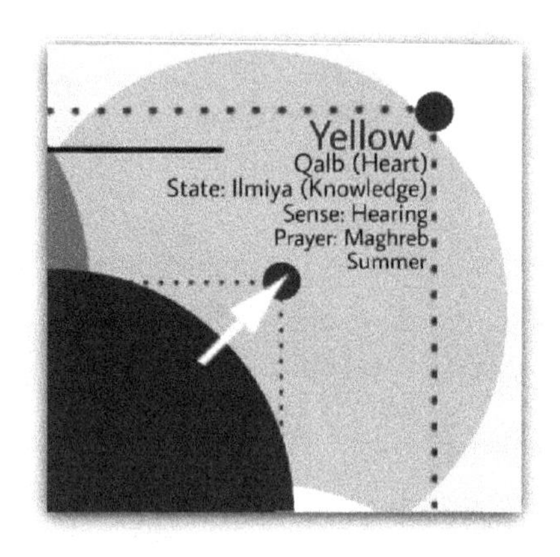

The *Qalb's* secret doesn't open until the *muttaqeen* begin to teach that you have to enter a perpetual state of fasting with your hearing, so that you can hear your consciousness and so you can hear your Lord. This is because all the hearing that you are doing is just from the *waswas* and whispering. All of the hearing is of entertainment that is trying to entertain the *nafs* (ego). It means that is not hearing. Allah ﷻ says, "They have ears but they don't really hear."

It means there is a reality and a second level of hearing. The *muttaqeen* are asking us to enter a state in which I am trying, *yaa Rabbi,* to abstain from hearing that which is of no benefit to me. Abstain from sounds that are of no benefit to my heart, from discussions and dialogue that only bring darkness to my heart and belief, such as backbiting, whispering and gossiping. All of these bad characteristics *Shaytan* inspires within a believer and a non-believer and within humanity, to darken the heart so that the reality of hearing never opens and that reality of the *Qalb* never opens. It means if they don't have *yaqeen* (certainty) of hearing there is no way that the *lataif* of the *Qalb* has opened.

2. Sense of Seeing
at the Station of *Sir* (Secret)

To Open the *Sir's* Secret, Control the Eyes

Then they begin to remind that you have these senses, the five senses for *hidayat* (guidance) for the body but these senses are (also) controlling the soul. It means every sense has two doors, one for the body and one for the soul. You are seeing but yet you don't see. We use the eyes to be engaged in everything from the material world. Everything that you see with your eyes, you are capturing into your heart and darkening your heart. You are accountable for what your eyes see. Now *Shaytan* makes everything available through your phone, to see things that will completely darken the heart. It brings darkness to the heart so again the heart won't open.

Nazar Bar Qadam – "Keep Your Eyes Upon Your Feet"

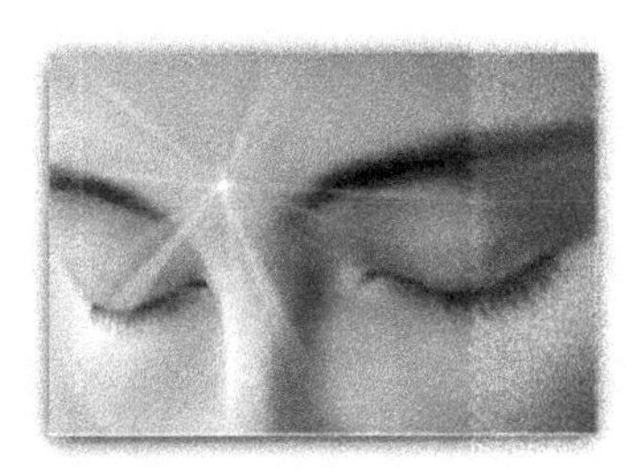

It means the *lataif* of the *Sir*, and its secret, won't open until the believer has control over their sight. They are trained to keep their *nazar bar qadam*, "keep your eyes upon your feet." Don't worry about the left or right; don't worry about who is in front or who is behind, who has what or what is happening. You keep your eyes upon your feet in life and pray that those feet take you to holy places. If these feet are not under guidance, you will be in all the wrong places at the wrong time. You find every holy association but your feet will take you somewhere else that is not holy. It means our whole life is that, *yaa Rabbi,* let my eyes be upon my feet and inspire these feet to always move in Your direction.

Fast With Your Eyes

Next, they begin to train that if you want to control your sight and the hunger that comes through your eyes, then keep your eyes closed and make them fast. As your stomach is fasting from all the nice treats that you like to eat, your eyes have to enter a state of fast, in which you sit often and close your eyes. I am not going to give you from the candy of this world. I am not going to give you from all these entertainments and you begin to close your eyes.

Only at the time when you fast with your ears and your eyes, you can begin to open the sense of your consciousness, that I am hearing my voice speak to me because I am fasting with my ears. I am hearing my consciousness and something is trying to be said to me; some inspiration is trying to come to me when I enter a state of fasting.

As soon as I fast with my eyes, I begin to close my eyes often and imagine, *yaa Rabbi,* I am in my *qabr*, my grave. That this world is an illusion and what would the next world hold for me? As soon as you begin to close your eyes you become subtle through your soul; you may begin to see things, experience things, and begin to feel things.

3. Sense of Touch (Soul's Subtlety) at the Station of *Sirr e Sir* (Secret of the Secret)

To Open *Sirr e Sir,* Control the Four Enemies of the Body: Material World, Desires, Ego, and Satan

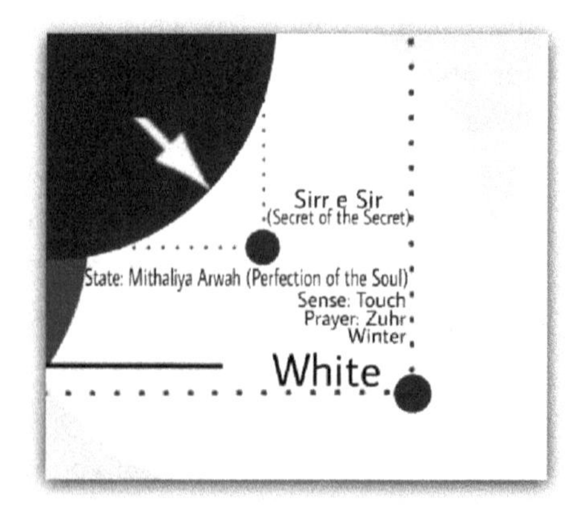

It means they begin to teach from the *Sirr e Sir* (Secret of the Secret). From hearing and from seeing, is now the sense of touch. For *Sirr e Sir* to open its reality, it has to enter into a state of touch. To come against your *nafs*, your *hawa*, your *dunya* and *Shaytan,* (Material World, Desires, Ego, and Satan) come against these enemies of the body, so that you can bring the power of your soul back. The *Sirr e Sir* has to do with *Alam al Mithal* in the World of Light.

DISCIPLINE THE PHYSICALITY WITH HARDSHIP

If you are not able to enter a state in which you put a hardship upon your physicality, the fasting of touch and sensation, *hawa* is the pleasures of your physicality; if you can't control that *hawa* and enter into a state, the *Sirr e Sir* can't open.

It means they put a hardship upon their physicality. They come and say, "O shaykh, this is going to be hard!" That is exactly the prescription. When they sit in a position that increases the difficulty and pain within their contemplation, that is the solution. The pain wouldn't let you sleep, so you would be able to sit for long periods of time in *tafakkur* (contemplation) because the pain just agitates you. It is not about entering a state of complete comfort and sleeping.

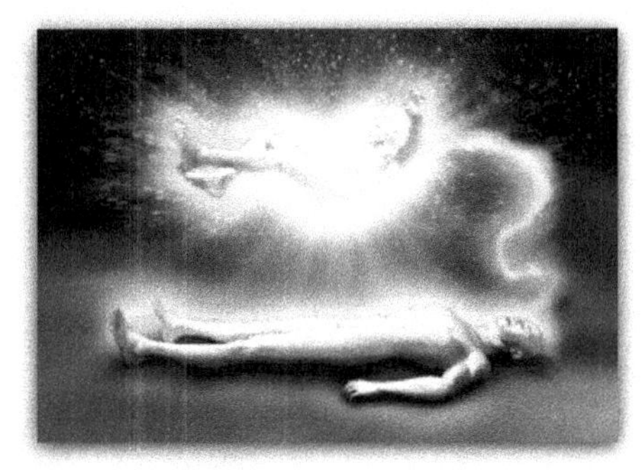

FASTING OF THE SENSES LEADS TO SPIRITUAL SUBTLETY, THE SOUL'S TOUCH

It is like a lock, all these three, four, five of these locks are moving and the senses of the body are now under abstinence and fasting. So it means they are fasting with their hearing, so that they can open, *sami`na wa ata`na.*

إِنَّمَا كَانَ قَوْلَ الْمُؤْمِنِينَ إِذَا دُعُوا إِلَى اللَّـهِ وَرَسُولِهِ لِيَحْكُمَ بَيْنَهُمْ أَن يَقُولُوا سَمِعْنَا وَأَطَعْنَا ۚ وَأُولَـٰئِكَ هُمُ الْمُفْلِحُونَ

24:51 – "Innama kana qawlal mumineena idha du'ao ilAllahi wa Rasulihi liyahkuma baynahum an yaqolo sam'ina wa ata'na, wa olaika humul muflihoon." (Surah An-Nur)

"The only statement of the [true] believers when they are called to Allah and His Messenger to judge between them is that they say, 'We hear and we obey.' And those are the successful." (The Light, 24:51)

We hear and we obey; not we hear ourselves and we obey, but we hear the call of Allah ﷻ and what the higher conscious is calling us. Our conscious, our greater soul, is always in the presence of Allah ﷻ. He didn't give us that Trust to destroy. It is only a portion of that light that is sent into your body; the greater portion is always in Divinely Presence so that we can hear. The fasting should be so that I open my hearing, I open my seeing, I open my sense of touch to become *latif* and subtle. That is not the physical but to be spiritual, to feel spiritual energy. If Allah ﷻ is opening, that means you begin to feel what others don't feel and your senses become subtle. You feel the energy of people around you.

4. Sense of Smell
at the Station of *Khafa* (Hidden)

To Open *Khafa*, Safeguard Your Breath

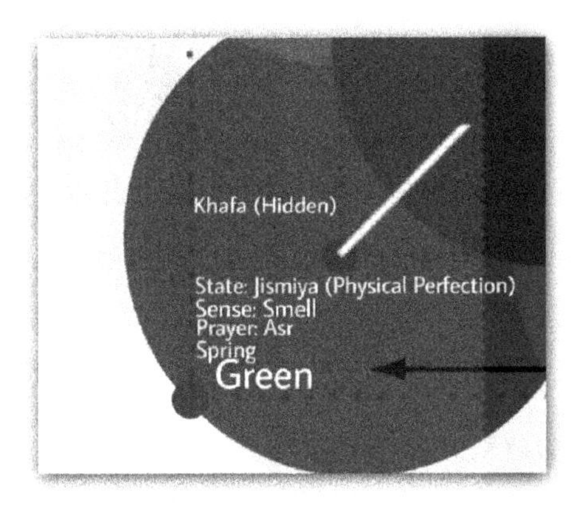

Next is the station of smell, which means that the *Khafa* (Hidden) point is based on the sense of smell and entering a state in which you are fasting with your smell. It means the importance of your breath, your *nafas*. What you are breathing in of realities, you are conscious of that breath; you are conscious of that fragrance and you are conscious of that cleanliness. This reality of smell and the reality of the breath have to do with the *Malaika*, because the angels are of a subtle nature. What they call in the west, 'aromatherapy', this was all from the Prophet ﷺ. Prophet ﷺ described that Allah عز وجل made dear for me, *attar* (fragrance), because it is a state of cleanliness.

عن أنس بن مالك رضي الله عنه أن رسول الله ﷺ قال:حُبِّب إليَّ مِنْ دُنْيَاكُمْ :اَلطِّيبُ؛ وَالنِّسَاءُ؛ وَجُعِلَتْ قُرَّةُ عَيْنِيْ فِي الصَّلَاةِ

"Hubbi ilaya min dunyakum: Attayib, wan Nisa, wa ju'ilat qurratu 'ayni fis Salat."

"An Anas bin Malik عليه السلام *narrated from Prophet* ﷺ*, 'Made beloved to me from your world are perfume/Purity, and Women, and the coolness of my eyes is in prayer." (Jami'al-Saghir, Hadith 5435. Classified as Sahih by Albani)*

It is a deep state of reality. When you are sensitive through your breath and are bringing in the energy of your breath, that sensitivity from fasting is that you safeguard what you are breathing. You don't take yourself where people are poisoning themselves, breathing in poison and you breathe freely in there! They say that second-hand smoke kills you more than first-hand smoke. Either first or second-hand you shouldn't be around it. The breath you are bringing in is from the Divine Power, the Divine Grace, and the Divine Blessing.

CONTAMINATED BREATH KILLS THE HEART

That breath that comes in comes with the secret of all *Qudrah* (Divine Power). That *Qudrah* goes into the lungs, and from the lungs, it mixes with the blood and then into the heart. If that power is real and clean, it enters into the heart, and from the heart it dresses all the organs. If that breath is contaminated, it will kill the heart and that is all that *Shaytan* wants; to destroy the heart of the believer.

Once they begin to safeguard their breath and cherish their breath, then they begin to sense that through the *siyaam* (fasting) of their breath, they smell what people can't smell. They can smell the bad characteristics of other people because everybody puts a fragrance (or smell) within their heart. If the heart is bad and the character is bad, they produce a smell worse than the toilet. That is why when pious people go by graveyards the smell is very extreme because most people who have died, their condition is very bad and they release a horrific smell because their soul was never fragranced with good actions. It means then the perfumes are important, the *attars* and all the fragrances that you are putting on, is for a realm that appreciates that reality. The spiritual realm of their life and their existence is through that fragrance.

MUTTAQEEN'S DU'A IS THROUGH A FRAGRANCE, NOT BY WORDS

Each of these levels of the heart have tremendous realities. Now when the *muttaqeen* are entering the realities of the *Khafa* level of their heart, their *du'a* is not by *kalam* (words), and their prayer is not by tongue. There is no tongue in Paradise; there is no body, so why do you have to have a tongue? It is light, in the World of Light there is only light. The *du'a* (supplication) at the *Khafa* reality is from the *Malaika.* That is when the heart of the *ashiqeen* (lovers) produce a fire. When the fire of their heart is lit, they merely begin to make a *du'a,* like a fragrance, an *attar;* the *attar* hits their heart and the *Malaika* are immediately attracted to that fragrance and they carry that fragrance into the Divinely Presence. That is why their prayers are accepted in Divinely Presence. It is not at the level of the *kalam.* It is beyond the level of *Iman* and now into the oceans of *Maqam al Ihsan* (Station of Moral Excellence).

أَنْ تَعْبُدَ اللهَ كَأَنَّكَ تَرَاهُ، فَإِنْ لَمْ تَكُنْ تَرَاهُ فَإِنَّهُ يَرَاكَ

"Ant ta'bud Allaha, Ka annaka tarahu, fa in lam takun tarahu fa innahu yarak."

"It (Ihsan – Station of Excellence) is to serve Allah as though you behold [See] Him; and if you don't behold [See] him, (know that) He surely sees you." (Prophet Muhammad ﷺ)

They are operating through their light and through realities. Their hearts are burning; they are *ashiqeen* with the love of Prophet ﷺ. It is with love for Allah عز و جل which is supreme, and love of Prophet ﷺ, and love of *Awliyaullah* (saints). Their heart is always like a charcoal and they keep burning it (charcoal) to show you, that the heart is like a charcoal. We have the *bukhoor* (fragranced incense), in which you light the charcoal, to burn the incense. When the charcoal is lit, the heart of the believer is lit. As soon as they make a *du'a,* it releases a fragrance upon their heart and the angels are attracted to the fragrance and carry the fragrance into the Divinely Presence. They don't carry the words of the servant because Allah عز و جل says, when I get you back up there I am going to seal your mouth.

الْيَوْمَ نَخْتِمُ عَلَىٰ أَفْوَاهِهِمْ وَتُكَلِّمُنَا أَيْدِيهِمْ وَتَشْهَدُ أَرْجُلُهُم بِمَا كَانُوا يَكْسِبُونَ (٦٥)

36:65 – "Al yawma nakhtimu 'ala afwahehim wa tukallimunaa aydeehim wa tashhadu arjuluhum bima kanoo yaksiboon." (Surah Yaseen)

"That Day, We will seal over their mouths, and their hands will speak to Us, and their feet will testify about what they used to earn." (Yaseen, 36:65)

That is the first thing Allah عز و جل said. He is going to seal the mouth because the mouth says many things and has nothing of any truth in it. What is true is the heart of the believer.

5. Sense of Taste
at the Station of *Akhfa* (Most Hidden)

To Open *Akhfa,* Fast From the Taste

It means then fasting from the sense of smell and opening the reality of the sense of smell. Then, the highest level, which is *Akhfa,* is the fast of the taste. That is why Allah ﷻ ordered *Ramadan* for us, the highest level of all the senses. When they are sensing with their hearing, sensing what they are seeing, sensing their life of touch and life of pleasure to themselves. And begin to fast with the breath, and appreciate the breath that is coming in, and the fragrance of that breath that is dressing them. Then Allah ﷻ opens for them the reality of taste. Now you will taste what you are hearing, you will taste what you are seeing, and you will taste what you are touching. For them everything is real at the level of taste.

Muttaqeen Taste the Heavenly Realities and Speak From Their Experience

This is not from reading books nor is not from reading from the scholars of the past. The *muttaqeen* are tasting and are in that ocean of reality. There is no permission in *Naqshbandiya* to take something, read something and tell people something. You are a liar because it is not real for you! You only have permission to speak the truth which you are experiencing and you have permission to speak from it. If you are not experiencing it, you have no permission to speak from it. You can hear the shaykh's teaching but you cannot give that teaching to other people when you are not tasting from that and understanding that reality.

It means then at the *Akhfa* (Most Hidden) reality, everything Allah عز وجل begins to open for them to taste. They taste the *dhikr*, they are not just saying the *dhikr*, but every cell in their body is moving with that *dhikr*. They taste from those realities that Allah عز وجل opened for them, to see it, to smell it, to understand it, to taste it and it is burnt upon their heart as a reality for them.

Then *Ramadan* is much greater than just being hungry for a few hours. It is a tremendous gift from Allah عز وجل to open for us a perpetual state of abstinence. Abstaining from everything that is bad and opening the great realities that God has given to us as our potential, and not the physical being that we are walking upon the Earth. Right now we are like the "Planet of the Apes" movie; we are a few monkeys that can talk and people are fascinated by the fact that we can talk. But this was not the reality that God had intended for us. It means we have devolved in who we are today.

We pray that this holy *Ramadan* opens for us a reminder, *wa laqad karamna bani Adam.*

وَلَقَدْ كَرَّمْنَا بَنِي آدَمَ وَحَمَلْنَاهُمْ فِي الْبَرِّ وَالْبَحْرِ وَرَزَقْنَاهُم مِّنَ الطَّيِّبَاتِ وَفَضَّلْنَاهُمْ عَلَىٰ كَثِيرٍ مِّمَّنْ خَلَقْنَا تَفْضِيلًا

17:70 – "Wa laqad karramna banee adama, wa hamalna hum filbarri wal bahri wa razaqnahum minat tayyibati wa faddalnahum 'ala katheerin mimman khalaqna tafdeela." (Surah Al-Isra)

"And We have certainly honored the children of Adam and carried them on the land and sea and provided good and pure sustenance and bestow upon them favours, and preferred them over much of what We have created, with [definite] preference." (The Night Journey, 17:70)

Allah عزّ وجلّ has given us a tremendous gift and that gift to be dressed and blessed upon us. And that we reach what Allah عزّ وجلّ wanted us to reach, what Prophet صلى الله عليه وسلم wanted us to reach, and what *Awliyaullah* are continually inspiring within our hearts to reach. Don't waste this time that has been given to you for something that has no value, but seek your eternal reality before your time is finished and no one knows when their time is finished!

Subhana rabbika rabil 'izzati 'ama yasifoon, Wa salamun 'alal mursaleen wal hamdulillahi rabbil 'alameen. Bi hurmati Muhammadil Mustafa wa bi siratil Suratil Fatiha.

OPENING SPIRITUAL SENSES

HEARING, SEEING, TOUCH, SMELL, AND TASTE

It is a reminder for people that we want a life in which we are accompanying the *Ahlul Basirah*, the people whose hearts are open. If their heart is not open then what are you going to do with them? It means we find people in our life and accompany people whose hearts are not open. It doesn't matter what their *madhhab* (religion) or what they claim they are or who they aren't. If their heart is not open and they are twenty, thirty, forty years doing what they are doing. It is not going to open for you either because whatever they did, it did not open for them. So it means the description of insanity is to do the same thing and expect a different result.

ACCOMPANY PEOPLE WHOSE HEARTS ARE OPEN – *AHLUL BASIRAH*

Allah's ﷻ *ni'mat* and blessing is to guide, to give us *isharat* and signs that go to those whose hearts are open and they see through their hearts because they have been dressed. This *zawiya* and all *Ahlul Haqqaiq* (People of Reality), they live by these certain *Hadith* (saying of Prophet Muhammad ﷺ). If you take one *Hadith* and live it, it is enough of an ocean that you will be lost. Where Allah ﷻ describes they completed their *fard*, what is mandatory from them, but they are servants of Mine who approach Me with voluntary worship.

...وَلَا يَزَالُ عَبْدِي يَتَقَرَّبُ إِلَيَّ بِالنَّوَافِلِ حَتَّى أُحِبَّهُ، فَإِذَا أَحْبَبْتُهُ كُنْت سَمْعَهُ الَّذِي يَسْمَعُ بِهِ، وَبَصَرَهُ الَّذِي يُبْصِرُ بِهِ، وَيَدَهُ الَّتِي يَبْطِشُ بِهَا، وَرِجْلَهُ الَّتِي يَمْشِي بِهَا، وَلَئِنْ سَأَلَنِي لَأُعْطِيَنَّهُ، وَلَئِنْ اسْتَعَاذَنِي لَأُعِيذَنَّهُ." [رَوَاهُ الْبُخَارِيُّ]

"..., wa la yazaalu 'Abdi yataqarrabu ilayya bin nawafile hatta ahebahu, fa idha ahbabtuhu kunta Sam'ahul ladhi yasma'u behi, wa Basarahul ladhi yubsiru behi, wa Yadahul lati yabTeshu beha, wa Rejlahul lati yamshi beha, wa la in sa alani la a'Teyannahu, ..."

"...My servant continues to draw near to Me with voluntary acts of worship so that I shall love him. When I love him, I am his hearing with which he hears, his seeing with which he sees, his hand with which he strikes and his foot with which he walks. Were he to ask [something] of Me, I would surely give it to him..." (Hadith Qudsi, Sahih al-Bukhari, 81:38:2)

The Religion of *Malakut* (Heavens) is Love and *Muhabbat*

It means they come through the door of love and *muhabbat*. Their *madhhab* (creed) is *muhabbat* because the *madhhab* of the *samaa* of *malakut* (heavens) is *muhabbat*. There is nothing but love in the world of light. Everything in the world of *mulk* (earth) becomes separate, that is the nature of *mulk*. Every *fitna* is upon the *mulk*, *Shaytan* is on the *mulk*. In *malakut* (heavens), it is only *tasleem*, it is only submission, and that submission is based on love and *muhabbat*. It means then to reach towards that reality they are teaching us, that to take that path in which you want to reach to that reality.

Then Allah ﷻ describes those servants I become their hearing with which they hear. Allah ﷻ will dress the hearing, which is *Hadith al-Qudsi,* "I will dress the eyes with which they see, the breath with which they breathe, the hands with which they touch, the feet with which they move." So much so they become *Rabbaniyoon* (Lordly) and they say *Kun faya kun* (Be and it is) because their will is matching the Will of Allah ﷻ; they don't have a will separate from Allah ﷻ.

AWLIYA (SAINTS) ARE THE PEOPLE OF AUTHORITY ON EARTH, THEY ARE THE *ULUL AMR* AND *ULUL IRADA*

إِنَّمَا أَمْرُهُ إِذَا أَرَادَ شَيْئًا أَن يَقُولَ لَهُ كُن فَيَكُونُ (٨٢

36:82 – "Innama AmruHu idha Arada shay an, an yaqoola lahu kun faya koon." (Surah Yaseen)

"His command is only when He intends a thing that, He says to it, "Be," and it is." (Yaseen, 36:82)

They are walking *ulul amr* (People of the Command) and *ulul irada* (People of the Will). The *ulul amr* are those who are trying to perfect themselves with what Allah ﷻ wants from *atiullah wa ati ar Rasula wa ulul amri minkum.* It means they must be under the authority of real *ulul amr.*

يَاأَيُّهَا الَّذِينَ آمَنُوا أَطِيعُوا اللَّهَ وَأَطِيعُوا الرَّسُولَ وَأُولِي الْأَمْرِ مِنْكُمْ

4:59 – "Ya ayyu hal ladheena amanoo Atiullaha, wa atiur Rasola, wa Ulil amre minkum…" (Surah An-Nisa)

"O You who have believed, Obey Allah, Obey the Messenger, and those in authority among you…" (The Women, 4:59)

That is the *taqleed* (imitation), for us it is *wajib* to be under *taqleed*, under guidance, under *itibah* (obedience) means to be under obedience, under guidance, why? Because they want to open this *Hadith.*

We have said many times before that the schools of *tarbiyya* are the schools of this holy *Hadith.* They want to open these *Hadiths* because the *Hadith* of Prophet ﷺ are real and living. It is not a story from old but that the *Hadith* must be real, must be living, and there must be servants who resemble that reality; they live, they walk, they talk in that reality.

Don't Take a School of Ideology That is Based on Hate

It means they come into our lives and begin to teach that from *malakut* you want to reach to the world of light. Then your *madhhab* (creed) is the *madhhab* of *muhabbat* because Allah عزَّ وجلَّ loves all His Creation. Don't take a *madhhab* of *Shaytan* and *hizb ash Shaytan* (party of Satan). It means don't take a school, an ideology, based on hate. It is based on love. Anywhere you go where people want to divide and want to make *la'nat*, curse, is *hizb ash Shaytan* because *Shaytan* is busy trying to take everybody into *jahannam* (hellfire). And *Ahlul Muhabbat* (People of Love) are busy trying to fit everybody into Paradise. So whatever you think, that teaching coming, they are busy trying to take people into Hell. For what?

We busy our life trying to take people back into Paradise. What Allah عزَّ وجلَّ loves, what Prophet ﷺ loves, what *ulul amr* love, is love. Not romance, and people touching themselves for no reason and touching other people. But it is *muhabbat*, is love, it's tolerance, is patience, is all the good character. That no matter how much Allah عزَّ وجلَّ squeezes you stay sweet; no matter how much people bother you, stay sweet. No matter how much *imtihaan*, tests, come into your life, into our lives, we stay sweet. If the test changes you, then what was the value? If a test comes and you become of a bad character, you become an angry character, you become a cursing character, then Allah ﷻ is not in need.

Awliya (Saints) Are the Mobile Phones for the Heaven

All the schools of *tarbiyya* (manners) are to perfect that love. So then they teach all this testing is coming, testing is coming, it is a science, that Allah ﷻ wants to open. First I am going to open for you your hearing. *Awliyaullah*, and there are 124,000 *Awliya* (saints) on this Earth. *Ahlul Basirah*, 124,000 *Awliya* on this Earth. They are mobile phones for the Heavens. If you come into their presence they hear, which means the *malakut* they hear through the phone, because who is on the other side of that phone? Whomever in *malakut* (heavens) that Allah ﷻ wants, there is a phone in that presence and there is *insaan* (human being) on this *mulk* (Earth).

Whatever Allah ﷻ Gave You, Give It Back in Allah's ﷻ Way

When *insaan* (mankind) comes to *tasleem* and submit themselves they are handing over everything Allah ﷻ gave to them, they give it back; that is *tasleem* (submission). Other than *tasleem,* it is a crook because whatever Allah ﷻ gave to them, they stole it, they ran with it. What Allah ﷻ wants in *tasleem*, "I gave you hearing, give it back to Me," *sami'na wa atana. Yaa Rabbi,* I heard and I obey.

سَمِعْنَا وَأَطَعْنَا غُفْرَانَكَ رَبَّنَا وَإِلَيْكَ الْمَصِيْرُ

2:285 – "…Sam'ina wa ata'na, ghufranaka Rabbana wa ilaykal masir." (Surah Al-Baqarah)

"…We hear, and we obey: (We seek) Thy forgiveness, our Lord, and to Thee is the end of all journeys." (The Cow, 2:285)

I gave you *rizq* (sustenance) now give it back to Me, I gave you sight, give it back to Me, whatever I gave you, *ilm* (knowledge), give it back to Me. It means put it all back to Allah ﷻ and surrender it and nothing in Allah's ﷻ way will be lost. But *dunya* comes and makes us fear, *yaa Rabbi,* if I put it there I will lose it, it will be gone. And the people of *haqqaiq* (reality) they realize that whatever you give to Allah ﷻ, He multiplies it. Whatever knowledge you thought you had, give it to Allah ﷻ and claim yourself to be nothing. Allah ﷻ will continually bestow upon you fountains of reality. Whatever sustenance Allah ﷻ gave to you, give it to Allah ﷻ and He will make a fountain of sustenance to float to you. It means whatever Allah ﷻ gave you – Allah ﷻ gave you will, then surrender your 'will' back to Allah ﷻ and Allah ﷻ will open *samawati wal ardh* (heavens and earth) to you.

But *Shaytan* comes and brings fear which is the opposite of faith. Satan comes and begins to say, "No, fear, whatever you do from that will be lost, it won't come back." And *iman* (faith) is that no, whatever you do in Allah's ﷻ way Allah ﷻ will multiply beyond imagination.

So it means they come and begin to teach, you want to be from the mobile phone? Do you want to be from the *ulul amr* and the people of realities? Their *madhhab* is the *madhhab* of love, their character is of patience and tolerance. Their reality is to bring everybody back to Paradise. Not to make one person to run into the hands of *Shaytan.*

GUIDE PEOPLE TO GOODNESS, DON'T SAY YOUR *SALAH* DOESN'T COUNT!

We went to the *masjid* for one of the events and a lady came to the ladies side and told one of the ladies, "Your outfit is not correct for *salah* (prayer). Sit down, don't pray, your prayer doesn't count." Is this *hizb ash Shaytan* (Party of Satan) or *hizb ar Rahman* (Party of The Most Merciful)? It is *hizb ash Shaytan* because you made the biggest *shirk* (partner) with Allah ﷻ because Allah ﷻ says, "I guide My Nations, I judge My Creation, not you. You haven't an eye to judge them, you haven't a heart to judge them, you don't know what their intention is. You don't know how patient I am with My servant. I am patient with them." And *insaan* (human being), who has no good character, no perfection, no permission for guidance, tells somebody, "sit down, don't pray." That is what *Shaytan* would do, to tell people, "Don't pray, it is not going to count." Who are you to say it is going to count or not count?

Our job is to guide people towards goodness. Say, pray whatever condition you are in, pray because Allah ﷻ owns your heart, not me. The Owner of that heart, He will guide you. Come with love, come with *muhabbat*, come however you want. The One who owns your heart, He guides you. If He likes that prayer, it is but an instant *Kun fayakun* and your heart can see the Seven Heavens and you will be completely in *tasleem* (submission). When is that going to come? That is up to Allah ﷻ. The guides begin to teach to have love and patience because Allah ﷻ guides His Creation. We are just people of *muhabbat*, we give a fountain of *muhabbat*, make people feel safe and feel loved.

1. Open Sense of Hearing at the Station of *Qalb* (Heart)

Surrender Your Hearing to the Spiritual Guidance, Not to Your Ego

They begin to teach, you want this reality, *sami'na wa atana* (we heard and we obey), open your ears, surrender these ears to these guides. Not what you hear, you want to do but what I heard of guidance. Not what you heard from yourself. "*Yaa Rabbi,* I heard I want a chocolate I am going to have a chocolate, I heard I want to bother people, I am going to go and bother them."

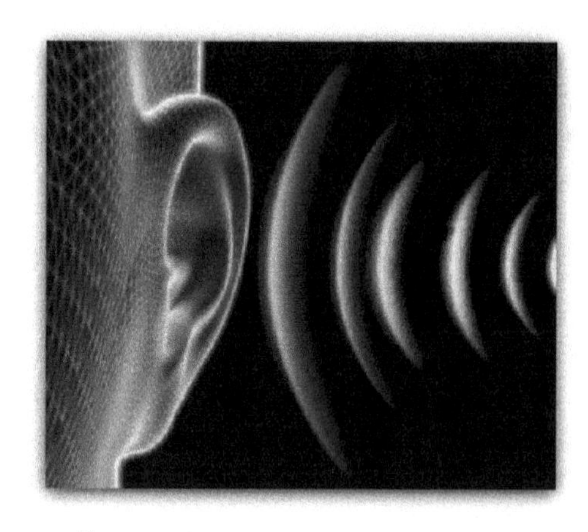

The ocean of *itibah* (obedience) is to open the reality, to be a mobile phone, to be from *Ahlul Basirah*. Then Allah عزّ وجلّ says, these ears you have, give it to them. Surrender your hearing and enter into the ocean of what Prophet صلى الله عليه وسلم brought for the *Sahabi* (Companions), *sam`ina wa atana.*

سَمِعْنَا وَأَطَعْنَا غُفْرَانَكَ رَبَّنَا وَإِلَيْكَ الْمَصِيْرُ

2:285 – "…Sam'ina wa ata'na, ghufranaka Rabbana wa ilaykal masir." (Surah Al-Baqarah)

"…We hear, and we obey: (We seek) Thy forgiveness, our Lord, and to Thee is the end of all journeys." (The Cow, 2:285)

The Companions perfected it, what they heard from Prophet صلى الله عليه وسلم, and were in complete obedience because they surrendered their ears.

Yaa Rabbi, I give you my physical ears, through your training and practices of physical ears, Allah ﷻ opens your spiritual hearing. Allah ﷻ describes, We have a lock placed upon their ears.

أَفَرَأَيْتَ مَنِ اتَّخَذَ إِلَـٰهَهُ هَوَاهُ وَأَضَلَّهُ اللَّـهُ عَلَىٰ عِلْمٍ وَخَتَمَ عَلَىٰ سَمْعِهِ وَقَلْبِهِ وَجَعَلَ عَلَىٰ بَصَرِهِ غِشَاوَةً فَمَن يَهْدِيهِ مِن بَعْدِ اللَّـهِ ۚ أَفَلَا تَذَكَّرُونَ (٢٣)

45:23 – "Afara ayta manit takhadha ilaha hu hawahu wa adallahu Allahu 'ala 'Ilmin wa khatama 'ala sam'ihi wa qalbihi, wa ja'ala 'ala basarihi ghishawatan faman yahdeehi min ba'di Allahi, afala tadhakkaron."
(Surah Al-Jathiyah)

"Have you seen he who has taken as his god his [own] desire, and Allah has sent him astray due to knowledge and has set a seal upon his hearing and his heart and put over his vision a veil? So who will guide him after Allah (has withdrawn Guidance)? Then will you not be reminded?" (The Kneeling, 45:23)

Who Owns Your Ears? Ear Piercing is a Sign

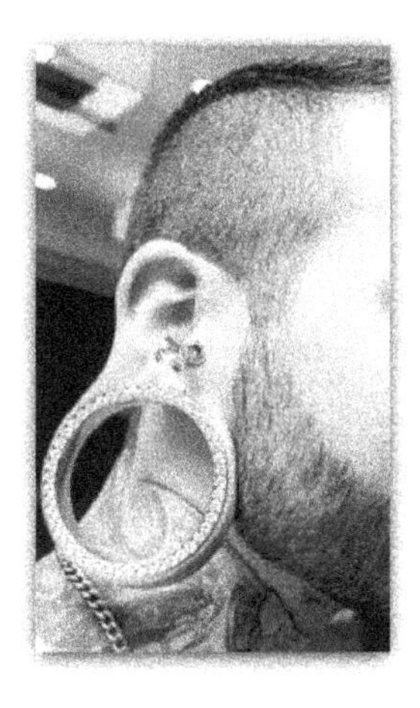

Why *Shaytan* has so many people with all their ears pierced? If you want to know the reality look to *Shaytan,* he has more advertising but *Rahman* (The Most Merciful) is more hidden. Now everybody has something on their ears. Men, not women, for women that is part of their fashion, but only one. Now they have like five hundred on their ears. Men, they even put in their ears, something that looks like a hockey puck, this big! That *Shaytan*, not the person, the person is innocent, they have a soul, but *Shaytan* is showing everybody, "Those ears are for me, I have yoked it, I have held his ears, his ears are for me" and you see the sign everywhere. Their entire being is being marked and shown they are not for *Rahman* but they are for the lower desires.

Then our whole life is to find a school in which I can submit my ears. Not to find a school in which I don't have to listen. It means to find a school of *tarbiyya* (good character). Now through even live broadcast they are everywhere. If you find those whose hearts are open and their teaching is the way of *muhabbat* and not *la'nat*, they curse no one.

Don't Curse Anyone, Everyone is From Nation of Sayyidina Muhammad ﷺ

مَّا خَلْقُكُمْ وَلَا بَعْثُكُمْ إِلَّا كَنَفْسٍ وَاحِدَةٍ إِنَّ اللَّهَ سَمِيعٌ بَصِيرٌ

31:28 – "Ma khalqukum wala ba`thukum illa kanafsin wahidatin inn Allaha Samee'un Baseer." (Surah Al-Luqman)

"Your creation and your resurrection will not be but as that of a single soul. Indeed, Allah is Hearing and Seeing." (Luqman, 31:28)

If you know that all Creation is under *Nur Muhammad* ﷺ, there is nothing outside of *Nur Muhammad* ﷺ. *Rabbil mu'mineen wa rabbal kafireen* (Lord of the Believers and Lord of the Unbelievers), Allah عزّ وجلّ is Lord over all Creation. If every light is from the light of Sayyidina Muhammad (ﷺ) how could you possibly curse someone? Tomorrow he or she might be coming into faith.

So they understood; they have a *taqwa* (consciousness) and fear. That Prophet ﷺ has a nation that accepted his *da'wah* (invitation). And all of Creation that didn't accept that *da'wah*, they are the *Ummah* that needs *da'wah*. That Message has to go to them because all that Creation is coming back to Prophet ﷺ.

WHAT YOU HEAR OF GOSSIP AFFECTS YOUR HEART

It means they have the best of character, the most of love, they are not here to judge anyone. So the guides begin to exhibit the characteristics of patience and tolerance and love. They begin to teach that, "Listen and begin to open your ears." Watch out for what is coming into your ears, of bad sound, of bad gossip, of bad talking. It means have a vigilance over your ears, like fasting. As soon as you go somewhere and someone is talking bad, don't think it is something small. When somebody is talking bad it is affecting your heart. Never the person, this is not an insult to any person, but when you go and someone is talking bad, you have to visualize as if *Shaytan* has little arrows and he is hitting the ear… bing, bing, bing, bing. Because the person is saying things but could be bringing doubt into your heart, and *ghaibat* (gossip), bringing a bad impression of somebody into your heart. It means changing your character from being sweet and loving to exhibiting all these bad characteristics.

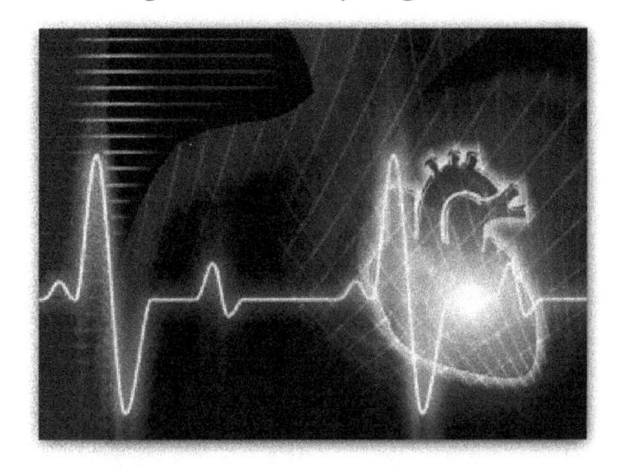

So it means this way of *tazkiya* (purification) is very difficult. *Ramadan* is not only you don't eat and become hungry but your ears are fasting. That, *yaa Rabbi,* perfect my ears, let me hear the good sounds of Your Holy Qur'an and *salawats* and to attend the *majlis* of *dhikr* and to keep the company of those who are also trying to clean their ears and purify.

The Ears Are the Door to the Soul

Then this lock of *sami`na wa atana* (We hear and we Obey) begins to open off the ears. If that lock opens upon the ears, this ear is the *baab* and the door of the soul. The eyes are the window of the soul, and the ears are the door of the soul. If Allah ﷻ releases the lock from the ear, it means that a door of the soul has now been opened.

That is why in the *dhikr* and *tafakkur* when they begin to teach you to make *tafakkur* (contemplation) the more you sit and listen, sit and listen, Allah ﷻ gives a permission to unlock that door. Soon as they unlock that door they can bring the soul of that person out where they begin to feel the energy of that *dhikr*. They feel the energy of the *tafakkur* because Allah ﷻ begins to give a permission that lower that door and this power of that soul can come out. The soul and the light is something that can't be imagined. Only a small part of that has been given to *insaan*, the greater part of that soul is always with Allah ﷻ; only a small light has been given to the body.

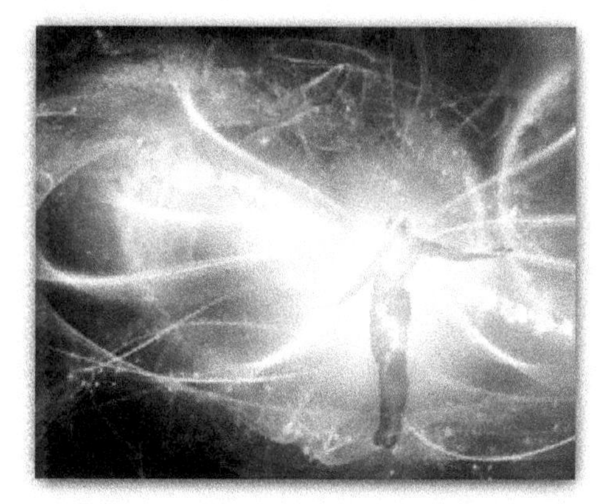

In *Salah* the Soul Could Go to the Presence of the Divine

Through *sam`ina wa atana* – even in the *salah* why are you going like this, raising both hands to your ears saying *"Allahu Akbar"* (Allah is Great)? Because only *siffat Allahu Akbar* can bring the fire of bad character and ignorance off of these locks. Because the *salah* is the time in which you should have been able to send your soul into Allah's ﷻ Presence. So by saying, *"Allahu Akbar,"* it means that Allah says, from whatever I gave you *ana al Akbar*, I am even greater than what you have even understood of me. Only My *Izza* and My Might can destroy what *Shaytan* is trying to put upon your ears.

Awliya (saints) free their soul, as soon as they say, *"Allahu Akbar,"* their soul is in that presence. It's according to their *darajat* (rank), some, their souls go to *Madinah*, some souls go to *Makkah*, some souls go into the Heavens, depending upon what Allah ﷻ opened from the *darajat* of that one's soul. So it means then their whole life is how to open the concept of their hearing, to hear good to open the reality of their soul.

2. Open the Sense of Seeing
at the Station of *Sir* (Secret)

What You See Can Darken the Heart

If the ears begin to open, then Allah ﷻ begins to focus upon their eyes. That give back your sight, give back what you are trying to see with your eyes and take a path of *tafakkur* and meditation. As much as you feed these eyes, as much this heart becomes darker. So all day long what does *Shaytan* want? Look at the internet, look at everything forbidden, look at every type of image, why? Because those images are going to the heart, they are darkening the heart, they are loading the heart.

So as soon as you sit for *tafakkur* it's all those images that you are now trying to get out of your mind. You keep saying, "*Yaa Rabbi, astagfirullah, astagfirullah, astagfirullah, astagfirullah.*" How can you sit for *tafakkur* (contemplation) when you are seeing all this bad in your eyes. Then you say, "O Shaykh I don't want to do this, I don't want to do *tafakkur.*" So then safeguard the sight.

Keep Your Eyes Upon Your Feet – *Nazar Bar Qadam*

For *Naqshbandiyya*, it is *nazar bar qadam*, keep your eyes upon your feet, which means that to safeguard your vision. What your eyes are seeing is not for this *dunya* (material world); these eyes should be for seeing the Heavens. When the eyes are kept clean, this is an inheritance from the Companions of Prophet ﷺ. *Karram Allahu Wajha*, (May Allah honour his face), Imam Ali عليه السلام is representing the purified eyes, the perfected eyes, he is the master of *Ahlul Basirah* (People of Spiritual Vision), to see all of the Heavens, of what Allah عز وجل wants to bestow upon the servant.

It means then the whole path is the perfection of the eyes. Live a life in which you lower your gaze. Live a life in which you perfect what you are seeing and life a life in which you are continuously cleansing. Even those whose eyes are taking in too much, they can meditate in water, in the shower. When they go into the shower they are supposed to close their eyes and see their soul washing and whirling. That by the power of the water, it washes away all the sins. The more they can control that and begin to meditate and make *tafakkur* under the water, they can wash even what this garbage and these images are trying to put upon the soul. It means even through their washing, their *ghusl*, their *wudu* everything to take away those images, they begin to safeguard their vision.

When You Cleanse Your Eyes, You See With Your Soul

When you block out that vision Allah عز وجل will begin to open the vision of the heart.

ثُمَّ لَتَرَوُنَّهَا عَيْنَ الْيَقِينِ

102:7 – "Thum ma la tara wun naha 'ayn al yaqeen." (Surah At-Takathur)

"Then you will surely see it with the eye/vision of certainty."
(The Rivalry in World Increase, 102:7)

Where you begin to see with the power of your soul, you will see the *ulul amr* (People of Command /Authority), who are in front of you. You will see through the Heavens, you will see into the *Diwan al Awliya* (Association of Saints), and into the heart of Sayyidina Muhammad صلى الله عليه وسلم which goes into the Divinely Presence of Allah عز و جل. Allah's عز و جل Divinely Presence can only be found in the heart of Sayyidina Muhammad صلى الله عليه وسلم. There is nothing outside the heart of Sayyidina Muhammad صلى الله عليه وسلم.

It means the whole *mi'raj* (ascension), the whole focus is towards Prophet صلى الله عليه وسلم, in the heart of Prophet صلى الله عليه وسلم. *Qalbun mu'min baytullah,* Allah عز و جل says, "I am not on the Earth but I am in the heart of My believer."

قَلْبَ الْمُؤْمِنْ بَيْتُ الرَّبْ

"Qalb al mu'min baytur rabb."

"The heart of the believer is the House of the Lord." (Hadith Qudsi)

مَا وَسِعَنِيْ لَا سَمَائِيْ ولا اَرْضِيْ وَلَكِنْ وَسِعَنِيْ قَلْبِ عَبْدِيْ اَلْمُؤْمِنْ

"Maa wasi`anee laa Samayee, wa la ardee, laakin wasi'anee qalbi 'Abdee al Mu'min."

"Neither My Heavens nor My Earth can contain Me, but the heart of my Believing Servant." (Hadith Qudsi conveyed by Prophet Muhammad ﷺ)

The only believer for Allah ﷻ is Sayyidina Muhammad ﷺ. It means that reality is in the heart of Prophet ﷺ. Once they begin to train, clean the eyes, lower the eyes, wash the eyes, lower the gaze, that, *yaa Rabbi,* I don't want from these eyes, I want from the eye of my heart, the eye of my soul. *Ya Rabbi,* begin to open that reality. By cleansing the physical Allah ﷻ begins to open the spiritual.

3. Open Sense of Spiritual Touch at the Station of *Sirr e Sir* (Secret of the Secret)

Through the spiritual seeing and the spiritual hearing, now begins to open up the *lataif*, the subtlety; you become subtle because now it is becoming a real *haqqaiq*. You are hearing the reality; you begin to hear your consciousness. You hear your soul from Allah's ﷻ Presence, it is getting all the advice from them, coming and begins to give you a *nisah*, an advice, "Do like this, do like that, do like this, do like that," all towards goodness. When they are hearing the advice and they begin to open their seeing, and see what Allah ﷻ wants them to see, that hearing and seeing is opening the *haqq* (truth) for them.

إِنَّ هَٰذَا لَهُوَ حَقُّ الْيَقِينِ

56:95 – "Inna hadha la huwa haq qul yaqeen." (Surah Al-Waqi'ah)

"Indeed, this is the true certainty." (The Inevitable, 56:95)

As they open the *haqq* (truth) for them they become more subtle, *latif*, they begin now to feel the sense of touch and feel is opening. They are hearing, because these are going to begin to open. When they are hearing and they are seeing they begin to feel everything.

So imagine the scary version because you can't see in the room. So all of a sudden if you see something frightening in the room and it sees that you saw it; it becomes very real for you because now it comes and runs after you. So it opens both sides, scary and not so scary. But with your practices and *dhikr* and all these realities, now that becomes *haqqaiq*. You are hearing the reality, you are beginning to train your soul to see the reality, and it becomes now a real reality. You are becoming subtle and the sense of touch is beginning to open.

4. Open Sense of Smell
at the Station of *Khafa* (Hidden)

If the sense of touch, the sense of hearing, and seeing is opening, then Allah ﷻ gives permission to begin to open the sense of smelling. Where they can begin to smell the fragrances of Paradise and they smell the fragrances of *shayateen* (devils). They go somewhere and they can smell something is not correct, because they are working through their soul.

The soul is very subtle; it picks up the fragrance of people. It can pick up when somebody has a bad thought, a bad intention in his heart, it is not putting out a *bukhoor*, (incense), but it is putting out a powerful odor of dirtiness. They can smell that and they understand what is happening.

Same with the good, they can go somewhere and have tremendous smell like a bouquet, like a *bukhoor*, because they are the *ashiqeen* (lovers). Their hearts are in love and it is burning like a charcoal, burning with love and Allah ﷻ keeps putting fragrances on it. That reality begins to open where these fragrances are opening from *malakut* (heavens) and from angels.

The smell and what they call aromatherapy is an angelic reality. The smell and the reality of smell is from the angelic reality. For them smell is very powerful because you are now entering into the angelic reality.

5. Open Sense of Taste at the Station of *Akhfa* (Most Hidden)

Then they are becoming more and more subtle and more and more in that dimension. Then the highest of realities, is that they are now beginning to taste the *haqqaiq*. They are hearing it, they are seeing it, they are experiencing it with all their senses, they are smelling it through the fragrance.

We said before, that the *du'a* of these *ulul amr* and *Ahlul Basirah* is not through the *kalam* (words), the *kalam* is the lowest level because Allah ﷻ says, I am going to seal your mouth when you come up into the Heavens.

الْيَوْمَ نَخْتِمُ عَلَىٰ أَفْوَاهِهِمْ وَتُكَلِّمُنَا أَيْدِيهِمْ وَتَشْهَدُ أَرْجُلُهُم بِمَا كَانُوا يَكْسِبُونَ (٦٥)

36:65 – "Al yawma nakhtimu 'ala afwahehim wa tukallimunaa aydeehim wa tashhadu arjuluhum bima kanoo yaksiboon." (Surah Yaseen)

"That Day, We will seal over their mouths, and their hands will speak to Us, and their feet will testify about what they used to earn." (Yaseen, 36:65)

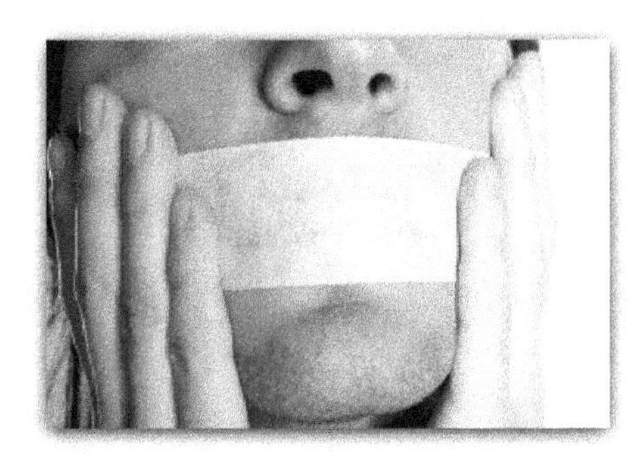

Because your mouth can be professional and can keep speaking, speaking, speaking but, the mouth doesn't tell you the condition of the heart. There are some people who have a very good mouth (speech) but they don't tell you the condition of the heart.

The *Malaika* only carry the *du'a* of the good fragrance. So it means as soon as the saints make a *du'a*, the heart puts out a fragrance to which the angels are attracted. They carry that fragrance to the Heavens, not what the servant said through their mouth but the fragrance that is being released through their heart.

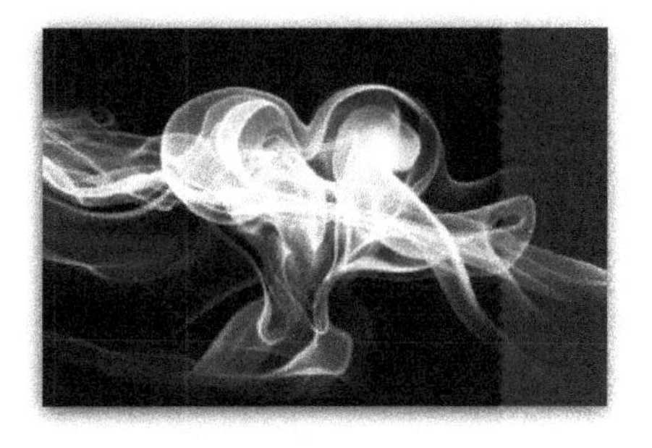

From that it opens up the reality of taste, in which every reality is dressing them and they become the mobile phones of the Heavens *inshaAllah.*

...وَلَا يَزَالُ عَبْدِي يَتَقَرَّبُ إِلَيَّ بِالنَّوَافِلِ حَتَّى أُحِبَّهُ، فَإِذَا أَحْبَبْتُهُ كُنْتُ سَمْعَهُ الَّذِي يَسْمَعُ بِهِ، وَبَصَرَهُ الَّذِي يُبْصِرُ بِهِ، وَيَدَهُ الَّتِي يَبْطِشُ بِهَا، وَرِجْلَهُ الَّتِي يَمْشِي بِهَا، وَلَئِنْ سَأَلَنِي لَأُعْطِيَنَّهُ، وَلَئِنْ اسْتَعَاذَنِي لَأُعِيذَنَّهُ." [رَوَاهُ الْبُخَارِيُّ]

"..., wa la yazaalu 'Abdi yataqarrabu ilayya bin nawafile hatta ahebahu, fa idha ahbabtuhu kunta Sam'ahul ladhi yasma'u behi, wa Basarahul ladhi yubsiru

behi, wa Yadahul lati yabTeshu beha, wa Rejlahul lati yamshi beha, wa la in sa alani la a'Teyannahu, …"

"…My servant continues to draw near to Me with voluntary acts of worship so that I shall love him. When I love him, I am his hearing with which he hears, his seeing with which he sees, his hand with which he strikes and his foot with which he walks. Were he to ask [something] of Me, I would surely give it to him…"
(Hadith Qudsi, Sahih al-Bukhari, 81:38:2)

Subhana rabbika rabil 'izzati 'ama yasifoon, Wa salamun 'alal mursaleen wal hamdulillahi rabbil 'alameen. Bi hurmati Muhammadil Mustafa wa bi siratil Suratil Fatiha.

COLOURS AND SEASONS OF THE LEVELS OF THE HEART

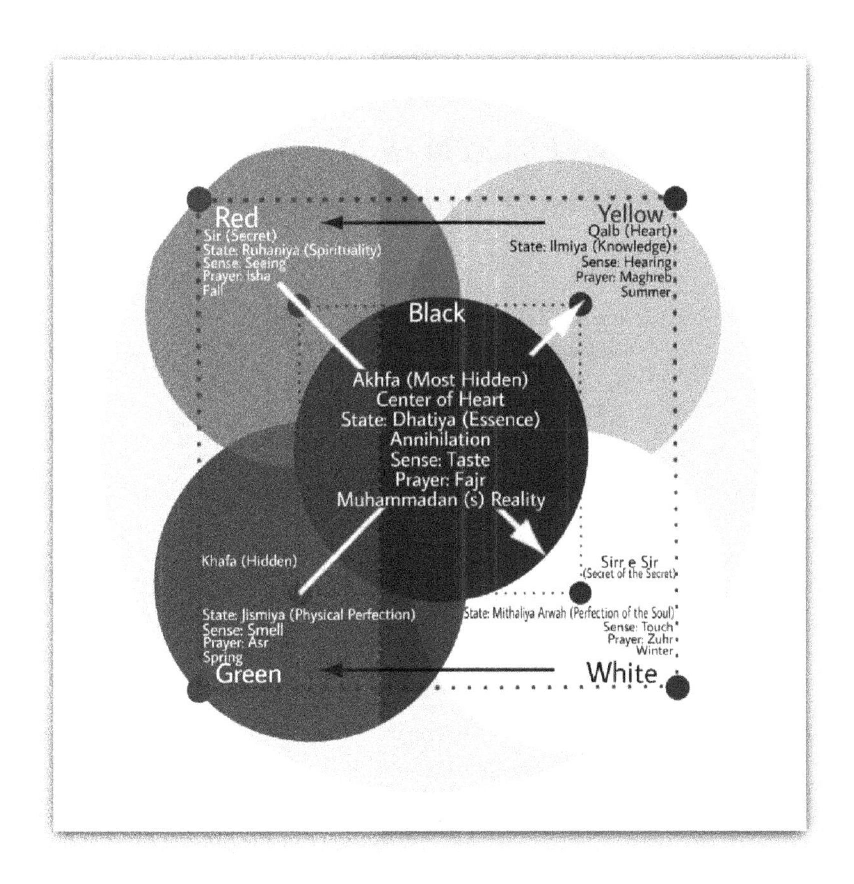

1. Yellow Represents Summer at the Station of *Qalb* (Heart)

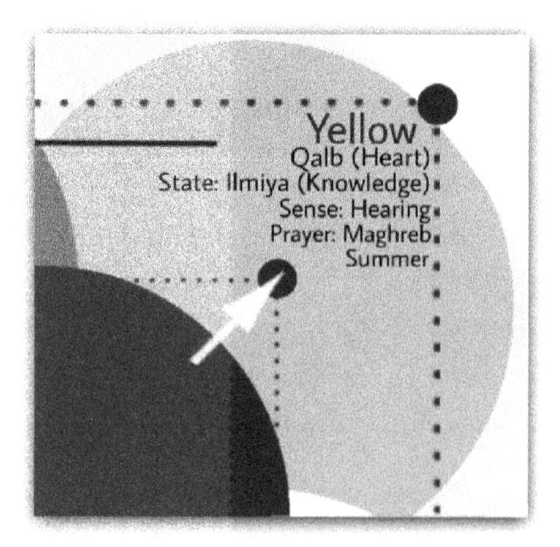

The first station of the heart, *Qalb* (Heart) is yellow and represents the season of summer and the reality of the Sun. Yellow has the reality of the height of life and the excitement of life. Yellow also represents the significance of knowledge.

2. Red Represents Fall at the Station of *Sir* (Secret)

You go from the season of summer to red, second station of *Sir* (Secret). The importance of red becomes the understanding of fall. In the height of life the coming of fall is a preparation for nature in the state of death. Whether it's one day or one year, or the cycle of life, the Divine is teaching you it's all the same. Everything is moving within that same reality. From summer time, everybody is happy, that is a season of one year. Then you come to fall and as soon as things become red, it's showing us it's preparing for death. Red is symbolic with war, with death, and with the process of dying.

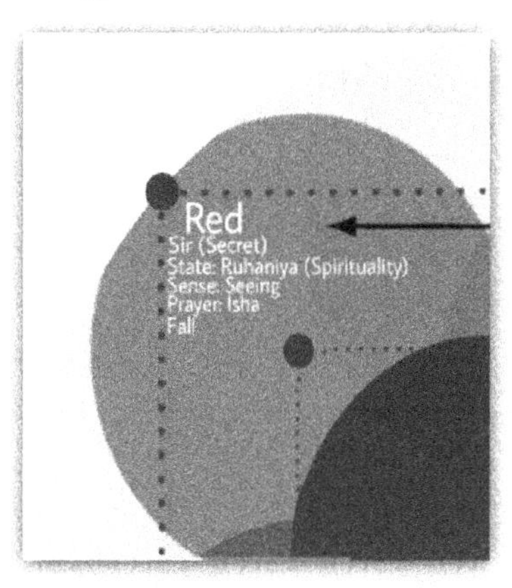

Then through this hourglass, you are going to pass into the black. Black is a state of no colour, no more existence, because the understanding of colours is that you see only what element was reflected out; the rest is absorbed in. You see yellow because yellow is what is left out; the rest of the colour spectrum went in. That is the understanding of colours. But when you

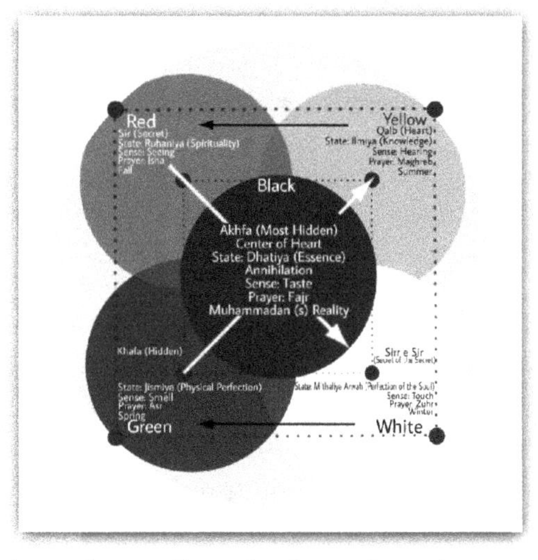

get to black, everything went in. For us that means the state of death; that is the time of non-existence. In the reality of the season, from fall coming to winter, there is a secret of death.

3. White Represents Winter
at the Station of *Sirr e Sir* (Secret of the Secret)

Then come into the white and the reality of white has to do with the preservation of life. The Divine is teaching us that winter is a state of preserving. We are trying to understand ourselves, so the Divine begins to teach to, 'Look upon the horizon and look upon yourself.'

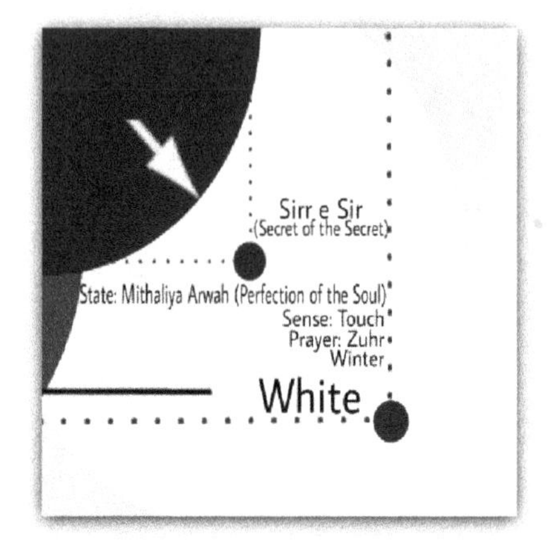

سَنُرِيهِمْ آيَاتِنَا فِي الْآفَاقِ وَفِي أَنفُسِهِمْ حَتَّىٰ يَتَبَيَّنَ لَهُمْ أَنَّهُ الْحَقُّ ۗ ... ٥٣

41:53 – "Sanureehim ayatina fil afaqi wa fee anfusihim hatta yatabayyana lahum annahu alhaqqu ..." (Surah Al-Isra)

"We will show them Our signs in the horizons and within themselves until it becomes clear to them that it is the truth..." (The Night Journey, 41:53)

Don't think that I can't preserve you and resurrect you; I'm doing it all around. Look at your summer, you are enjoying yourself. All of a sudden it's fall and all the trees are turning red and they are dying. They enter the state of death and by winter they are in a state of preservation. It is also the reality of *Barzakh.*

يُخْرِجُ الْحَيَّ مِنَ الْمَيِّتِ وَيُخْرِجُ الْمَيِّتَ مِنَ الْحَيِّ وَيُحْيِي الْأَرْضَ بَعْدَ مَوْتِهَا ۚ وَكَذَٰلِكَ تُخْرَجُونَ (١٩)

30:19 – "Yukhriju alhayya mina almayyitiwayukhriju almayyita mina alhayyi wayuhyee al-ardabaAAda mawtiha wakathalika tukhrajoon." (Surah Ar-Rum)

"It is He Who brings out the living from the dead, and brings out the dead from the living, and Who revives the earth and Gives it life after it is dead: and thus will you be brought out (from the dead/Resurrected)." (The Romans, 30:19)

So white is to preserve; white is symbolic that you are in the state of death and the purity of death. That's why all of our eastern traditions are white. It means you passed the death and now you are in the ritual purity of white. In many traditions they bury with white because you are in a heavenly-like state.

4. Green Represents Spring at the Station of *Khafa* (Hidden)

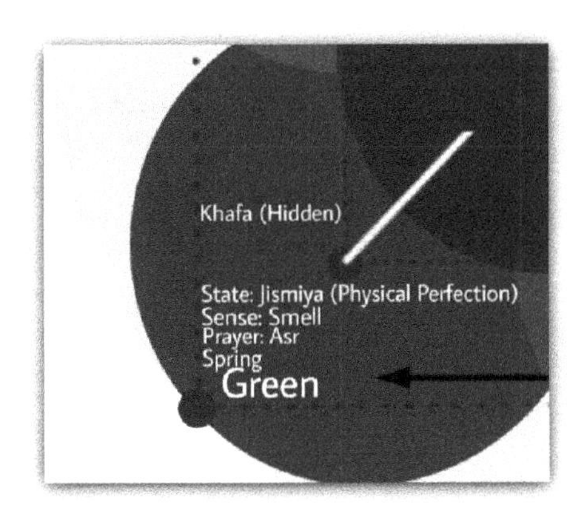

The Divine is showing that from the white you move to the green, because in nature, as soon as winter snow goes, now comes spring. From those same trees comes the next colour, green representing spring, the fourth station of the heart *Khafa* (Most Hidden).

Spring is the reality of resurrection. The rains of April and the reality of spring, is the Divine showing that with that Divinely water that falls from the sky, everything is resurrected. So then the plants and the trees that looked like they were dead to us before, they are now resurrected with these lights.

وَآيَةٌ لَّهُمُ الْأَرْضُ الْمَيْتَةُ أَحْيَيْنَاهَا وَأَخْرَجْنَا مِنْهَا حَبًّا فَمِنْهُ يَأْكُلُونَ

36:33 – "Wa ayatun lahumul ardul maytatu ahyaynaha wa akhrajna minha habban faminhu yakuloon." (Surah YaSeen) Wa ayatun lahumul ardul maytatu ahyaynaha wa akhrajna minha habban faminhu yakuloon." (Surah Yaseen)

"A Sign for them is the earth that is dead: We do give it life, and produce grain from it, of which you do eat." (Yaseen, 36:33)

Then again from spring we move towards the reality of summer. It means then the colours have a tremendous importance for us. Many understandings of the yellow have to do with the significance of knowledge, the height of the material life. Red has to do with the struggling and the state of death, the state of warfare, the state of struggling against yourself.

5. Black Represents the State of Annihilation at the Station of *Akhfa* (Most Hidden)

Black is a colour which absorbs everything because colours are what reflect back to you. The green is what didn't absorb and reflects back to your eye. The black, it absorbs everything. It is the reality and station of *fana*, station of annihilation, in the Divinely Presence.

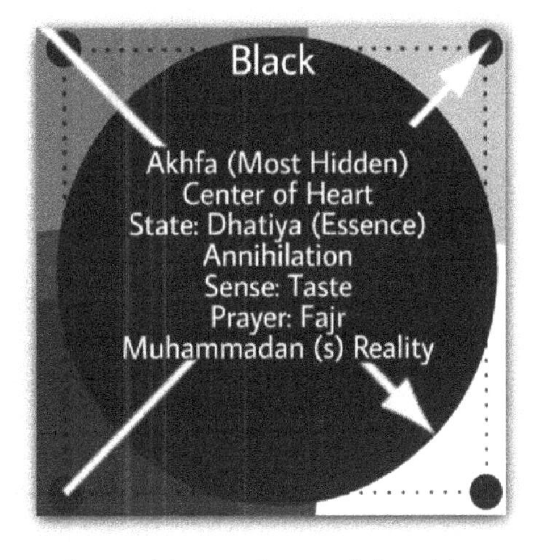

Black has to do with the state of annihilation, that if you died and annihilated yourself. You shouldn't be having an existence; you shouldn't be reflecting anything of yourself, of your character, of your personality. Then the black, being the highest point, means that the highest point is to enter into the Divine with no characteristic, with no identity, to be nothing; to be annihilated in the Divinely Presence.

THE COLOURS OF THE *LATAIF AL QALB* ARE INTERMIXED

Then there are tremendous realities of the colour white; the purity of the state of death. Green has to do with the power of resurrection, the beauty of spring and how the Divine brings everything back to life.

These are all intermixing colours; it's not just one colour. The yellow has infinite dimensions of colour when it begins to touch the red, when it begins to touch the black, it is touching the white. Inside it's also touching the green. It means the phases of these colours are the lights of the soul. They begin to teach that fall passes death and becomes winter. Then as soon as winter is finished, it enters spring and everything comes back to life, *InshaAllah.*

Subhana rabbika rabil 'izzati 'ama yasifoon, Wa salamun 'alal mursaleen wal hamdulillahi rabbil 'alameen. Bi hurmati Muhammadil Mustafa wa bi siratil Suratil Fatiha.

MURAQABAH (SPIRITUAL CONNECTION) AND LEVELS OF THE HEART

Alhamdulillah, there are many different realities in *tariqa* (spiritual path) and these are gifts from Allah's عزّ وجلّ Divinely Presence to the presence of Sayyidina Muhammad (صلى الله عليه وسلم) and from Sayyidina Muhammad صلى الله عليه وسلم to *Awliyaullah* (saints). From the teachings of the saints and guides and perfected ones, it is a reminder that out of the many oceans of realities that we have talked about is the meditation and *muraqabah.*

It means all of it is based on how to open the heart. The heart has its subtle openings, what they call *lataif*, like satellite dishes of energy that open the layers of the holy heart to the holy presence and the Divinely lights of the Heavenly Kingdom to come. It means we are asking from

Allah's ﷻ Heavenly Kingdom to come onto Earth and come into our hearts and to make our heart be a Heavenly Kingdom.

THE HEAD MUST SUBMIT FIRST, THEN THE HEART OPENS

SUBMIT THE 7 HOLY OPENINGS OF THE HEAD

For the heart to open, the holy head has to be in submission. It means that when the ears are in submission, the eyes are in submission, and the breath is in submission. Then the last and most difficult is the holy tongue; that all of it must be in submission. So all of the *tariqa* training comes to teach us that when we accompany the shaykhs, accompany our perfected masters, they teach us how to perfect our *samina wa atana*, "we hear and we obey."

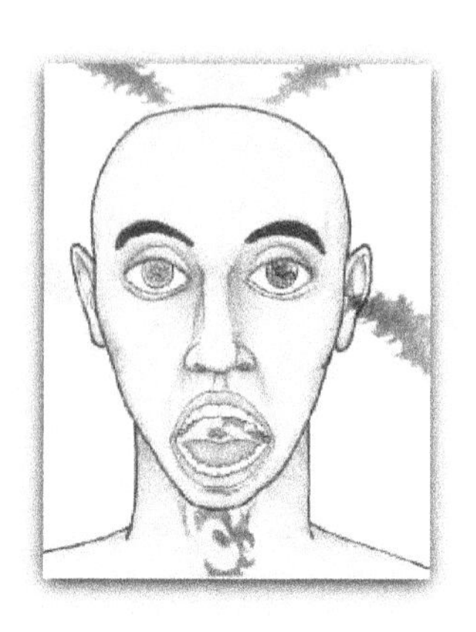

THE EARS HAVE DIRECT CONNECTION TO THE FEET – KEEP YOU BALANCED

سَمِعْنَا وَأَطَعْنَا غُفْرَانَكَ رَبَّنَا وَإِلَيْكَ الْمَصِيرُ

2:285 – "…Sam'ina wa ata'na, ghufranaka Rabbana wa ilaykal masir." (Surah Al-Baqarah)

"…We hear, and we obey: (We seek) Thy forgiveness, our Lord, and to Thee is the end of all journeys." (The Cow, 2:285)

So Allah ﷻ is teaching directly, your ears are locked to your feet. So if you have vertigo you can't walk. There are two levels of ears. We have an outer ear and an inner spiritual ear. Allah ﷻ describes they have ears but they don't use it, they use it like the animal kingdom but we don't really hear into the heart.

KEEP YOUR VISION UPON YOUR FEET – *NAZAR BAR QADAM*

Keep your vision upon your feet, *nazar bar qadam*, why? Because your *nazar* has your *hawa*, your desires. You don't see blind people have *dunya* (material world) desires. There is no blind person out there trying to conquer the Earth and buy a Ferrari, he can't see, he can't use it. There are no blind people with material desires.

Then seeing is directly connected to your desires. Keep your desire closed and keep your vision on your feet. It means watch where your feet are taking you in life. If these feet go dancing we have got trouble. If these feet go to *masjid* to worship and do prayers, *alhamdulillah,* we are on the footsteps of piety and on the footsteps of Sayyidina Muhammad صلى الله عليه وسلم *qadam al Haqq, wa qadam as Siddiq* (The Footstep of the Truthful). And those who are inheriting from holy Companions and *Ahl al-Bayt an-Nabi* صلى الله عليه وسلم, inherit the footsteps of Prophet صلى الله عليه وسلم.

TAFAKKUR (CONTEMPLATION/MEDITATION)

IN *TAFAKKUR* (MEDITATION) SEE YOUR *IMAM* IN FRONT

From the previous teachings, if all of the head openings are understood and are submitting from its animal nature, and coming down towards its heavenly reality, immediately at that time they begin to teach us in the meditation and in the *tafakkur* (contemplation). That when you are making *tafakkur* and contemplation, you have to always be with the people of light. You always have to be with your *imam.* It means there is never a time that we accompany physically the shaykh and that spiritually we are not with him.

It means every concept of our life is of that nature, that, *yaa Rabbi,* the biggest *imam* (spiritual leader), the greatest *imam* is Sayyidina Muhammad صلى الله عليه وسلم. When we teach ourselves – or Sayyidina Isa عليه السلام or Nabi Musa عليه السلام or whatever nation they are from, and whichever prophet they are following – our life is based on, 'The Prophet is always in front of me.' That my life is always behind them, I pray that God accepts me to be dust under their feet.

But because we are not at that time then Allah ﷻ gives to us guides. So our holy shaykh is always my *imam*, whether I am accompanying him and praying behind him, and memorizing in the vision of my eye in my heart. It means I try never to leave that presence. It means that you are keeping the love of the shaykh. And that love of the shaykh, because we accompany based on love, not by force. Nobody can force us to sit here at spiritual associations; nothing will open by force.

Love Opens The *Hudur* (Presence) of the Shaykh

We accompany by love and they begin to teach with that love you begin to have a *hudur*, you feel a presence. That presence means you merely look at them and when you close your eyes you can see them with the eye of the soul, with the eye of the heart. That you see them and you build the relationship physically with them, and spiritually with them. That to always be in their company, that *muhabbat* and love for that reality, begins to develop the *hudur* and the presence of the shaykh. It means the physical presence of accompanying these masters and their

spiritual presence, because Allah ﷻ says; go through every house through the correct door.

...وَلَيْسَ الْبِرُّ بِأَن تَأْتُوا الْبُيُوتَ مِن ظُهُورِهَا وَلَٰكِنَّ الْبِرَّ مَنِ اتَّقَىٰ ۗ وَأْتُوا الْبُيُوتَ مِنْ أَبْوَابِهَا ۚ وَاتَّقُوا اللَّهَ لَعَلَّكُمْ تُفْلِحُونَ

2:189 – "... wa laysal birru bi-an tatol buyoota min zuhooriha wa lakinnal birra manit taqa, wa' tol buyoota min abwabiha, wat taqollaha la'allakum tuflihoon." (Surah Al-Baqarah)

"... And it is not righteousness to enter houses from the back, but righteousness is [in] one who fears Allah. And enter houses from their doors. And be Conscious of Allah that you may succeed." (The Cow, 2:189)

MURAQABAH (SPIRITUAL CONNECTION)

CONNECT WITH THE SHAYKH AT THE LEVEL OF SOUL

The house of Allah ﷻ is *qalbun mu'min baytullah* which means come through the heart not through the head. It means open the soul and make a connection with them through the level of the soul.

قَلْبَ الْمُؤْمِنْ بَيْتُ الرَّبْ

"Qalb al mu'min baytur rabb."

"The heart of the believer is the House of the Lord." (Hadith Qudsi)

There are people who accompany the Shaykh fifty years, forty years, ten years physically but they never attempted to connect spiritually. And that is the great error that is the great difficulty because all you are taking is from his physicality and it is such a small reality compared to the spirituality of the shaykh. That is the light and the eternal presence of the shaykh, he is the reflection of Sayyidina Muhammad ﷺ and Sayyidina Muhammad ﷺ is the Divinely reflection upon Earth.

The perfection of what Allah ﷻ wants is known through all the prophets. All the attributes of the Divine reflect through the prophetic reality and from the prophetic reality to the pious servants. *Atiullah wa ati ar rasula wa ulul amri minkum.*

يآأَيُّهَا الَّذِينَ آمَنُوا أَطِيعُوااللَّه وَأَطِيعُواْلرَّسُول وَأُوْلِي الأَمْرِ مِنْكُمْ

4:59 – "Ya ayyu hal ladheena amanoo Atiullaha, wa atiur Rasola, wa Ulil amre minkum…" (Surah An-Nisa)

"O You who have believed, Obey Allah, Obey the Messenger, and those in authority among you…" (The Women, 4:59)

The *ulul amr* (those with heavenly authority) inherit that reflection. So they begin to teach by keeping their presence, by meditating and contemplating that my Lord I never want to be without them, that I am always with them.

Realm of the Heart is Spiritual and Requires Spiritual Connection

As soon as you begin to learn to make *tafakkur* (contemplation), we are now leaving the level of the mind and the level of the physicality. Through the head at the initial stage, it was to discipline the physicality.

Now when we enter into the realm of the heart it is the realm of faith. This is no longer of a physical nature, this is of a spiritual nature, and we have to make a spiritual connection with our guide. Sultanul Awliya Mawlana

Shaykh Nazim ق, is the ultimate in that connection but, *alhamdulillah,* Allah عز وجل gave for us a perfect example of that reflection and making connection with that and asking always to be in the presence of Mawlana Shaykh Hisham Kabbani. For us in this region we seek his example, we seek his travelling, we hear his *suhbahs*, we hear all the teachings.

At First Stage We Try to Connect With the Shaykh

By that example we are asking, *yaa Rabbi,* let me to serve the one who is serving the *sultan* who is serving Prophet ﷺ. Let me have access to that one and be able to travel to see him, to take *bayah* (allegiance) with him, to accompany them, to serve them. That begins to open the concept that as soon as we are meditating and contemplating, *yaa Rabbi,* let me always be with him, from Your Holy Qur'an, *ittaqullah wa konu ma as-sadiqeen.*

...اتَّقُوا اللَّـهَ وَكُونُوا مَعَ الصَّادِقِينَ ١١٩

9:119 – "...ittaqollaha wa kono ma'as sadiqeen." (Surah At-Tawba)

"...have conscious of Allah and be with those who are truthful/pious/sincere (in words and deed)." (The Repentance, 9:119)

I am asking to always accompany Your pious servants. As soon as I am meditating and contemplating, asking, *yaa Rabbi,* I want to be with the soul and its reality, and you begin to visualize as if you are there physically with them. Their soul is right there in the presence, their soul is right in front of us and asking, *yaa*

Rabbi, let me open my heart and build my connection from soul to soul with my guide.

At the first stages it is me trying to connect. There is no way to hear him until he has given permission that the connection is correct. I merely send out the line, send out the request, it is for them to find acceptance. If they accept, they feel it to be sincere, they deem it to be correct, then they begin to send their *nazar*. *Nazar* means their spiritual attention upon the soul.

As soon as they send their spiritual attention it means all of this knowledge is based on the heart, based on the spiritual connection. We begin to learn the physical is what we are hearing through our ears, but it is opening a spiritual connection of the shaykhs.

KA'BAH AND THE HEART

FOUR CORNERS OF *KA'BAH* REPRESENT FOUR CATEGORIES

NABIYEEN, SIDDIQEEN, SHUHADA AND *SALIHEEN*

They are teaching us, for that (spiritual connection) reality to open up Allah ﷻ says, if you want to be with Me, you have to be with four categories; the *Nabiyeen, Siddiqeen, Shuhada* and *Saliheen* (Prophets, Truthful, Witness/Martyrs, and Righteous).

وَمَن يُطِعِ اللَّهَ وَالرَّسُولَ فَأُولَـٰئِكَ مَعَ الَّذِينَ أَنْعَمَ اللَّهُ عَلَيْهِم مِّنَ النَّبِيِّينَ وَالصِّدِّيقِينَ وَالشُّهَدَاءِ وَالصَّالِحِينَ وَحَسُنَ أُولَـٰئِكَ رَفِيقًا

4:69 – 'Wa man yuti' Allaha war Rasola faolayeka ma'al ladheena an'ama Allahu 'alayhim minan Nabiyeena, was Siddiqeena, wash Shuhadai, was Saliheena wa hasuna olayeka rafeeqan." (Surah An-Nisa)

"And whoever obeys Allah and the messenger, then those are with the ones on whom Allah bestowed his softness amongst the prophets, the highly Righteous [Truthful], the Witnesses to the truth, and the Righteous. And excellent are those as companions." (The Women, 4:69)

That is why the *Ka'bah* is a symbol from them. If you want to be with Allah عزوجل, you have to be with the *Nabiyeen* (Prophets) which is the *Hajar al-Aswad* (Black stone in *Ka'bah*), with the *Siddiqeen* (Truthful), the corner that is closest to Prophet صلى الله عليه وسلم. The *Shuhada* (Martyrs) because they see and those *Shuhada* produce the *Saliheen* (Pious People).

1. *Nabiyeen* (Prophets) – Corner of *Hajar al Aswad.* (*Nabiyeen* are all the 124,000 prophets).

2. *Siddiqeen* (Truthful Ones) – Corner close to Prophet صلى الله عليه وسلم. *Siddiqs* are the big Companions of Prophet صلى الله عليه وسلم.

3. *Shuhada* (Those Who Witness) – The martyrs. Not only the people who died in battle, but those who die in their physical world. It means the big *alims* (scholars) of reality, who were able to destroy their characteristic. They are deemed not to be very much alive in this *dunya* because they are alive in the Divinely Presence.

The *Shuhada* are witnessing. If not a *Shuhada* and not from one who sees in their association, they are never going to reach to be the *Saliheen.* It is just the formula which Allah عزوجل is creating that reality.

4. *Saliheen* (Righteous Ones) – So by entering in and finding the groups of *Saliheen,* they must have from amongst them *Ahlul Basirah* (People of Spiritual Vision), whom they have trained and their desires have dropped. As a result of the desires dropping Allah عزوجل describes, We took the lock of their ears, We took the lock of their eyes which is the *ayn* (vision) of the heart, and We removed the *Kiswah*, the veils that are blocking them.

It means by keeping their company their whole purpose is not the physical association but by means of the physical they are able to pull the souls of people. So from *'Malakut kulli shay' it* means we come into a physical association and we seek out a physical association but these *Ahlul Basirah* are from the people of light. That immediately their soul in the room is able to grab all the souls of everyone present, and takes them to what Allah ﷻ wants from the fulfilling of the Contract.

فَسُبْحَانَ الَّذِي بِيَدِهِ مَلَكُوتُ كُلِّ شَيْءٍ وَإِلَيْهِ تُرْجَعُونَ

36:83 – "Fasubhanal ladhee biyadihi Malakutu kulli shay in wa ilayhi turja'oon." (Surah Yaseen)

"Therefore Glory be to Him in Whose hand is the [heavenly] dominion/ kingdom of all things, and to Him you will be returned." (Yaseen, 36:83)

Seek Support From Pious Souls at the Levels of the Heart

What we say in our *Naqshbandi Dhikr; yaa Sayyid, yaa Sahib, yaa Siddiq, yaa Rasul, yaa Allah.* We want their *madad* and support.

1. ***Ya Sayyid*** (O Master), ***Saliheen*** (Righteous) – at *Qalb* (Heart)

2. ***Ya Sahib*** (O Owner), ***Shuhada*** (Martyrs/Witness) – at *Sir* (Secret)

3. ***Ya Siddiq*** (O Truthful One), ***Siddiqeen*** (Truthful) – at *Sirr e Sir* (Secret of the Secret)

4. ***Ya Rasul*** (O Messenger), ***Nabiyeen*** (Prophets) – at *Khafa* (Hidden)

5. ***Ya Allah*** (O Allah) – at *Akhfa* (Most Hidden)

It is the same from Holy Qur'an and Allah ﷻ is saying, if you want to be with Me you must be with *Nabiyeen* (Prophets), *Siddiqeen* (Truthful Ones), *Shuhada* (Martyrs/Those Who Witness), *wa Saliheen* (Righteous).

So *Shuhada* are witnessing. One way of becoming a witness is you die and now you witness the light Allah ﷻ wanted to show. Or your desires drop and your heart begins to open; your soul begins to see what Allah ﷻ wants it to see, and now you are from the *Shuhada* and *Ahlul Basirah* (People of Spiritual Vision), those whose hearts are open.

Allah ﷻ says you have to be from these four realities, from the *Saliheen*, from the *Shuhada*, the *Siddiqeen* and they are all connected to Sayyidina Muhammad ﷺ, *Nabiyeen.*

HOLY *KA'BAH* AND THE FOUR INNER AND OUTER POINTS OF *LATAIF AL QALB*

It means then there are the levels of the heart. Before we go into the understanding of the *Lataif al Qalb*, you will see that around the heart encompassing the circle of reality is a square which each points to, the outermost point of each *lataif*, makes four. That four is the *Ka'bah*, *qalbun mu'min baytullah.*

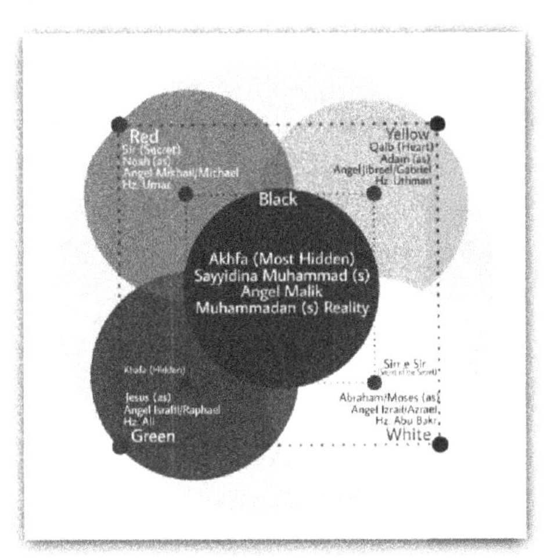

قَلْبُ الْمُؤْمِنْ بَيْتُ الرَّبْ

"Qalb al mu'min baytur rabb."

"The heart of the believer is the House of the Lord." (Hadith Qudsi)

There is an outer four and an inner four. The outer four is the *Ka'bah* of the physicality. The inner four is the innermost reality, the *Baytul Mamur*, the Divinely House in the oceans of light.

They teach us to accompany the guides, to learn and understand from them, to open our souls into their presence. Then Allah ﷻ begins to open the reality of the soul, and the true connection of the soul. And only at that time can this conveyance begin to open.

Opening the Heart Requires *Tafakkur* (Contemplation)

Until that time we learn and understand, so that when we are meditating we start to study, what is the *Qalb* (Heart), what is the *Sir* (Secret), what is the *Sirr e Sir* (Secret of the Secret), what is the *Khafa* (Hidden), and what is the *Akhfa* (Most Hidden), the inner most secret dimension of that *lataif*. But it requires somebody who is interested in studying it and is very strong on their meditation because it is the combination of these two realities.

In *Muraqabah*, Focus on the Lights of Each Station

As soon as you study it, you read about the first station, the *Qalb* (Heart), and you see it as a yellow colour, the *lataif* of the *Qalb*. It means then you envision that you are focusing just on the *Qalb* (Heart). *Yaa Rabbi* (O my Lord), I want to open the reality of the *Qalb*. Its yellow and you see everything around you like an ocean of yellow and you are sitting with your connection with the shaykh.

Once that connection begins to open you feel that you are in their presence. And keep asking, "Send from your light, send from your blessing, send from what Allah ﷻ has granted to you of these realities. *Sayyidi* (my Master), I am a weak servant, and just keeping my presence, "waiting, waiting for your *fa'iz* and blessing to begin to dress me."

You begin to see everything in that ocean of yellow that send from that light. I want to see myself in that light. How you focus is to see yourself inside the *lataif*. That everything around is yellow and you are focusing on that. Then you begin to understand that reality; that yellow and the reason for the yellow and you begin to study its realities. One understanding of that it is the opening of the *Qalb* (Heart) and has to do with the reality of knowledge. Then you begin to see the realities.

Subhana rabbika rabil 'izzati 'ama yasifoon, Wa salamun 'alal mursaleen wal hamdulillahi rabbil 'alameen. Bi hurmati Muhammadil Mustafa wa bi siratil Suratil Fatiha.

OPENING THE HEART THROUGH LOVE, PRESENCE, AND ANNIHILATION

DON'T MIX SHAYKHS (GUIDES) AND DIFFERENT SCHOOLS OF THOUGHT

With *tafakkur* (contemplation) and the way of *tafakkur*, each shaykh may have a different understanding depending upon the school which they are following. It is very important why we don't mix between the different shaykhs. An example for us is if you take a course of Math at UBC (University of British Columbia) and there is a course of Math at SFU (Simon Fraser University). Each may get you to a point of graduation but each one is teaching a different course, at a different time, at a different schedule, and in a different way.

Marif'ah (Gnosticism) is completely like that, where Prophet صلى الله عليه وسلم gives them a secret and says, "Via this *awrad* (daily practice), which is your dial-up, via this practice, from these shaykhs, they will uplift you." So if you take from other shaykhs and say, "In Pakistan we were thinking the *Sir*, the *Qalb*, the *Ruh*," and they have all these different names for *Lataif al Qalb*, "that it is like that." We say, okay, but you have to ask that shaykh who gave you that *awrad* on how to uplift you, via what he was given by Prophet صلى الله عليه وسلم, if he was given by Prophet صلى الله عليه وسلم.

LATAIF AL QALB – ENERGY POINTS OF THE HEART ACCORDING TO *NAQSHBANDIYA NAZIMIYYA*

Through *Naqshbandiya til Aliya* from Shaykh AbdAllah Fa'iz ad-Daghestani ق to Sultan al-Awliya Mawlana Shaykh Nazim al-Haqqani ق and *Sultanul Quloobana* Mawlana Shaykh Hisham Kabbani, they are teaching through their system and through their *lataif.*

They have the *Qalb* (Heart), *Sir* (Secret), *Sirr e Sir* (Secret of the Secret), *Khafa* (Hidden), and *Akhfa* (Most Hidden). The colors for these are based on many realities. You will see many of our *dhikrs* are based on these. The *salah* (daily prayer) is based on understanding these five *lataifs*. The angels are based on this; the *Sahabi* (Companions of Prophet Muhammad صلى الله عليه وسلم) are based on these *lataif.* Every reality that we can possibly imagine, must have an understanding from the *Lataif* of the *Qalb*. That from the great prophets of Allah عز وجل, each are standing upon these *lataifs*; Sayyidina Adam عليه السلام, Sayyidina Nuh عليه السلام, Sayyidina Ibrahim عليه السلام, Sayyidina Musa عليه السلام, Sayyidina Isa عليه السلام, and Sayyidina Muhammad صلى الله عليه وسلم.

Adamic Reality At the First Station of the *Qalb* (Heart)

If we just understand the Station of the *Qalb* (Heart), and to enter into the *Qalb* then Sayyidina Adam عليه السلام begins to teach, *walaqad karamna bani Adam.*

وَلَقَدْ كَرَّمْنَا بَنِي آدَمَ...

17:70 – "Wa laqad karramna bani adama..." (Surah Al-Isra)

"And We have certainly honored the children of Adam..." (The Night Journey, 17:70)

It means many *ayat* of Qur'an are specific to that; we have an Adamic reality in which we are always coming from Paradise to Earth. Not one time that Sayyidina Adam عليه السلام came, but all Adams, all humans are continuously coming onto the Earth. So you have the Adamic reality.

There is No *Mi'raj* (Ascension) to the Divinely Presence Without Prophet Muhammad صلى الله عليه وسلم

It means there is an eternal reality that is timeless, and every prophet came for a timed message but more important they came to complete the cycle of Creation with the *khatim* (seal) being Sayyidina Muhammad صلى الله عليه وسلم. That all of them are carrying the *Muhammadan* Light and Prophet is صلى الله عليه وسلم coming to seal it. That, "Now I am going to take you all on a *mi'raj* (ascension)," because nobody can enter (to Divine Presence) without the presence of Sayyidina Muhammad صلى الله عليه وسلم.

That no *mi'raj*, no deep reality about themselves nor the Lord, until the master of that (Divinely) Presence arrives. That is why they all waited on the *Isra* (Prophet Muhammad's ﷺ Journey to Jerusalem) to take the hand of Prophet ﷺ, to complete their faith. They prayed *salah* in the form of Sayyidina Ahmad عليه السلام. They prayed the Islamic prayer and gave *Shahada* (Testimony of Faith) to Prophet ﷺ.

أَشْهَدُ أَنْ لَا إِلَهَ إِلاَّ الله وَأَشْهَدُ أَنَّ مُحَمَّدًا عَبْدُهُ وَرَسُولُهُ

"Ashhadu an la ilaha illa-lah, wa ashhadu anna Muhammadan rasulu hu."

"I bear witness that there is no god but Allah, and I bear witness that Muhammad is the messenger of Allah."

It means then they are all from *Ummatun Muhammad* ﷺ and behind Prophet ﷺ like a comet. The thrust of the energy is the Prophet ﷺ and the tail of the comet are all the prophets, all the *Sahabah*, all the *Ahlul Bayt*, all *Awliyaullah* are moving continuously in a *mi'raj* (ascension) with Prophet ﷺ.

ADAMIC REALITY IS A *MIZAAN* (SCALE): TO BALANCE OUR ANGELIC AND FIERY NATURE

It means from an eternal reality, the Prophets are standing on the *lataif* of the heart to teach us. So it is an infinite ocean. Sayyidina Adam عليه السلام is teaching if you want to enter into the *Qalb* I am standing on that reality and it is the doorway to knowledges. That is why, *"ismaa kullaha."*

وَعَلَّمَ آدَمَ الْأَسْمَاءَ كُلَّهَا... ٣١

2:31 – "Wa 'allama Adamal Asma a kullaha…" (Surah Al-Baqarah)

"And He taught Adam the names of all things…" (The Cow, 2:31)

That Allah ﷻ describes this Adamic reality, which is a vessel and a vehicle for the *Muhammadan* Light, that Allah ﷻ wants to deposit that Light. And it is the great *mizaan*, the great Scale of Allah ﷻ, which Adam carries an angelic light, and carries a *jinn* light. Because of his *teen* (soil), and the reality of his physicality, he is able to balance these two realities. Because the angelic light is the water, so *Malaika* (angels) are born from water. The *jinn* are the fire within *insaan* (human being).

If he doesn't take care of that fire, it becomes *naar* and he becomes an angry person. If he controls that fire, it becomes a *himmah* (zeal) in which to achieve what Allah ﷻ wants you to achieve. It means their whole life is balancing this light. That I want to bring excess amount of angelic lights which is the reality of my soul, and I want to control all of the *jinn* and the bodily understanding, which is very turbulent, and to bring them all together.

All the Universes Are Contained Within Sayyidina Muhammad ﷺ

It means every *lataif* has a deep reality of how to dress from that knowledge, how to be blessed from that knowledge and how to open from these realities the internal reality of *Insaan Kamil* (Perfected Being). That all the

universes are contained within Sayyidina Muhammad ﷺ. Every reality is contained within Sayyidina Muhammad ﷺ. So the guides want us to go back to the ocean of Prophet ﷺ. If we lose the form, the drop becomes the ocean.

Then how *Awliyaullah* have *uloomul Awwaleen wal Akhireen* (Knowledge of the Beginning and the End) is from taste. So they don't describe the water but they tasted the water. They lost the form, destroyed the form, crushed the form, but not by themselves. It means through the *nazar* (gaze) of their shaykh which Allah ﷻ has dressed these guides. That they come with their spirituality, and through their *nazar*, they are hitting and destroying and destroying, and destroying, because that is the reality of their light.

People Don't See the Reality of the Shaykh, Just Like They Can't See the Rays of the Sun

That is why when we were describing the Sun because some people are so physical that they say, "No, when I see a human being, I see him as myself." I say, "But you see the Sun and you don't see its rays," because "*layli wan nahar.*"

إِنَّ فِي خَلْقِ السَّمَاوَاتِ وَالْأَرْضِ وَاخْتِلَافِ اللَّيْلِ وَالنَّهَارِ لَآيَاتٍ لِّأُولِي الْأَلْبَابِ

3:190 – "Inna fee khalqis Samawati wal ardi wakhtilafil layli Earth around Sunwan nahari, la ayatin li Olel albab." (Surah Al-Imran)

"Indeed, in the creation of the heavens and the earth and the alternation of the night and the day are signs for those People of understanding (People of the Door of Knowledge)." (Family of Imran, 3:190)

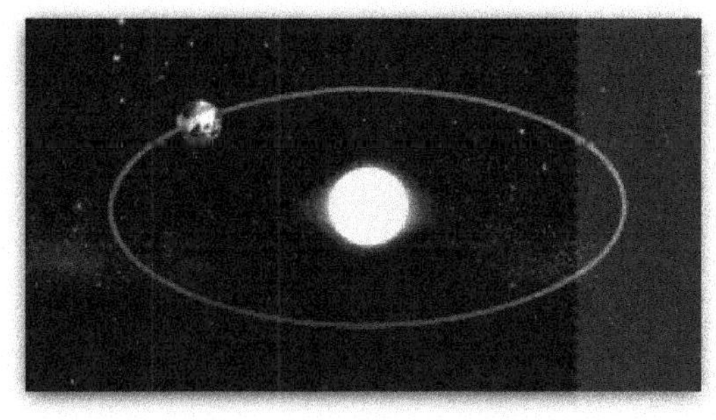

It means the Sun is always shining and it's 360 degrees shining. Then why is the sky black? Why is it not illuminating the entire skies? Only when it enters *hadd ad dunya* (limits of Earth) we begin to see the light of the Sun. It is shining and has many different rays, gamma rays, the infrared. They are all the different spectrums that the Sun is shining, but we have not the eyes to see it.

MUHAMMADAN AWLIYA (SAINTS) INHERIT FROM PROPHETS

So those who don't understand and they say, "What I see is what I believe," means there is everything around us is of that example. The Sun is shining and we haven't yet seen it. So imagine when *insaan* (human being), that Allah عَزَّ وَجَلَّ opens the heart of these *rijalAllah* (men of God), their hearts are more powerful than the physical Sun. Their hearts are more powerful, why? Allah said, *walaqad karamna bani Adam.* He didn't say, I honoured the Sun and the Moon, He said I honoured *Bani Adam* (Children of Adam).

وَلَقَدْ كَرَّمْنَا بَنِي آدَمَ...

17:70 – "Wa laqad karramna bani adama..." (Surah Al-Isra)

"And We have certainly honored the children of Adam..."
(The Night Journey, 17:70)

Sayyidina Yusuf عليه السلام said, "They are under my feet," the Sun, the Moon and the eleven stars are under my feet," which means under my control.

إِذْ قَالَ يُوسُفُ لِأَبِيهِ يَا أَبَتِ إِنِّي رَأَيْتُ أَحَدَ عَشَرَ كَوْكَبًا وَالشَّمْسَ وَالْقَمَرَ رَأَيْتُهُمْ لِي سَاجِدِينَ

12:4 – "Idh qala Yosufu li abeehi ya abati innee raaytu ahada Ashara kawkaban wash Shamsa wal Qamara raaytuhum le sajideen." (Surah Yusuf)

"[Of these stories mention] when Joseph said to his father, "O my father, indeed I have seen [in a dream] eleven stars and the sun and the moon; I saw them prostrating to me." (Joseph, 12:4)

And the *Awliya* (saints) of Prophet صلى الله عليه وسلم are *warith al-Anbiyaa*, they are the inheritors of the stations of the Prophets of *Bani Israel.*

عُلَمَاءِ وَرِثَةُ الْأَنْبِيَاء

"Ulama e warithatul anbiya."

Prophet Muhammad صلى الله عليه وسلم *said: "My scholars are the inheritors of the prophets."*

عُلَمَاءِ أُمَتِيْ كَأَنْبِيَاءِ بَنِيْ إِسْرَائِيلْ

"Ulama e Ummati ka anbiya e Bani Israel."

"The scholars of my ummah are like the Prophets of Bani Israel."
(Prophet Muhammad صلى الله عليه وسلم*)*

Prophet ﷺ wants to say, "Whatever you are reading of the Qur'an are the stories and *qisas* of *Bani Israel*, and Prophet ﷺ is saying, "My *Awliya* are inheriting all of them." The ring they carry is from the ring of Sayyidina Sulaiman عليه السلام, the *asaa* (staff/cane) they carry is the *asaa* of Nabi Musa عليه السلام. They can part an ocean, they can move a mountain but, they don't do anything until the order and *isharat* (indication) of Prophet ﷺ.

It means every *Sunnah* is the *Sunnah* of Prophet ﷺ. Their shirt they can put it to heal you. If the shirt of Sayyidina Yusuf عليه السلام can heal, what about the *Awliya* of Sayyidina Muhammad ﷺ? It means every *Sunnah* is the *Sunnah* of Sayyidina Muhammad ﷺ.

OCEANS OF *MUHABBAT* (LOVE), *HUDUR* (PRESENCE), AND *FANA* (ANNIHILATION)

It means these are the Treasures they want to describe. So they say, "These are the Treasures," but we are running after *dunya*. So the only way to receive these Treasures is to make *tafakkur* with them *(Awliya)*. The concept of the *tafakkur* is that the guides have the Ocean of Love, *muhabbat*, the Ocean of *Hudur*, and the Ocean of *Fana*.

1. *MUHABBAT* (LOVE)

ONLY THROUGH LOVE A SPIRITUAL BOND IS CREATED

The understanding of *muhabbat* is that a tremendous bond will take place, but only through love. That is why all our great shaykhs, all they talk about is love. If not for the love of Prophet ﷺ, and love of these pious people, there is not going to be any relationship. This is not *aql* (mind), this is not like "Okay you seem like a clever guy and I am a clever guy, so we can be clever." But this is through *muhabbat* because the bond can only take place through love. When a chemical bond from our atomic reality takes place, it becomes a solid and fixed bond. That is why this *Hadith* of Prophet ,ﷺ, these *Hadiths* are all oceans, that (Prophet ﷺ said), "You will be with who you love." It means then it's the love that will connect everything.

الْمَرْءُ مَعَ مَنْ أَحَب

"Almar o, ma'a man ahab."

Prophet Muhammad ﷺ said: "One is with those whom he loves."

BE LIKE A FLOWER AND GIVE FRAGRANCE TO THE HAND THAT CRUSHES YOU

Then by coming into their presence, and building the love for these *Awliyaullah*, it is a romance; that you love them. That they are the lights of Prophet ﷺ; that you just want to be around them, you want to be absorbed in them. This light is allowing their hearts to be opened and the soul to move, because if the love is not there your heart doesn't open. So when the heart opens it is like a flower that begins to give its fragrance.

That is why in nature we see it; the flower has innocence and has such a love for the Sun, that as soon as the Sun shines, because many flowers stay closed; as soon as the Sun shines, the petals are opening and as a result it gives its fragrance. Even if you crush the flower it gives its fragrance out of love. It means that bond of love is so important that is why the crushing.

That is why Imam Ali ﷷ said, "Be loving and keep good character even to the hand that crushes you," because he knows that hand is Allah ﷻ. That is the *bayah* (allegiance)! Allah ﷻ says your hand over their hand but My Hand is over all of them.

إِنَّ الَّذِينَ يُبَايِعُونَكَ إِنَّمَا يُبَايِعُونَ اللَّـهَ يَدُ اللَّـهِ فَوْقَ أَيْدِيهِمْ ۚ فَمَن نَّكَثَ فَإِنَّمَا يَنكُثُ عَلَىٰ نَفْسِهِ ۖ وَمَنْ أَوْفَىٰ بِمَا عَاهَدَ عَلَيْهُ اللَّـهَ فَسَيُؤْتِيهِ أَجْرًا عَظِيمًا

48:10 – "Innal ladheena yubayi'oonaka innama yubayi'on Allaha yadullahi fawqa aydeehim, faman nakatha fa innama yankuthu 'ala nafsihi, wa man awfa bima 'ahada 'alayhu Allaha fasayu teehi ajran 'azheema." (Surah Al-Fath)

"Indeed, those who give Baya (pledge allegiance) to you, [O Muhammad] – they are actually giving Baya (pledge allegiance) to Allah. The hand of Allah is over their hands. So he who breaks his pledge/word only breaks it to the detriment/Harm of himself. And he whoever fulfills their Covenant (Bayat) that which he has promised Allah – He will grant him a great reward." (The Victory, 48:10)

When Tests Come, Don't Exhibit Bad Character – Keep the Love

We accepted complete *tawheed* (oneness of Allah عزَّ وجلَّ), that my faith is that whatever I am doing in this way of Sayyidina Muhammad ﷺ, Allah's عزَّ وجلَّ Hand is over their hand. Even when the crushing comes, be like a flower and give your fragrance. Never exhibit craziness, never exhibit bad character, never exhibit harshness in your character; then they understand this love is true.

Otherwise it is like this *dunya*, I love you today, I hate you tomorrow, I love you today, I hate you tomorrow. That becomes a *munafiq* (hypocrite) because the minute a *munafiq* becomes angry, he hates the person. Anybody who moves from a state of love to an instant state of hate is a *munafiq* because he is not able to control. He uses the state of love only for whatever goal he wants to take out of it.

So what they want from us is the state of real love. You will be crushed; you go through difficulty but still have love for Allah عزَّ وجلَّ, love for Sayyidina Muhammad ﷺ, love for *Awliyaullah*. That is the *muhabbat* (love).

Guard Your Heart to Keep the Love of Your Shaykh

Our life is then to keep that *muhabbat*. So it means you guard your heart to love that shaykh and that shaykh is everything. He is everything to you, to reach towards that reality. That as soon as your soul begins to move, it is bonding with his soul. That is why *wa hamalna durriyatahum fil fulkil mashhoon.*

وَآيَةٌ لَّهُمْ أَنَّا حَمَلْنَا ذُرِّيَّتَهُمْ فِي الْفُلْكِ الْمَشْحُونِ (٤١) وَخَلَقْنَا لَهُم مِّن مِّثْلِهِ مَا يَرْكَبُونَ (٤٢)

36:41-42 – "Wa ayatul lahum anna hamalna dhurriyyatahum fil fulkil mashhooni. (41) "Wa khalaqna lahum mim mithlihi ma yarkabon. (42)" (Surah Yaseen)

"And a sign for them is that we have carried their atoms/forefathers in the loaded ship. (41) "And We have created for them similar (vessels) on which they ride. (42)" (Yaseen, 36:41-42)

Wa hamalna means they carry us in the *fulukul mashhoon,* where Allah ﷻ states, *wa mithlihi,* We created the likes of them. These are the smaller ones going around to catch people to bring them back to these big *Awliyaullah. Wa hamalna dhurriyatahum. Hamalna* (carried) through what? Through their soul. So it means their souls are so powerful, when it comes out it immediately catches the soul of everybody in the room and catches their energy and carries it upon themselves and they immediately go back into the presence of Prophet ﷺ. It means unimaginable reality of keeping that *muhabbat.* From that Ocean of *Muhabbat* it begins to prepare us.

2. *HUDUR* (PRESENCE)

THE PROCESS OF KEEPING THE PRESENCE OF THE SHAYKH

Then the process of *hudur* means we have to make our way towards them. So they become like a mountain, these are like *Awtad.*

وَالْجِبَالَ أَوْتَادًا ٧

78:7 – "Wal jibala awtadan." (Surah An-Naba)

"And Mountains like Pegs." (The Tidings, 78:7)

They don't move, their belief is not going to change based on anyone; they are like a mountain, firm and straight. But we are like one day this way, one day that way, one day this way, one day that way changing direction. So the *hudur* means I have to keep their company, I have to keep their presence. I have to keep their way so that I can learn their way. What are their characteristics, what is their way, how do they talk? How do they interact? What do they want in my life and that becomes then the ocean of *itibah*, of obedience.

YOUR WILL AND CHOICES CORRUPT THE *HUDUR* (PRESENCE)

When you want to enter into real *hudur* (presence), you have to completely obey them. Because you only will know then why your 'will' is here and his 'will' is there. Why your will is here and his will is there in a different direction. Why your will is here and his will is still there. So then our lives are to lose my will. I keep losing what I want to chose, and the directions I want to do, and then you have no more choice. It means the choices are coming from my will, the decisions I am making are coming from my will. Those are all corrupting the *hudur*.

That is why we said before the shaykh runs you around. He doesn't run you around on secrets, "O, give me the secrets of *Surah Yaseen* and bring it back." Shaykh will say, "Go get me two pizzas and make sure there are no mushrooms on them." You say, "What!? I have to go get pizzas?" Mawlana Shaykh is giving a *suhbah* and says to one student, 'go give me two pizzas for the kids and make sure one has mushroom and one is just cheese.' And he would be so upset and he would go out there so upset and bring back the wrong pizza! Because he was doing it from anger.

When the shaykh wants to test, "I am not going to test from the secrets of the Holy Qur'an, "Bring them for me, and to do some free sort of majestic Islamic reality." You can't even handle two pizzas! You can't do that without getting angry?" You should make it as if the king of the Heavens has asked for pizza, I will bring the best pizza, I will bring ten pizzas of what you wanted, to show love, this is *muhabbat.* Thinking that, "I don't need to be there. The shaykh is sending me; he is dressing me with a different secret at that time." It means everything was the *hudur.*

First Stage of *Hudur* is Like a Wet Log, You Don't Feel the Burning

You are trying to keep their company. The first stages of keeping the shaykh's company, you are like a wet log. Everything is very exciting for you; everything is just amazing for you because you are not feeling their heat yet because you are wet. You are coming in, "Oh, this is so fantastic!"

As soon as that log becomes dry, it now feels the fire. Every time it sits, "Oh, I am feeling like I am heated up. Whatever the Shaykh is saying is beginning to annoy me, is beginning to agitate me. I can actually now begin to feel the fierceness of his fire." Right? Yeah, because you begin to feel, you feel the energy, and begin to become aggravated real quick.

Ah that is the wood that is the state they want to take you. Make yourself like a piece of dry timber and let us begin to burn you. [This is not physical for anyone reading, "Oh, these guys want to burn people," no, this is all spiritual]. This is spiritual that when you are wet, you don't feel anything. When you sit and sit and sit and through the *hudur* (presence) you are trying to keep their company, keep their company. Every night you are trying to meditate so that the company (*hudur*) is 24 hours. I keep his company when I pray, I keep his company when I do *dhikr*, I keep his company when I drive, I keep his company when I am sitting at home. I keep his company when I am in his company.

Then you begin yourself to feel dry, like you are drying, immediately you can catch. His energy comes and you begin to feel it. At that time, that *tafakkur*, that contemplation is then to be consistent. Keep yourself calm, do your *dhikr*, breathe, let that energy begin to come until the student can catch fire. At the point of catching fire they feel themselves igniting. That all their body is heating up specifically their hands and their neck, because their spine is like an electrical wire. That their spine is on fire from the energies that are coming onto them. Immediately their neck will be lit and their hands will be heated. That is why at that time they can even do healing, because there is a tremendous amount of energy coming from their hands. It is through the *hudur*.

Don't Complain Through the Tongue or the Heart

By keeping the *hudur* (presence) and be nothing, be nothing, be nothing; keep his presence because you have to feel a state of burning. You have to begin to test yourself that don't complain through your tongue and definitely never complain through your heart. If you can't control your tongue imagine then what complaint is coming through the heart? It means I am keeping their company and I am not going to comment; "he sat at the table and I didn't sit at the table," "he had tea in a glass and I had tea in Styrofoam."

Everything is meant to agitate and aggravate. We told you many times in our life we would travel with Mawlana Shaykh. He would say, "Sit here with me," and I would sit. Then he would say, "Get down, I have to bring somebody else," in front of 500 people. Because people would say, "Oh, you are lucky, you got to sit with the Shaykh." Then five minutes later, "Sit on the floor." You had to take your plate and go to the floor. Or you had to wait in line because you thought you were going to get fed at the table. He would say, "Get out and go in other line." Really, now? You go back in the line and there are 500 people who ate everything. It is testing, to crush you, crush you, crush you, until your mind is spinning that these shaykhs, what are they doing?

He would say, "Go here, go there. You are going to run a market, you are going to run a gas station, you are going to run a motel." Every minute the co-ordinance would change, because my Lord in every moment is in a new *tajalli* (manifestation). It means every *tajalli* that was coming was always different. Constantly to grind, to grind, to grind, to grind so that you don't use your *aql* (logic) with him. You don't use the faculty of mind to think that, "Maybe he doesn't know what he is talking about, maybe I know better." They want it to be complete *tasleem* (submission), complete *tasleem*, until you feel yourself like you are burning. As soon as that is burning the student catches. When the student catches means now their heart is being lit, that is the *Qalb*.

LATAIF AL QALB ARE STATIONS OF THE STAR – THE SUN

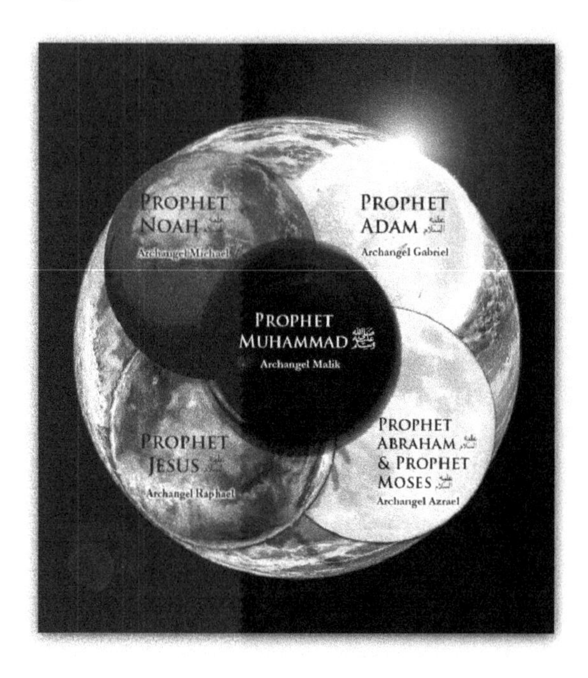

This is the *Qalb* (Heart) and the *lataif* of the heart; these are the stations of the star. The first star is a sun, then the red are the Big Red Giant. So even when we study the birth and the life cycle of a star, it is based on the *Lataif al Qalb*. That is why Prophet ﷺ described, "My Companions are like stars."

أَصْحَابِيْ كَالنُّجُــومْ بِأَيِّهِمْ اقْتَدَيْتُمْ اهْتَدَيْتُمْ

"Ashabi kan Nujoom, bi ayyihim aqta daytum ahta daytum."

"My companions are like stars. Follow any one of them and you will be guided." (Prophet Muhammad ﷺ)

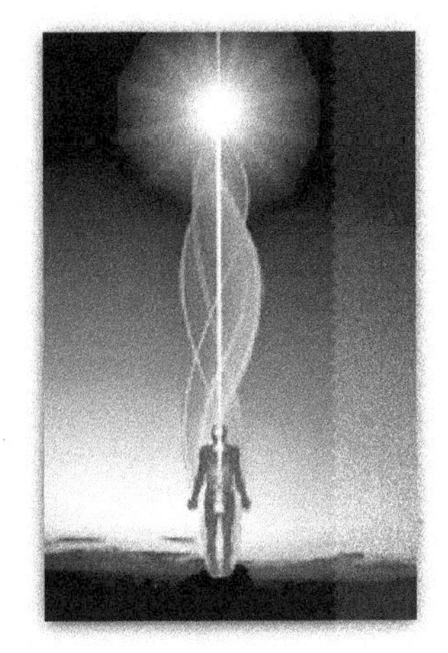

If they are like stars what is Prophet ﷺ? He is the star maker! So it means then the station of *Awliya* (saints), they are stars. As soon as the student begins to catch fire, it means they can immediately heat up, and they are entering into the state of a sun. Their *Qalb* (Heart) is like a *shams* (sun), it is now being lit and Allah عزّ وجلّ is lighting that heart, Prophet ﷺ is lighting the heart, *ulul amr* are lighting the heart. Because now that *fa'iz* is coming through the good character, through the *muhabbat*, and the *hudur*, the student is now matching. Because he is not continuously conflicting, no, no, no, you don't know what you are talking about, I know.

3. *FANA* (ANNIHILATION)

***Muhabbat* (Love) + *Hudur* (Presence) = *Fana* (Annihilation)**

So through that crushing, as soon as the student becomes aligned with his Shaykh that now entered into *fana* (annihilation). He is now in the *fana* of the shaykh because with his love and his *hudur* and all his testing, the shaykh's *fa'iz* and the light is dressing upon that student, dressing upon that student. They begin to feel heated, begin to feel energized and electrified. As much as they can carry that, they are carrying the light of the shaykh which is the light of Sayyidina Muhammad ﷺ; they are all *Muhammadan* Lights. There is only but one Sun making all these suns.

It means there is only one light of Prophet ﷺ. That light that makes *Awliyaullah* is the *Muhammadan* Reality.

When You Become Nothing, Shaykh's Light Will Dress You

So the students keep their *muhabbat*, they keep the way of love; they are constantly in that *tafakkur* and *hudur.* That not only I am in your presence, *yaa Sayyidi,* but I want to be with you always, that you are in front of me and I am a dust in your pocket. So when the *fana* (annihilation) begins to dress, as soon as you make your *salah*, you don't want to be the one praying. Why would I want to pray when I don't know anything, I don't do anything? I want him to pray, I don't want to be anything. I want to be dust in your pocket.

Immediately with his *tajalli* he begins to pray. So when he begins to pray, you pray at his station, not at your station because you are asking to be dressed from them. This is not *shirk* because this is not worshiping. If you surrender yourself, *wa koonu ma as-sadiqeen, ittaqullah.* Accompany them.

يَا أَيُّهَا الَّذِينَ آمَنُوا اتَّقُوا اللَّـهَ وَكُونُوا مَعَ الصَّادِقِينَ ١١٩

9:119 – "Ya ayyuhal ladheena amanoo ittaqollaha wa kono ma'as sadiqeen." (Surah At-Tawba)

"O you who have believed, Have consciousness of Allah and be with those who are truthful/ Pious / sincere (in words and deed)." (The Repentance, 9:119)

IT IS A BINARY CODE – YOU MUST BE OFF FOR SHAYKH TO BE ON

Allah ﷻ says have a *taqwa*, consciousness, have such a level of purity, keep the company of these pious people. If you keep their company and be nothing in their company, it means this is the Binary Code. You turn off, they will turn on. If you are on, they are off. If you are going to be 'on' they immediately would turn off and there is nothing else to convey.

So we took a way in which to be nothing. As soon as I turn 'off' I am nothing, I am completely non-existent, *nasiyan mansiyya*, that I wish to be something unknown. That is what Sayyidatina Maryam (Mary) عليها السلام was saying. *Nasiyan mansiyya*, "I wish I was something unknown."

قَالَتْ يَا لَيْتَنِي مِتُّ قَبْلَ هَٰذَا وَكُنتُ نَسْيًا مَّنسِيًّا...

19:23 – "... qalat ya laytanee mittu qabla hadha wa kuntu nasyam mansiyya." (Surah Maryam)

"…. She cried (in her anguish): "Oh, I wish I had died before this! And I was a thing forgotten and out of sight!" (Maryam, 19:23)

AWLIYA (SAINTS) ARE *RABBANIYOON* WITH DIVINELY HEARING, VISION, SPEECH

It means let me go back into my Adamic reality, *yaa Rabbi.* All these names people gave me, I am nothing, let me to be just a drop back in that ocean. If you are nothing and call upon their *madad* (support), then the *salah* is real from them. So as soon as they pray then imagine where they are looking when they are praying? It means they dress you and that is the *Hadith* that comes now, "When My servant comes through voluntary worship,"

...وَلَا يَزَالُ عَبْدِي يَتَقَرَّبُ إِلَيَّ بِالنَّوَافِلِ حَتَّى أُحِبَّهُ، فَإِذَا أَحْبَبْتُهُ كُنْت سَمْعَهُ الَّذِي يَسْمَعُ بِهِ، وَبَصَرَهُ الَّذِي يُبْصِرُ بِهِ، وَيَدَهُ الَّتِي يَبْطِشُ بِهَا، وَرِجْلَهُ الَّتِي يَمْشِي بِهَا، وَلَئِنْ سَأَلَنِي لَأُعْطِيَنَّهُ، وَلَئِنْ اسْتَعَاذَنِي لَأُعِيذَنَّهُ." – رَوَاهُ الْبُخَارِيُّ.

"..., wa la yazaalu 'Abdi yataqarrabu ilayya bin nawafile hatta ahebahu, fa idha ahbabtuhu kunta Sam'ahul ladhi yasma'u behi, wa Basarahul ladhi yubsiru behi, wa Yadahul lati yabTeshu beha, wa Rejlahul lati yamshi beha, wa la in sa alani la a'Teyannahu, ..."

"...My servant continues to draw near to Me with voluntary acts of worship so that I shall love him. When I love him, I am his hearing with which he hears, his seeing with which he sees, his hand with which he strikes and his foot with which he walks. Were he to ask [something] of Me, I would surely give it to him (Rabbaniyoon)..." (Hadith Qudsi, Sahih al-Bukhari, 81:38:2)

They (saints) carry the *Hadith* of Prophet ﷺ. What Allah عز وجل described for Prophet ﷺ? "I become your hearing, I become your seeing, I become your breathing, I become the tongue with which you speak, the hand with which you touch, the feet with which you walk." That was *Rabbaniyoon*, so much so you became power of *kun fayakun*. This is an inheritance from Prophet ﷺ to *Awliyaullah.*

إِنَّمَا أَمْرُهُ إِذَا أَرَادَ شَيْئًا أَن يَقُولَ لَهُ كُن فَيَكُونُ (٨٢)

36:82 – "Innama AmruHu idha Arada shay an, an yaqola lahu kun faya koon." (Surah Yaseen)

"His command is when He intends a thing, He says to it, "Be," and it is!" (Yaseen, 36:82)

"His command is only when He intends a thing that He says to it, "Be," and it is.

"Verily, when He intends a thing, His Command is, "be", and it is!" (Yusuf Ali)

So when you make the *madad* (ask support) and negate yourself, he is coming with the voluntary worship; he is coming by Allah عز وجل to reward you with love. That if I am coming, I am going to dress you from Allah's عز وجل hearing, I am going to dress you from Allah's عز وجل faculty of seeing. Allah عز وجل is not saying that I am going to dress you with ears from My Heaven, but your *sami*, your hearing, will eternally be dressed upon you, upon your soul. Your seeing will see what no eyes can see. Because each *wali* (saint) has his own unique vision of what Allah ﷻ is dressing him. He may think he has reached where no *wali* has gone before, and other *Awliya* came back and said, "No, we are all on the other side, you are only on this side." It means they have a unique vision that Allah ﷻ has given to them. All is from that *Hadith*.

AWLIYA (SAINTS) DRESS THEIR STUDENTS WITH THE DIVINELY HEARING, VISION, SPEECH

The *Awliya* (saints) that you are making *fana* with, he is coming with that dress. And these are the big *Qutbs*, these are the big *Awliyaullah* which, *Alhamdulillah*, we are under the flag of Sultan al-Awliya Mawlana Shaykh Muhammad Nazim Adil al-Haqqani ق and the big *Qutb al-Mutasarrif*, Mawlana Shaykh Hisham Kabbani. They carry that dress and that reality. If he brings the light of Allah ﷻ from *ati ullah wa ati ar-rasula wa ulul amri minkum*, that *ulul amr* carries that reality.

يآأَيُّهَا الَّذِينَ آمَنُوا أَطِيعُوااللهَ وَأَطِيعُواْلرَّسُولَ وَأُوْلِي الْأَمْرِ مِنْكُمْ

4:59 – "Ya ayyu hal ladheena amanoo Atiullaha wa atiur Rasola wa Ulil amre minkum…" (Surah An-Nisa)

"O You who have believed, Obey Allah, Obey the Messenger, and those in authority among you…" (The Women, 4:59)

It means as soon as you negate yourself 'to go out' he comes with the hearing from Allah ﷻ, he comes from the seeing of Allah ﷻ, he comes with *ya'dullah* (Hand of Allah), which means the real *bayah* (allegiance). That my hand is on the hand of Prophet ﷺ and Allah's Hand is upon our hand.

إِنَّ الَّذِينَ يُبَايِعُونَكَ إِنَّمَا يُبَايِعُونَ اللَّهَ يَدُ اللَّهِ فَوْقَ أَيْدِيهِمْ ۚ فَمَن نَّكَثَ فَإِنَّمَا يَنكُثُ عَلَىٰ نَفْسِهِ ۖ وَمَنْ أَوْفَىٰ بِمَا عَاهَدَ عَلَيْهُ اللَّهَ فَسَيُؤْتِيهِ أَجْرًا عَظِيمًا (١٠)

48:10 – "Innal ladheena yubayi'oonaka innama yubayi'on Allaha yadullahi fawqa aydeehim, faman nakatha fa innama yankuthu 'ala nafsihi, wa man awfa bima 'ahada 'alayhu Allaha fasayu teehi ajran 'azheema." (Surah Al-Fath)

"Indeed, those who give Baya (pledge allegiance) to you, [O Muhammad] – they are actually giving Baya (pledge allegiance) to Allah. The hand of Allah is over their hands. So he who breaks his pledge/ word only breaks it to the detriment/ Harm of himself. And he whoever fulfills their Covernant (Bayat) that which he has promised Allah – He will grant him a great reward."
(The Victory, 48:10)

It means wherever your hands go, Allah's عزّ وجلّ Hand is upon your hand. Wherever your feet go, Prophet's ﷺ feet are there, Allah عزّ وجلّ is powering that *qadam*. So much so you become *Rabbaniyoon*, whatever you put into your heart, *kun fayakun*, it begins to manifest in this world of Creation.

It means these realities are so immense and unimaginable and all it requires is to keep love and get out of the way! To enter into their *hudur* and be nothing. But all the *nafs* (ego) wants is that it wants to control; it wants to drive, it wants to take the power. As much as we can negate to be nothing, as much as they can dress us from that reality.

This Path Only Opens Through Love and *Tafakkur* (Contemplation)

The guides can begin to open the reality of that Holy *Hadith*. It means every reality is from Holy *Hadith*. "Be with whom you are going to love."

الْمَرْءُ مَعَ مَنْ أَحَب

"Almar o, ma'a man ahab."

Prophet Muhammad ﷺ *said: "One is with those whom he loves."*

Only that love opens this way. That inherit from this power, so that this heart can begin to open and then the *Lataif al Qalb,* the Levels of the Heart can begin to open. So then the meditation and *tafakkur* is to bring that light. When we have that down, when we understand how to make the *tafakkur,* how to make contemplation, our life is based on that. Continuous *tafakkur* and then you begin to see the shaykh in front of you and the light begins to come. You begin to see a yellow light from his heart coming to your heart, a red light coming to your heart from his heart.

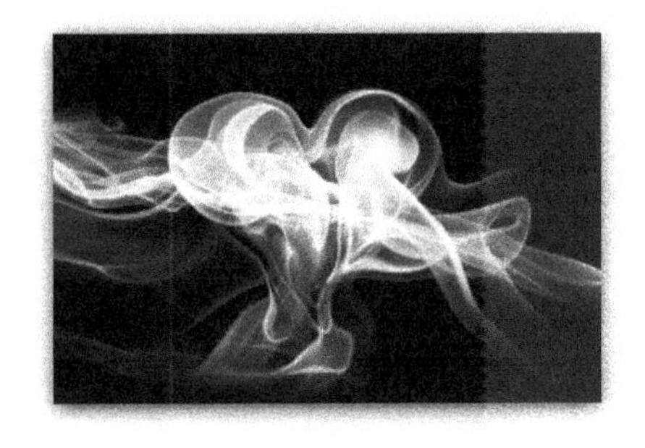

The white light, especially for *Naqshbandiyya* it starts where all *Turuq* stop. They stop at understanding the *Sultanate* of Sayyidina Muhammad ﷺ. Sayyidina Abu Bakr as-Siddiq عليه السلام, at *Aalam al-Mithaal,* is then opening from the world of Light the *Naqshbandiyya* realities, at the station of *Sirr e Sir* (Secret of the Secret) and from the *Khafa* realities. Then from the *Akhfa* realities of the greatness

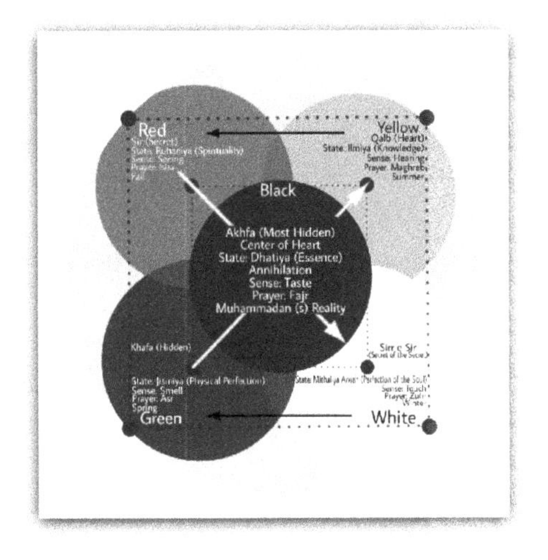

which Allah عز وجل dressed Sayyidina Muhammad ﷺ. These realities are so immense and unimaginable.

External and Internal Realities of *Asma ul Husna* (Beautiful Names of Allah عز وجل)

Even *Asma ul-Husna,* its external understanding is related to Allah عز وجل externally. Internal understanding of *Asma al-Husna* is related to Sayyidina Muhammad ﷺ.

So anyone who wants to talk about Allah عز وجل and say, *"Siffat ar-Rahmaan.* which means Allah is Compassionate." When Allah عز وجل wants you to know the reality of that *Siffat* (attribute), He brings you to the Muhammadan Reality of it. That each of the *huroof* (Arabic letters) is a description of Prophet ﷺ. Everything is based on that.

Prophet ﷺ brought you the *dhikr* of "Allah" عز وجل. Allah عز وجل brought us *dhikr* of Sayyidina Muhammad ﷺ. *InnAllaha wa malaaikatahu Yusaluna.*

إِنَّ اللَّهَ وَمَلَائِكَتَهُ يُصَلُّونَ عَلَى النَّبِيِّ يَا أَيُّهَا الَّذِينَ آمَنُوا صَلُّوا عَلَيْهِ وَسَلِّمُوا تَسْلِيماً

33:56 – "InnAllaha wa Malaikatahu yusalluna 'alan Nabiyi yaa ayyuhal ladhina aamanu sallu 'alayhi wa sallimu taslima." (Surah Al-Ahzab)

"Allah and His angels send blessings on the Prophet [Muhammad ﷺ]: O you that believe! Send your blessings on him, and salute him with all respect. " (The Combined Forces, 33:56)

It means our *dhikr* is from Prophet ﷺ. So when they speak of Prophet ﷺ they are speaking from the highest realities. When they speak from what they believe or perceive to be Allah عزّ و جلّ, it is at a different reality because they are talking from external understanding. When Allah عزّ و جلّ wants the servant to know its inner reality it is related to Prophet صلى الله عليه وسلم. And only in the heart of Prophet صلى الله عليه وسلم can it bring out the real realities of Allah عزّ و جلّ.

Subhana rabbika rabil 'izzati 'ama yasifoon, Wa salamun 'alal mursaleen wal hamdulillahi rabbil 'alameen. Bi hurmati Muhammadil Mustafa wa bi siratil Suratil Fatiha.

EMPTY YOUR CUP AND CONNECT WITH THE SPIRITUAL GUIDES

يٰاأَيُّهَا الَّذِينَ آمَنُوا أَطِيعُوااللهَ وَأَطِيعُواالرَّسُولَ وَأُوْلِي الْأَمْرِ مِنْكُمْ...

4:59 – "Ya ayyu hal ladheena amanoo Atiullaha wa atiur Rasola wa Ulil amre minkum…" (Surah An-Nisa)

"O You who have believed, Obey Allah, Obey the Messenger, and those in authority among you…" (The Women, 4:59)

ADMIT THAT YOU ARE *ZALIM* (OPPRESSOR) TO YOURSELF

In their way of *haqqaiq* (realities) the guides open from the realities of Holy Qur'an. But they can't open until the student is in a state of *tasleem* (submission), where you admit to yourself that you are *zalim* (oppressor). *Laa ilaha illa anta subhaanaka inni kuntu min az Zhalimeen,* "Glory be to Allah عزَّ وجلَّ and for sure I am an oppressor to myself." *(Holy Qur'an, 21:87)*

If you are *zalim,* and you believe you are *zalim* (oppressor), then we don't count anything. You pray but you don't think that it's counting. You are not proud, the *zalim* shouldn't be proud of his prayer because that was the door. If Sayyidina Yunus (Jonah) عليه السلام is repeating that (prayer), that he had to go with anger. When you read the *ayat* (verse) of the Qur'an, it describes that he left angry.

وَذَا النُّونِ إِذ ذَّهَبَ مُغَاضِبًا فَظَنَّ أَن لَّن نَّقْدِرَ عَلَيْهِ فَنَادَىٰ فِي الظُّلُمَاتِ أَن لَّا إِلَٰهَ إِلَّا أَنتَ سُبْحَانَكَ إِنِّي كُنتُ مِنَ الظَّالِمِينَ

21:87 – 'Wa dhan Nooni idh dhahaba mughadiban fazhanna al lan naqdira 'alayhi fanada fizh zhulumati an la ilaha illa anta Subhanaka, innee kuntu minazh zhalimeen." (Surah Al-Anbiya)

"And [mention] Zun-nun [Yunus (Jonah) (as)], when he went off in anger and thought that We had no power/ decree over him! But he cried out through the depths of darkness, "There is no god/ diety except You; Glory to you: Indeed I have been of the wrongdoers/ Oppressor to Myself!" (The Prophets, 21:87)

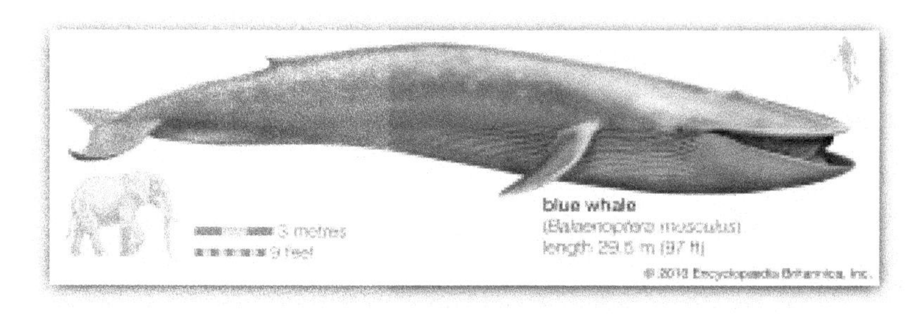

It means anyone with *ghadab* (anger) is a *zalim* (oppressor). And Allah ﷻ had to have him (Yunus عليه السلام) swallowed by a whale. So Allah ﷻ is not happy with anger. Anyone who shows anger at any moment enters a state of *kufr*, or disbelief. That is what they talk about, *thumma amano thumma kafaro* (believe, then disbelieve, then believe). You can't say you are a big believer, if you are getting angry; you are a *kafir* (disbeliever), in a nice and polite sense. So we are not *mukhlis* where they don't get angry.

Don't Be Proud Performing 5 Pillars of Islam

So you admit to Allah ﷻ, "*Yaa Rabbi,* I am a *zalim*, I am getting angry, I have all sorts of bad character. I know You are not counting my *salah* (daily prayer), I am coming through the Door of Your *Maghfirah, yaa Rabbi.* I am imitating what Prophet ﷺ asked me to imitate, I am praying through imitation.

If you devalue it leave it for Allah ﷻ to value it. If you value it, leave it to Allah ﷻ to devalue it. Hey, that's a nice quote. Right? Isn't it more polite to go to Allah ﷻ and say, "*Yaa Rabbi*, it's nothing. You asked me and all my *amal* (actions), my *Shahada* (testimony) is a lie."

Are you witnessing anything when we say, *"Ashadu an la ilaaha ilAllah wa ashadu ana Muhammadan `abduhu wa habeebuhu wa rasuluhu?"*

أَشْهَدُ أَنْ لَا إِلَهَ إِلاَّ الله وَأَشْهَدُ أَنَّ مُحَمَّدًاعَبْدُهُ وَرَسُولُهُ

"Ashhadu an la ilaha illa-lah, wa ashhadu anna Muhammadan rasulu hu."

"I bear witness that there is no god but Allah, and I bear witness that Muhammad is the messenger of Allah."

Did you witness anything? It means it is a lie and so you are a liar too! You are praying *salah*, but you are praying and thinking of all the different things, all the *waswas* (whispering) and anger. This one and that one, this beautiful person, this ugly person, this person did this, this person did that, that *salah* is not for Allah ﷻ.

With the *zakat* (charity), "Oh, I don't want to give, maybe it will come back, maybe it won't come back. I am never going to have it again, it is going to lower my account; it is not going to increase my account." The *zakat* didn't count.

Hajj, "Oh, it's too far, it is going to be too long." *Hajj* didn't count. *Siyam* (Fasting)? "Oh, it was just thirty days of complaints. Oh, how long is this day? *Yaa Latif*, when is it going to be *iftar* (time of breaking fast)? Why is it so long? Why is it so hard?" So fasting was all thirty days of complaints.

Be True With Allah ﷻ, Admit Your Nothingness

Then they come and teach, "Be true with Allah ﷻ; you can't lie with Allah ﷻ, you can't make a facade with Allah ﷻ. Be truthful with Allah ﷻ, *ana `abduka ajiz, wa daeef wa miskeen wa zalim wa jahl* (I am a servant that is weak, poor, oppressor, and ignorant). If not by Your *Rahma, yaa Rabbi,* nothing is going to happen for me. My prayer doesn't count, my fasting didn't count, my *Shahada* was a lie, my *zakat* is with trembling hands, my *Hajj* is too far; everything, *yaa Rabbi*, is nothing, nothing, nothing.

They want the student to admit his nothingness. As soon as he becomes nothing, his cup becomes empty. Every spiritual way, every prophetic way, every reality was to be nothing, be nothing, be nothing in the face of your Lord, Most High.

"My Lord, I Wish I Was Nothing"

If you are truly entering a state of nothingness then Sayyidatina Maryam's ﷺ prayer, *"Nasiyam manshiyya."*

...قَالَتْ يَا لَيْتَنِي مِتُّ قَبْلَ هَٰذَا وَكُنتُ نَسْيًا مَّنسِيًّا...

19:23 – "... qalat ya laytanee mittu qabla hadha wa kuntu nasyam mansiyya." (Surah Maryam)

".... She cried (in her anguish): "Oh, I wish I had died before this! and I was a thing forgotten and out of sight!" (Maryam, 19:23)

O my Lord, I wish I was nothing, something completely forgotten because even my name and what is going to come from my name, is going to make a *fitna* (confusion) on this Earth." When she realized that they would call Sayyidina Isa (Jesus) ﷺ 'God', she was trembling. "How am I going to be in the Heaven and people are going to be calling my son, the Creator? *Astagfirullah al 'Azeem.* With this destiny, I wish I was nothing, *yaa Rabbi*, I wish I was non-existent, whatever the *hikmah* (wisdom) is I am still wishing to be nothing, nothing, nothing."

If You Are an Oppressor, How Could You See Problems in Others?

So it means everything came to us, to be nothing. So *Awliyaullah* come into our lives and remind, "If you are truly accepting to be nothing, then we will come and show you." If you are nothing, then don't see any problem in how people pray because you said you were a *zalim* (oppressor). Can a *zalim* talk about how other people pray? You have to worry about your *zulumat.* How other people pray, how other people look, their appearance. You are a *zalim*, you have to hope Allah ﷻ doesn't punish you in *jahannam* (hellfire).

So why do you worry about other people? Worry only about yourself. If you worry only about yourself, you will be set in life because you will truly be humble. *Yaa Rabbi,* grant me Your *Maghfirah* (forgiveness), *yaa Rabbi,* grant me Your *Maghfirah,* I am nothing, I am nothing. Only at that time you begin to negate everything that you don't look to anything. You don't look to your left or your right, I negate myself, I negate myself; I know nothing because I am only concerned about the one who is going in the grave and that is my grave. Every grave has one person. I am only interested in this person and what is going to happen in my grave.

TAKE THE HAND OF *ULUL AMR*, THEY HELP YOU COMPLETE YOUR COVENANT – *BAYAH* (ALLEGIANCE)

Then, at that level, the student is ready. When the student is ready and has negated himself, because the self is the one who is going to be fighting with the shaykh. From *ati ullah*, to obey Allah ﷻ, *ati ar Rasul,* to obey Prophet ﷺ and the third order, *wa ulul amri minkum,* to obey those in authority.

يَاأَيُّهَا الَّذِينَ آمَنُوا أَطِيعُوااللَّهَ وَأَطِيعُواالرَّسُولَ وَأُوْلِي الأَمْرِ مِنْكُمْ...

4:59 – "Ya ayyu hal ladheena amanoo Atiullaha wa atiur Rasola wa Ulil amre minkum..." (Surah An-Nisa)

"O You who have believed, Obey Allah, Obey the Messenger, and those in authority among you..." (The Women, 4:59)

How are you going to obey *ulul amr* when you are obeying yourself? That is why you have to negate. When you negate yourself, I am nothing, I am nothing, I am nothing, then you put your hand into their hand and say, "You take care of me." I am nothing and I agreed that I was nothing." So be in the hands of the *ulul amr*. They take your hand and say, "Come, we are going to start to train you on how to complete your covenant with Allah عزّ وجلّ."

إِنَّ الَّذِينَ يُبَايِعُونَكَ إِنَّمَا يُبَايِعُونَ اللَّـهَ يَدُ اللَّـهِ فَوْقَ أَيْدِيهِمْ ۚ فَمَن نَّكَثَ فَإِنَّمَا يَنكُثُ عَلَىٰ نَفْسِهِ ۖ وَمَنْ أَوْفَىٰ بِمَا عَاهَدَ عَلَيْهُ اللَّـهَ فَسَيُؤْتِيهِ أَجْرًا عَظِيمًا (١٠)

48:10 – "Innal ladheena yubayi'oonaka innama yubayi'on Allaha yadullahi fawqa aydeehim, faman nakatha fa innama yankuthu 'ala nafsihi, wa man awfa bima 'ahada 'alayhu Allaha fasayu teehi ajran 'azheema." (Surah Al-Fath)

"Indeed, those who give Bayah (pledge allegiance) to you, [O Muhammad] – they are actually giving Bayah (pledge allegiance) to Allah. The hand of Allah is over their hands. So he whoever breaks his pledge/oath, only breaks it to the detriment/Harm/loss of himself. And whoever fulfills their Covenant (Bayah) that which he has promised Allah – He will grant him a great reward." (The Victory, 48:10)

You took your *bayah* that you would have your allegiance to Allah عزّ وجلّ through the hand of Sayyidina Muhammad ﷺ brought to you by the *ulul amr* (saints). *Awliyullah* are the walking hands and feet of Prophet ﷺ on this *dunya*. They are the *Muhammadan* guides and the *Muhammadan* representatives.

KEEP THE COMPANY OF THE *SADIQEEN* (TRUTHFUL SERVANTS OF ALLAH)

They begin to teach then that the Holy Qur'an has all of those realities but you have to be nothing to begin to see it. *Ittaqulla wa konu ma'as Sadiqeen.*

يَا أَيُّهَا الَّذِينَ آمَنُوا اتَّقُوا اللَّـهَ وَكُونُوا مَعَ الصَّادِقِينَ ١١٩

9:119 – "Ya ayyuhal ladheena amanoo ittaqollaha wa kono ma'as sadiqeen." (Surah At-Tawba)

"O you who have believed, be conscious of Allah and be with those who are truthful/ sincere (in words and deed)." (The Repentance, 9:119)

"Have a consciousness and accompany the *sadiq*." It means then in the world of light which is their world, they are the people from the world of light and they don't care for the material world. So their guidance and their realities of Holy Qur'an are from the *Malakut*, the Heavenly Realm which is the superior realm. This is the false and the perishing graveyard of *insaan* (human being). This *dunya* (material world) is the graveyard; the Heavens is where the reality is.

'Wa koonu ma`as Sadiqeen, ittaqulla' means they have such a level of consciousness, then accompany Allah's عزَّ وجلَّ truthful servants. So it means then you will be taught how to accompany them physically, and more importantly how to accompany them spiritually. They have a physical body which you accompany; you see and you eat and you

drink and you pray with them, but they have a spiritual body which is more superior.

They have a spiritual body that you should be feeling; you should be connecting with that spiritual body. Then Allah's عز و جل Words are true, no time, no limit and Allah عز و جل does not care for *dunya.* So what does Allah عز و جل mean when He عز و جل says, "Be conscious of Me and keep the company of the *siddiqeen* and the *sadiq.*" It means at every moment you should be training that, "*Yaa Rabbi,* wherever I am, let me be in the company of those who are truthful." If they are truthful these are the servants who are with Allah عز و جل, *Nabiyeen, Siddiqeen, Shuhada wa Saliheen,* Prophets, Truthful, Martyrs, and Righteous.

وَمَن يُطِعِ اللّهَ وَالرَّسُولَ فَأُوْلَـئِكَ مَعَ الَّذِينَ أَنْعَمَ اللّهُ عَلَيْهِم مِّنَ النَّبِيِّينَ وَالصِّدِّيقِينَ
وَالشُّهَدَاء وَالصَّالِحِينَ وَحَسُنَ أُولَـئِكَ رَفِيقًا

4:69 – 'Wa man yuti' Allaha war Rasola faolayeka ma'al ladheena an'ama Allahu 'alayhim minan Nabiyeena, was Siddiqeena, wash Shuhadai, was Saliheena wa hasuna olayeka rafeeqan." (Surah An-Nisa)

"And whoever obeys Allah and the messenger, then those are with the ones on whom Allah bestowed his softness amongst the prophets, the highly Righteous [Truthful], the Witnesses to the truth, and the Righteous. And excellent are those as companions." (The Women, 4:69)

Allah عز و جل says, They are with Me and those are the best of company. I will dispatch from those who are with Me to be with you. They are *al hayyu al-qayyum,* their souls are alive in their graves and their light is everywhere. They watch over you and you watch over them. Keep their company means you will be trained. "*Yaa Rabbi,* they must be with me at all times, I want to feel their presence," but you have to be nothing. Otherwise if your ego is saying, "No it is the boss, it knows that you don't want to be with them."

ACCOMPANY *AWLIYA* (SAINTS) WITH YOUR SOUL AND BODY

Allah ﷻ says, "Hold tight to the rope of Allah ﷻ."

وَاعْتَصِمُوا بِحَبْلِ اللَّـهِ جَمِيعًا وَلَا تَفَرَّقُوا

3:103 – "Wa'tasimo bihab lillahi jamee'an wa la tafarraqo." (Surah Al-Imran)

"And hold firmly to the rope of Allah all together and do not separate." (Family of Imran, 3:103)

It means in every instant Allah ﷻ is giving that you have to be with these people from the spiritual world. The physical world is the best. If your physical world is eating with pious people, praying with pious people, drinking with pious people, *Alhamdulillah,* it is a good sign that you are probably in a good place in Paradise. But if you are with the worst of people in *dunya* and you are expecting to be with the best of people in *akhirah* (hereafter) that is not going to happen! This *dunya* is just a sign for us.

So, *Alhamdulillah,* we all eat and drink and we are following our beloved shaykh, Mawlana Shaykh Hisham under the flag of Sultan al Awliya Mawlana Shaykh Muhammad Nazim al-Haqqani ق, under the

flag of Mawlana Shaykh 'AbdAllah Fa'iz ad-Daghestani ق. All *Sultan al Awliyas*, the cream of the creams, the chairmen of the board. What better company than that?

But, I don't want to follow them only by my body, my body is not important, I want to be with them with my soul. Allah ﷻ says, hold tight to their rope.

Souls of Pious People Are Everywhere, Connect With Them

It means then you begin to train that if you truly believe that you are nothing and every time you say, "*Yaa Rabbi* I am nothing, I am nothing, let me to be with them." Allah ﷻ then begins to train, Prophet ﷺ begins to train, that every sense you have has a sense and a reality from your soul. It means your ears have a physical ear but you also have a spiritual ear. So you begin to train yourself when you close your room and make your *itikaaf* (seclusion) every day. You close your room and close everything off and spend a few minutes contemplating, making *tafakkur* that, "I am nothing, let me to be with them."

Madad yaa Sayyidi, madad yaa Sayyidi what Allah ﷻ gave you of your power, your soul is *al hayy al qayyum* (Ever-Living, and Self-sustaining), it is not limited to your body. Your soul has its power everywhere. And Allah ﷻ said to be with you, to be with the *Nabiyeen* to be with the *Siddiqeen* to be with the *Shuhada wa Saliheen.* I want to be with Prophet ﷺ. I want to be with the *Saliheen*, who are *Ahl al-Bayt* and *Ashaab an-Nabi* ﷺ. I want to be with the *Shuhada*, those who martyred their desires and their hearts are open. *Yaa Rabbi*, I want to be with them now when I make *salah*.

We Give *Salaam* to *Ibadullahi Saliheen* in Our *Salah*

These are Allah's ﷻ Words, this is not *shirk*. Worship is only for Allah ﷻ. You make your *tafakkur* that they are there, I am saying it in my *salah* (daily prayer), I am saying *asalaamu `alayka ayyu hanNabi* (Peace be upon you, O Prophet ﷺ), and I am not seeing Prophet ﷺ.

السلام عليك أيها النبي ورحمة الله و بركاته. السلام علينا و علي عباد الله الصالحين

"Assalamu alayka ayyu hanNabi wa rahmatullahi wa barakatuhu. AsSalamu alayna wa ala Ibadullahi Saliheen."

"Peace be upon You O` Prophet (Muhammad ﷺ, His Mercy and His blessings too. Peace be on us and on all righteous servants of Allah."

I have to train myself that Prophet ﷺ must be there, *ibadallah saliheen* must be all around me. But let me start with the easiest rope because the rope that is reaching to me is my *Saliheen* and my beloved guides.

Do *Muraqabah* – Connect With Your Shaykh Spiritually

"Madad yaa Sayyidi, yaa Mawlana Shaykh, unzur halana wa ishafalana Sayyidi (O my master, support me, gaze upon me and intercede for me). I know that you are with them and that you are watching over me, I want to feel your presence. I want to feel your light and your

energy that you are always with me, *Sayyidi.* I am not worthy of seeing you but I know your light is with me."

You build a relationship with the Shaykh, just like it is physical. It's no difference for you if you are from the *malakut* (heavens), the spiritual realm is more important than the physical realm. As we are seeing the shaykh is praying, as you are sitting down to pray, then spiritually he must be present right there in front of you. You are saying it; you are giving *salaam* to Prophet ﷺ and *ibadillahis-saliheen* (Righteous Servants) in every prayer. These are Allah's عزَّ وجلَّ *Saliheen.*

So you are training yourself, "*Madad yaa Sayyidi, yaa* Mawlana Shaykh, let your light be with me. That from your *fa'iz*, from your light dress me, and bless me from what Allah عزَّ وجلَّ has given to you. What Allah عزَّ وجلَّ has dressed upon you, dress it upon me." You train yourself and visualize yourself in their presence. Stay in a state of quietness and calmness and then begin to make a *hisaab* (accounting).

Then their *fa'iz* and their light begins to dress you. They begin to teach that every time you begin to do something bad you lose the *fa'iz*. Their light is coming to dress you from Prophet ﷺ. Every time you do something bad that light goes and the connection will be lost. Every time you keep yourself to be good and that becomes your *muhasabah* (taking an account of yourself).

People don't know that if you do your *muhasabah* without connecting to these lights. Without understanding the presence of these lights it's not going to open anything to you. You are not going to open anything from yourself. You are not going to be able to pull from your reality and break through all of these problems, but you need the *Awliyaullah* to be present with you to begin to sign off on what you are doing.

The *Saliheen* and Shaykhs Are Watching You

Allah ﷻ says in the *salah, ibadillahis-saliheen.* These *Saliheen* must be there, they are watching but there is a *hijab* that is veiling you from their presence. Of course they accompany you everywhere you go. The angels accompany you, the *jinn* are accompanying you. Why? The *Saliheen*'s light has a difficult time and doesn't find a bus to get there? Their light is everywhere! People don't think. They think they need to find a bus to find where you are. No, their light is accompanying you. Allah ﷻ is saying that in every *salah* you make, you are giving *salaam* to them. Allah ﷻ is teaching you the best, *yaa Nabi salaam 'alayka…*

يَا نَبِي سَلَامْ عَلَيْك يَا رَسُولْ سَلَامْ عَلَيْك

يَا حَبِيبْ سَلَامْ عَلَيْك صَلَوَاتُ الله عَلَيْك

Ya Nabi Salaam 'Alayka *Ya Rasul Salam 'Alayka*
Ya Habib salam 'Alayka *Salawatullah 'Alayka*

O' Prophet, peace be upon you, O' Messenger, peace be upon you
O' my beloved, peace be upon you, Praises of Allah be upon you

Allah ﷻ is teaching you the best of manners so give them *salaams*, they are always with you. Give *salaams* to your beloved Prophet ﷺ, he is your *imam*. Your *salah* is not even coming to Me without mentioning Sayyidina Muhammad ﷺ. And who is with Prophet ﷺ? The *Saliheen*, all *Awliyaullah*, all the lovers of Sayyidina Muhammad ﷺ are accompanying Prophet ﷺ.

Every Night Do *Muraqabah*, Connect With *Saliheen* and *Siddiqeen*

They are there; they must be training on how to connect with the world of light. They say, "Yes, sit, close your eyes and spend a few minutes every night when the system is off," and Allah ﷻ says, We made the day as busy, business time for you but the night is quiet and peaceful. In *Salat at-Tahajjud* Allah ﷻ describes then in *Surah Al-Isra* that there is the gate of the *Siddiq's*, "*Yaa Rabbi* let me to enter from the gates of the *Siddiq's* and to exit from the gate of the *Siddiq's* and *Sultanun Naseerah*."

وَقُل رَّبِّ أَدْخِلْنِي مُدْخَلَ صِدْقٍ وَأَخْرِجْنِي مُخْرَجَ صِدْقٍ وَاجْعَل لِّي مِن لَّدُنكَ سُلْطَانًا نَّصِيرًا ٨٠

17:80 – "Wa qul Rabbi adkhelni mudkhala Sidqin wa akhrejni mukhraja Sidqin waj'al li min ladunka Sultanan NaSeera." (Surah Al-Isra)

Say: "O my Lord! Let my entry be by the Gate of Truth and Honour, and likewise my exit by the Gate of Truth and Honour; and grant me from Your Presence a King to aid (me)." (The Night Journey, 17:80)

So there is a *baab* (door), there is an opening. In which at night you are meditating and contemplating, "*Yaa Rabbi*, let me to be in the presence of these great *Siddiq's*. Let my soul to be in their presence, let their *fa'iz* and their lights be dressed upon me." And you are visualizing their presence and asking from your soul to feel them.

Then you begin to realize and they say, "If you want to feel us then correct yourself because *haqq* (truth) and falsehood can't be together."

وَ قُلْ جَآءَالْحَقُّ وَزَهَقَ الْبَٰطِلُ، إِنَّ الْبَٰطِلَ كَانَ زَهُوقًا

17:81 – "Wa qul jaa alhaqqu wa zahaqal baatil, innal batila kana zahoqa." (Surah Al-Isra)

"And say, "Truth has come, and falsehood has perished. Indeed falsehood, [by its nature], is ever perishing/ bound to perish." (The Night Journey, 17:81)

You don't do crazy things and think that I am going to feel the shaykh. No, they put an iron door and say, "Forget it for you!" No, you do good things, good *amal* (deed), completely listen to what they are teaching, have good actions, so that this *pardah* (veil) can be moved away. So it is all about good characteristics. Those good characteristics are going to begin to open all their *fa'iz*, their lights.

EVERY NIGHT MAKE A *MUHASABAH,* TAKE AN ACCOUNT OF YOURSELF

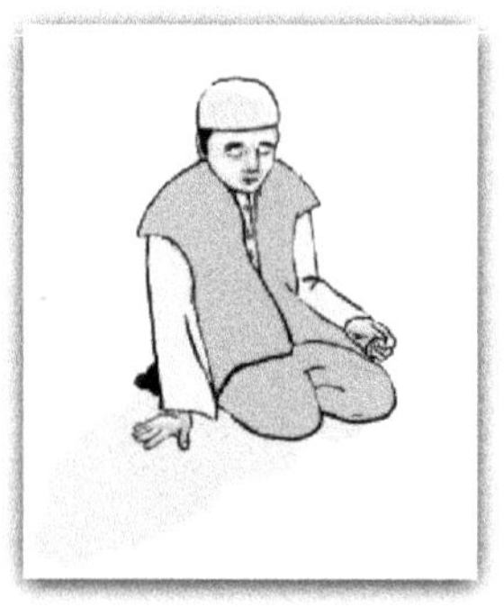

Then they say, "When you are doing the *muraqabah* (contemplation), do *muhasabah* (accounting)." As soon as you are sitting and contemplating late at night, put a little bit of *salawat* (prophetic praisings), so that you feel the love of Prophet ﷺ. And with the *salawat* playing they are taking away the *waswas* (whispering) that are coming into the ear, "Oh, you have to go check your email, you have to do this, and you have to do that." No, knock all of that off. You are listening to *salawat* and you are sitting and contemplating that Mawlana Shaykh must be in front of me, he must be watching me, his light is all around from the *ibadillahis-saliheen.*

Who am I to connect with Prophet ﷺ? Let me first be humble and I said I was nothing, I was a *zalim* (oppressor). *InshaAllah,* this shaykh accepts me in my *zulumat* and that he washes me and cleanses me. As soon as you begin to connect with them, they inspire from the teaching, "Now make a *hisaab*, an accounting of yourself. What did you do that night? What did you do that day? What did you do throughout the day? Correct your actions."

OUR BAD ACTIONS CREATE A VEIL THAT BLOCK US FROM OUR SHAYKH

If the actions are incorrect, this wall is going to be solid steel. If the actions are correct and the training is correct, this wall begins to melt; the wall that separates us from them begins to melt, and every night we begin to take a *hisaab*. Every night we connect our heart and say, "*Sayyidi,* dress me from your *fa'iz*, dress me from your light. I am not doing anything right, I know Allah ﷻ is going to be angry with me."

Again they inspire within us, "Take your *hisaab*, take your *hisaab*, what are you doing wrong within that day? Did you harm anybody with your speech? Did you break anybody's heart with your actions? Those are what count for Allah ﷻ."

And the guides continue to inspire, inspire, inspire so this *pardah* (veil) goes, this *pardah* goes, this *pardah* goes. And as the actions become correct, the *amal* becomes correct, then you begin to feel their *fa'iz*. Their energy is very powerful and you begin to feel that energy. The vigilance they are talking about is that, you vigilantly meditate that dress me from your light, dress me from your light.

Empty what is in your head, empty everything about your understanding. The active mind is blocking the heart, because the mind is filled with *waswas*, (whispering of Satan), it is filled with *shak*, doubt. It has doubt in every action they do, in every understanding and every reality. That doubt will not let anything to enter in.

That is why the Prophet ﷺ said, "Take your head off if you are coming to the Divinely Presence." It means the *dhikr* is *laa ilaaha ilAllah*, *La* to the head; don't use your head to think, "How is this going to be possible?" How will you reach to the Heavens with this head? It has to be through the heart.

YOU MUST CONNECT TO THE LIVING SHAYKH (GUIDE)

It has to be the living guide who has the authority and is holding to an electrical line. Because if you are not connected to the living guide it is very difficult to connect to the ones who have passed. That is not how the system works. Allah عز وجل wants us to be connected to the living guide so that we have safety on Earth. That the *fa'iz* reaches us in our existence on this *dunya*. It means then we seek out the living guides.

We take a way of being nothing and begin to train every night on how to be nothing, how to be nothing, how to take that *hisaab*. And how to be dressed from their lights, blessed from their lights. As the action becomes better and better and we begin to ask, "*Yaa Sayyidi,* dress me from your light, bless me from your light." You begin to feel their light dressing. You begin to feel their energies dressing. Then they begin to teach that, you be nothing, you said you are nothing.

I am saying I am nothing, I am nothing, let me be a dot in your *jubbah* (robe), like a piece of dust. That is why when you read these *du'as* that let me just be dust under the feet of Prophet ﷺ, then just let me be dust in your *jubbah.* I am not asking, I don't want my existence, I don't want to be around, I want to be nothing, to be nothing.

That *muhabbat*, that love, brings us to the *turuq*. The Shaykh is the symbol of the Prophet ﷺ coming, this love is bringing us. They are teaching and training that whatever you know, even you think you know, you know nothing. You empty out. You know nothing and you become empty. Through the *muraqabah* and the practices and meditation and contemplation you are slowly trying to connect and get closer.

It is like a jet trying to connect with another jet in mid-air. You are constantly balancing, until your good character is correct. Then the love is coming, and then there is a connection. Because you have negated, you loved, you obeyed, and you gave all the teachings the way they wanted it to be taught. They said, "Relieve yourself of the bad characteristics." As soon as there is connection it means your love and their soul is connected.

If that soul reaches out and connects with the student through their good character, not proximity to them but through their good character, there is a bond, this light bonds. Through that bond they can bring that student to be closer and closer and closer into the reality.

As soon as the student becomes closer in the reality they are being dressed by that light, blessed by that light and that is what they call the *fana* (annihilation). It means with *muhabbat*, you came with love, you kept the *hudur,* the presence, the *hudur* is physical and spiritual. You have to keep their spiritual presence.

Be Vigilant – Whatever You Do, Shaykh is Right There

"They are with me wherever I am. If I am on the bus talking bad to people, my shaykh is sitting right there," If I am talking to people I should not be conversing with, my shaykh is right there. I am cheating people, my shaykh is right there. Whatever I am doing, I am believing that my shaykh is right there, that light is right there. Allah عزّ وجلّ sees, the angels see, the *jinn* see. You don't think the light of Prophet صلى الله عليه وسلم is seeing? They are seeing!

So then you are constantly keeping your vigil. You are vigilant that they are with me; I have to govern myself accordingly. As much as I govern myself accordingly, their light stays. If I do crazy things, their light goes, their light goes.

If You Do Wrong Things, Prophet's صلى الله عليه وسلم Light Leaves You

The Shaykh's light is *Haqq* (truth). *Haqq* and falsehood don't go together. If you capture a few minutes of light and go out and do false and bad things, their light leaves. It can't be together. You can't take a *Muhammadan* Light and go out and do crazy things. So you govern yourself.

Your whole character begins to change because at night they begin to teach in the meditation, "No, no you can't do that. Prophet's ﷺ light is not going to stay with that." As soon as you lose your temper that light is gone. How then are you going to capture it? You have to start all over again.

That is why it is the good character. If these people are able to keep the love of Prophet ﷺ, it is through their good character, through their love, through their humbleness, that light stays. That light stays and it begins to bless them and begins to nourish them and begins to change everything. That is what the real *taqwa* (consciousness) is.

If somebody doesn't have that light, they have no understanding of *taqwa*. They don't care, they are like being behind steel walls; it could be another seven inches of steel for all they care. But if you are feeling that light, feeling their presence, feeling their love, are you going to go do something crazy and risk all of that? No.

So then the guides have very humble character. They have a lot of *khushiya* in their heart. They are fearful that Allah عز وجل and Prophet ﷺ is going to be upset with them, *Awliyaullah* will be upset with them and lose all the *fa'iz*, lose all the emanations that are coming to them. So it builds beatific characteristics. As a result whatever comes to them they stay quiet, they have the best of character and more is being dressed upon them.

GIFT FROM ALLAH عز وجل – THE LIGHT OF *AWLIYA* THAT IS FROM *NUR MUHAMMAD* ﷺ

The light that they are sending is the light of Sayyidina Muhammad ﷺ because it is all from *Tawheed, laa ilaaha ilAllah Muhammadun Rasulullah* ﷺ (There is no God but Allah and Muhammad ﷺ is the Messenger of Allah).

So *Awliyaullah* (saints) are not a light separate for themselves. Some people say, "No, no I follow this *wali*, not this *wali*." They are all *Muhammadan Wali*, they are all *Muhammadan* lights, their *darajat* (level) of strengths is what is important. There are some small suns and there are some very big powerful suns.

And we need the one that is alive now that is constantly dressing, constantly blessing, because the *fa'iz* is coming to him, Prophet's ﷺ support is coming to him. It comes to the living saints of this *dunya*, of this *zaman*. Those living saints carry the authority of Prophet ﷺ on Earth.

IT IS ALLAH'S عز وجل GIFT TO HAVE A SAINTLY GUIDE (*WALIYUN MURSHIDA*)

When you connect with them and keep them into your life, it is like sunshine where you have your own sun. Allah عز وجل gives you your very own sun, wherever you go this sun is shining. Who has no sun has no sun at all, no *waliyan murshida*, (Allah عز وجل says),

ذَٰلِكَ مِنْ آيَاتِ اللَّـهِ ۗ مَن يَهْدِ اللَّـهُ فَهُوَ الْمُهْتَدِ ۖ وَمَن يُضْلِلْ فَلَن تَجِدَ لَهُ وَلِيًّا مُّرْشِدًا...

18:17 – "... Dhalika min ayati Allahi, man yahdillahu fahuwal Muhtadi, wa man yudlil falan tajida lahu waliyyan murshida." (Surah al Kahf)

"...That was from the Signs of Allah: He whom Allah, guides is rightly guided; but he whom Allah leaves to stray,- for him you will never find Saintly Guide to the Right Way." (The Cave, 18:17)

Whom We didn't give a guide, they have no *wali murshid*, the guide who is a saint of Allah ﷻ. Whom Allah ﷻ gives is then a huge *ni'mat* (blessing).

That *wali,* the light he is sending out is the light of Prophet ﷺ. It increases your love of Sayyidina Muhammad ﷺ, it increases your consciousness of Sayyidina Muhammad ﷺ, it increases every knowledge within the heart of the love of Sayyidina Muhammad ﷺ. Why? Because he is *feekum*, he is amongst you and spreading your heart, spreading your soul, filling your soul with all the love of Prophet ﷺ. So then they become *ashiqeen*, they become the lovers of Sayyidina Muhammad ﷺ.

كَمَا أَرْسَلْنَا فِيكُمْ رَسُولًا مِّنكُمْ يَتْلُو عَلَيْكُمْ آيَاتِنَا وَيُزَكِّيكُمْ وَيُعَلِّمُكُمُ الْكِتَابَ وَالْحِكْمَةَ وَيُعَلِّمُكُم مَّا لَمْ تَكُونُوا تَعْلَمُونَ (١٥١)

2:151 – "Kama arsalna feekum Rasulam minkum yatlo 'Alaykum ayatina wa yuzakkeekum wa yu'Allimukumul kitaaba walhikmata wa yu'Allimukum ma lam takono ta'Alamon." (Surah Al-Baqarah)

"Just as We have sent among (within) you a messenger from your own, reciting to you Our Signs, and purifying you, and teaching you the Scripture/Book and

Wisdom and teaching you New Knowledge, that which you did not know."
(The Cow, 2:151)

We pray that Allah عز وجل grants us more and more understanding on how to truly use this body He gave us. How to keep it in its surrender and how to dress the soul with its reality. Those who think they can do it by themselves they have a very difficult path ahead of them. Those who acknowledge they are nothing and they have been defeated by their own *Shaytan*, as soon as they tap out and surrender, *Shaytan* got me in a headrest and I can't get out of it, then the *waliyan murshida* will appear; the *Awliya* will appear in their lives to rescue them.

ASK FOR *AWLIYA'S* SUPPORT, YOU CAN'T WIN THIS BATTLE WITH *SHAYTAN*

Allah's عز وجل love for *Bani Adam* (Children of Adam) and this Creation in this *Nur Muhammadi* صلى الله عليه وسلم just requires us to surrender. You know nothing and *Shaytan* (Satan) gets you in a big headlock, then Allah عز وجل sends that one who can defend us. They begin to come and teach that "If you think you are going to fight it, *Shaytan* is going to defeat you in an instant."

But if you want their support, then take the way of training on how to bring their light how to bring their *fa'iz*, how to bring their emanations upon our life. And that will change us, our families and our whole community will be under their dress.

Now in days of difficulty it is needed more than ever. If anyone thinks they have the ability to protect themselves from what is coming upon the Earth, God help them, Allah عز وجل help them. Those who agreed they are helpless and said, *yaa Rabbi,* we need *rijalAllah* (Men of God). We need to be amongst the *rijalAllah* whom, *yaa Rabbi,* You have blessed and You supported. And those whom Your hand and Prophet's ﷺ hand is upon, we need that hand, *yaa Rabbi,* and that we are nothing.

Subhana rabbika rabil 'izzati 'ama yasifoon, Wa salamun 'alal mursaleen wal hamdulillahi rabbil 'alameen. Bi hurmati Muhammadil Mustafa wa bi siratil Suratil Fatiha.

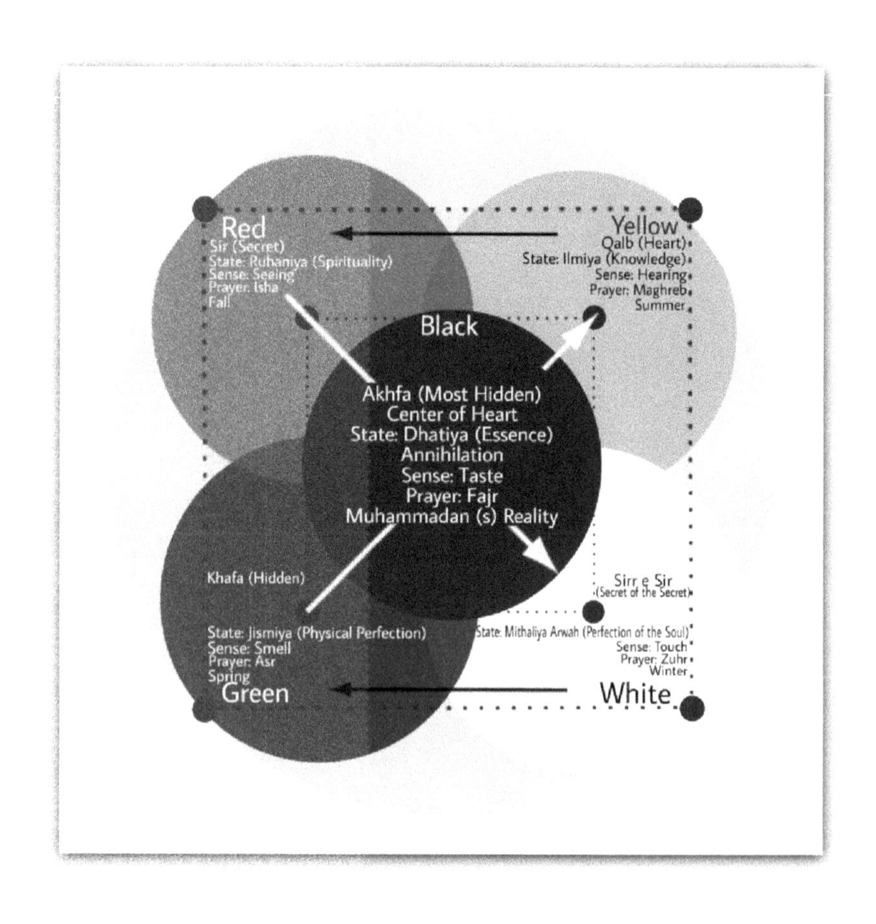
Red
Sir (Secret)
State: Ruhaniya (Spirituality)
Sense: Seeing
Prayer: Isha
Fall
Yellow
Qalb (Heart)
State: Ilmiya (Knowledge)
Sense: Hearing
Prayer: Maghreb
Summer
Black
Akhfa (Most Hidden)
Center of Heart
State: Dhatiya (Essence)
Annihilation
Sense: Taste
Prayer: Fajr
Muhammadan (s) Reality
Khafa (Hidden)
State: Jismiya (Physical Perfection)
Sense: Smell
Prayer: Asr
Spring
Green
Sirr e Sir
(Secret of the Secret)
State: Mithaliya Arwah (Perfection of the Soul)
Sense: Touch
Prayer: Zuhr
Winter
White

LEVELS OF THE HEART AND THE 9 POINTS

SECRETS OF THE CAVE
THE ENNEAGRAM, THE 9 POINTS, AND 9 *SULTAN AL AWLIYA*

Adapted from the Naqshbandi Sufi Way Book
By Mawlana Shaykh Hisham Kabbani

Shaykh Sharafuddin ق asked Shaykh 'Abdullah ق to host their guest. Shaykh 'Abdullah ق recounted the events of the meeting to several of his *murids* (students) many years later. As soon as they met, Shaykh 'Abdullah ق said, "You are interested in the knowledge of the Nine Points. We can speak on it in the morning after *Fajr* prayer. Now you eat something and rest." At *Fajr* time Shaykh 'Abdullah ق called Gurdjieff to come and pray with him. As soon as the prayer finished, the Shaykh began to recite *Surah Yaseen* (36th chapter) from the Holy Qur'an. As he finished reading, Gurdjieff approached him and asked if he could speak of what he had just experienced.

A MEETING WITH GURDJIEFF

Through your spiritual power I was able to ascend to the knowledge of the power of the Nine Points. Then a voice, addressing me as *'Abd an-Nur*, said, 'This light and knowledge have been granted to you from the Divine Presence of Allah ﷻ to bring peace to your heart.

However, you must not use the power of this knowledge.' The voice bid me farewell with the salutation of peace and the vision ended as you were finishing the recitation from the Qur'an.

The enneagram image above holds the secret of the 9 Points, 9 States of Humanity, 9 *Sultan al Awliya*. Shaykh 'Abdullah ق replied, "*Surah Yaseen* was called 'the Heart of the Qur'an' by the Holy Prophet صلى الله عليه وسلم and the knowledge of these Nine Points was opened to you through it."

The vision was by the blessings of the verse, 'Peace! A Word (of salutation) from a Lord Most Merciful' *(Holy Qur'an, 36:58)*. "Each of the Nine Points is represented by one of nine Saints who are at the highest level in the Divine Presence.

They are the keys to the untold powers within man, but there is no permission to use these keys. This is a secret that in general will not be opened until the Last Days, when the Mahdi عليه السلام appears and Prophet Jesus عليه السلام returns. This meeting of ours has been blessed. Keep it as a secret in your heart and don't speak of it in this life. *`Abd an-Nur*, for that is your name with us; you are free to stay or go as your responsibilities allow. You are always welcome with us. You have attained safety in the Divine Presence. May Allah عز و جل bless you and strengthen you in your journey.

His States and Discourses After His Second Seclusion at 30 Years of Age

Shaykh Abdullah ق was ordered to enter a second long seclusion for five years. During that seclusion, many visions and states were granted to him, which would be impossible to describe within the span of this book. After he completed this second seclusion, the power of his spiritual attraction increased. He became so renowned that even during his Shaykh's lifetime, people used to come from everywhere to learn from him.

Following are some of his discourses. "I do not speak to you about any *maqam* (station), *tajalli* (manifestation), or *rutbah* (rank) without my having already entered that station or position and experienced that manifestation. I am not like many others; I do not speak separating my sight from my heart, enumerating the *maqamat* (stations) for you without my knowing their *haqqiqat* (reality). No! First of all I followed that path and saw what it was. I learned those realities and secrets which may be found along it, and I worked my way along it until I obtained the Knowledge of Certainty *(Ilm al-yaqin)*, the Eye of Certainty *(ayn al-yaqin)*, and the Truth of Certainty *(Haqq al-yaqin)*. Only then do I speak to you, giving you a tiny taste of what I have tasted, until I am able to make you reach that station without tiring you and without difficulties.

STATIONS OF THE HEART – *LATAIF AL QALB*

There are five stations of the Heart: *Qalb, Sir, Sirr e Sir, Khafa* and *Akhfa.*

- ***Qalb*** is the Heart,
- ***Sir*** is the Secret,
- ***Sirr e Sir*** is the Secret of the Secret,
- ***Khafa*** is the Hidden, and
- ***Akhfa*** the Most Hidden.

The secret of this *tariqa* is based on these five *lataif* (subtle things), the stations of the heart.

Latifat al-Qalb, the stage of the Heart, is under the authority of Sayyidina Adam ﷺ, because it represents the physical aspect of the heart.

Latifat as Sir, the station of the Secret, is under Sayyidina Nuh عليه السلام, because it is the vessel which is saved from the ocean of darkness, salvation from the flood of ignorance.

Latifat Sirr e Sir, the station of the Secret of the Secret, is under two Prophets: Sayyidina Ibrahim عليه السلام and Sayyidina Musa عليه السلام, who represent Allah's عز وجل Divine Presence on Earth. Allah عز وجل made Sayyidina Ibrahim عليه السلام the symbol of all His *khalifs* on this Earth, as mentioned in the verse of the creation of mankind, "I will create a vicegerent on earth." *(Holy Qur'an, 2:30).* Sayyidina Musa عليه السلام was blessed with hearing and speaking to Allah عز وجل which are the two essential attributes of knowledge.

Latifat al-Khafa, the Hidden Station, is under Sayyidina Isa (Jesus) عليه السلام. Because of his relationship with Hidden Knowledge, he represents spiritual understanding.

Latifat al-Akhfa, the Most Hidden Station, is under the reality of Sayyidina Muhammad صلى الله عليه وسلم, because he was granted a station high above that of all other Prophets and messengers. He was the one who was raised up, in the Night of Ascension, to the Divine Presence. This is represented by the *Kalima* (Sacred Phrase), because there is no *la ilaha illallah* without *Muhammadun Rasulullah*. The lights of these stations have been shown to me.

- The light of the Heart is a yellow hue;
- the light of the Secret is red;
- the light of the Secret of the Secret is white;
- the light of the Hidden Station is green; and
- the light of the Most Hidden Station is black.

These Five Stations Are the Center of the Nine Points

They represent the locus of revelation and inspiration of the Divine Presence in the heart of the human being. These Nine Points are located on the chest of each person and they represent nine different hidden states in every human being. Every state is connected to a saint, who has the authority to control that point.

If the seeker in the Naqshbandi Way is able to unveil and to make spiritual contact with the authorized master controlling these points, he may be given knowledge of and power to use these nine points.

The conditions related to opening these nine points can only be alluded to obliquely.

1. The first station involves the power of imprisoning the ego.
2. The key to the second state is *dhikr* with *la ilaha illallah.*
3. The third state consists in witnessing the engraving of Allah's ﷻ name on the heart (*naqsh*).
4. The fourth state relates to the meaning of that engraving on the heart.
5. The fifth state is to imprint the engraving with your *dhikr.*
6. In the sixth state the heart is made to stop pumping at will and to start pumping at will.
7. The seventh state is to be aware of the number of times one stops the heart from pumping and the number of times one restores the pumping of the heart.
8. In the eighth state one mentions the phrase *Muhammadun Rasulullah* in every cessation of the heart and every restoration of its pumping.
9. The ninth stage is to return to your Cave, as Allah ﷻ mentioned in *Surah al-Kahf*, "When ye turn away from them and the things they worship other than Allah, betake yourself to the Cave: your Lord will shower His mercies on you..." *(Holy Qur'an, 18:16).* (9:40 This is the Power of 9, Importance of the King, Return to the King, 12 Veils of Power 9 in Holy Qur'an *Tauba* Surah 9 Verse 40 is the Beginning of entrance to the *Thawr* Cave).

The Cave is the Divine Presence. Here one utters the cherished prayer of the Prophet ﷺ, 'O God, You are my destination and Your pleasure is what I seek.' The heart, as it cycles between the cessation and restoration of its pumping, is existing at the level of the essence of the Divine Presence. Because that Divine Essence is the source of all created being, that heart will be at one with every minutest creation in this universe. The heart which has reached the secrets of the nine points will be able to see everything, hear everything, know everything, taste everything, sense everything, 'Until He will be the ears with which he hears, the eyes with which he sees, the tongue with which he speaks, the hand with which he grasps, and the feet with which he walks. He will be Lordly, he only need say to a thing Be! and it will be.' (This is Perfectly Manifested in Sayyidina Muhammad ﷺ, Our Eternal Messenger of Allah).

Why did he go to that cave? The 'Cave of Silence' as it has been called? Indeed, it is the 'Cave of Silent Secrets'. Why was the Prophet ﷺ ordered by God to go to that cave, which is one day's travel from *Makkah*, when he had a distance of fifteen days journeying to go?

"29" – When the Prophet ﷺ went into that cave, a spider and a dove came and made a house over the door in order that no one would know what was inside. (The Spider is the 29th *Surah* directing us that the secrets of 29 and the *Lam Alif* is the seal for the entry into the Divine Presence and The Dove is the Angelic Realm and Eggs are the story of Creation.) 29 secretly encoded *Surahs*.

This is common knowledge. As for the secret, look to love. When love for someone is pure, God will never forget that person. Before leaving *Makkah* for *Madinah*, the Prophet ﷺ put someone in his bed because the ignorant people came to his door intent on killing him. He put Sayyidina Ali ﵇ in his bed. There is a secret to that; it means that he made Sayyidina Ali ﵇ his representative, in his place. He did not put Sayyidina Umar ﵇ there. He did not put Sayyidina Uthman ﵇ – none of the Companions, but someone of his own flesh and blood.

THE FULL MOON HAS TWO FACES

The full moon has two faces, one that shines on earth and the other dark side is hidden. The Prophet ﷺ took with him as company his other mirror-image, Sayyidina Abu Bakr ﵇, to the cave. He said, "I am the city of knowledge and Ali is the door." You must be *Ahl Bayt*, either pure blood line or by way of Sayyidina Saliman Farsi ﵇ in Service to the Rasul ﷺ. The door is something physical, external. When you want to enter the house, how do you enter? Through the door. In order to enter to the Prophet ﷺ and to come to the knowledge that the Prophet ﷺ is giving, you have to enter through the door. That door is Sayyidina Ali ﵇. The Prophet ﷺ also said, "Whatever God has poured into my heart, I poured into the heart of Sayyidina Abu Bakr as-Siddiq ﵇. The Prophet ﷺ referred again to the secret of Abu Bakr ﵇ when he said, "Abu Bakr does not surpass you because of fasting or praying more, but because of a secret that took root in his heart." So inside the house, we find Sayyidina Abu Bakr ﵇ and outside the house, we find Sayyidina Ali ﵇.

That is why, of the two sources of Sufi knowledge, one came from Sayyidina Abu Bakr ﵇ and the other from Sayyidina Ali ﵇. From the time of the different schools of Divine Law, Muslims have agreed that the knowledge of the heart came from these two paths. Justice and laws, on the other hand, came from Hadrat Umar ﵇ . The Prophet's ﷺ comment about Sayyidina Abu Bakr ﵇ is the secret of the cave. To represent his body, the Prophet ﷺ put Sayyidina Ali ﵇ in his bed prior to his departure from *Makkah* to *Madinah*. This means that Sayyidina Ali ﵇ represented the external. But he took Abu Bakr ﵇ to the cave for the cave represents what is interior.

Shaykh Sharafuddin ق On Will and Destiny

It is known that there are two types of destiny. The first kind of destiny is termed *qada'an mucallaq*, which means 'suspended or mutable destiny.' It is written on the *Lawh al-Mahfoudh* (the Preserved Tablet). This will varies according to will and behavior, cause and effect. All saints can change this kind of destiny for their *murids*, in order to train them and to influence their destiny by changing their actions and behavior. The authority to change the Mutable Destiny is given to the Shaykhs for their *murids* (students) because they are connected to each other by Divine Will. The second type of destiny is contained in *Umm al-Kitaab*, the Mother of the Book, as mentioned in the *ayat*:

يَمْحُو اللَّـهُ مَا يَشَاءُ وَيُثْبِتُ ۖ وَعِندَهُ أُمُّ الْكِتَابِ

13:39 – "Yamho Allahu ma yashao wa yuthbitu, wa 'indahu ommu al kitaab." (Surah Ar-Rad)

"Allah eliminates what He wills or confirms, and with Him is the Mother of the Book." (The Thunder, 13:39)

It is called *qada'an mubram*, which means Fixed Destiny. Saints never interfere in that Fixed Destiny, which is in the Hand of the Creator. Allah عزّ وجلّ gave the authority to change the Fixed Destiny only to the Nine Saints who are at the highest level in the Divine Presence by permission from the Prophet صلى الله عليه وسلم who is first to take that power from Allah عزّ وجلّ.

They control the Nine Points of human consciousness related to the different stages of the ascent of an individual on his path to the Divine Presence. Allah عزّ وجلّ gave these Nine Saints, whose number has not changed from the time of the Prophet صلى الله عليه وسلم until today, the power to use *Sultan adh-Dhikr*, the Greatest Remembrance.

Everyone knows that *dhikr* is primarily the repetition of *la ilaha illallah*, and that is what is practiced by all *tariqas*, including the *Naqshbandiyya*. But the *Sultan adh-dhikr* is a completely different type of *dhikr*.

إِنَّا نَحْنُ نَزَّلْنَا الذِّكْرَ وَإِنَّا لَهُ لَحَافِظُونَ

Allah said, "Inna nahnu nazzalna-dh-dhikra wa inna lahu la-hafidhun [15:9]"

"We have revealed the Dhikr, and we are the One to protect that Dhikr in you."

The *dhikr* mentioned here is the Holy Qur'an. The *dhikr* of these nine saints, besides *la ilaha illallah*, is the secret of the Holy Qur'an. They recite the Qur'an, not as we recite it, reading from beginning to end, but they recite it with all its secrets and inner realities. Because Allah ﷻ said,

...وَلَا رَطْبٍ وَلَا يَابِسٍ إِلَّا فِي كِتَابٍ مُّبِينٍ

6:59 – "...Wala ratbin wala yabisin illa fee kitaabin mubeenin."
(Surah Al-An'am)

"Nor is there anything fresh or dry but is inscribed in a clear Record."
(The Cattle, 6:59)

None of God's creations in all the created universes has not been mentioned already, with all its secrets, in the Clear Book, the Qur'an.

The saint reciting the Qur'an in *Sultan adh-Dhikr* is therefore reciting it with all the secrets of every creation, from beginning to end. Allah ﷻ gave every letter of the Qur'an, according to the Nine Highest Masters of the Naqshbandi Order [this was the first time the Shaykh ever mentioned this secret], twelve thousand knowledges.

The Qur'an contains around 600,000 letters, so for every letter, these saints are able to take 12,000 knowledges! Each of these nine saints differs from the other in his level as well. We may see that one of them, for example, was able to recite the Holy Qur'an by the power of *Sultan adh-Dhikr*, which is to grasp 12,000 meanings on every letter, only once in his life. Another was able to recite it three times in his life. The third was able to do it nine times in his life. Another was able to recite it 99 times in his life. This secret differed from one saint to another.

Shah Mawlana Naqshband ق was able to do it 999 times in his life. Our Master Ahmad al-Faruqi ق was able to recite it 9,999 times in his life. Shaykh Sharafuddin ق was able to recite it 19,999 times. Here Shaykh 'Abdullah ق stopped. Shaykh Nazim ق said, "In every breath Grandshaykh 'Abdullah Daghestani ق was exhaling with *Sultan adh-Dhikr* and inhaling with *Sultan adh-Dhikr*. He used to complete the secret of Qur'an twice in every breath." Mawlana Shaykh Nazim is Inheritor of this Trust.

Grandshaykh Abdullah al-Fa'iz ad-Daghestani ق at over age of 85.

Fig. 129. Shaykh Abd Allah al-Faiz ad-Daghestani in 1970.

Subhana rabbika rabil 'izzati 'ama yasifoon, Wa salamun 'alal mursaleen wal hamdulillahi rabbil 'alameen. Bi hurmati Muhammadil Mustafa wa bi siratil Suratil Fatiha.